DISJOINTED PLURALISM

PRINCETON STUDIES IN AMERICAN POLITICS:
HISTORICAL, INTERNATIONAL, AND COMPARATIVE
PERSPECTIVES

SERIES EDITORS
Ira Katznelson, Martin Shefter, Theda Skocpol

A list of titles
in this series appears
at the back of
the book

DISJOINTED PLURALISM

INSTITUTIONAL INNOVATION
AND THE DEVELOPMENT OF THE
U.S. CONGRESS

Eric Schickler

PRINCETON UNIVERSITY PRESS

PRINCETON AND OXFORD

Copyright © 2001 by Princeton University Press
Published by Princeton University Press, 41 William Street,
Princeton, New Jersey 08540
In the United Kingdom: Princeton University Press,
3 Market Place, Woodstock, Oxfordshire OX20 1SY
All Rights Reserved.

Library of Congress Cataloging-in-Publication Data

Schickler, Eric, 1969–
Disjointed pluralism : institutional innovation and the
development of the U.S. Congress / Eric Schickler.
p. cm. — (Princeton studies in American politics)
Includes bibliographical references and index.
ISBN 0-691-04925-4 (alk. paper)—ISBN 0-691-04926-2 (pbk. : alk. paper)
1. United States. Congress—History. 2. Organizational change—
United States—History. 3. Legislators—United States—History.
I. Title. II. Series.
JK1021 .S35 2001
328.73'09—dc21   00-058487

This book has been composed in Galliard

Printed on acid-free paper. ∞

www.pup.princeton.edu

Printed in the United States of America

2 4 6 8 10 9 7 5 3 1

2 4 6 8 10 9 7 5 3 1

(Pbk.)

Contents

Figures

Tables

Acknowledgments

THIS BOOK began when I was a graduate student at Yale University, and I owe a great debt to many people there. David Mayhew went above and beyond a dissertation adviser's call of duty in sharing his many insights into Congress with me and in spending numerous hours commenting on chapter drafts, suggesting sources, and discussing the project. I have also learned much from Donald Green and Stephen Skowronek, each of whom served on my dissertation committee and provided advice and support at every stage of the project. Several other Yale faculty and graduate students also gave much-needed help along the way, including Alan Gerber, Andrew Rich, Michael Ebeid, and Terri Bimes.

Since leaving New Haven, I have received considerable help from numerous individuals. Special thanks are due to David Brady, Joe Cooper, Larry Dodd, Bryan Jones, and Steven S. Smith, each of whom provided extensive comments on the entire manuscript. I also would like to thank Chris Ansell, Doug Arnold, Bruce Cain, Jack Citrin, Jon Cohen, Rui de Figueiredo Jr., Steve Finkel, Brian Humes, Scott James, Sam Kernell, Keith Krehbiel, Eugene Lewis, Karen Orren, Kathryn Pearson, Paul Pierson, Nelson Polsby, Brian Sala, Pablo Sandoval, Ken Shotts, Charles Stewart, Kathy Thelen, and Ray Wolfinger for their comments and encouragement. I also benefited greatly from the help of David Rohde, Jeffery Jenkins, Thomas Hammond, and the other participants in the Political Institutions and Public Choice seminar at Michigan State University, who provided many valuable suggestions. At Princeton University Press, Chuck Myers, Anne Reifsnyder, and Richard Isomaki were invariably supportive and helpful.

Special gratitude is owed to John Sides, who provided exceptional research assistance from the moment I arrived in Berkeley. I also thank Eric McGhee, who joined the project later and provided critical help revising the manuscript. The financial support of the Institute of Governmental Studies at the University of California, Berkeley, is also gratefully acknowledged.

Finally, I would like to thank my parents, Sonya and Abraham, my brother Eliot, and Terri for their love and support over the years.

DISJOINTED PLURALISM

CHAPTER 1

Disjointed Pluralism and
Institutional Change

WHATEVER ELSE a national legislature may be, it is a complex of rules, procedures, and specialized internal institutions, such as committees and leadership instruments. Particular configurations of these rules, procedures, committees, and leadership instruments may serve the interests of individual members, parties, pressure groups, sectors of society, or the legislature as a whole. As a result, as any legislature evolves through time, little is more fundamental to its politics than recurrent, often intense, efforts to *change* its institutions. Congressional politics has depended crucially on such innovations as the "Reed rules" of 1890, the Senate cloture rule adopted in 1917, the creation of congressional budget committees in 1974, the House breakaway from seniority rights to committee chairmanships in 1975, and the package of reforms adopted by Republicans when they took over the House in January 1995.

What explains the politics of institutional change in Congress? How is it that congressional institutions have proven remarkably adaptable to changing environmental conditions and yet a never-ending source of dissatisfaction for members and outside observers? This book addresses these questions. The answers, I argue, can be found in the multiple interests that undergird choices about legislative institutions. Members have numerous goals in mind as they shape congressional rules and procedures, the committee system, and leadership instruments. Entrepreneurs who seek reform can devise proposals that simultaneously tap into an array of distinct member interests. But conflicts among competing interests generate institutions that are rarely optimally tailored to meet any specific goal. As they adopt changes based on untidy compromises among multiple interests, members build institutions that are full of tensions and contradictions.

The claim that members have multiple goals is by no means new. Fenno's *Congressmen in Committees* (1973) is but one of several important studies that have explored how members' electoral, policy, and power goals shape legislative behavior and institutions.[1] Nonetheless, an increasingly popular way to think about legislative institutions uses a single collective interest to explain the main features of legislative organization across an extended span of congressional history. Examples of this approach include Cox and McCubbins's (1993) partisan model of legislative organization,

Krehbiel's (1991) informational theory of committees, and Weingast and Marshall's (1988) distributive politics model. Each of these theories attempts to show how legislative institutions are tailored to achieve a collective interest shared by members.

While such models have proven valuable in isolating important causal variables and in explaining specific features of legislative politics, focusing on the relationships among multiple interests generates additional insights into congressional organization. This involves much more than the claim that one has to look at everything—all imaginable interests and coalitions—to understand Congress. Instead, I argue that analyzing the interplay among multiple interests produces new generalizations about how congressional institutions develop. Such an analysis can help us understand both the adaptability and the frustrations that characterize congressional organization.

Based on an analysis of important institutional changes adopted in four periods, 1890–1910, 1919–32, 1937–52, and 1970–89, I argue that members' various interests makes "disjointed pluralism" a central feature of institutional development. By *pluralism,* I mean that many different coalitions promoting a wide range of collective interests drive processes of change. My analysis demonstrates that more than one interest determines institutional change within each period, that different interests are important in different periods, and, more broadly, that changes in the salient collective interests across time do not follow a simple logical or developmental sequence. Furthermore, no single collective interest is important in all four periods. Models that emphasize a particular interest thus illuminate certain historical eras, but not others.

These pluralistic processes of change do not in themselves require a dramatic revision in how we think about legislative institutions. Even if no model focusing on a single interest can explain everything about congressional institutions, critical insights may well emerge from a series of such models, each explaining a few key components of legislative organization. Eventually, a theory that synthesizes these approaches may be possible, providing a fuller understanding of the dynamics of congressional institutions.[2]

The qualifier *disjointed* suggests why that approach is only partly satisfying. By disjointed, I mean that the dynamics of institutional development derive from the *interactions* and *tensions* among competing coalitions promoting several different interests. These interactions and tensions are played out when members of Congress adopt a single institutional change, and over time as legislative organization develops through the accumulation of innovations, each sought by a different coalition promoting a different interest.[3]

This disjointedness calls into question the utility of a series of simple models that each seeks to explain a particular facet of legislative organization, and it also complicates efforts at theoretical synthesis. Models that focus on a single organizational principle, though valuable in many respects, deflect attention from how the relationships among multiple interests drive processes of change. Integrated theories that encompass several interests are potentially helpful but should not assume, as is sometimes apparently their implication, that institutions fit together comfortably to form a coherent whole (see, for example, Shepsle and Weingast 1994). Instead, my case studies suggest that congressional institutions are often ambiguous or contradictory.

Because the conceptual value of disjointed pluralism hinges on the many collective interests that motivate members, I first review prominent models of collective interests and the expectations that these models generate for institutional development. I then detail the implications of these multiple interests for understanding congressional change. Finally, I summarize the research design and review the findings from each period.

COLLECTIVE INTERESTS

Five distinct and partially contradictory kinds of collective interest could motivate the design of legislative institutions (see table 1.1). The first is rooted most directly in members' reelection interest, which potentially unites incumbents behind devices that increase their electoral security. The second consists of broad, institutional interests that also may unite all members: bolstering the capacity, power, and prestige of their chamber or of Congress as a whole. By contrast, the other interests are likely to divide members into competing groups. The third, members' interest in access to institutional power bases, can generate conflict between those who currently have disproportionate access and those who lack access. Similarly, the fourth, members' party-based interests, pits majority party members against members of the minority. Finally, the fifth, policy-based interests, is rooted in the connection between institutions and policy outcomes. Institutions may favor certain policies at the expense of others; as a result, ideological, sectional, and sectoral divisions over policy may spill over into conflicts about institutional design.[4]

In his classic study, *Congress: The Electoral Connection* (1974), David Mayhew argues that virtually every facet of congressional organization can be understood in terms of members' shared *reelection* goal. As Mayhew and others point out, a variety of institutional arrangements promote reelection, including staffing and franking privileges (Mayhew 1974; Fiorina 1977); credit-claiming opportunities gained most often through pork-

TABLE 1.1 Summary of Collective Interests

Collective Interest	Group for Whom It Is a Good	Predicted Authority Structure
Reelection	Incumbents (vs. challengers)	
perks for incumbents (Mayhew 1974; Fiorina 1977)		Decentralized incumbent cartel
particularistic goods and pork (Mayhew 1974; Fiorina 1977; Fenno 1973)		Decentralized incumbent cartel
opportunities for individual entrepreneurial action (Mayhew 1974; Loomis 1988)		Individualistic entrepreneurship; decentralized committee system
position-taking devices (Mayhew 1974; Arnold 1990)		Decentralized incumbent cartel
Congress-centered		
congressional capacity and power (Dodd 1977; Sundquist 1981; Cooper 1988; Davidson and Oleszek 1976)	Congress as a whole (vs. executive)	Integrative mechanisms and central leadership instruments
policy expertise (Krehbiel 1991; Maass 1983)		Informationally efficient committee system controlled by floor
congressional prestige and popularity (Matthews 1960; Born 1990; Jacobson 1993)	Congress as a whole	Predictions unclear
chamber capacity and power (Diermeier and Myerson 2000)	Chamber (vs. other chamber)	Integrative mechanisms; multiple veto points
Individual power bases (Dodd 1977; Loomis 1988)	Juniors (vs. seniors)	Individualistic entrepreneurship; decentralized committee system
Party-centered		
majority party reputation and effectiveness (Cox and McCubbins 1993; Rohde 1991)	In-party (vs. out-party)	Party cartel or conditional party government
Policy-based		
ideological success (Krehbiel 1998; Schickler 2000)	Ideological bloc (vs. opposing bloc)	Rules promote policy positions of median voter on floor
sectional benefits (Bensel 1984; Holcombe 1925)	Regional bloc (vs. other regions)	Predictions unclear
sectoral benefits (Shepsle and Weingast 1984; Weingast and Marshall 1988; Hansen 1990; Burns 1949)	Bloc based on producer interests (vs. consumers or other producers)	Decentralized committee system

barrel, distributive policies (Mayhew 1974; Fenno 1973); opportunities for individual entrepreneurial activity (Loomis 1988); devices to avoid taking positions on difficult issues (Arnold 1990); and platforms for position taking on popular issues (Mayhew 1974). More generally, reelection-based models typically predict that Congress will have a decentralized committee system that spreads influence widely, thereby providing members with numerous opportunities to cultivate constituent support (Mayhew 1974; Fiorina 1977).

On observing the many incumbent-protection devices embedded in congressional institutions, Mayhew (1974, 81–82) suggests that "if a group of planners sat down and tried to design a pair of American national assemblies with the goal of serving members' electoral needs year in and year out, they would be hard pressed to improve on what exists." This raises the question: why do we need to go beyond members' shared stake in reelection to understand congressional development? Why is the reelection interest, on its own, not sufficient? Part of the answer to this challenge is empirical: in the chapters that follow, I provide considerable evidence that other interests shaped important changes in congressional organization. But there are also strong theoretical grounds for the importance of multiple interests.

Notice first that the same member careerism that makes reelection a powerful influence on congressional organization has the potential to make other interests salient as well. The value of reelection hinges in part on Congress's status as a powerful and prestigious institution.[5] Maintaining congressional power is not something that members can simply take for granted. Indeed, the twentieth century has witnessed the decline of numerous elected legislatures (Huntington 1965). The most prominent threat to congressional power has been the rise of the modern presidency and the surrounding executive establishment. Therefore, one can expect careerist members to act in concert to defend congressional power, particularly following major episodes of executive aggrandizement. Examples include the committee consolidation brought about by the Legislative Reorganization Act of 1946 (Cooper 1988; Dodd 1977) and the more centralized budget process provided by the Budget Act of 1974 in the wake of the battle over impoundments with President Richard Nixon (Sundquist 1981).[6]

A focus on *congressional capacity and power* can lead to two somewhat different expectations about congressional organization.[7] Dodd (1977) and Sundquist (1981) argue that centralized leadership—typically in the hands of party leaders—is necessary for Congress to formulate coherent, broad-reaching policies and therefore to compete effectively with the executive branch. In their view, a fragmented, committee-dominated system has been the main source of congressional weakness. Sundquist in particular praises the 1974 Budget Act as an example of a centralizing change intended to safeguard congressional power.

In contrast to Dodd's and Sundquist's emphasis on centralization, Krehbiel's (1991) informational model suggests that a strong committee system facilitates congressional policymaking, provided that the committees are supervised by floor majorities.[8] Krehbiel argues that committees are not autonomous entities but agents of the floor, supplying information that reduces legislators' uncertainty about the consequences of proposed bills. The floor creates committees that are representative of its own policy preferences, because representative committees are most likely to specialize and to transmit their information to the rest of the chamber (Krehbiel 1991). All members benefit from such a committee system, which boosts congressional capacity and power.[9]

Viewing Krehbiel in the context of Dodd and Sundquist reveals a tension: The need for specialized policy expertise leads to strong committees, but using this information in a coherent manner requires coordinating the activities of these committees. Whereas Dodd and Sundquist believe strong party leaders are essential for this coordination, Krehbiel's model suggests that floor majorities rein in and channel committee activities. Notwithstanding these differences, both Dodd and Sundquist and Krehbiel argue that members have an incentive to design institutions that promote congressional policymaking capacity.

While Congress-centered interests have led to several major reforms, members have at times defined institutional power more narrowly, in terms of their chamber rather than Congress as a whole. Interchamber rivalry has received little attention from congressional scholars, but Diermeier and Myerson (2000) have recently developed a formal model that highlights this dynamic. They conclude that the members of one chamber can increase their collective access to desired resources, such as campaign contributions, by adding more veto points in their chamber. In other words, House members stand to gain a greater share of contributions or other favored resources if lobbyists face more institutional hurdles in the lower chamber than in the Senate. Though none of the cases I examine fit this precise dynamic, there are several examples of institutional changes intended to empower one chamber relative to the other. For example, Joseph Cannon's (R-Ill.) revitalization of the speakership in the early 1900s derived bipartisan support from representatives' dissatisfaction with their chamber's decline relative to the Senate.[10]

Whereas all members may have a similar commitment to defending congressional power (or at least the power of their chamber), other collective interests divide members into competing groups. As Fenno (1973) and Dodd (1977) have pointed out, one of the reasons that members seek reelection is to exercise power as individuals. This ambition creates the potential for conflict between members with disproportionate access to *institutional power bases* and those, such as junior backbenchers, who lack such access and therefore share an interest in decentralization (Dodd 1986). Indeed, several instances of institutional reform analyzed in this book derived support from junior members—often drawn from both parties—who advocated a greater dispersion of power bases (see Schickler and Sides 2000). Along these lines, Diermeier's (1995) model of floor-committee relations suggests that a sudden influx of junior members can undermine existing arrangements, leading to major institutional changes.

Power bases are also particularly salient to careerist members. A member who plans to leave Congress soon is less likely to carve out a niche in the House or Senate than is one who plans to spend many years in Washington. This is not only because power bases can facilitate reelection, but also because careerist members may value power within Congress for its own sake. Therefore, members' power base goals, like the goal of safeguarding congressional capacity and power, have probably become more potent as careerism has increased.

At the same time, members' power base goals are often in tension with their interest in congressional capacity and power. Dodd (1977) argues that the drive for individual power leads to a highly fragmented authority structure.[11] Members end up placing policymaking responsibility in "a series of discrete and relatively autonomous committees and subcommittees, each having control over the decisions in a specified jurisdictional area" (Dodd 1977, 272). Individual entrepreneurship flourishes because each member can use her committee or subcommittee to initiate new policies or oversight activities. But, as noted above, the difficulty, according to Dodd, is that the resulting fragmentation impedes workable responses to broad policy problems. This, in turn, erodes the influence of the legislative branch as the president and bureaucracy acquire power at the expense of Congress. In the end, members' pursuit of individual power saps Congress of its power as an institution (Dodd 1977, 1986). This is but one example of important tensions among members' multiple interests.

Another important cleavage affecting institutional design is *party*. In Cox and McCubbins's (1993) formulation, majority party members are united by their stake in the value of their common party label. Party members suffer electorally if voters believe the party failed to adopt needed legislation, just as they benefit if voters credit the party with many legislative accomplishments. Majority party members are by no means helpless to affect how voters perceive their party. Cox and McCubbins (1993, 112) assert that "party records often can be changed in ways that affect the vast majority of party members' reelection probabilities in the same way." Thus, individual members' desire for reelection generates a collective interest in their party's reputation.

But majority party members face a dilemma. While they would all benefit from cooperative action, each individual has incentives to pursue narrow gains that jeopardize the party's reputation (Cox and McCubbins
1993, 123–24). The party resolves this dilemma by creating leadership
posts that are both attractive and elective, thereby inducing its leaders "to
internalize the collective electoral fate of the party" (1993, 132–33). Party
leaders are charged with enforcing cooperation on matters important to
the party's reputation and with using their influence over legislative procedures to promote party interests.

With the assistance of party leaders, majority party members collude to
establish House institutions that provide built-in advantages for the party
throughout the legislative process. The majority party constitutes a "cartel" that usurps the rule-making power of the House and uses that power
to bias the legislative process in its favor. Rules are stacked in favor of the
majority party's policy preferences, and committees are agents of the party
(Cox and McCubbins 1993).

In contrast to Cox and McCubbins's portrayal of a consistent, strong
bias in favor of the majority party, Rohde (1991) emphasizes variations
over time in party strength (see also Aldrich and Rohde 1995; Binder
1997; Dion 1997).[12] Building on earlier work by Cooper and Brady
(1981), Rohde argues that party government depends on the degree of
majority party unity on the agenda items confronting Congress, and on
the level of polarization between the majority and minority parties.
Whereas Cox and McCubbins focus on members' common stake in their
party's reputation, Rohde points to policy agreement as necessary for
strong party action. When shared policy commitments exist, majority
party members will structure the legislative process to promote those
commitments. Therefore, Rohde's conditional party government model
implies that Congress will resemble a party cartel when the majority party
is unified on major policy issues, but that committees will enjoy considerable autonomy from partisan pressures when the majority party is divided.

Finally, *policy-based interests* may also divide members into conflicting
groups. Institutions can have important effects on policy outcomes. As
a result, members who share policy priorities can benefit by designing
institutions that promote those priorities (see Remington and Smith
1998). As with party interests, when some members receive benefits in
this category, others are likely to absorb costs.

It is plausible to conceptualize policy in terms of a single ideological
dimension (see Poole and Rosenthal 1997). Thus, one hypothesis that
emerges from a focus on policy goals is that changes in the chamber median—attributable to such events as big shifts in election results—will lead
to changes in institutions (see Krehbiel 1998).[13] Schickler (2000) argues
that as the median voter moves closer to the majority party, she will work

with the party to adopt rules that strengthen majority leaders' agenda control. By contrast, when the median voter moves closer to the minority party, she will work with members of the minority to adopt changes that weaken majority leaders' agenda control, thus enabling cross-party coalitions to adopt their favored policies. An example of a change derived from such a shift in the "ideological power balance" would be the reforms launched by progressive Republicans and Democrats to weaken Speaker Cannon in 1909–10.[14]

Policy-based goals also may divide members into sectional or sectoral blocs. The Senate farm bloc of 1921 is a classic example of an institution serving the policy interests of a single sector (Hansen 1991). Pluralist models of iron triangles (Cater 1964) and rational choice distributive theories (Shepsle and Weingast 1984; Weingast and Marshall 1988) emphasize the effect of sectorally based policy interests on Congress's committee system. Both sets of models depict committees as unrepresentative bodies dominated by members who support programs in their committee's jurisdiction.

These are the five families of models. Congress's institutional arrangements can promote a variety of different collective interests: *reelection* for all incumbents; *congressional capacity, power, and prestige,* or more narrowly, the power and prestige of one chamber; plentiful access to *institutional power bases;* each *party's interest* in its reputation and effectiveness; and members' shared *policy interests.* An individual member may find several of these interests salient and as a result may move in and out of multiple, distinct coalitions, each of which prioritizes a particular interest.

In addition to highlighting the importance of a specific interest, each of the models described above can also be used to derive hypotheses about the conditions under which a given interest will be more or less prominent:

Electoral interests will matter more as member careerism increases (Mayhew 1974).

Congressional capacity and power will be more salient following episodes in which the president has gained influence at Congress's expense (Dodd 1977; Sundquist 1981).

Members' interest in institutional power bases will generate pressure for decentralization following an influx of junior members that substantially alters the seniority distribution (Dodd 1986; Diermeier 1995).

Majority party interests will be particularly important when the majority party is internally unified and has policy preferences that are sharply different from those of the minority (Rohde 1991).

Policy-based interests will generate pressure for institutional changes when electoral shocks and other exogenous factors substantially shift the location of the median voter on the floor (Krehbiel 1998; Schickler 2000).

The chapters that follow include some evidence that is consistent with each of these hypotheses, and the concluding chapter assesses their relative contributions. But while such hypotheses about particular collective interests are helpful, focusing on the relationships among competing interests can produce a fuller understanding.[15] A single interest has only rarely proven sufficient to generate a major change in legislative institutions. Instead, intersections among multiple interests typically drive individual changes and the process of institutional development more generally. Thus, analyzing how different combinations of interests come together to promote and shape institutional change can lead to important new insights into congressional development. Disjointed pluralism takes up this challenge.[16]

A THEORY OF DISJOINTED PLURALISM

If a single collective interest dominated battles over legislative organization, institutions should be well tailored to achieve that specific goal. If, for example, members' shared interest in reelection dominated, then Congress would look like the cooperative cartel of incumbents described by Mayhew (1974). Virtually all aspects of legislative organization would promote reelection. Similarly, if majority party members' shared interest in their party's reputation and success dominated—perhaps as in the contemporary British House of Commons—then every important aspect of congressional organization would be stacked in the party's favor.

Contrast this to a situation in which no single collective interest is dominant. Any institutional change that promotes one interest is likely to affect other interests that some members find important. On the one hand, these interdependencies create problems: designing institutions to achieve a particular goal is complicated by the need to balance that goal against competing interests. On the other hand, multiple goals create opportunities for coalition building: if institutions were evaluated along a single dimension, a single organizational outcome preferred by a majority would be likely, and it would be impossible to split that majority without changing individual members' underlying preferences. By contrast, as Riker (1986) has pointed out, it is easier to find a proposal that defeats the status quo if there are multiple evaluative dimensions present (see Arrow 1951; McKelvey 1976).

Disjointed pluralism attempts to generalize about both these problems and opportunities. Four claims are central to my argument.

Claim 1: *Multiple collective interests typically shape each important change in congressional institutions.* With few exceptions, the process by which Congress adopts a specific institutional change reflects not just a single collective interest but multiple interests, and the interactions among coalitions promoting these interests typically determine the effects of each change. The "unintended effects" of an institutional innovation often derive not from the failure of members seeking a single goal to anticipate the consequences of their actions, but rather from the tensions among the *multiple interests* that produced the change in question.

In many cases, a confluence of interests allows a specific change to serve as a "common carrier," whereby several groups support the change, but each group believes it will promote a different interest. As Lindblom (1965) points out, different groups can agree on a course of action for very different reasons (see also March 1994). To assume, therefore, that each group interprets a given reform in the same way is to ignore powerful mechanisms through which political actors can coordinate their efforts. A proposed institutional change will more likely be adopted if it taps into multiple bases of support.

An example of a common carrier change is the Legislative Reorganization Act of 1970, which united backbenchers in both parties. Liberal Democrats hoped the LRA would serve their policy interests by limiting the power of conservative Democratic committee chairmen, and junior Republicans hoped it would promote their individual power goals by providing more opportunities for rank-and-file participation. Republicans and liberal Democrats shared a temporary interest in passing the Reorganization Act, but they each emphasized distinct consequences of the reform that were not fully compatible. Understanding the complex implications of the Reorganization Act is impossible without attention to this conjunction of interests. It is noteworthy that liberal Democrats' and junior Republicans' demands were complementary in this case. More generally, a group is more likely to be in the winning coalition if its interests can be seen as complementary, rather than contradictory, to the interests of other groups (see March 1994).

While the common carrier model is based on a (perhaps temporary) confluence of interests, multiple interests may also shape institutional changes in more conflictual ways. Although those initiating a change may have a single, clear goal in mind, they often are forced to make concessions to opponents of this goal, or to members who are not hostile to the basic purpose of the reform but nonetheless believe it might adversely affect some other interest. One cannot equate the initiators' goals with the final outcome of these compromises.

If one envisions institutional design as simply selecting a policy from a unidimensional continuum, this is not necessarily an important point. For example, if reformers want to require 100 signatures on a discharge petition, while opponents prefer 218, and neither side is strong enough to enact its preferred solution, a compromise figure of 150 might be adopted.[17] In such a case, the resulting policy outcomes will presumably be somewhere in between the positions favored by the two camps.

But institutions and institutional changes are rarely unidimensional. A change in one element of a complex reform proposal may affect other elements of the proposal in significant ways. For example, proponents of the Legislative Reorganization Act of 1946 sought to enhance Congress's position relative to the executive by strengthening congressional committees and by providing new integrative devices, such as party policy committees and a centralized budget process, to coordinate committee activities. The moves to strengthen committees succeeded, but the integrative devices were dropped from the bill. Foes of these features supported the general goal of challenging executive primacy, but also wanted to protect committee autonomy and limit the role of legislative parties. Strengthening committees without providing integrative devices reinforced the developing "feudal" system of committee power centers. Chapter 4 shows that in the long term these changes had only ambiguous effects on congressional power. Thus, the conflicts among competing collective interests may result in institutions that are poorly suited to achieving some widely shared objectives.

This does not mean that institutional changes are typically failures. The interactions among competing interests need not produce undesirable outcomes. Furthermore, when these interactions do lead to negative consequences, members will likely have opportunities to find new institutional solutions. The point, however, is that such institutional solutions do not embody a single, specific principle of legislative organization, and it cannot be assumed that they achieve any *particular* goal very well.

Claim 2: *Entrepreneurial members build support for reform by framing proposals that appeal to groups motivated by different interests.* Common carriers do not happen spontaneously. Instead, entrepreneurial members define issues so as to facilitate cooperative action among legislators who might normally oppose one another. Many of the changes I analyze were made possible by innovators who devised proposals that tapped into several distinct member interests. For example, in 1894, minority leader Thomas Reed (R-Maine) relentlessly filibustered to force majority party Democrats to accept his rules for limiting minority obstruction. While Reed believed these rules would promote congressional capacity and would help a future GOP majority govern effectively, his dramatic filibuster induced an urgent partisan interest in reform among Democrats, who feared that they otherwise would appear incompetent.

What drives individual entrepreneurs, such as Reed, to promote institutional changes that benefit some larger group? As Cox and McCubbins (1993) note, party leaders may have incentives to pursue changes that help their party because they will gain additional power and perquisites if the party retains (or captures) majority status. Again, the leader receives rewards that lead him to internalize the collective fate of his party. But party leaders are not the only entrepreneurs. The initiator of a nonpartisan change may also receive special benefits from its adoption. For example, a member who proposes the creation of a special committee generally becomes chair of that committee and thereby stands to gain personal power or an electoral benefit. Indeed, there are numerous cases in which entrepreneurs promulgate changes that promote a broad collective interest and that simultaneously provide a narrower, special benefit for themselves.[18] The efforts of entrepreneurs thus can help overcome collective action problems and advance the interests of groups that, unlike parties, lack the advantages of a formal organization (see Frohlich, Oppenheimer, and Young 1971).

Entrepreneurs' promotion of common carriers also gives us new leverage on the role of individual leaders in shaping congressional institutions. By the 1980s, most congressional scholars viewed institutional context as the primary determinant of leadership style (Cooper and Brady 1981; Rohde and Shepsle 1987; Sinclair 1990). Yet recent studies of specific committees and leaders suggest that individual leaders can make a substantial difference (Strahan 1990; Reeves 1993; Evans 1991; Peters 1998). The challenge then becomes incorporating leadership into a broader theoretical perspective. Entrepreneurial leaders exercise influence not chiefly by command or force of personality (though these occasionally are useful). Rather, the case of Reed, among others, suggests that entrepreneurs succeed by devising proposals and framing issues in ways that appeal to distinct member interests.[19] Thus, leadership is not an idiosyncratic residual that defies systematic analysis. Strategic innovation by would-be leaders is endemic to legislative politics and rooted in the pluralism of member interests.[20]

Claim 3: *Congressional institutions typically develop through an accumulation of innovations that are inspired by competing motives, which engenders a tense layering of new arrangements on top of preexisting structures.* A third feature of congressional development illuminated by a focus on multiple interests is the layering of new arrangements on top of preexisting structures intended to serve different purposes (see Orren and Skowronek 1994). At any point in time, Congress's authority structure consists of elements intended to favor the most salient interests during past moments of institutional creation. New coalitions may design novel institutional arrangements but lack the support, or perhaps the inclination, to replace preexisting institutions established to pursue other ends. While each individual change is consciously designed to serve specific goals, the layering of successive innovations results in institutions that appear more haphazard than the product of some overarching master plan.[21]

This layering process is in some ways path-dependent (Pierson 1998; North 1990; Aldrich 1994; Hughes 1991). The options available to decision makers today depend on prior choices. Preexisting institutions often create constituencies dedicated to the preservation of established power bases (see Remington and Smith 1999). As a result, institution-builders often attempt to add new institutions rather than dismantle the old.

If legislative institutions were geared toward a single collective interest, then this historical dynamic might not matter: a unique optimal solution to institutional design questions would likely emerge. But when multiple dimensions are relevant to members, a single dominant solution is less likely. As Aldrich (1994) points out, in such a situation the outcome will depend on the path followed (see also March and Olsen 1984).

An example of this path-dependent layering process occurred in 1974, when Congress created budget committees to provide an integrated fiscal policy. The Congressional Budget and Impoundment Control Act of 1974 superimposed the new budget committees on a decades-old structure of authorization, appropriations, and revenue committees. The budget committees' task of integrating fiscal policy was complicated because they had to work with committees that did not have a stake in the success of the new process. Sundquist (1981, 438) underscores this temporal dimension: "if the Congress were being organized anew, it may be doubted that a three-tier structure would be designed, with budget, authorizing, and appropriations committees all involved in the major decisions on every program every year." But too many members had a stake in their existing power bases to allow the dismantling of the old budgetary system.

The effects of an institutional change are thus mediated by tensions between that new arrangement and an entrenched authority structure designed to serve other interests. Along these lines, Riker (1995, 121) observes that "no institution is created *de novo*. Consequently, in any new institution one should expect to see hangovers from the past. . . . There is no reason to expect these hangovers to be internally consistent or to fit perfectly with the goals of reformers." Thus, congressional institutions generally are not well-tailored solutions to particular collective interest problems, and instead often embody contradictory purposes.

Claim 4: *Adoption of a series of changes intended to promote one type of interest typically will provoke contradictory changes that promote competing interests.* While the concept of path dependence illuminates the layering of successive innovations, its emphasis on continuity underestimates the incidence of major changes in congressional institutions (see Thelen 2000 for a related argument). Rather than pushing Congress in one particular direction, the multiple interests motivating members produce a more wayward, or even oscillatory, trajectory.

More specifically, successful innovations that promote a specific member interest tend to generate a reaction in which members seek to protect competing interests. The exclusive pursuit of one interest means other interests are neglected, eventually provoking legislators to change tacks and aggressively pursue these other interests. In particular, those members who are disadvantaged by current organizational arrangements will have strong incentives to seek reform. They can appeal to a subset of the current winning coalition by offering them a gain in terms of some objective that is not well served by existing institutions (see Riker 1986). Therefore, even when one interest reigns, it is setting up a predictable reaction. The multiple interests that motivate members are ultimately irreconcilable and preclude the triumph of a majority party cartel, rampant member individualism, or any other coherent model of organization.[22]

The resulting pattern of innovation and response should be evident when a series of changes push congressional organization in a single direction. The 1890–1910 period is perhaps the best example. Republicans pursued their partisan interests through several changes centralizing control in the House in the early to middle 1890s. However, this threatened competing interests, in particular members' power as individuals. The resulting dissatisfaction led to the 1899 election of a figurehead Speaker, David Henderson (R-Iowa), who members hoped would provide less aggressive leadership. But Henderson's weakness sparked further dissatisfaction as the House soon began to lose influence to the Senate. Joseph Cannon capitalized on this discontent in 1903, gaining wide support for reinvigorating the speakership. But his alleged excesses eventually led to a new round of decentralization in 1909–10 as progressive Republicans and Democrats "revolted" against Cannon. The 1970s–1980s also fits this pattern nicely: the extreme fragmentation brought about by the reforms of the early 1970s prompted Democrats to enact countervailing measures that strengthened majority party influence. This, in turn, provoked minority Republicans to embrace a far more confrontational strategy. By contrast, innovation-and-response is less evident in the 1920s and 1937–52 because there was no comparable push in a single direction.[23] Thus, if a series of changes promote one specific interest at the expense of others, members who share those other interests are more likely to organize to defend their priorities.

This does not mean that members' diverse interests always bring legislative institutions back to some stable, compromise equilibrium. In contrast to traditional pluralism, which views institutions as "pillars of order" in politics (Orren and Skowronek 1994, 312), *disjointed* pluralism portrays institutions as multilayered historical composites that militate against any overarching order in legislative politics. Congressional development is disjointed in that members incrementally add new institutional mechanisms, without dismantling preexisting institutions and without rationalizing the structure as a whole (see Braybrooke and Lindblom 1963). The resulting tensions mean that significant numbers of members will ordinarily be dissatisfied with established ways of doing business. This enables entrepreneurs to devise innovations that serve as common carriers, momentarily uniting those dissatisfied with the status quo. As a result, institutional development is an ongoing, open-ended process. The interplay of coalitions promoting contradictory objectives produces institutions that are tense battlegrounds rather than stable, coherent solutions.

ASSESSING INSTITUTIONAL CHANGE

Ultimately, the relationship between members' interests and institutional development is an empirical question. To begin to answer this question, I focus on four periods: 1890–1910, 1919–32, 1937–52, and 1970–89. These periods have been selected based on three criteria. First, I focus on the time since the House became a fully (or almost fully) majority-rule-based institution in 1890. This strategy allows comparisons between the majoritarian House and the nonmajoritarian Senate, while avoiding the additional complexities pertaining to the pre-1890 quasi-majoritarian House. A second criterion is that each period extends at least one decade and can appropriately be viewed as a single unit with common themes throughout.[24] A final criterion is that the periods include eras of Republican as well as Democratic majorities. The first two periods encompass much of the long era of Republican national hegemony, and the latter two periods most of the recent era of Democratic dominance.[25]

Within each period, I focus on changes in any of three main elements of the congressional authority structure:

Changes in the rules, procedures, and practices governing how matters reach the floor and how they are considered on the floor in the House or Senate.

Changes in the committee system. These include the creation of new committee units (or the abolition of existing units), changes in committee jurisdictions, changes in the powers or mode of operations of a specific committee (or of committees in general), and changes in methods of appointment that determine how representative committees are and whether assignments are used to induce loyalty.

Changes in leadership instruments. These include changes in the types of members who become leaders and changes in the roles played by leaders. Possible roles include, but are not limited to, punishing dissidents, enforcing agreements, acting as impartial brokers, keeping peace in their party or chamber, and defending the prerogatives and prestige of the institution. Leadership instruments are not limited to formally designated party leaders or official party organizations but can in principle serve a party, a faction, or the floor. The criterion for selection is importance, not who is served.

I focus on change because it offers an important window into the dynamics of legislative institutions. When members seek to change legislative organization, they test the control of competing coalitions over these institutions and bring the effectiveness of these institutions in promoting specific collective interests into sharp relief. Scholars have a unique opportunity to investigate institutions when they are "up for grabs." Furthermore, efforts to change institutions are a major part of legislative politics. However, our understanding of how members coordinate to enact such changes is limited. Yet it is precisely these processes—in which members with different interests interact to create new institutions—that affect the kinds of changes adopted and their long-term implications.

I attempted to identify important changes in rules, the committee system, or leadership instruments by reviewing approximately thirty secondary sources on each period. These sources are varied and therefore should not bias case selection in favor of a particular theoretical camp or collective interest. I included an institutional change in this study if five or more sources suggest that the change substantially affected congressional operations.

This case selection method has the drawback of relying on scholars who may cite one another about the importance of a change. If the first scholar cited was mistaken, then subsequent authors who rely on the first scholar's account will perpetuate this misimpression.[26] To mitigate this problem, I supplement these secondary sources with primary sources and with more specialized secondary accounts. This prevents overemphasizing a change that a handful of secondary sources too eagerly label important.[27] Appendix A includes a more detailed discussion of case selection, including a list of the sources used and a few examples of changes that narrowly failed to qualify for consideration.

For each change, the key questions are who sought the change, what interest or interests were pursued through the change, how was the change adopted, and what its implications were for congressional operations and outcomes. I also evaluate the changes within a given period more broadly in terms of whether they sought to (and in fact did) create, augment, or destroy an authority structure that approximated an incumbent cartel (Mayhew 1974), a majority party cartel (Cox and McCubbins 1993), a system of decentralized committee baronies (Shepsle and Weingast 1984;

Weingast and Marshall 1988), a set of informationally efficient committees that are agents of the floor (Krehbiel 1991), a system of individualistic entrepreneurship (Dodd 1977; Loomis 1988), or a series of centralized integrative mechanisms. In addition, I examine the relative significance of different kinds of control coalitions, including universalistic, majority party, ideological, issue-specific, distributive, and junior-member coalitions.

There are two main units of analysis in this study: the individual change and each period as a whole. With respect to each case, the null hypothesis is that a single collective interest accounts for the change in question. The alternative hypothesis is that multiple collective interests played a *significant* role in generating the change. As noted in the first claim above, there are two main scenarios in which multiple collective interests play a significant role: two or more distinct interests can reinforce one another, as in a common carrier change, or alternatively a change intended primarily to serve a single interest may be compromised by concessions to competing interests. The null hypothesis is a reasonable baseline, given that it is parsimonious and that numerous important studies attempt to show that a single member interest can explain key features of legislative organization (Mayhew 1974; Weingast and Marshall 1988; Krehbiel 1991; Cox and McCubbins 1993).[28] In order to reject the null hypothesis, a single interest must be insufficient to explain the content and adoption of the change in question. If a single interest is sufficient and additional interests played only a minor role in buttressing that dominant interest, then the null hypothesis cannot be rejected.

What counts as sufficient evidence to reject this null hypothesis? Obviously, if one defines each interest narrowly, then it will be much easier to find multiple interests operating than if one or two interests are defined so broadly as to encompass all possible motivations. The most important question is how broadly to define the reelection interest. One might argue that it is the source of most of the other interests that I identify, such as partisan, policy, or power interests, because pursuing these other interests is simply a strategy to achieve reelection. Indeed, Cox and McCubbins's party cartel model is rooted in the reelection drive: members seek a positive party reputation because it increases their reelection chances. But a key point is that the reelection interest, in isolation, does not divide majority party from minority party members (or liberals from conservatives, westerners from easterners, juniors from seniors, and so on). Only in the context of party-based divisions does the reelection interest produce a collective interest among some members in their party's reputation. While this collective interest may be derived from individual members' electoral calculations, it nonetheless leads to different expectations about congressional organization than those generated by the reelection interest in isolation. Similarly, policy interests and power base interests—though perhaps rooted in electoral calculations—divide members into competing camps, and as a result generate different expectations from incumbents' shared goal of reelection. Therefore, it is appropriate to distinguish between the reelection interest and other collective interests, which though perhaps rooted in electoral goals, nonetheless unite a subset of legislators against another group of members.

To sum up, an institutional change will be considered partisan if members of one party support the change because they believe it will enhance the reputation or effectiveness of their party (which in turn may be expected to increase party members' reelection chances). Policy interests will be cited when policy preferences have a significant impact on support for reform.[29] Similarly, power base goals will be cited when the evidence indicates that a subset of members favored a change because it would increase their access to power. By contrast, a change will be considered to serve members' electoral interests if it promotes reelection in a way that at least potentially unites all incumbents, rather than splitting members along partisan, ideological, sectional, or sectoral lines.[30] Finally, congressional (or chamber) capacity, power, or prestige will be considered significant if the evidence indicates that members supported a change because it would boost the institutional standing of Congress or their chamber.[31]

Given this definition of each interest, several types of data will be used in determining whether multiple interests were involved in a change. In some cases, I analyze roll call votes or cosponsorship data quantitatively to estimate the contribution of different interests. In such a situation, one test of the null hypothesis would be whether two or more variables—where each is a valid indicator for a distinct collective interest—have a significant impact on members' votes or cosponsorship behavior. One difficulty is that even when roll call data are available, the impact of certain collective interests may be impossible to estimate quantitatively. In particular, it is difficult, if not impossible, to measure members' interest in congressional capacity and power.[32]

When appropriate data are unavailable for a quantitative test, I rely on qualitative evidence, including floor debate, committee hearings, newspaper accounts, members' biographies, and other specialized works by historians and political scientists. In evaluating this information, I use several decision rules:

> **1.** A member statement that cites a collective interest is *not sufficient* to establish that this interest motivated a change. For obvious reasons, members have incentives to justify their actions as beneficial to the institution or to the public, even if those actions have a more

partisan or parochial motivation. In judging whether members' statements citing broad, institutional interests are merely masking a narrower motivation, I use two primary criteria:

　　a. If several members from opposing parties or ideological factions cite a common motivation for a change, then it is reasonable to conclude that the members' statements are not merely camouflaging a partisan or ideological motivation.

　　b. If a member consistently supports a given change, even as that member's own direct political interests shift over time (such as when the member moves from majority to minority party status), then it is more plausible that the member's statements are not camouflaging a partisan motivation.

　　2. In evaluating information from secondary sources, I emphasize specialized studies of the change in question more than general-interest works. For example, in evaluating the Joint Committee on Atomic Energy in 1946, I rely more on Green and Rosenthal's *Government of the Atom* (1963), which focuses almost entirely on the JCAE, than on *Congressional Quarterly's* (1982) general history of Congress from 1776 to 1981.

　　3. Furthermore, I consider evidence from secondary sources more convincing if multiple sources independently reach similar conclusions. If several sources agree that a particular interest played an important role, and the later sources are not all simply citing the same earlier source as the basis for their judgement, then there are stronger grounds to conclude that interest played a significant role.

More generally, regardless of whether quantitative data are available for a specific case, to understand its causal dynamics I draw upon as wide a variety of sources as possible, from member statements to specialized scholarly studies. To the extent feasible, I avoid relying upon a single source—be it a single member's statement or the findings of a single historian or political scientist—to establish the relevance or irrelevance of a collective interest. That said, the cases obviously vary in the amount of information available. When the evidence base is thin, I reach more tentative conclusions. Such cases are clearly identified in the substantive chapters.

Much the same logic is involved in establishing whether an entrepreneur played an important role in devising common carriers. In evaluating this claim, it is first necessary to determine whether a change in fact did tap multiple interests. If so, the next question is what role, if any, an entrepreneurial member played in building the coalition behind the change. Was the change simply an obvious move that most members easily grasped, or did it entail significant creativity in agenda setting, framing, or other forms of manipulation by an entrepreneur? Evidence for evaluating this possibility will be drawn from the same types of sources and evaluated using the decision rules outlined above.

To evaluate the third and fourth claims about disjointed pluralism, I focus on each period as the unit of analysis. In each period, I examine to what extent a single interest dominated congressional development, or alternatively, whether multiple collective interests produced the patterns of path-dependent layering and innovation and response identified in claims 3 and 4. This involves, in part, counting the number of changes that are accounted for by each interest. But it also involves analyzing the relative importance of the various changes and their aggregate effect on congressional operations. Furthermore, evaluating these claims requires examining the temporal dynamics of the changes: in what way, if any, do earlier changes lead to and shape the effectiveness of later changes? Claim 3 generates the expectation that tensions between an innovation and pre-existing institutions will often compromise its effectiveness. Claim 4 generates the expectation that successful changes promoting one member interest will provoke further changes that safeguard competing interests.

A final methodological issue is the definition of the dependent variable, institutional change. As noted above, I define *institution* broadly to include leadership instruments, the committee system, and rules and procedures. Such a broad definition is necessary because there are many alternative organizational paths by which members can pursue their interests. Understanding congressional organization requires dealing with each of these types of change.

Still, defining institutional change broadly means that some cases simply are not fair tests for certain theories. For example, Cox and McCubbins's (1993) majority party cartel model cannot be expected to explain changes in minority party organization, such as the creation of the Conservative Opportunity Society in 1983. Furthermore, as the COS illustrates, not all of the changes required majority approval. These changes may not feature the same dynamics as changes that require approval on the floor. In the empirical chapters, I note when a case is not relevant to assessing a specific theory. In chapter 6, I consider the question of whether certain theories better account for one type of change than other types of change and attempt to show that the four claims of disjointed pluralism hold if one examines only those changes that required approval by a floor majority.

INSTITUTIONAL CHANGE IN THE FOUR PERIODS

Even in 1890–1910, a period encompassing the longest successful era of party government in congressional history, multiple collective interests shaped institutional development. Majority party interests were, of course, critical, but minority party interests and concerns about congressional capacity also shaped House rules in 1891–95, when the Democrats were briefly in the majority. Moreover, the 1909–10 reforms that brought this period to a close were dramatic triumphs for a cross-party coalition of minority Democrats and insurgent Republicans that was united by a confluence of ideological, partisan, and power base concerns.

However, the 1909–10 rules changes did not repeal most of the innovations adopted by Republican majorities under Speakers Thomas Reed and Joseph Cannon, but rather added new devices, such as the consent and discharge calendars, that protected the minority and individual members. Thus, the reforms layered new mechanisms that empowered cross-party coalitions on top of a structure that still advantaged the majority party in other ways.

The main tension throughout the 1890–1910 period was between Republicans' shared interest in maintaining control of Congress, and progressive Republicans' interest in working with like-minded Democrats to pass legislation opposed by conservative Old Guard Republicans. House Republicans were able to mitigate this tension until the pressure for progressive policy departures became too great in 1909–10. Although Senate Republicans also built a party cartel of sorts, members were determined to protect their individual prerogatives and thus limited Republican successes in shaping Senate institutions.

From 1919 to 1932, the House majority party was once again more successful than the Senate majority in promoting its interests. Five of the ten significant institutional changes were initiated by House Republicans and were at least partly intended to improve the GOP's effectiveness. But some of these Republican moves were also responses to pressure for decentralization in the ideologically divided GOP. Cross-party coalitions rooted in ideological and sectoral interests also shaped institutional changes during this period, particularly in the Senate. Even in the House, cross-party coalitions enjoyed notable victories in 1924 and in 1931. In both cases, ideological concerns interacted with members' personal power interests to promote reforms that loosened majority leaders' agenda control.

From 1937 to 1952, majority party interests receded further in importance. The main collective interests were defending Congress from presidential aggrandizement and promoting the cross-party conservative coalition. Those were distinct interests: the congressional-executive rivalry, which motivated the Legislative Reorganization Act of 1946 and the 1940s boom in congressional investigations, cannot be reduced to policy differences between congressional majorities and the president. Liberals as well as conservatives backed these changes and expressed similar concerns about Congress's institutional viability. But other, competing interests also shaped each of these changes. As noted above, the Reorganization Act's integrative devices were removed because of concerns about committee and individual member prerogatives.

The onset of loyalty investigations in 1938 and the transformed role of the Rules Committee in the late 1930s were above all cross-party coalition successes. These investigations benefited conservatives in both parties and undermined the Democratic party nationally. Democrats responded with a few institutional changes of their own, but these were mostly compromised by competing interests. The 21-day rule of 1949–51, for example, temporarily countered Rules Committee obstruction, but did not eliminate many of the strategic advantages that the committee accorded conservatives.

One of the major tensions in this period was between Democratic leaders who saw themselves as largely responsible to Presidents Roosevelt and Truman, and the rank and file in both parties who believed their leaders were not adequately defending Congress as an institution. A second tension was that efforts to challenge executive primacy had to accommodate members' desire to expand individual entrepreneurship and protect their committee power bases.

In the 1970s–1980s, party interests returned to prominence, but they interacted with junior members' power base interests and with a renewed concern that Congress had lost too much ground to the executive branch. The result was an array of institutional changes that augmented majority party influence and helped coordinate spending decisions, but also facilitated entrepreneurship by junior members. Although Democrats' party-building efforts were compromised by the need to accommodate pressures for decentralization, they nonetheless successfully reinvigorated party government. This success, however, led Republicans to embrace Newt Gingrich's (R-Ga.) strategy of launching aggressive new attacks on Democrats and the House as an institution. These attacks led not only to Jim Wright's (D-Tex.) resignation as Speaker in 1989, but also to a more general decline in the standing of the House.

Chapters 2 through 5 provide a detailed analysis of each of these periods, while chapter 6 assesses the evidence and discusses the implications of disjointed pluralism for legislative institutions. The epilogue briefly discusses how disjointed pluralism illuminates developments in the 1990s. One final point warrants emphasis: the argument that disjointed pluralism characterizes congressional development does not imply that generalizations about institutions and institutional change are impossible. Instead, disjointed pluralism calls attention to features of congressional institutions that are generalizable across historical eras. Multiple collective interests typically shape individual institutional changes. Institutional development repeatedly appears disjointed as new arrangements are layered on top of preexisting structures intended to serve competing interests. While the mix of collective interests salient to members has shifted over time, the institutional and societal pressures that inform those interests remain sufficiently diverse to ensure that no single member interest dominates for long. As a result, institutional change is consistently characterized by the interplay of competing coalitions promoting multiple, potentially conflicting interests.

CHAPTER 2

Institutional Development, 1890–1910:
An Experiment in Party Government

SCHOLARS have repeatedly described 1890–1910 as the high-water mark for party government in the United States (Brady and Althoff 1974; Mayhew 1974, 175; Rohde 1991, 4–5). Unusually strong party cohesion, particularly among Republicans, coincided with intense interparty conflict for most of these two decades. Political commentators of that time could credibly speculate that congressional politics would become more and more like the strong party regimes of England and other parliamentary systems (Follett 1896).

The two parties were evenly matched as the 51st Congress convened in December 1889, with neither enjoying a clear hold on the allegiances of most voters. Nevertheless, the narrow Republican majority in the House embarked on an ambitious agenda of tariff increases, pension hikes, voting rights initiatives, and legislation to increase the value of silver.[1] To pave the way for these measures, Republican Speaker Thomas Reed of Maine undertook a "revolutionary" reinterpretation of House rules, famously stripping the minority of its ability to obstruct House business.[2] Voters seemed to register their disapproval of the GOP's legislative accomplishments by electing a huge Democratic majority in the November 1890 midterm elections. The new Democratic majority promptly repealed (if only temporarily) the bulk of Reed's rule changes. But in the midst of a deep recession prompted by the Panic of 1893, the Democrats proved unable to bridge the growing gap separating eastern, conservative "gold Democrats" from agrarian Democrats sympathetic to Populism and free silver. The Republican electoral sweep of 1894–96 gave the GOP a relatively secure hold on the House, Senate, and presidency that endured for the rest of the 1890s and the first decade of the 1900s. For a brief period following the 1896 realignment, Republicans enjoyed an unusual degree of unity on the major policy issues facing the country. It was not long, however, before sectionally based divisions over the tariff and corporate regulation created serious troubles for Republican leaders. The "Revolution of 1910," which deprived Speaker Joseph Cannon (R-Ill.) of his control of the House Rules Committee, signaled the end of Republican experiments with strong party government.[3] Reed's rules had inaugurated a twenty-year period in which institutional development was dominated by struggles between majority rule and minority rights, and between strong party leadership and cross-party coalitions seeking to promote new policy directions and a broader distribution of power.

Applying the criteria for case selection outlined in chapter 1 to the 1890–1910 period yields a list of ten important institutional changes:

1. Adopting the Reed rules of 1890 to curtail minority obstruction
2. Repealing the Reed rules in January 1892
3. Restoring Reed's quorum rule in April 1894
4. Increasing the prerogatives accorded to the House Rules Committee in 1892–95
5. Rising Senate centralization under William Allison (R-Iowa) and Nelson Aldrich (R-R.I.)
6. Decentralizing Senate Appropriations in 1899
7. The declining prestige and centrality of the speakership under David Henderson (R-Iowa) during his tenure from 1899 to 1903
8. The revival of the Speaker's power with Joseph Cannon's (R-Ill.) ascension to the office in 1903
9. Reforming the House rules in 1909 by creating a consent calendar, strengthening Calendar Wednesday, and guaranteeing the minority the opportunity to offer a motion to recommit
10. Overthrowing Speaker Cannon in 1910 through rules changes enlarging the Rules Committee, barring the Speaker from the committee, and making Rules an elected body

Appendix B.1 summarizes the floor votes that directly pertained to these changes, while table 2.1 notes the collective interests that were significant in each case and briefly describes the main effects of each institutional change. Seven of the ten cases involved formal changes in rules that were voted on in the House or Senate. Three cases—increasing Senate centralization in the late 1890s, the decline in the speakership under Henderson, and Cannon's revitalization of that office in 1903—were more informal in nature. While these three changes manifest patterns similar to those of the other cases, the available evidence with respect to the informal changes is less extensive, and as a result, the analysis of these changes is more tentative.

Notwithstanding the common portrayal of the 1890–1910 era as the heyday of majority party government, I will show that disjointed pluralism illuminates key features of institutional development during this period and helps make sense of patterns that are obscured by a narrow focus on majority party interests. Consistent with the first claim about institutional development, multiple collective interests typically shaped each individual change. Of the ten changes in this period, two or more member interests played an important role in nine cases (see table 2.1).

TABLE 2.1 Summary of Collective Interests Associated with Institutional Changes, 1890–1910

Case	Primary Interest	Common Carrier for Other Interests?	Compromised by Other Interests?	Coalition Shaping Change	Main Effects of Change
Reed rules, 1890	Majority party (effectiveness and reputation)	Congressional capacity and prestige		Majority party	Greatly increased Speaker power; regularized House procedures; stopped obstruction
Repeal of Reed rules, 1892	Majority party		Reed's bill introduction process retained (individual electoral interests)	Majority party	Revived ability of minority to obstruct business
Restoration of quorum rule, 1894	Minority party (reputation)	Majority party (reputation and effectiveness); cong. capacity		Cross-party, bipartisan leadership	Ended minority obstruction in House
Rise in Rules Committee prerogatives	Majority party (effectiveness)	Cong. capacity	Right to report at any time extended to more committees (individual power bases)	Bipartisan leadership	Added element of central control countering decentralizing thrust of 1892 rules
Rise of centralized Senate party leadership, 1897	Majority party (effectiveness)			Majority party	Created interlocking directorate of party and committee leaders

TABLE 2.1 Summary of Collective Interests Associated with Institutional Changes, 1890–1910 (cont.)

Case	Primary Interest	Common Carrier for Other Interests?	Compromised by Other Interests?	Coalition Shaping Change	Main Effects of Change
Decentralization of Senate appropriations	Individual power bases (junior senators)	Policy (sectionally based)	SAC allowed to keep part of its jurisdiction (power base interests)	Bipartisan reformist (antileadership)	Limited SAC influence and boosted role of substantive comms.; a blow to party leaders
Henderson and decline of speakership	Individual power bases	Senate leaders' power goals			Boosted position of committee chairmen and Senate leaders
Cannon's revival of the speakership	Majority party (effectiveness)	House power and prestige (vs. Senate)	Minority leader granted influence over committee assignments	Majority party	Returned to centralized House operations; ended Senate dominance
1909 rules reforms	Policy (progressives)	Individual power bases	Key reforms defeated by GOP leaders	Cross-party reformist (vs. majority party)	Limited dispersal of power; improved process for locally oriented, minor bills
1910 rules reforms	Policy (progressives)	Minority party; individual power bases	Amendments to protect party influence over Rules Committee (Democrats' partisan interests)	Cross-party reformist	Took away major power lever from Speaker; established Rules Committee as power base in its own right

Supporting the second claim of disjointed pluralism, entrepreneurial members were often critical in generating a confluence of multiple interests in favor of change. For example, as a member of the minority party in 1894, Reed aligned members' partisan goals and their interest in congressional capacity behind his rules for ending minority obstruction. In this and other cases, the relationships among multiple member interests played a critical role in enabling institutional innovation.

The cases examined in this period also provide ample support for the claim that legislative institutions tend to develop through an accumulation of innovations rooted in competing interests. As a result, the implications of any specific change can only be understood in relation to prior changes. For example, the centralized party leadership that arose in the Senate in the late 1890s coexisted with a strong respect for seniority and with rules that allowed prolonged filibusters. Party leaders' power was mitigated by the persistence of these preexisting arrangements, which empowered the individual member. Furthermore, party leaders' tightening hold provoked a reaction among rank-and-file members, who believed that their individual power bases had been diminished. This sentiment contributed to the 1899 decision to disperse control of appropriations (Schickler and Sides 2000). The 1899 change added another centrifugal force to the Senate authority structure, complicating the task of the apparently ascendant GOP leadership.

Finally, the changes in this period support the fourth claim, that a series of changes intended to promote one interest tends to provoke contradictory changes that promote competing interests. Repeatedly, Republicans pursued their partisan interests by enhancing central control over congressional operations. But in each case, centralization threatened other priorities, such as individual members' power bases, leading to rebellions geared toward dispersing control. In the same year when restive senators defeated the leaders of both parties by decentralizing appropriations, House members rebelled against "Czar" Reed by electing a "figurehead" Speaker, David Henderson (R-Iowa). In the end, Henderson proved so weak that he set the stage for Cannon's reinvigoration of party leadership in 1903. But members soon began to chafe once again under Cannon's leadership. A range of member interests shut out by the Cannon-led regime of party government eventually provoked the 1909–10 revolt that brought the era of "czar rule" to an unmistakable close. Yet these member rebellions left in place many of the centralizing changes adopted previously, such that the congressional authority structure came to include elements that served opposing purposes. A focus on the interactions and tensions among multiple member interests helps us to understand these dynamics of institutional development.

To facilitate analysis of the temporal dimension underlying the 1890–1910 changes, I present the cases in chronological order. I first discuss the 1890–97 innovations that empowered congressional party leaders. I then consider the initial reaction against this move toward centralization: the weakening of the speakership under Henderson and the dispersal of Senate appropriations. Finally, I turn to Cannon's restoration of strong leadership in the House and the 1909–10 revolt provoked by the Speaker's perceived excesses. The discussion of each case will explore the member interests that led to and shaped the change, the processes through which the change was adopted, and the impact of the change on congressional operations.

PARTY-BASED CHANGES AND THE PUSH FOR CENTRALIZATION, 1890–1897

Partisan interests played an important role in motivating and shaping each of the five institutional changes adopted from 1890 to 1897. With the exception of the Democrats' repeal of the Reed rules in 1892, each of these changes helped centralize power in the hands of party leaders. Broad, institutional concerns about congressional capacity also shaped these moves toward centralization. For example, the increase in the Rules Committee's powers in 1892–95 garnered substantial bipartisan support because minority-party Republicans believed that strong agenda control was required for Congress to function effectively. Minority party Republicans also drove the decision to restore the Reed rules in 1894. Thus, even in this period of strong parties, understanding institutional development requires a focus on how majority party interests intersected with potentially competing interests—minority party interests and members' stake in congressional capacity—to facilitate change.

Reed Rules, 1890

Adoption of the Reed rules in 1890 is without question one of the most significant events in the institutional development of the Congress. No single change did more to secure majority rule in the House. The two most important features of the Reed rules were the provisions instructing the Speaker not to entertain dilatory motions and putting an end to the "disappearing quorum." The dilatory motions ban empowered the Speaker to deny motions made solely to delay business. The "disappearing quorum" involved members' refusing to vote on a roll call even if actually present, thereby depriving the House of the quorum needed to do business. Reed's rules authorized the Speaker to establish a quorum by counting those members who were present but refused to vote. In the fifteen years after the end of Reconstruction, dilatory motions and the disappearing quorum had reached epidemic proportions, often bringing House business to a halt. The Reed rules rendered such tactics unavailable, and no equally effective substitutes have since been devised. The rules also included several other changes that promised to streamline House operations: reducing the quorum in the Committee of the Whole from half of the House to one hundred members, revamping the calendar system, and simplifying the bill introduction process.[4]

The collective interest most often cited as the motivation for the Reed rules is Republicans' interest in promoting their ambitious agenda (Dion 1997; Forgette 1997; Peters 1990). The Reed rules are thus commonly interpreted as support for conditional party government theory, which predicts that a unified majority party will seek to centralize power in the hands of its leaders (see, e.g., Wolf 1981). This theory has considerable merit: Reed would not have succeeded had Republicans not stuck together on a series of party line votes that began with Reed's initial rulings and concluded with final adoption of the new rules (see appendix B.1). Indeed, if one focuses solely on the 1890 roll calls, partisanship explains *all* of the variance in members' votes.

Nonetheless, two important caveats should be added to a purely partisan interpretation of the Reed rules. First, there is good reason to doubt whether Republicans actually enjoyed the near-consensus on major policy objectives that recent scholarship has attributed to them. Conditional party government theory may therefore be insufficient for understanding the 1890 changes.[5] A second, perhaps more important caveat, is that evidence from the fights surrounding minority obstruction both before and after 1890 suggests that concerns for congressional capacity also played a significant role in these recurrent battles.[6]

Turning first to the evidence concerning conditional party government, it is critical to note that the Reed rules were adopted in the 51st Congress, well *before* the realignment of 1896 settled the currency issue and brought about increased GOP homogeneity and party polarization.[7] The early 1890s were a time of intraparty dissension rather than an era of homogeneous majorities (Sundquist 1983). One way to see this is to examine constituency-based measures for majority party homogeneity and party polarization. Manufacturing production levels are generally considered one of the most important district-level characteristics in the late nineteenth century, as the American political economy was increasingly divided between industrial and agrarian districts with opposing policy priorities (see Bensel 1984; Cooper and Brady 1981). Figure 2.1 displays a measure of district-level homogeneity and party polarization that uses per capita manufacturing activity in each district for the 47th through the

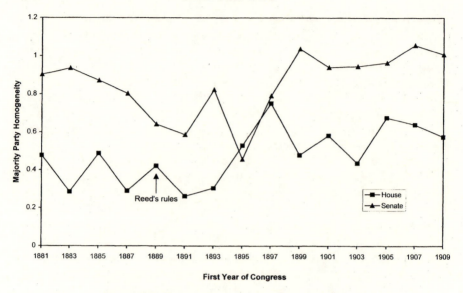

Figure 2.1 Party polarization and homogeneity
in the House and Senate, 1881–1910

61st Congresses (1881–1910). The measure, which parallels roll call–based measures devised by Aldrich and Rohde (1998), assesses the difference between the mean level of per capita manufacturing production in Republican as opposed to Democratic districts, divided by the standard deviation of per capita manufacturing production in majority party districts. The virtue of this measure is that it accounts for both the distance separating the parties and the internal divisions in the majority party. High scores on the measure indicate a majority party composed of members from homogeneous districts that differ sharply from minority-party districts. It is clear from figure 2.1 that Republican districts did not become increasingly homogeneous, and that Republicans and Democrats did not become more polarized, until several years *after* passage of the Reed rules.[8]

This conclusion is reinforced by an examination of the legislative agenda in the 51st Congress (1889–91). The three most important issues were the tariff, silver, and the federal elections bill (Wellborn 1928; Morgan 1969).[9] Republicans experienced significant factional divisions on all three issues, contrary to the argument that GOP unity on key policy issues motivated party members' embrace of the Reed rules. Below I delineate the GOP divisions and then offer an alternative interpretation of the Reed rules that focuses on Reed's successful fusion of Republicans' legislative and reputational concerns with their interest in congressional capacity.

The elections bill, which aimed to protect blacks' voting rights from southern efforts to disenfranchise them, barely gained approval by the GOP caucus over the opposition of a large minority of Republicans (*Washington Post*, June 17, 1890; McCall 1914; Hirschson 1962). With only two exceptions, the dissenters nonetheless chose to abide by the caucus vote to approve the bill.

Silver was an even more divisive issue for Republicans. Dunn (1922, 1:36) claims that "there were enough Republicans in each House who held silver above everything else to have turned the apparent Republican majority into a minority." More than twenty House Republicans voted for free silver on the floor, and Reed saved President Benjamin Harrison from a politically damaging veto only by delaying a key roll call until the support of gold Democrats could be secured. Several accounts suggest that even more Republicans favored free silver, but nonetheless went along with GOP leaders (McCall 1914; Dunn 1922, 1:37–42; Wellborn 1928). The Sherman Silver Purchase Act of 1890, though enacted on a near party-line vote, amounted to an effort to compromise differences that in the long run could not be compromised.

Even the tariff spawned sectional cleavages among Republicans.[10] Farm-state Republicans represented constituencies that were skeptical of the GOP's high tariff policy. Faulkner (1959, 104) writes that "there was little enthusiasm in the West" for maintaining high tariff duties, while Williams (1978, 26) argues that in the Midwest and the Plains states, "restive farmers openly wondered what the [protective] system offered them." Republican Joseph Medill's influential *Chicago Tribune* led a strong movement in the Midwest away from protectionism. Ways and Means Committee chairman William McKinley (R-Ohio), author of the 1890 tariff bill, sought to mollify farm-state Republicans by extending protection to agricultural products, but the economic benefits of such duties were suspect and did little to satisfy frustrated farmers.[11]

This midwestern discontent produced some Republican resistance to the McKinley bill. For example, on the day that the bill passed the House, Benjamin Butterworth (R-Ohio) criticized the Republican-controlled Ways and Means Committee for depriving rank-and-file members of the chance to amend the proposed legislation, since "we have not had time to secure a consensus of opinion even on this side of the House to enable us to legislate intelligently" (*Chicago Tribune*, May 22, 1890, 5; see also *New York Sun*, May 14, 1890). Yet Butterworth joined all but two Republicans in voting for the bill. In fact, it is remarkable how many Republicans bucked the rising tide among their constituents. After the bill passed the House, the *Tribune* charged that thirty to forty western Republicans had voted for a bill that "they had repeatedly denounced" and that they "were anxious should not pass" (May 23, 1890, 4; see Wellborn 1928, 471, for a similar assessment). While it is difficult to document how many members succumbed to party pressure, there is little doubt that the unified Republican support on the floor belied the considerable risks facing farm-state members who voted for higher tariffs. The independent *Minneapolis Journal*, among other midwestern newspapers, attacked the bill for its bias against farm products, and warned that "the Northwest will not be so easily satisfied with the measure as Northwestern Congressmen appear to be" (September 27, 1890; see also *Indianapolis News*, October 18, 1890).

In short, while political scientists have generally treated 1890 as the beginning of an era of GOP unity (Brady and Althoff 1974; Wolf 1981), historians and contemporary observers depict a much different reality.[12] Socolofsky and Spetter (1987, 78) claim that "factionalism within Republican ranks, which Harrison had been able to avoid in 1888, was rife by the time that elections were held in 1890." Mayer (1964, 224) argues that prior to the 51st Congress, "sectional economic disputes had been compromised with a minimum of disturbances. Henceforth, however, the [Republican] party would have to deal with a chronically disgruntled minority of Westerners which it was unable either to assimilate or to exclude permanently from its counsels." The staunchly Republican *New York Tribune*, in its summary of the first session of the 51st Congress, gives a sense for how attentive observers viewed the GOP in 1890: "It has been the custom to represent the Republican party as torn with internal dissensions, enervated by corruption, and dying or about to die. But no living party, in the plenitude of its highest vigor and might, has ever overcome greater obstacles, achieving thereby greater benefits for the Nation, than the Republican party in the enactment of the new tariff" (September 29, 1890). While the GOP had accomplished much, even its friends acknowledged these fierce factional divisions.

The burgeoning divisions at the constituency level suggest the need to look beyond partisan interests for a full understanding of the Reed rules. It is plausible that many members supported reform because they believed that the House's inability to process important legislation endangered congressional capacity and prestige. By the 50th Congress of 1887–89, minority obstruction was generating massive press criticism. For example, the *Washington Post* observed that "no other body in the world takes up so much time and spends so much money doing nothing. . . . The system of rules . . . is the prime cause of the wonderful inertia of this unwieldy and self-shackled body" (January 19, 1888). The *Post* even ran a series of front-page stories that compiled attacks on the rules from more than twenty other newspapers (see *Post*, April 22 and May 6, 1889). Furthermore, House organization appeared increasingly anachronistic in the context of Congress's rising workload, as the federal government took its first hesitant steps to regulate the expanding corporate economy (Cooper and Young 1989). Members thus had legitimate grounds to believe that rules reforms were necessary to enhance Congress's capacity to legislate and to defend the institution's standing.

Evidence for concerns about congressional capacity and power comes from several sources. Prominent Republicans, such as Reed and Henry Cabot Lodge (R-Mass.), wrote magazine articles in 1889 arguing that the House needed to reform its rules in order to safeguard its capacity to act (Lodge 1889; Reed 1889). Lodge (1889, 301, 295) claimed that the public was "disgusted" by the lower chamber's "impotence and stagnation" and that rules changes were needed to transform the House "from dead rot to vitality." Several Republicans struck a similar tone during floor debates on the Reed rules. Byron Cutcheon (R-Mich.) claimed that "new fields of legislation have opened upon us unknown to [the Founders]. With new necessities we must adopt new methods [that] . . . economize the time of the House for the transaction of business" (*Congressional Record* [hereafter CR], February 12, 1890, 1236). Similarly, Benjamin Butterworth—the same Ohio Republican who later fiercely attacked the McKinley tariff on the floor—argued that the new quorum rule was urgently needed "in order to enable the House to discharge the constitutional duties that devolve upon it" (CR, January 30, 1890, 989).

One might wonder whether such statements were merely rationalizations offered by majority party members to defend a change that they favored for purely partisan reasons. Against this view, it is noteworthy that GOP leaders pushed to streamline the legislative process while in the minority as well as when in the majority. In 1884, during the Democratic 48th Congress, Reed proposed rules changes that anticipated many of the scheduling reforms adopted six years later. Defending these proposals on the floor, Reed argued that "we are doing no business, because under our rules we deliberately sacrifice our time in such a way that it is impossible to do business. . . . Let us provide machinery for giving people decisions" (CR, April 17, 1884, 3064).[13] More than 90 percent of House Republicans and nearly 20 percent of Democrats voted for the proposed changes in 1884, but they were defeated by the overwhelming majority of Democrats (CR, February 8, 1884, 1000). Reed also lamented the House rules in private conversations, claiming in 1884 that Democratic Speaker John Carlisle "is not naturally ineffective. . . . But no Speaker could do any better with his hands tied by the rules we are working under . . . if we can't do business with the rules we have, we ought to frame some others which will meet our needs" (as quoted in Leupp 1910, 37). As discussed below, Republican leaders continued to push for rules that limited minority

obstruction, not only in the 51st Congress, when they were in the majority, but also in 1892–94, after the party lost its majority. This consistency
gives reason to doubt that Republican statements about congressional capacity were mere posturing.

The question is this: why did Republicans prove far more responsive
than Democrats to such institutional concerns? To be sure, Democrats
supported some of the Reed rules. Alexander (1916, 206) writes that most
of Reed's rules were not controversial, as "members generally approved of
the readjustment of the order of business, the reduction of the quorum in
Committee of the Whole to one hundred, and the relief of the morning
hour by filing bills and reports with the clerk." Some Democrats even
privately agreed with Reed's view that dilatory motions and the disappearing quorum were bad for the House. For example, in an anonymous
article in the *North American Review* ("Speaker and His Critics" 1890,
237), a Democratic leader acknowledged that the unrestrained obstruction of recent years has "awakened in many minds serious doubts as to the
future of parliamentary governments," and that absent an effective ban
on the disappearing quorum, the House would likely fail "either to assert
its power or to preserve its dignity" (246). This Democrat noted that
Reed's quorum rule "at least gives the House the means of proceeding
with its business" (247; see also Williams 1978, 24, 178). Similarly, Democrat Thomas Norwood of Georgia, who served in the House during the
49th and 50th Congresses, issued a strong attack on the rules in May
1889, calling on the House to end minority obstruction and thus allow
the chamber to do business more effectively (*Post*, May 6, 1889). Such
Democratic statements suggest that there were members in both parties
who viewed a crackdown on obstruction as essential for the House's institutional standing.

Nevertheless, Reed correctly doubted that Democrats, whose leaders
openly planned to use relentless obstructionism in the 51st Congress,
would provide him with much support. Reed would demonstrate later in
the 1890s that the minority party does not inevitably oppose rules designed to facilitate House business. But in 1890, Reed played a crucial role
in fusing concerns about congressional capacity with the GOP's partisan
interests, rallying Republicans around the idea (which proved incorrect)
that the party's reputation would be enhanced by reforming House institutions. Reed and his allies repeatedly contrasted the efficiency of their
methods to the hapless Democratic rules. Members of both parties came
to perceive that the Republican party's electoral reputation depended on
making the House appear a well-functioning, productive institution. Peters (1990, 62) argues that "in spite of their marginal situation, many
in the Republican hierarchy were convinced that the re-establishment of
Republican political dominance . . . required that the party prove itself

better able to govern than the Democrats." Reed emphasized that this meant reforming the House rules—even as the GOP's policy divisions instead could have led Republicans to conclude that they should avoid reforms that would help pass controversial (and hence politically dangerous) legislation.

Many observers have pointed to Reed's forceful, determined personality as a key factor leading to the 1890 changes (Galloway and Wise 1976; Low 1906). This view was endorsed by Reed's own colleagues, including Cannon, who denied that either he or McKinley—the two other leading House Republicans—would have had the strength and courage to push through the reforms (Busbey 1927). Reed's consistent advocacy of reform, even while in the minority (1884–89, 1891–94), adds further support for taking the Speaker's role seriously and suggests that his motivations were not simply partisan.[14] Indeed, Reed's commitment to limiting obstruction had become so strong that he was prepared to resign as Speaker should he have been defeated in the rules fight (Strahan 1999). Reed also did more than any member to publicize the evils of minority obstruction and to build popular support for reform, writing articles in the *Saturday Evening Post*, *North American Review*, and other magazines.[15]

Yet political scientists have been reluctant to deal explicitly with Reed's role because it appears too idiosyncratic for systematic analysis (Strahan 1999 and Riker 1986 are important exceptions). This is a mistake: Reed's actions are but one example of how entrepreneurs fuse member interests in novel ways that facilitate institutional change. Reed timed consideration of the rules and dramatized the issue in such a manner that Republicans developed an immense stake in his reforms. Reed's achievement was to align his abiding interest in Congress's institutional capacity—as demonstrated by his commitment to reform even when he was in the minority—and his belief in majority party government, with Republicans' shared interest in their party's reputation for competence and legislative success.

Reed relied on a heresthetical maneuver, to use Riker's (1986) term, to unify the Republicans.[16] Rather than attempting to adopt new rules at the opening of the 51st Congress, Reed waited to make his move until party passions were most salient. That moment came when the House began consideration of contested election cases. In 1890, election cases were still regarded as purely partisan affairs (Polsby 1968), and Reed knew that Republicans would be loath to allow Democrats to obstruct the seating of GOP members. Without warning even fellow Republicans of his plans, Reed ruled on January 29, 1890, that the Speaker could count nonvoting members as present for the purposes of a quorum, as long as they were in the House chamber. Following a tumultuous daylong debate in which Democrats loudly accused Reed of tyranny, the Speaker was upheld on appeal by a perfect party vote (see appendix B.1). The next day, he ruled that the Speaker would not entertain motions that he judged dilatory. Once again, the Democrats cried foul, but Republicans upheld Reed on another party-line vote. Dunn (1922, 1:23) argues that had Reed taken his proposal to a party caucus, pivotal Republicans would have "refused to follow him in such a radical step . . . but he sprang his new system at a time when party feeling ran high over a contested election case and the fierce denunciations of the Democrats solidified his own party" (see also Robinson 1930, 220). Two weeks later, the Rules Committee brought to the floor a new code of rules that incorporated Reed's two rulings, as well as the other changes described above. The rules once again sparked an intense debate but were adopted on another straight party vote.

Reed's timing was crucial not only because the contested election case provided an unmistakable partisan backdrop for his decision, but also because his surprise maneuver received immense press attention. By taking such a prominent public stand before having received assurances of support from his Republican colleagues, Reed put party members in the position of either "winning" by publicly backing their leader, or surrendering to Democrats' denunciations.[17] Reed's defeat would have embarrassed the GOP in front of an attentive, engaged national audience.

Perhaps more importantly, had Reed waited until the House undertook a detailed debate on the rules as a whole, he risked entangling the rules controversy in other substantive issues that divided Republicans. Reed's dramatic ruling instead created momentum that greatly facilitated the passage of his reforms. Robinson (1930, 220) writes that "in matters of tariff and currency, where sectional differences were likely to assume serious proportions, it was especially desirable to avoid all preliminary clashes. A protracted wrangle over the rules would have given any petty group of obstructionists within the party an unprecedented opportunity for the levy of political blackmail." This, in fact, is what happened during the same Congress in the Senate. When Democrats obstructed the federal elections bill, Aldrich and other GOP leaders sought to enact a cloture rule that would have had similar effects to Reed's reforms. But a faction of silver Republicans reneged on an earlier commitment to do whatever it would take to pass the elections bill and instead shelved it and the cloture resolution in order to collaborate with Democrats on free silver legislation.[18]

Reed's success in holding Republicans together was so complete that few compromises among competing interests were made en route to the adoption of his reforms. As a result, the Reed rules had relatively unambiguous effects. Most importantly, the reforms greatly enhanced the power of the Speaker and inaugurated an era of strong majority party leadership in the House. Galloway and Wise (1976, 168) express the widespread view that "the net effect of the Reed rules was a great increase in the powers of the Speaker. Reed ruled the House with an iron hand for six years."

Some scholars interpret this increase in the Speaker's influence as but one important step in a gradual process of accumulating leadership prerogatives (Follett 1896; Peters 1990), while others treat it as a sudden, dramatic break with earlier developments (Galloway and Wise 1976). Starting with Speakers James Blaine (R-Maine) and Samuel Randall (D-Pa.) in the 1870s, and continuing throughout the 1880s, various precedents gave the Speaker increasing control of floor recognition and enabled the majority party to use special orders from the Rules Committee to shape the House agenda. Yet in the face of dilatory motions and the disappearing quorum, these changes only modestly empowered the Speaker and the majority party (Wolf 1981).

Reed's rules heightened the importance of these earlier reforms. By eliminating minority obstruction, the new rules removed the final barrier to the incipient "majority despotism" that had begun to take shape under Reed's predecessors (Peters 1990, 69). The Reed rules did far more than simply limit minority obstruction, because the new rules were superimposed on those earlier changes that had granted the Speaker increased agenda control. Thus similar, compatible member interests motivated a series of incremental changes, such that the net rise in Speaker influence far outpaced that contemplated in any single change.

The paradox, then, is that in an era of relatively heterogeneous majorities, a series of innovations empowered the speakership and helped achieve an unprecedented level of majority party government. How did this come to pass? Although a more detailed examination of each step in this process is needed, a hypothesis that emerges from this examination of the Reed rules is that members' concerns about congressional capacity in the context of a growing House and rising workload interacted with partisan interests. Prior to 1890, party-based reforms had only limited impact because they were layered on top of preexisting arrangements that accorded substantial obstructive powers to dissenters. Reed's predecessors had provided the Speaker with tools to manage the House agenda in an environment of intraparty strife and a potent opposition party; but the earlier reforms did not enable the Speaker actually to overcome concerted House opposition. It was only with Reed's rules, which swept away the longstanding precedents favoring minority rights, that the Speaker and majority party could enact major programs in the face of intense opposition. These rules, in turn, were made possible by Reed's skillful timing, which induced an intense partisan interest in major reform.

In addition to bolstering the Speaker's influence, the Reed rules regularized House procedures and enabled the lower chamber to process more legislation (Cooper and Young 1989). The 51st Congress was unusually productive (Morgan 1969), and the Senate quickly replaced the House as the locus of minority obstruction and the target of criticism about unwieldy congressional organization. Although the majority party could expect disproportionate legislative benefits from this productivity, there were nontrivial benefits for all members. For example, the bill introduction system proposed by Reed, which specified that members introduce bills by filing them with the clerk, provided credit-claiming and advertising opportunities for all members (Cooper and Young 1989).

Ironically, Republicans' impressive record in the 51st Congress ended up imposing immense electoral costs on party members. Democrats gained 75 House seats in the 1890 elections, while the number of Republicans dropped almost by half, to just 88. Most scholars have joined contemporary observers in attributing the GOP defeat primarily to the McKinley tariff (*Harper's Weekly*, November 15, 1890; *Post*, November 5, 1890; Faulkner 1959). Western constituents believed the bill perpetuated the pro-eastern bias of the GOP's protectionist policies (*Public Opinion*, November 15, 1890, 123–25; *Minneapolis Journal*, September 27, 1890). This exacerbated the GOP factional divisions described above. Furthermore, because of Senate delays, the tariff did not gain final approval until just a month before the election. Stanwood (1903, 287) calls this "a tactical blunder of the most stupendous character." The increased duties took effect on October 6, 1890, but the main benefit of the bill for consumers, cheaper sugar, did not take effect for another six months. Democrats could thus easily blame price increases on the measure.

The Reed rules contributed to Republicans' electoral undoing both indirectly and directly. Indirectly, the rules enabled Republicans to push through legislation without any Democratic support. This tied Republicans closer together so that western members were unable to distance themselves from their eastern brethren. Moreover, it allowed controversial programs to pass, while placing full responsibility for those measures in GOP hands (see Dunn 1922, 1:16).

More directly, the Reed rules helped Democrats depict the GOP as the party of centralization and federal interference. Williams (1978, 41) notes that voters became "restive, uncertain about the activism of the Fifty-first Congress," as well as concerned that certain state-level Republican initiatives would curtail religious liberties and access to liquor. Democrats "skillfully exploited the opening, pointing out the larger pattern. In both nation and state—whether it was the McKinley tariff, prohibition, the [federal] election bill, Reed's tyrannical rules, or the Bennett [education] law—the Republicans seemed bent on abusing power and encroaching on individual liberties" (Williams 1978, 46).[19] Jensen (1971) describes how Wisconsin Democrats successfully linked the Reed rules and other examples of centralization at the national level with local Republican educational initiatives that alienated swing German voters, producing an unprecedented Democratic sweep of all but one major office in the state.

Contemporary accounts also noted how the Reed rules undermined the GOP: the *New York Times* argued that controversies surrounding Reed's methods, the tariff, and the federal elections bill each tainted the GOP's reputation (*NYT*, November 5, 1890; see also *Harper's Weekly*, November 15, 1890).

Reed had used his considerable skills to push Republicans to adopt new rules that greatly empowered party leaders. But the resulting mode of party government depended on a level of constituent homogeneity that simply did not exist. Members were pressured to vote for policies that lacked support at home, and suffered collectively from an extreme party image. Given Republicans' internal divisions, they may have been better off with a less ambitious legislative agenda and with more modest rules reforms that still allowed minorities within the party to block highly controversial bills. This case illustrates both the potential influence of partisan interests and the risks to members of allowing such interests to trump constituency opinion.[20]

The Reed rules also demonstrate that important institutional changes can hinge on an entrepreneurial leader's ability to manipulate the strategic situation to align multiple interests. In addition, the confluence of Reed's rules and earlier, party-based innovations suggests the importance of the relationships among institutional changes that are layered on top of one another. Unlike many other cases of institutional development, however, the interests that motivated the Reed rules were quite compatible with the earlier changes, and, as a result, the Reed rules actually compounded the importance of these changes.

Repeal of Reed Rules, 1892

While in the minority, Democrats vehemently condemned the Reed rules. When the party won a huge majority in the 1890 elections, its members wasted little time in repealing the quorum rule and the dilatory motions ban, along with most of the rest of Reed's handiwork. Democrats' partisan interests were the driving force behind repeal, though the electoral interests of members of both parties forced amendments retaining provisions of Reed's rules that facilitated individual credit-claiming.[21]

Notwithstanding the prevalence of majority party interests, this change raises difficult questions for partisan theories. Why would an incoming majority party enact rules that protect the minority? Why would the minority oppose these changes and actually support rules that take away its ability to obstruct business? The answer has to do with the complexity of members' party-based interests, which included a mix of potentially conflicting legislative and reputational considerations.

A partial explanation for the Democrats' decision to drop the Reed rules derives from conditional party government theory: a heterogeneous majority party prefers rules that diffuse agenda control among all majority party members (Rohde 1991). Wolf (1981), in particular, has argued that the Democrats' internal divisions, centering on the tariff and currency, forced party members to deprive their leaders of much power. Indeed, the Democrats feared that any legislating would damage their party's fragile unity. Consistent with this view, the *New York Times* scolded the Democrats for delays in organizing the 52nd Congress and charged that many Democrats "earnestly wish that their party shall do nothing because they are convinced that if it does do anything it will be something that they can get no advantage from" (February 1, 1892). But while Democratic divisions likely created a party interest in some loosening of Reed's rules (and thus making it difficult to pass legislation that divided the party), the reforms themselves appear to have gone further than the Democrats' legislative interests required.[22] In particular, by repealing Reed's disappearing quorum rule and failing to provide even a partial substitute, the Democrats empowered the Republican minority to obstruct business even when Democrats had an urgent need for action. As events in 1894 made clear (see below), the new Democratic rules allowed Republicans to do just that.

Understanding this outcome requires attention to Democrats' reputational interests, as well as their directly legislative goals.[23] The party had made such an issue of the Reed rules in the 1890 campaign that maintaining them would have been politically damaging. As the new Congress convened, Democratic newspapers were confident that the incoming majority would repeal the Reed rules. Thus, the *Detroit Free Press* predicted that "Reedism in the chair will not find favor in a Democratic House, and one of the first things to go will be the odious rules [of the 51st Congress]" (December 8, 1891). The new Speaker, Charles F. Crisp (D-Ga.), had built his reputation by leading the battle against the Reed rules, and the *Boston Globe* declared that his election meant that "the era of Czarism, with its arbitrary recognitions and 'vote counting,' is over" (December 8, 1891; see also, *Post*, January 22, 1892). Future Democratic congressman George McClellan of New York later wrote (1911, 597) that "as Mr. Crisp had been one of the loudest denouncing the 'tyranny' of the Reed rules, he was obliged on taking the Chair, if he wished to preserve even the semblance of consistency, to find some other method of asserting his power." While House rules are rarely salient to voters, the Democrats' attacks on the Reed rules prevented them from emulating their Republican predecessors—whatever their party's legislative interests required.

The coalition that enacted the 1892 rules changes was partisan and included few, if any, Republicans (see appendix B.1). Democrats from all wings of the party—pro-silver, pro-gold, free traders, and protectionists—

united to support the new rules, which had been proposed by Democrats on the Rules Committee. Republicans proposed amendments restoring the main features of the Reed rules but failed.

Therefore, the decision to drop Reed's rules was rooted most directly in Democrats' partisan interests and was passed by a party-based coalition. But it is doubtful that repealing the Reed rules helped stack the legislative process in ways beneficial to Democrats. After all, two distinct Democratic objectives drove the 1892 changes. While Democratic heterogeneity generated a party interest in decentralization, the specific form of decentralization—namely, empowering obstructionists in both parties—derived from the Democrats' need to maintain a consistent image. Though few Democrats expressed opposition to the general idea of decentralizing power, several did question the wisdom of allowing concerns about hypocrisy to shape legislative organization.

Indeed, more than a few Democrats favored retaining Reed's rules. The productivity of Reed's Congress had set a daunting example, and the dangers of allowing rampant obstruction became apparent early in the session. As the debate on the rules dragged on, press coverage of the Democratic Congress became increasingly critical, with headlines such as "The Do-Nothing Congress" and "Dilatory Democrats" gracing the *New York Times* (January 29, 1892, 5; February 1, 1892, 4). The *Times*, then a Democratic newspaper, claimed that "not a few of the Democrats are convinced that Mr. Reed is more than half right in his views regarding the suppression of dilatory motions, but the larger number are unwilling to alter their attitude toward the man and his parliamentary opinions" (January 29, 1892, 5). Several Democrats argued on the floor that the House should restrict minority obstruction. Bourke Cockran (D-N.Y.) asserted that the House has the right "to ascertain the existence of a quorum or perform any other function of the House in any method that seems to it proper" (CR, February 1, 1892, 741). Benjamin Enloe (D-Tenn.) acknowledged, "I see something good in the rules of the Fifty-first Congress . . . the rules of the Fiftieth Congress were do-nothing rules" (CR, January 29, 1892, 680). William Bynum (D-Ind.) moved to amend the Democrats' proposed rules to deprive dissenters of the most effective dilatory motions. His amendment lost, 87–161, but it received the support of 31 Democrats and all but three Republicans (see appendix B.1), suggesting that a significant number of Democrats, along with nearly all Republicans, opposed minority obstruction. A logit analysis of this roll call shows that the 31 Democrats who voted for the change did not differ significantly from other Democrats in their ideology, region, committee membership, or seniority.[24] Instead, based on their floor statements, they appear to have been united by the belief that the Reed rules had genuinely improved House operations.

Although dissident Democrats failed to amend those proposed rules that affected minority rights most directly, they did succeed in preserving Reed's streamlined bill introduction process. Prior to the Reed rules, which established an automatic means for introducing proposed legislation, the bill introduction process was notoriously inefficient, hindering members' ability to use bill proposals to advertise and credit-claim (Cooper and Young 1989). Democratic leaders wanted to rescind the new process because it enhanced the Speaker's control of bill referral decisions. But individual members were unwilling to surrender the electoral benefits that the Reed innovations provided, despite the additional prerogatives granted to the Speaker. While one of two amendments restoring the Reed provisions passed on a voice vote, the other was the subject of a roll call (see CR, February 1, 1892 and February 3, 1892). Democrats split 105 to 74 in favor of retaining Reed's bill introduction system, while Republicans were unanimous in their support (see appendix B.1). A logit analysis of this roll call suggests that the Democrats who voted to retain Reed's system did not differ in ideology, region, or committee assignments from other Democrats, but did tend to be slightly more senior (b = .14; SE = .09; p = .12, two-tailed). This suggests, albeit tentatively, that careerist members in particular wanted a system that promoted individual member credit-claiming.[25] The amendments restoring the bill introduction process were important exceptions to the general thrust to reduce the Speaker's power.

The repeal of the Reed rules was replete with ironies for both parties. Repeal made the majority party an advocate for minority rights, and the minority an advocate for effective majority rule. This role reversal stemmed in part from constraints that the Democrats' own 1890 campaign tactics placed on their subsequent decisions about congressional organization. Repeal also led to other changes that granted the Rules Committee increased control of the House agenda, thereby contributing to the long-term trend toward centralization that Democrats for the most part opposed (see discussion below). Finally, the Democrats' failure to govern effectively absent the restrictions imposed by the Reed rules would ultimately doom minority obstruction in the House.

Restoration of the Quorum Rule

Cockran's and Bynum's concern about the House majority's ability to conduct business turned out to be prescient. The Democrats' new rules embarrassed the party during both the 52nd and 53rd Congresses. While the Democrats' large majority in the 52nd Congress mitigated these ill effects somewhat, Republicans used obstruction to great effect in the

53rd Congress, when the Democratic margin was reduced to a still-substantial 220 to 126 advantage. In September 1893, the House adopted some of the less controversial features of Reed's rules, such as the provision setting the quorum in the Committee of the Whole at one hundred. Later in that same Congress, a Republican filibuster forced the Democrats to adopt the quorum rule, with only cosmetic changes from the original Reed version. Restoring the quorum rule was made possible by an intriguing confluence of member goals: Republicans' interest in embarrassing the Democrats and in legitimizing Reed's innovations, Democrats' interest in showing they could govern, and all members' interest in Congress's capacity to legislate.[26]

As the Democrats became increasingly divided amid the fights over silver and the tariff in the 53rd Congress, Reed saw the opportunity to force the beleaguered majority party to endorse his methods. He and his Republican colleagues began an extended obstruction campaign in February 1894, which continued with few interruptions for over two months. The Republicans relied most heavily on the disappearing quorum tactic, which proved effective because the Democrats could not keep their members in the Capitol. Reed made it clear that Republicans would not relent until Democrats admitted the need to count a quorum.

Reed's success depended on his aligning several member interests. In part, Reed drew upon Republicans' expectation that their party would soon be in the majority and thus would no longer benefit from minority obstruction. By forcing the Democrats to adopt the quorum rule, Reed saved the Republicans from having to impose the controversial procedure in the next Congress and thereby preempted Democratic accusations of GOP tyranny. But even as late as April 1894, it was not certain that Republicans would gain majority status in the upcoming November elections. Given this uncertainty, skeptical Republicans wondered whether it was wise to support the quorum rule "and thus pave the way for the easy accomplishment of whatever purpose the leaders of the majority may form" (*Post*, April 16, 1894, 2; see also *Post*, April 12, 1894, 1).

Reed nonetheless kept Republicans unified. He convinced his fellow partisans that they would gain by making the Democrats choose between legislative paralysis and the institutional arrangements that they had so recently condemned. For weeks, the press attacked the Democrats for their inability to legislate. The *Washington Post* charged that the Democrats "have deliberately refused to follow the dictates of their better judgment lest they should be charged with now upholding that which they once denounced" (April 14, 1894, 4). Cockran, one of the few Democrats to oppose minority obstruction with some consistency, argued that "there seems to be a feeling that the counting of a quorum of members present would be an endorsement of Reed's rules. Mr. Reed, in my opinion, is not such a powerful person that he should be allowed to drive a party into a ridiculous, illogical, and obstructive course, merely for the sake of remaining in opposition to him on a popular question" (*Post*, April 13, 1894, 1). Republicans stood to gain from the Democrats' embarrassment and from the vindication that would come from adoption of Reed's rules. Accordingly, Atkinson (1911, 47) points out that Reed "thought it would be good politics to justify in this way . . . the parliamentary principles for which he stood."

In addition to tapping into these Republican goals, Reed made the quorum rule a common carrier for members' broader interest in Congress's capacity to legislate. Reed's own steadfast advocacy of reform—while in the minority as well as the majority—contributed to the slowly emerging consensus that majority rule would benefit all members. Furthermore, the 1894 filibuster showed how the minority could wreak havoc upon the House without strong rules to restrict obstruction. Members of both parties came to view the quorum rule as necessary for Congress to function (*Post*, April 14, 1894, 1, 4; McClellan 1911). Democrat William Springer of Illinois, echoing earlier statements by Republicans, expressed this new-found bipartisan sentiment: "We have tried the old system. We have been here a month without doing two days' actual business, and our constituents are tired of this delay. . . . If we shall adopt this rule, we will from this time forward have it in our power to discharge the duties which our constituents have confided to us" (CR, April 17, 1894, 3790; see CR, April 17, 1894, 3789–92, for similar statements by Reed and by Democrats Joseph Outhwaite of Ohio and Thomas Catchings of Mississippi).

Finally, Reed foisted upon reluctant Democrats a partisan interest in rules reform: escape from the prolonged filibuster that had made a mockery of the party's ability to govern. Reed could not have generated this Democratic interest if not for the majority party's dismal failure to keep its members in Washington, rather than in their districts. Democrats desperately sought to end the GOP filibuster without counting a quorum, but urgent pleas for better attendance failed to generate a quorum of just Democrats. The party caucus even proposed to fine absent members. But Republicans blocked the proposal, forcing a full-scale surrender to Reed's rules (*Post*, April 13, 1894, and April 18, 1894).

That surrender did not come without a fight from some Democrats. At a Democratic caucus meeting, William Jennings Bryan (D-Nebr.) complained that the party "had enough to answer for without being called upon to explain why they now adopted tactics for which they had denounced Mr. Reed" (*Post*, April 14, 1894, 1). Richard Bland (D-Mo.) mused that "if we are to have Reedism we might as well go home" (*Post*, April 14, 1894, 1). But following a stormy debate, the caucus approved the quorum rule by an 80 to 44 vote. The Democrats' long delay in accepting the quorum rule and their urgent search for alternatives—even in the face of mounting embarrassment and intense press criticism—suggest the extent to which concerns about maintaining a consistent image (not to mention genuine principled opposition) motivated party members.

Reenactment of the quorum rule, therefore, was brought about by the minority party. The floor vote on its passage united all Republicans with 125 of 170 voting Democrats (see appendix B.1).[27] Despite the bipartisan support, there was no mistaking who had won. As Wolf (1981, 348) observes, "the divided Democratic majority had been driven to accept a measure of central control through Republican prodding, rather than by the wishes of its own membership." Dissident Democrats decried the "humiliating spectacle" (*Post*, April 18, 1894, 1). Meanwhile, Republicans applauded the change, and Reed congratulated the House.

The fight over the quorum rule and over the Reed rules more broadly has important implications for our understanding of institutional change. First, it suggests that entrepreneurial leaders can successfully take advantage of different member interests. Reed, who from the start was motivated by a mix of partisan and institutional objectives, aligned several distinct interests to support his vision of how Congress should operate. In 1890, he framed the issue of the balance between majority rule and minority rights as largely a partisan concern; but just four years later, Reed's persistent obstruction turned that same issue into a bipartisan matter that united most Democrats and Republicans. Although many Democrats were unhappy with the quorum rule, 1894 marked the end of their party's long-standing commitment to the "right" of the House minority to obstruct business. As Peters (1990, 73) concludes, with the April 1894 decision, "the quorum issue was settled for good."

Second, the quorum fight shows that the minority party can substantially influence institutional development, even during an era that rightly qualifies as the premier instance of strong majority-party government in congressional history. The 1894 adoption of the quorum rule makes little sense from the perspective of party government models that focus on the interests of the majority party to explain rules changes that affect minority rights. Whereas Dion (1997), Binder (1997), Rohde (1991), and Cox and McCubbins (1993) lead one to expect a cohesive majority party to clamp down on minority obstruction, in this case an increasingly divided majority embraced majority rule only at the insistence of the minority.

Third, understanding the quorum battle requires attention to each party's reputational concerns as well as its purely legislative interests. Democrats' 1892 decision to repeal the Reed rules and their reluctance in 1894 to adopt the quorum rule reflected party members' concerns about maintaining a consistent image with the public. But when such reputational concerns intrude heavily into members' calculations about what arrangements best serve their interests, it is unlikely that the resulting institutions will be optimally tailored to achieve the *legislative* interests of either party. Instead, institutions emerge as products of a complex battle in which entrepreneurs seek to manipulate individual members' interests to suit a range of potentially conflicting goals.

Increase in House Rules Committee Prerogatives

The additional prerogatives granted to the Rules Committee in the early 1890s derived from Democrats' partisan interests and from broader concerns about congressional capacity. Leaders of the majority Democratic party championed each of these prerogatives. The Democrats on the Rules Committee sponsored the February 1892 change granting the committee the privilege of immediate consideration of its reports, with no dilatory motions allowed. This protected bills carrying the Rules Committee's endorsement from many filibuster tactics, but not from the disappearing quorum. Most Democrats supported the new rule, believing that it would limit obstruction without requiring complete acceptance of Reed's rules (CR, January 29, 1892, 675–83). Similarly, Rules Committee Democrats, seeking to protect the party from minority obstruction, sponsored the September 1893 change allowing the Rules Committee to sit while the House was in session. Together, these changes enabled the Rules Committee to block filibusters quickly. Finally, Speaker Crisp issued a ruling in February 1895 that extended the Rules Committee's jurisdiction to bills still pending in legislative committees (CR, February 4, 1895, 1740–52).[28]

Several Democrats opposed these new prerogatives, arguing that they surrendered too much influence to a single committee and undercut the party's criticisms of Reed's rules. Joseph Bailey (D-Tex.) called the 1892 move "an essential departure from the traditions and the usages of the Democratic party" (CR, January 29, 1892, 676) and charged that "if you adopt this rule, you are estopped hereafter to criticise [Reed]. . . . It embodies the very essence of his philosophy in transacting the public business" (677). Democrat Warren Hooker of Mississippi even sponsored an amendment to delete the new Rules Committee powers from the package of rules approved in 1892; while a handful of Democrats spoke for the amendment, it garnered no Republican support and was defeated on a division vote, 139–21.[29] The opposition to the 1893 change was less heated, consisting primarily of amendments intended to loosen party leaders' agenda control. For example, rank-and-file Democrats proposed to enlarge the Rules Committee, to require reports within three days on all measures referred to it, and to reduce legislative committees' dependence on the Rules Committee by extending the privilege of reporting bills "at any time" to more legislative committees (see CR, August 30, 1893, 1084, and August 31, 1893, 1106–9; *Post*, September 2 and 3, 1893).[30] Personal power goals likely motivated much of this Democratic opposition: the dissidents' floor statements emphasized the fear that an empowered Rules Committee would diminish the role of other committees and individual members.[31]

Democratic dissidents did not find allies among the GOP leadership. Republicans provided no support for Hooker's effort to delete the 1892 change protecting the Rules Committee from minority obstruction (see CR, January 29, 1892, and February 1, 1892). Instead, GOP leaders and most rank-and-file Republicans backed the Democratic leadership's proposals to empower the Rules Committee. This Republican embrace of centralized agenda control in the House evidently stemmed from their interest in boosting Congress's capacity to legislate, rather than from the benefits of public posturing. Unlike the Reed rules, the powers of the Rules Committee did not seem to interest the public, so there was little to gain from posturing on this issue. Rather, many Republicans genuinely believed in a powerful Rules Committee, given the demands of Congress's increasingly complex agenda. Reed called the 1892 increase in the Rules Committee's powers a "very great advance . . . henceforth we shall have some governing and responsible power in the House" (CR, January 26, 1892, 556), and GOP leader Nelson Dingley of Maine praised the 1893 Democratic proposals for moving "in the right direction," though "they do not go as far as they should" (CR, August 30, 1893, 1077). Republican Charles Grosvenor of Ohio concluded that the House had "practically agreed that the Committee on Rules shall control the business of the House. . . . That is really what we must come to—I do not object to it" (CR, August 31, 1893, 1108).

Several Democrats also argued that a strong Rules Committee was necessary. Springer noted that "we must leave this authority" to schedule legislation with the Rules Committee, "if we expect to do business" (CR, January 29, 1892, 676). Similarly, Catchings of Mississippi claimed that it is "absolutely necessary that some committee or some portion of this House should have some power as to the arrangement of the order of business. There would be chaos without it" (CR, January 26, 1892, 555). The consistent message from numerous members of both parties was that the House's growing workload necessitated a strong Rules Committee.

Observers have repeatedly attributed the Rules Committee's new powers to this broad member interest in congressional capacity (Luce 1922, 478; Atkinson 1911, 65). Yet critics of this "workload" perspective argue with considerable force that increases in workload do not correspond to the specific dates that reforms were adopted to improve the management of House business (Dion 1997).

Questions about timing suggest that these changes were not simply functional responses to exogenous workload demands. Instead, the pluralism of member interests played a key role. Partisan concerns intersected with members' interest in congressional capacity—an interest stirred by such critics of House operations as Reed—to create the momentum for specific reforms. Democrats advocated new prerogatives for the Rules Committee in 1892–95 because of GOP obstruction and because of their perceived ineffectiveness compared to Reed's 51st Congress. This partisan interest is critical for understanding the timing of the Rules Committee reforms. But the changes attracted bipartisan support because of broader concerns about workload and capacity. In January 1896, when the new Republican Congress decided to retain the Rules Committee's prerogatives, minority leader Crisp praised the GOP, demonstrating the bipartisan consensus (at least among congressional leaders) on centralized agenda control (see CR, January 10, 1896, 566).

Empowering the Rules Committee required compromises with competing member interests in 1893, but not in 1892 or 1895. The Rules Committee's critics were strong enough in 1893 to amend the proposed rules by allowing the Banking and Currency Committee and the Coinage Committee to report their bills at any time. This limited the Rules Committee's control of the agenda since these committees could now gain consideration of their measures without the Rules Committee's help. The privilege to report at any time enhanced the value of individual members' committee power bases and, in this particular case, promised to help currency legislation reach the floor. The Democrats on Rules opposed granting these two committees this power, but the amendment passed on a division vote, 102–58. The only roll call dealt with adding the Coinage Committee to the initial proposal conferring the privilege upon Banking and Currency. That amendment passed by a 138–97 vote, with Democrats voting 98–64 in favor, and a slim majority of Republicans concurring as well. A logit analysis of the roll call indicates that western support for free silver and membership on the Coinage Committee provided the impetus for this amendment's passage—suggesting the relevance of policy-based and personal power motivations.[32] But Republicans and most Democrats opposed other proposals that would have further limited the influence of Rules.

More broadly, the new Rules Committee powers were part of a disjointed set of changes that embodied tensions rooted in competing member interests. When they became the majority party in December 1891, Democrats had to accommodate their intense factional divisions and their prior advocacy of minority rights, while at the same time appearing competent and effective as the majority party. Democrats could not simply repeal Reed's rules and offer no substitute, for fear of appearing a "do-nothing" Congress. This peculiar mix of Democratic interests explains why the rules of the 52nd Congress simultaneously moved in two directions: resurrecting minority rights through repeal of Reed's quorum and dilatory motions rules, and enhancing the Rules Committee as a centralized leadership instrument partially immune from obstruction. This combination of centralizing and decentralizing moves only makes sense when one views legislative institutions as products of competing member interests, rather than as well-tailored tools to achieve a particular objective.

The primary effect, then, of the Rules Committee changes was to introduce a modicum of centralization and strong agenda control into the newly decentralized House of the Crisp years. Reed's 1894 filibusters demonstrated that the Democratic rules did not ensure the majority party would control the legislative agenda. But as long as the Democrats could maintain a quorum on the floor, party leaders could use the Rules Committee to gain prompt consideration of favored measures. While restrictive special orders did not become common immediately following the 1892 rules (Bach 1990), House leaders did increasingly depend on resolutions from the Rules Committee to bring controversial matters to the floor.

It is ironic that the Democrats, with their sharp internal divisions and long-standing commitment to minority rights, helped centralize power under the auspices of the Speaker and Rules Committee. Democrats sponsored these innovations in large part to avoid adopting Reed's rules, and, in the absence of those rules, the Democratic innovations gave only a limited boost to the majority party. But once the Reed rules were restored and thus layered on top of the Democratic changes, a set of institutions resulted that dramatically tightened party control. The House had empowered the Rules Committee and virtually eliminated minority obstruction. The Democrats clearly had not intended to create such a potent combination when they augmented the Rules Committee's powers. This again exemplifies how congressional institutions develop through a series of innovations, inspired by competing motivations, with results that do not neatly correspond to any single member interest. An innovation providing an element of centralized agenda control in an otherwise fragmented system became much more potent when combined with the newly consolidated Reed rules.

The Emergence of Centralized Senate Leadership, 1897

The dramatic increase in the power of party leaders in the House was paralleled, though in somewhat muted form, by changes in the Senate in the last decade of the nineteenth century. In particular, burgeoning centralized leadership in the GOP under the so-called Senate Four—

Nelson Aldrich, William Allison, Orville Platt (R-Conn.), and John Spooner (R-Wis.)—brought about important changes in the Senate. In most accounts, 1897 was a crucial year in the Senate Four's rise to power because Allison became chairman of the GOP Caucus and Steering Committee. The committee assignment process and other levers of Senate power were soon largely in the hands of Allison, Aldrich, and their allies.[33]

Unfortunately, the evidence base on this change is relatively thin. As a result, my findings are tentative.[34] The primary conclusion is that Republicans' partisan interests were responsible for the development of centralized leadership under Allison and Aldrich: Republicans' shared goals of enacting conservative policies, blocking Populist-inspired reforms, and appearing to be an effective majority party were predominant.

Events in the Senate are reasonably consistent with the insight, drawn from conditional party government theory, that increasing homogeneity in majority party members' policy views leads party members to delegate more power to their leaders (Rohde 1991). While centralization gained considerable ground in the House before the parties became significantly more homogeneous (see my discussion of the Reed rules above), the Senate changes occurred as the Senate parties became more homogeneous. This is borne out by the data presented in figure 2.1, which tracks party homogeneity in the House and Senate over time.

Even as late as the 54th Congress of 1895–97, the Senate Republican party had a substantial number of dissident members, mostly westerners dedicated to the cause of free silver. In fact, seventeen of forty-six Senate Republicans voted for a free silver bill in that Congress (CR, February 1, 1896, 1215–16; *Post*, February 4, 1896, 6). In December 1895, western Republicans forced GOP Caucus Chairman John Sherman of Ohio to submit his selections for the party's Committee on Committees to the caucus for approval. This unprecedented move reflected the westerners' distrust of party leaders, and resulted in increased representation for western silverites on the Committee on Committees (Rothman 1966, 49–50, 298). However, less than two years later, following the 1896 campaign in which six Republican senators formally left the party to become "Silver Republicans" (and a handful of other Republican silverites were defeated), the GOP dissidents lacked the numbers to impose any such conditions on party leaders (*Post*, March 7, 1897; Rothman 1966, 50).[35]

The Republican party that emerged from the 1896 election faced less internal division than had existed at any other time in the post–Civil War era (Brady, Brody, and Epstein 1989, 210; see also figure 2.1). Not coincidentally, in 1897 the Allison-Aldrich faction gained unmistakable control of the Senate GOP machinery and became the dominant force in Senate politics.

Members may also have been more willing to accept centralized leadership because of changes in recruitment. By the 1880s and 1890s, more and more senators had come up through the ranks of state political machines, and their training at the state level led them to appreciate party discipline (Swenson 1982; Rothman 1966). Many of these "machine" senators were far more concerned about patronage and particularistic benefits for their states—a crucial resource for the machines that selected them—than with matters of broad public policy. For example, New York boss and Republican senator Thomas Platt focused almost exclusively on local issues and patronage (Thompson 1906, 99) and thus was willing to defer on most policy matters to party leaders. In a telling 1899 letter, he confided to Allison that "I consider the interests of the Government as embodied in you and Senator Aldrich. What you say goes" (quoted in Rothman 1966, 47). While Republicans' homogeneity made it easier for senators like Platt to defer to Allison and Aldrich on policy matters, the training and local orientation of such senators were likely important resources for party leaders. After all, the Democrats experienced similar, though slightly weaker, developments in party leadership under Arthur Pue Gorman (D-Md.) in the middle to late 1890s, even as the party continued to be plagued by substantial internal divisions (Rothman 1966). The key was party leaders' ability to convince members that centralization did not threaten their particularistic credit-claiming opportunities and instead might ensure a steady supply of benefits for their constituents (Swenson 1982).

It is plausible that concern about the Senate's capacity and power also motivated the centralization. In the early 1890s, the Senate was beset by filibusters on high-profile issues such as the federal elections bill and repeal of the Sherman Silver Purchase Act, and it also appeared more vulnerable to logrolling than the newly centralized House (see, e.g., Williams 1973 on the Wilson-Gorman tariff). Yet by the end of the nineteenth century, the Senate once again had surpassed the House as the leading force in the federal government. Byrd (1988, 1:368), among others, argues that Aldrich's and Allison's efforts made the Senate a more cohesive, formidable institution (see also Brown 1922; Merrill and Merrill 1971). Rothman (1966, 265) notes that in the face of challenges posed by industrialization and an increasingly complex legislative agenda, "the Senate, rather than flounder and abdicate power, transformed its procedures and traditions. Parties and leaders assumed unprecedented authority, bringing new practices to the chamber." Still, the evidence for the importance of congressional capacity and power is too indirect to conclude that it was a cause of the 1890s Senate changes. Instead, it is safer to conclude that party leaders capitalized on the reduced resistance to central control that stemmed from

Republicans' homogeneity and perhaps on the lower salience of broad issues of public policy to "machine" senators.

These leaders managed to create a more centralized Senate authority structure through a series of maneuvers over several years. But as noted above, 1897 emerges as a key date in the process. Prior to 1897, the overlap between party leadership offices and committee leadership had been uneven, and formal party leaders did not generally use their influence to benefit a specific faction (Brady, Brody, and Epstein 1989). Because the Republican caucus chairmanship had yet to become a powerful leadership instrument, Allison's seniority was a sufficient criterion for his selection as chairman in March 1897 (Rothman 1966, 44). But Allison then dramatically extended the importance of the caucus chairmanship. In the past, the caucus chairman had typically appointed someone else to chair the Steering Committee, but Allison retained that post for himself. Furthermore, he placed his allies on Steering and expanded the committee's role in determining the Senate's order of business (CQ 1982, 225). Allison also made sure that his allies controlled the Committee on Committees, and he appointed his friend James McMillan (R-Mich.) as its chairman. As a result, for the first time a single faction controlled both floor scheduling and committee assignments. Rothman (1966, 50) observes that "various members of the Allison-Aldrich circle intermittently occupied key Senate positions before 1897, but after Allison assumed power they monopolized party offices." This shift occurred by design, not by accident. Shortly before he became caucus chairman, a friend of Allison advised him that "both in the committees and in the offices, we should use the machinery for our own benefit and not let other men have it" (Rothman 1966, 44). Allison followed this course, and he and his allies "firmly maintained Republican unity, effectively dispensing rewards and promoting their friends" (Byrd 1988, 1:366).

With Allison's ascension to the caucus chairmanship, party and committee leaders formed an interlocking directorate in which a limited number of members derived immense influence from a potent combination of positions. Starting in 1897, a series of Allison intimates chaired the Committee on Committees: McMillan, Aldrich, Orville Platt, and Eugene Hale (R-Maine). While leading the GOP caucus and Steering Committee, Allison also chaired the Appropriations Committee and was a high-ranking member on Finance. Aldrich became chairman of the Finance Committee in 1899 and also served on Rules and Interstate Commerce. Platt and Spooner served together on Finance and Judiciary; Spooner also became chairman of the Rules Committee in 1899. As Byrd (1988, 1:365) concludes, "seldom in the history of the Senate . . . had the major committees been so monopolized by the party leaders." In addition to the leverage provided by this monopoly, Aldrich and Allison derived influence from their role in financing campaigns. Aldrich, in particular, "made his position as a powerful influence on the campaign-contribution habits of corporations clear to his fellow Republican senators" (Ripley 1969a, 29; see also Stephenson 1930).

Although there is no evidence that Republicans anticipated that Allison would extend the prerogatives of party leaders when they elected him caucus chairman, the Iowa senator was uniquely qualified for his role.[36] Unlike Aldrich, who was identified with the eastern, financial wing of the GOP, Allison had ties to both the eastern-industrial and midwestern-agrarian wings. These ties made him acceptable to a wider range of party members than any other Republican leader. Allison's Iowa constituents demanded that he at least appear to represent "western" or agrarian concerns, yet he invariably managed simultaneously to service the eastern, financial interests. A cynical account would be that Allison "gave business the substance of what it wanted without seeming to do so" (Mayer 1964, 277). However, Mowry (1958, 116) provides a more balanced interpretation: though a conservative, Allison was sensitive to "the agrarian unrest in his home state and consequently was always a little more willing to bend before a storm of popular protest." Allison mediated between the contending wings of his party, forcing conservative eastern leaders to address the concerns of western farmers, while not allowing those concerns to derail the conservative course favored by the easterners. After Allison's death in 1908, Republican leaders became less receptive to the claims of the midwestern agrarians—precisely at the time that those demands became increasingly vociferous (Merrill and Merrill 1971). But during Allison's tenure, his ties to the West elicited wider acceptance for a centralized leadership structure primarily controlled by the GOP's conservative eastern wing.

The most important impact of the rise of centralized party leadership was that political parties assumed a level of influence that has rarely been achieved in the Senate. The percentage of roll calls that pitted at least 90 percent of Republicans against 90 percent of Democrats increased dramatically in the 55th Congress and stayed at unusually high levels for the next eight years (see data in Hurley and Wilson 1989, 229). The traditionally individualistic Senate became a more disciplined body, as disputes were worked out in the Republican party caucus, rather than on the more unpredictable Senate floor. Even on issues where policy divisions cut across party lines—such as the Hepburn railroad regulation bill in 1906—key deals were often made within the GOP caucus rather than on the floor.[37] Members clearly sensed that it "paid" to work within party mechanisms rather than ally themselves with opposition Democrats. For example, Albert Beveridge (R-Ind.), who ran for the Senate as a something of an insurgent, immediately tried to win over Allison and Aldrich following his January 1899 election so that he would have the opportunity to serve on an important committee (Rothman 1966, 56–57).

Yet this element of centralization was superimposed on a Senate authority structure that gave considerable leverage to individual members. Independent-minded committee chairmen repeatedly challenged the Republican Steering Committee's floor-scheduling decisions (Gamm and Smith 1999). Furthermore, the new leadership arrangements did not eliminate the potential for filibusters. Even in this era of strong party leadership, dissident members could bring Senate business to a halt, either blocking a controversial measure or forcing acceptance of a favored amendment.[38] In addition, respect for seniority in selecting committee chairmen was extremely high among Republicans in the 1880s and 1890s (Ripley 1969b, 44; Price 1975). By the time Allison and his allies came to power, they could have disregarded seniority only with great opposition and strife (Rothman 1966, 52). This imposed only limited direct costs on the Allison-Aldrich circle, as their allies tended mostly to be senior members. But the seniority system nonetheless reduced their flexibility and provided some independence to party dissidents.

Therefore, while the interlocking of party and committee leadership elevated the Republican party and made the Senate more centralized, this development had a limited impact because of the persistence of arrangements, such as the filibuster and seniority system, that fulfilled competing objectives, such as safeguarding individual senators' power bases. Institutional development occurred through a tense layering of new arrangements on top of preexisting ones designed to serve different objectives. The result was a disjointed authority structure, rather than simply a centralized or decentralized system. Thus, a journalist writing in 1906 concluded that the House could be led much more easily than the Senate, which "despite its coterie of bosses, is often uncontrollable" (Thompson 1906, 155; see also Gamm and Smith 1999).

On the whole, the institutional changes adopted from 1890–97 empowered congressional party leaders, especially in the House, but the majority party did not simply dominate processes of institutional change. Instead, the interactions and tensions among multiple member interests shaped institutional development. First, the Democrats' 1892 decision to repeal most of Reed's rules reflected complex interests. Democratic campaign rhetoric had induced a reputational interest in defending minority rights, which inhibited the party's control of business. Second, minority party Republicans played a critical role in forcing the Democratic majority to restore Reed's quorum rule in 1894. Thus, even in the 1890s, a cohesive, committed minority could shape key features of legislative institutions. Third, more than one collective interest typically shaped each change. Thus, broadly based concerns about congressional capacity often intersected with partisan interests to promote changes that centralized control. The GOP's consistent advocacy of majority rule in the 1890s—including party leaders' willingness to support Democratic moves that increased the power of the Rules Committee—reflected Reed's success in convincing Republicans that minority obstruction was detrimental to all members.

INDIVIDUAL POWER BASES AND THE REACTION AGAINST CENTRALIZATION (PART 1)

The push toward strong party leadership and centralization in 1890–97 threatened competing interests and as a result rather quickly provoked a reaction. Restive members pushed for changes that empowered individual members by weakening party leaders. These changes did not repeal the 1890–97 leadership advances but did mitigate some of their effects. The resulting House and Senate authority structures contained elements of both fragmentation and centralization. Changes rooted in members' power base concerns, among other factors, thus compromised the effectiveness of Reed, Aldrich, and Allison's party-based innovations, illustrating the disjointed, pluralistic character of congressional development.

Decentralization of Senate Appropriations, 1899

Just as Allison and Aldrich were consolidating their hold over the Senate GOP machinery, resistance to centralization emerged in the solidly Republican upper chamber. The most visible manifestation of this resistance was the effort to decentralize control of appropriations. In a series of moves from 1877–85, the House had distributed its appropriations bills among eight committees. The Senate considered similar actions as early as 1879, and again in 1884 and 1896, but failed to decentralize each time (Robinson 1954). By 1899, the pressure for change became too great, and the Senate adopted a slightly watered-down compromise. The Agriculture, Commerce, Indian Affairs, Military Affairs, Naval Affairs, Pensions, and Post Office and Post Roads Committees acquired the privilege of reporting appropriations for matters in their jurisdiction. The Senate Appropriations Committee retained jurisdiction over only a handful of areas, such as spending on the legislative, executive, and judicial branches.[39]

This change is puzzling for conditional party government theory: senators decentralized appropriations even as the majority party's homogeneity and party polarization were peaking in the wake of the 1896 realignment (see figure 2.1; Brady et al. 1989). This would normally lead us to expect a steady move toward centralization rather than a reform to decentralize power. Again, attention to the pluralism of member interests helps make sense of this otherwise anomalous reform.

The appropriations decentralization primarily served junior senators' interest in enhanced access to power. The 1896–99 debate over appropriations vividly illustrates the widespread belief that reform had become necessary so junior members could participate equally in Senate deliberations. Newton Blanchard (D-La.) declared that "it is sought by this resolution to change the distribution of power in the Senate, to emancipate the Senate from the monopolistic dominance of about 20 men"—those who served on the Appropriations and Finance Committees (CR, February 4, 1896, 1288). The resolution's chief sponsor, Republican Fred Dubois of Idaho, added that, by custom, junior senators "are not expected to take much, if any, part in general debate. This leaves them ample time for committee work. By dividing the appropriations, their abilities could be utilized. . . . I think that each member of the Senate should perform as much of the work, share as much of the care, enjoy as much of the honor, and be as much of a leader as possible" (CR, December 11, 1896, 133). Senators David Hill (D-N.Y.), John Daniel (D-Va.), Knute Nelson (R-Minn.), Jacob Gallinger (R-N.H.), and James George (D-Miss.), among others, voiced similar sentiments. These members believed decentralizing appropriations would make committees populated by junior members more potent. Gallinger argued that "with the proposed distribution, minor committees will become important and desirable. Some of the older Senators will stay on them, and there will be a greater sprinkling of new men on what are now leading committees, and in this way the new element, to which I belong, will be under proper influence and instruction" (CR, February 5, 1896, 1326).

This reference to the "new element" is intriguing. The floor debates suggest that junior members saw themselves as a group with interests distinct from those of their senior colleagues. Press accounts also treat junior members in this way: the *Washington Post*, for example, noted that "the younger, newer blood in the Senate, which has no respect for traditions when those traditions are not in harmony with equality and fairness, has asserted itself with an emphasis which is not to be mistaken" (February 5, 1896, 5; see also February 8, 1896, 4).

An analysis of the series of votes taken on the proposed change in 1896 shows that junior members were far more likely to support the appropriations decentralization than were more senior members. At the bivariate level, the correlation between number of Senate terms served and a summary measure of roll call support for the 1896 proposal is an impressive $-.63$. As table 2.2 shows, this relationship holds up after controlling for membership on Appropriations, region, ideology, and party.[40] By contrast, there is no evidence that party affiliations structured members' preferences

TABLE 2.2 Ordinary Least Squares Analysis of Votes on Senate
Appropriations Decentralization, 1896 (SE in parentheses)

Independent Variable	Model 1	Model 2
Length of Service (# of two-year terms)	−.30**	−.26**
	(.08)	(.08)
West	.81	.29
	(.55)	(.54)
First-dimension D-NOMINATE score	−1.24	−.63
	(1.02)	(.97)
Second-dimension D-NOMINATE score		−2.88**
		(.97)
Member of Appropriations	−1.78*	−1.64*
	(.91)	(.85)
Gain Jurisdiction	.23	.37
	(.81)	(.76)
Republican	1.33	.71
	(1.29)	(1.22)
Constant	3.23	3.66
	(1.12)	(1.06)
Adj. R^2	.48	.55
N	56	56

Note: The dependent variable is a six-point scale constructed from senators' votes on the five roll calls on the decentralization issue (see Appendix B). Poole and Rosenthal's (1991) D-NOMINATE scores are used to measure ideology; they range in value from −1 to +1. "Gain Jurisdiction" is a dummy variable coded as 1 if the member served on one of the standing committees that was promised additional jurisdiction under the Dubois proposal and the member did not serve on the Appropriations Committee. Otherwise, it is coded as 0.

$*p < .05$ (one-tailed test). $**p < .01$ (one-tailed test).

on the appropriations matter (see appendix B.1 and table 2.2). Unlike the party-based rules changes of 1890–97, the appropriations reform pitted Republican and Democratic leaders against rank-and-file members drawn from both parties. This is a much different cleavage.

Decentralization was also driven by sectionally based divisions over economic policy. Dubois, the sponsor of the 1896 reform bid, was an Idaho Republican who believed the West urgently needed increased federal funding and the free coinage of silver. He hatched the plan to decentralize appropriations in consultation with several other western silver Republicans (Graff 1988, 169–71). These westerners wanted to undermine conservative, eastern Republicans and bolster the power of their faction. Inclusion of a dummy variable for the West is one way to tap into this sectional cleavage (see model 1 of table 2.2). But as model 2 of table 2.2 shows, the estimated effect for the West variable drops substantially when

members' second-dimension NOMINATE scores are added to the model.
The NOMINATE scores, which correlate at .56 with western residence,
are one of the strongest predictors of members' votes on the reform. More
detailed analysis of the votes on decentralization by Schickler and Sides
(2000) indicates that the significant effect for the second-dimension
NOMINATE scores is attributable to the deep cleavages over economic
development policy that divided the advanced, industrialized Northeast
and upper Midwest from the more agrarian South and West (see Bensel
1984). Hungry for federal funds to fuel regional development, western
and southern senators were particularly eager to curb conservative eastern
party leaders' Appropriations Committee power base.[41]

Resistance to the reform emanated from Appropriations Committee
members, who stood to lose considerable influence, and party leaders, such
as Aldrich, who did not want power dispersed among numerous committees (*Post*, February 8, 1896, 4; December 23, 1898, 4). The Appropriations Committee, like the Finance Committee, was closely identified with
the party leadership. Chaired by Allison, it also included other top Republicans and the Democratic leader Gorman. Foes of the change successfully
delayed its adoption for several years and forced some compromises into
the final version adopted in 1899. As table 2.2 shows, Appropriations members were far more likely to oppose the change than were other senators.[42]

The reformers won a partial victory in February 1896, when the Senate
voted 44 to 25 to sidetrack a deficiency appropriations bill and consider
the Dubois proposal. Dubois had caught the leaders of both parties by
surprise, and Aldrich, Allison, and Gorman worked to delay consideration
of the measure while they lobbied members to oppose it. It initially appeared that Dubois would win easily (CR, February 4, 1896, 1277; *Post*,
February 5, 1896), but over the next few days, party leaders made various
appeals that convinced more than a dozen members to switch sides. On a
40–28 vote, the resolution was referred to the Rules and Administration
Committee, which spelled its doom since all but one of that committee's
members opposed it. The *Post* reported that a mix of "personal appeals,"
"promises of various kinds," "social considerations," and "presidential
politics" won converts to the leadership's side (February 8, 1896, 4).[43]
The leaders' success suggests the ways in which foes as well as proponents
of a reform can manipulate the pluralism in members' interests.

Although Allison, Aldrich, Hale, and Gorman continued to oppose decentralization in 1899 (*Post*, December 23, 1898, 4; Rothman 1966), they
were not so successful. William Chandler (R-N.H.) introduced the resolution on the floor and threatened to force its consideration should the Rules
Committee detain it for long. Chandler gathered the signatures of forty-
six senators—a majority of the full Senate, drawn almost equally from the
two major parties—on a petition urging decentralization. Rather than
allowing Chandler to bring the resolution to the floor for consideration,

Aldrich had the Rules Committee limit its scope. The Appropriations Committee retained control of spending on foreign relations, the District of Columbia, and coastal fortifications, in addition to the few areas that Chandler had willingly left to the committee.[44] Aldrich then brought the resolution to the floor, where it was accepted on a voice vote. The compromise kept the basic idea of the Chandler proposal but left the Appropriations Committee with control over a slightly greater share of the budget.

A logit analysis of the decision to sign the petition suggests the same pattern of results as in 1896: seniority, sectionalism, and membership on Appropriations drove members' decisions on signing the petition, while party played no role (Schickler and Sides 2000). It is noteworthy that the New Hampshire Republican Chandler had latched onto a proposal initiated by western silverites. Chandler—who served on two committees that gained jurisdiction from decentralizing appropriations—likely supported the reform with much different goals in mind than the silver Republicans, again illustrating that changes gain adoption by serving as common carriers for multiple interests.

The most important effect of the decentralization was limiting the influence of the Appropriations Committee, while boosting the importance of substantive committees. Robinson (1954, 298) argues that the Senate "in effect broke the power of the Appropriations Committee," and Ripley (1969b, 27) adds that the "decision obviously enhanced the [legislative] committees' power." Thus, while the 1897 consolidation of power in the hands of Allison, Aldrich, and their allies added an important centralizing element to the Senate, this 1899 change dispersed power among a far greater number of senators. It seems quite likely that the final impetus for successful adoption of the 1899 change was members' dissatisfaction with the ever-increasing centralization that Allison, Aldrich, and Gorman had introduced in recent years. Institutional development took on a disjointed cast as changes serving party-based interests provoked a reaction defending competing interests.

Analyses of the 1890s have emphasized changes with a centralizing thrust but have virtually ignored reforms with opposing implications. The result has been an exaggerated assessment of the degree of centralization reached in the turn-of-the-century Senate (see Brady et al. 1989; Rothman 1966). Yet a focus on the intersections among multiple, competing member interests allows us to see how the Senate authority structure came to embody conflicting imperatives: unlimited debate, a strong seniority system, dispersed control of appropriations, and a high level of overlap between party and committee leaders. Rather than a coherent, party-based system, it appears instead a complex, multifaceted institution that at once elevated party, committee, and individual members in mutually contradictory ways.

Henderson and the Decline of the Speakership, 1899–1903

When Thomas Reed resigned as Speaker in 1899, the House presiding officer was widely, and appropriately, viewed as one of the most important political leaders in the country. But the tenure of Reed's Republican successor, David Henderson, saw a substantial diminution of the speakership. This change was essentially informal, involving shifts in the routine relations among the Speaker, House members, and the Senate. The evidence base for this change is less extensive than for most other changes analyzed in this book, and thus the conclusions reached are somewhat tentative. However, omitting this case would ignore an important change in institutional relationships and therefore distort our understanding of the period as a whole.[45]

Based on the available evidence, the decline in the speakership served as a common carrier for two interests: House committee chairmen and rank-and-file members' interest in a wider distribution of influence, and Senate Republican leaders' power goals. While most political scientists portray the 1890–1910 period as the apogee of Speaker power, both committee chairmen and Senate leaders gained influence at the Speaker's expense during the Henderson years. Thus, Ripley (1967, 90) observes that "Henderson is usually overlooked by those assuming the Reed-Cannon era to be typical of the pre-1910 House."

In the aftermath of Reed's "czar rule," House members did not want a presiding officer with a domineering personality or a commitment to strong, centralized leadership. Washington reporter William Wolff Smith (1906, 304) writes that "the House had grown restless under the iron hand of Reed. . . . Indeed, the House was ready to go to the other extreme and reduce the Speakership to the position of a mere presiding officer." Journalist Joe Mitchell Chapple (1899, 479) adds that "Congress [had] chafed under the Czar—it was only a question of time when the rebellion would occur and the older members of Congress welcome a change as a relief from the dictatorial policy of Reed." Similarly, Hoing (1957, 1), in a sympathetic account of Henderson's career, describes the "ill-feeling against [Reed's] domineering attitude" that characterized the House in 1899. He argues that Henderson's election "symbolized the unrest of the rebellious rank-and-file Republican members" dissatisfied with Reed's "autocratic" approach.

Representatives thus sought a wider distribution of institutional power under Henderson. A self-described "friend" of the new Speaker warned him that "members of the House, no longer having the fear of Mr. Reed before their eyes, and anxious to fatten after long privation, will press upon you" (*Forum* 1899, 62). While the friend advised against giving in to unwarranted demands, he added that Henderson ought to disperse influence, noting, "you have everything to gain and nothing to lose by inviting the cooperation of your fellow members."

In response to this rank-and-file sentiment, Henderson joined other prominent candidates for Speaker in distancing himself from Reed, proclaiming, "I have no desire to reign as a czar, or to undertake to control and direct legislation in the House" (*Post*, September 21, 1902, 16; *NYT*, May 25, 1899, 4). This commitment placed Henderson in a difficult position, one dictated by the restive members who had elected him: as Hoing (1957, 30) argues, Henderson had to manage "a rebellious House yet avoid any appearance of trying to follow Reed's autocratic ways."

The Senate's Republican leaders took advantage of House members' antagonism to strong leadership to help install a man that they could dominate. Journalist Otto Carmichael (1903, 4198) asserted in 1903 that Henderson's election had been "secured by the definite agreement between certain powerful Senators." Henderson's personal papers confirm that he had requested and received help from key senators (see excerpts in Hoing 1957; see also Stephenson 1930, 163). For example, Allison responded to Henderson's requests for help by promising to "look after" Aldrich and Spooner and by contacting other senators and representatives on Henderson's behalf (Hoing 1957, 5–10). Having consolidated their hold on the upper chamber, the Senate's GOP leaders could intervene in House affairs because they headed state political machines and therefore largely controlled the nomination of many House Republicans (Carmichael 1903; Ogden 1903). Furthermore, as noted above, Aldrich and his colleagues dispensed campaign funds critical for House members' reelection (Stephenson 1930, 206). The Senate leaders favored Henderson because he was a longtime ally of Allison, and because they feared that the "increasingly disgruntled" House Republicans would otherwise choose a "testy independent" such as Cannon, or perhaps even an advocate of lower tariffs (Merrill and Merrill 1971, 118).[46]

Henderson also benefited from the candidacy of Albert Hopkins (R-Ill.), which deprived Cannon of the complete support of the Illinois delegation (Dunn 1922, 1:310–12), and from westerners' determination to elect someone from their region. Henderson's most active supporters came from the upper Midwest and the West (Hoing 1957, 10–11). With the entry of new states and shifts in population, these westerners had increased leverage in national politics. Indeed, many observers took note of Henderson's status as the first Speaker from west of the Mississippi River (see " 'Czar' Reed's Successor" 1899, 19).

Nonetheless, Henderson's key asset was his lack of resemblance to Reed, which served the personal power interests of both individual House members and Senate leaders whose influence Reed had threatened. Henderson's anonymous "friend" described Reed's determination and strength in great detail, and went on to argue that the incoming Speaker is "in natural temperament and characteristics, [Reed's] very antithesis" (*Forum* 1899, 57; see Chapple 1899 for a similar assessment). A year later, a journalist noted that Henderson "lacks the political resourcefulness, the unyielding tenacity, and the profoundly intellectual force which combined to make his predecessor, Thomas B. Reed, in many respects the most remarkable Speaker in the history of the House" ("Contemporary Celebrities" 1900, 114). It is important to emphasize that these contemporary accounts—echoed by historians (Hoing 1957; Mowry 1958)—were not criticisms of Henderson, but rather pointed to the common sentiment that Reed had been too powerful.

In sum, the coalition that brought Henderson to power included an unlikely combination of rebellious House Republicans, westerners eager to elect one of their own, and ambitious senators. This does not mean that the speakership's temporary decline was the inevitable product of member preferences (or of a senatorial plot, for that matter). Alternative outcomes were possible. For example, had Cannon convinced his Illinois rival Hopkins to drop out of the race, he might have persuaded House Republicans to resist senatorial intervention and accept a kinder, yet still firm, version of czar rule. But in 1899, the obstacles confronting Cannon were greater than those he would face just four years later. Reed's achievements had become Cannon's handicap, just as Henderson's shortcomings would soon become Cannon's precious resource.

Within the House, the primary impact of Henderson's weak leadership was a broader distribution of influence. Reed had not relied much on committee chairmen, preferring instead to make decisions on his own after consulting a few close allies. By contrast, Henderson spread power "by organizing the chairmen of the committees into a sort of 'Cabinet' " (Smith 1906, 305). This Cabinet met regularly and deliberated on the merits of important bills, thus giving more members a significant say over House business. A relatively decentralized system thereby displaced the personal leadership of Reed (Ripley 1967, 83).

But the most striking effect of Henderson's tenure as Speaker involved the relationship between the House and the Senate. Henderson deferred to the Senate's GOP leaders, who took over strategic decision-making for congressional Republicans. Mowry (1958, 117) writes that "as often as not high policy was worked out by the [Senate] Four to be subsequently presented to Henderson." Contemporary observers took note of the declining position of the House and the speakership. Ogden claimed in 1903 (204) that the preceding session featured "a further abasement of the power of the House, as compared with the Senate. This has been partly due to its being in the hands of small men." Journalist Charles W. Thompson, writing a few years later (1906, 155), observed that during the Henderson years, House leaders "never forgot the Senate, and the House was a mere appendage to the other body." Furthermore, "The Deterioration of the House" became "a stock subject for newspaper and magazine moralizing" (Thompson 1906, 181; see also Carmichael 1903). The diminished position of the Speaker and of the House was vividly illustrated in September 1902, when President Roosevelt and leading senators met at the famous Oyster Bay Conference (Skowronek 1993, 240; Stephenson 1930). While Allison, Aldrich, Spooner, Platt, Lodge, and Marcus Hanna (R-Ohio) represented the Senate, the House lacked any representation, as the president and Senate leaders formulated GOP positions on such pressing issues as the tariff and trusts.

This combination of effects—distributing power more equally within the House even as it flowed out to the Senate—displeased many representatives even though it derived from the peculiar combination of interests that gave rise to Henderson's election.[47] Rager (1991, 17) argues that "Cannon and many of his colleagues were hugely dissatisfied with Henderson [as Speaker] because he seemed weak and allowed the House to take a subservient role to the Senate." Signs of revolt thus began to mount in Henderson's last months as Speaker (Thompson 1906, 154; *NYT*, September 18, 1902, 1).

In short, the House of 1899 to 1903 hardly resembled a centralized, Speaker-led system, as many scholars have characterized the 1890–1910 period (e.g., Brady and Althoff 1974; Cooper and Brady 1981; Sinclair 1990).[48] Reed's tightly controlled, party-based system threatened individual members' prerogatives, stimulating a reaction that fragmented power in the House. But when Senate leaders' harnessed this reaction to augment their own power, House members became even more disgruntled.

Members' eagerness to weaken the Speaker following the Reed years illustrates nicely that the dominance of a few collective interests—in this case, the partisan goals and boost in congressional capacity promoted by Reed's rules—will likely drive members to seek new institutions that safeguard competing interests. The result is a disjointed process of change in which institutions serving contradictory purposes are layered on top of one another. The Henderson speakership contributed a dissonant element to the developing regime of strong party leadership launched by Reed.

CANNON'S REVIVAL OF THE SPEAKERSHIP AND THE RETURN TO CENTRALIZATION

Henderson's unexpected announcement in September 1902 that he would not stand for reelection to the House brought issues of House organization and party leadership back to the fore. Henderson cited rising support for tariff reform in his home state as the reason for his retirement, though personal factors likely played a role as well (*Post*, September 20, 1902, 6; Hoing 1957). As House Republicans began to ponder who would replace Henderson, it was not clear whether the spirit of revolt and discontent would lead to a further dispersal of authority or to another round of centralization (Mayhill 1942, 49).

As the new Speaker, Joseph Cannon quickly resolved this uncertainty. Cannon simultaneously consolidated power within the House and forced the president and Senate leaders to consult with him as they framed legislative strategy. Within the House, committee chairmen once again lost stature, as Cannon and a small coterie of close allies largely controlled House business. While firsthand evidence on the sources of this informal change is relatively thin, it suggests that the entrepreneurial Cannon fashioned his revival of the speakership into a common carrier for Republicans' interest in managing their divisions through strong party leadership and all members' interest in empowering the House relative to the Senate.[49]

Scholars espousing "conditional party government" theory have argued that Cannon's strength stemmed from sharp policy differences between an unusually united Republican party and its Democratic opposition (Aldrich 1995, 227–28; Rohde and Shepsle 1987). But this account is only partly convincing. First, it is worth noting that House members elected Henderson to serve as a figurehead even as GOP homogeneity and party polarization were peaking in the immediate aftermath of the 1896 realignment (see figure 2.1). Second, although the GOP and Democrats continued to have very different constituency bases in 1903, Republicans nonetheless confronted rising internal divisions from the outset of Cannon's term. As Henderson's resignation made clear, by 1902 farm-state Republicans, who constituted more than one-fifth of all House Republicans, were under intense pressure to reduce tariffs and confront the trusts.[50] Progressive and Regular Republicans were fighting it out in Iowa and Wisconsin, two states represented by twenty House Republicans; tariff reform sentiment was also rife in Minnesota, Kansas, Nebraska, and Idaho.[51] Furthermore, polarization between the parties evidently declined during Roosevelt's administration, contrary to the conditional party government interpretation. The 1904 presidential campaign, which loomed as Cannon began his first term as Speaker in November 1903, featured a marked narrowing of party differences as Roosevelt made overtures to progressives and as the Democrats moved to the center by replacing William Jennings Bryan with Alton Parker of New York as the party's standard-bearer.[52] Roosevelt's own proposals attracted much Democratic support, which was crucial because conservative Republicans opposed many of the president's policies.

The developing schism between conservative and progressive Republicans might lead one to expect Henderson's decentralized mode of operations to continue. Thus conditional party government theory cannot fully explain Cannon's revitalization of the speakership; instead, I argue that the intersection between Republicans' partisan interests and all members' interest in the power and prestige of the House made this change possible.

Republicans had particular reason to be dismayed with the results of Henderson's leadership. The GOP had been ill prepared to manage its emerging divisions, as insurgencies caused major embarrassments for party leaders.[53] Party members stood to gain from electing a stronger Speaker who could rein in dissidents. Observers, as of 1903, expected Cannon to "keep his party together and secure results" (*Review of Reviews*, December 1903, 676).

But dissatisfaction with Henderson was not simply partisan. Cannon garnered bipartisan support for his early efforts to enhance the speakership because Democrats and Republicans alike stood to benefit from his "determination to regain for the House some of the prestige it had lost under Henderson" (Mowry 1958, 118). Members expected that Cannon would stand up to Senate leaders and defend the power of the House. Mayhill (1942, 30) points out that while some of Cannon's rivals for the speakership had sought support from key senators, "Cannon unhesitantly defied Senate authority" and thus "appealed to the group who believed that the House had been granting too many concessions to the Senate." During Henderson's final session as Speaker, when Senator Ben Tillman (D-S.C.) successfully filibustered to extract added appropriations for his home state, Cannon unleashed an unprecedented tirade against the Senate. Cannon accused Tillman of "legislative blackmail" and declared that the Senate "must change its methods of procedure, or our body, backed up by the people, will compel that change" (CR, March 3, 1093, 3058). Even the Democratic *New York Times* called this a "brilliant attack" that "electrified" the House and produced resounding applause (March 5, 1905). The *Nation*'s congressional correspondent agreed that Cannon had "uttered the thoughts of many hearts when he denounced" the Senate (Ogden 1903, 204). Because Tillman was a Democrat, Cannon could "defy the masters of the Senate and yet keep wholly free of any charge of disloyalty to the Republican party," a "*coup de theatre* that should become historic" (Stephenson 1930, 214; see also Carmichael 1903). Gwinn (1957, 73) expresses the common view that this speech "clinched" Cannon's election as Speaker.

Cannon also broadened his appeal by giving up one of the Speaker's prerogatives and allowing the minority leader, his close friend John Sharp Williams (D-Miss.), to name minority party members to House committees. Thompson (1906, 179–80) argues that such gestures fostered "a tempered tyranny" that generated less hostility than had the leadership of Cannon's predecessors.[54] Cannon's bold challenge to the Senate and his willingness to grant favors to the Democrats made the new Speaker unusually popular with members of both parties (see Thompson 1906; Rager 1991, 49).

In sum, Cannon recentralized authority by fusing Republicans' partisan interests with House members' concern about their institution's power and by making limited concessions to Democratic leaders. While Republicans made the key decision to elect Cannon, believing in part that strong leadership could better manage the party's developing divisions, Cannon also derived support from a bipartisan coalition concerned about the power of the lower chamber. This bipartisan backing added to the Speaker's leverage when dealing with the Senate, the president, and even his own party's dissidents. Cannon took advantage of a spirit of revolt that might have gone in several different directions and channeled it to strengthen his party and the House simultaneously.

In the short to medium term, Cannon's centralized leadership actually tempered GOP infighting. Republicans benefited as Cannon worked with Roosevelt to pass popular legislation and avoid divisive issues. Conservatives could trust Cannon to keep tariff reductions off the agenda for as long as possible (Mowry 1958). Progressive Republicans accepted Cannon's leadership because, at least through 1906, he did not obstruct new legislation that they supported, such as the Hepburn Act, the Pure Food Bill, and the Meat Inspection Act.[55] Conservative Republicans disliked these measures, but their adoption placated progressives without requiring the tariff to be addressed (Skowronek 1993; Peters 1990, 78). Therefore, the Republicans' cohesive voting record in the early twentieth century seems to have stemmed largely from negotiation among and skilled agenda control by Cannon, Roosevelt, and the Senate leaders, even as Republican districts appear to have become increasingly heterogeneous.

Cannon's leadership also transformed congressional politics by reversing the trends toward decentralization and toward Senate supremacy. Henderson's cabinet of committee chairmen gave way to Cannon's small, informal circle of lieutenants (MacNeil 1963, 80–81). Cannon consolidated and used vigorously the powers that Reed and his predecessors had developed. Among other things, he manipulated committee assignments to promote his policy ends. For example, in 1905, when his close friend James Tawney (R-Minn.) came under intense pressure from constituents to support tariff cuts, Cannon removed Tawney from Ways and Means and made him chair of Appropriations, where Tawney's tariff stance was irrelevant.

Cannon's impact on House-Senate relations was even more striking. Even before Cannon formally took office, Roosevelt and the Senate leaders realized that he would not simply accept their dictates. In August 1903, after the Senate Four met with Roosevelt to discuss financial legislation, Roosevelt sent Cannon a letter stating that he and the Senate leaders would not make definite plans until they had heard his views. Gwinn (1957, 75) notes that "this statement indicated a shift of power in the

GOP. Had Henderson still been Speaker, the Four might have sent him a mandate instead of an invitation for advice." Roosevelt and the Senate leaders consulted Cannon regularly because they knew that he "was not another David Henderson who could be expected to automatically rubber stamp decisions made without his input" (Rager 1991, 35). The Aldrich-Allison group were thus no longer the unchallenged leaders of congressional Republicans (Thompson 1906, 26–27). The *Washington Post* took note of the new House-Senate dynamics in a 1904 article headlined "House Gains Power" (April 30, 1904, 4). The *Post* reviewed a series of legislative battles from the preceding session and concluded that under Cannon, "the House has wielded a greater influence . . . than it had done at any session of recent years."

Cannon's House leadership and battles with the Senate were mutually reinforcing: his influence in the lower chamber made it imperative for Senate leaders to gain his support, while his influence with the president and Senate leaders improved his stature within the House (Mowry 1958, 118; Brown 1922, 115–16). Under Cannon, the House had become better organized and featured "a higher *esprit de corps* than at any other time in its history . . . [it] was proud of its place in the federal system and wary of encroachment" (Gwinn 1957, 78–79).

PROGRESSIVE INSURGENCY, INDIVIDUAL POWER, AND THE REVOLT AGAINST CENTRALIZATION

Support for Cannon's centralized mode of operations turned out to be fairly short-lived. As the Progressive movement gained momentum, Roosevelt jettisoned his strategy of conciliating GOP leaders. The president initiated an agenda of governmental activism that Old Guard leaders found unacceptable but that many rank-and-file Republicans and Democrats supported enthusiastically.[56] By December 1907, Roosevelt's relations with Republican leaders in the House and Senate were strained to the breaking point. Cannon became increasingly aggressive as he sensed that Roosevelt's forces threatened his leadership (Polsby et al. 1969). In turn, Republican insurgents and Democrats came to believe that Cannon was manipulating the rules to block their influence. This discontent led them to attack Cannon publicly. By constricting the opportunities for individual members and the minority party to shape House decision making, Cannon created an explosive situation where members were willing to attack the House to effect change.

These attacks culminated in the 1909–10 rebellion against Cannon. Although the rise of progressivism within the GOP and nationally is generally regarded as the primary cause of the rebellion, ideological interests alone are not a sufficient explanation. Less than a majority of House members were progressives or even leaned progressive in the 61st Congress of 1909–11. Instead, the rebellion derived from a confluence of member interests, including not only progressives' policy interests, but also individual members' power base interests and minority party interests. At the same time, however, Republican leaders successfully created a temporary coalition based on ideological affinity and side-payments that compromised the 1909 changes. Even the insurgents' ultimate victory in March 1910 was limited by Democrats' desire (as the likely majority party in the 62nd Congress) to contain decentralization.

Rules Reforms, 1909

In March 1909, at the outset of the Republican-controlled 61st Congress, Democratic leaders and insurgent Republicans proposed to enlarge the Rules Committee, to remove the Speaker from that committee, and to take away his control of assignments to most House committees. But a handful of dissident Democrats surprised their leadership by backing Cannon and helping to defeat this plan on the floor. These dissidents, led by John Fitzgerald of New York, then proposed a compromise that provided for a consent calendar, so that members sponsoring minor legislation would not need the Speaker's recognition; for a guarantee that the minority would be allowed a motion to recommit before final passage of legislation, so that a roll call vote could be obtained on the minority party's substitute language; and for a strengthened Calendar Wednesday rule (adopted days earlier at the close of the 60th Congress), which mandated a call of the committees once a week. Regular Republicans united with twenty-three Democrats to pass the compromise proposal over the heated objections of insurgents and their Democratic allies.[57]

Notwithstanding the absence of a progressive majority, the policy interests of progressive Republicans and their Democratic allies helped drive these reforms. As models 1 and 2 of table 2.3 indicate, first-dimension NOMINATE scores are a powerful predictor of members' votes on the 1909 reforms: progressives were far more likely to vote against Cannon than were conservatives. Progressives believed that Cannon's control of the Rules Committee and committee assignments stifled progressive legislation. Insurgent leader John Nelson (R-Wis.) had illustrated progressives' mounting frustration in 1908 when he argued that "President Roosevelt has been trying to cultivate oranges for many years in the frigid climate of the Committee on Rules, but what has he gotten but the proverbial lemons?" (CR, February 5, 1908, 1652). The 1906 and 1908 elections boosted the number of progressives, giving them leverage in the narrowly Republican 61st Congress. This is reflected in the big shifts in the floor

TABLE 2.3 Logit Analysis of Roll Call Votes on House Rules Reforms, 1909 and 1910 (SE in parentheses)

Independent Variable	Pass Clark Resolution, 1909 (all members)		Table Norris Resolution, 1910 (Republicans only)		
	Model 1	Model 2	Model 3	Model 4	Model 5
First-dimension NOMINATE score	−6.64*	−9.31*	−23.36*	−21.99*	−17.50*
	(.73)	(1.26)	(5.25)	(5.56)	(3.57)
Second-dimension NOMINATE score		10.82*		2.36	7.26*
		(2.14)		(3.65)	(2.89)
West	1.85*	−.27	1.21	.87	.60
	(.57)	(.76)	(.82)	(.97)	(.76)
Value of Committee Assignments	−1.00*	−1.04*	−.50	−.45	
	(.32)	(.37)	(.68)	(.65)	
Constant	.77	1.72	7.82	7.20	4.62
	(.43)	(.57)	(2.19)	(2.33)	(1.29)
Proportional Reduction in Error	.81	.88	.77	.77	.77
N	300	300	158	158	200

Note: The dependent variable in 1909 is members' votes on passage of Democratic leader Champ Clark's proposed rules reforms. The dependent variable in 1910 is members' votes on a motion to table George Norris's proposed reforms. Votes are coded so that a pro-Cannon vote is scored 0, and an anti-Cannon vote is scored 1. Similar results are obtained when other reform votes are used (such as passage of Fitzgerald's substitute in 1909 and passage of Norris's proposal).

$*p < .01.$

median away from the Republican median following each of these elections. While the floor median was still closer to the GOP median than to the Democratic median in the 61st Congress, the ideological power balance on the floor was now fairly close.[58]

Progressive policy goals were partly sectionally based, as progressivism was strongest in the West. For decades, western Republicans had distrusted the eastern industrial and finance capitalists who seemed to dominate their party (Sundquist 1983). No westerners served on Rules in the 60th Congress. Cannon did put Iowa Republican Walter Smith on the committee in the 61st Congress, but Smith had a conservative voting record and was hardly typical of western Republicans. As in the 1899 Senate appropriations decentralization, this sectional cleavage is largely captured by members' second-dimension NOMINATE scores: while westerners were significantly more likely to support reform when the second dimension is omitted from the model, the region variable is insignificant when the second dimension, which is strong and significant, is included (see models 1 and 2 of table 2.3). The substantial effects for the two NOMINATE dimensions underscore the importance of policy preferences as an impetus for the Cannon revolt.[59]

Still, progressive policy goals were not the only motivations for either Democrats or insurgent Republicans. Democrats and insurgents did not work together on major policy issues, belying the notion that their coalition was primarily ideological (Jones 1970). Conservatives, as well as progressives, stood to benefit from decentralization, which would enhance the power of individual members. Two of the leading insurgents, Augustus Gardner (R-Mass.) and Charles Fowler (R-N.J.) did not come from progressive districts and, particularly in Gardner's case, had fairly conservative voting records.[60] However, Gardner and Fowler were senior committee leaders who had each seen Cannon commandeer legislation from their committees.[61] Weakening the Speaker promised to safeguard committees from such incursions.

Members with poor committee assignments had particularly strong reasons to challenge Cannon. The Speaker controlled assignments and increasingly used them in a seemingly arbitrary way to reward supporters and penalize foes (Polsby et al. 1969, 799).[62] Insurgents argued that their proposal to take away the Speaker's committee assignment power would lead to a fairer distribution of highly valued committee slots, which would in turn foster a more egalitarian distribution of power (CR, January 18, 1909, 1056–58; February 13, 1909, 2324). The logit analysis illustrates the role of such personal power concerns. Groseclose and Stewart (1998) have developed a technique to calculate the value of individual members' committee portfolios, and Krehbiel and Wiseman (1999) recently applied this technique to the 50th through 62nd Congresses.[63] Drawing upon Krehbiel and Wiseman's estimates, I have computed committee portfolio values for all House members serving in the 60th Congress. Models 1 and 2 of table 2.3 show that these portfolio values are significant predictors of members' votes on the 1909 reforms: members with poor assignments were more likely to favor decentralization than were members with better assignments.[64]

Beyond taking away the Speaker's committee assignment power, individual members' power base concerns also drove other parts of the reform package. Calendar Wednesday, though adopted by Regular Republicans to hold off more ambitious changes, essentially copied an insurgent proposal to provide better floor access for lesser committees (Brown 1922). Similarly, the consent calendar empowered individual members by freeing them of their dependence on the Speaker for recognition when it came to local matters (Damon 1971, 215–16). Calendar Wednesday and the consent calendar were not designed to facilitate highly controversial, ideologically charged bills, but instead to process uncontroversial legislation that a subset of members deemed significant. Members' concerns about their personal power intersected with their ideological goals, since weakening the Speaker and the Rules Committee promised to both increase individual members' access to the floor and reduce the conservative Cannon's leverage.

Democrats' partisan interests also may have motivated reform, but the evidence for this interest is weaker than the evidence for ideological and power base interests. Democratic leaders came to believe that the Republican schism could give them a springboard to majority status in the House, and that targeting Cannonism could unite their party's agrarian and industrial factions (Morrison 1974). Champ Clark (D-Mo.), who succeeded Williams as minority leader in March 1909, later recalled, "I seized with delight the growing dissatisfaction among the Republicans in the House over the rules, as a wedge to weaken and finally split the Republican party wide open" (1920, 260). The Democrats had focused heavily on Cannonism in the 1908 campaign and planned to continue their attacks in the 1910 elections. They hoped to identify all Republicans with the unpopular Speaker and thereby improve the electoral chances of Democratic candidates.

Nonetheless, the extremely high correlation between party and first-dimension NOMINATE scores ($r = .94$) makes it impossible to statistically separate the impact of ideology and minority party interests. When party is substituted for the first-dimension NOMINATEs in the logit analysis, the results are much the same as those reported in table 2.3, and party is itself substantively and statistically significant. Including both variables generates a significant effect for the NOMINATE scores but a small and insignificant coefficient for the party variable. It is also worth noting that within each party, those members who voted against Cannon were to the left of their colleagues who stuck with the Speaker.[65] Thus, the ideology effect appears more robust than the party effect.

Subverting Cannon's power as Speaker, therefore, united members pursuing a mix of ideological, power base, and perhaps partisan objectives. This coalition did not simply occur by accident: entrepreneurs in both parties worked to create a reform package with the widest possible support. Led by George Norris (R-Nebr.) and John Nelson (R-Wis.), the insurgents became formally organized in December 1908. At that time, "the opponents of Cannon presented a sorry spectacle of disunity and cross purposes" (Hechler 1940, 44). Possible strategies included uniting with Democrats to unseat Cannon, replacing Cannon from within the GOP caucus, or weakening the Speaker through rules changes. However, replacing Cannon risked alienating nonprogressive insurgents who favored decentralization but did not want a new Speaker committed to progressive policies (Atkinson 1911). A focus on rules appealed to this swing group of "mild insurgents." The insurgents appointed a steering committee—including both "radical" and mild insurgents—which worked out a compromise that appealed to both groups. The proposal called for taking away the Speaker's control of committee assignments, enlarging the Rules

Committee and making it geographically representative, and setting aside one day a week for a regular call of committees. Twenty-nine insurgents signed a resolution backing these three proposals, enough for a majority when combined with all Democrats (Hechler 1940).

The insurgents' newfound unity and sheer numbers strengthened their case with Democratic leaders, who had initially feared that the insurgent Republicans would work out a compromise with the GOP leadership that included little for the minority party (Clark 1920). But the insurgents' resolution convinced Clark that they were worthy allies. Clark and Albert Burleson (D-Tex.) worked with insurgent leader Nelson to formulate strategy for the opening day of the 61st Congress. The coordinated efforts of insurgents and Democratic leaders produced a cross-party reformist coalition.

But Cannon recognized the threat to his authority and relied on Regular Republicans and a handful of Democrats to water down the proposed reforms. While several Regular Republicans already considered Cannon a liability by 1909, their conservatism and desire to maintain party control gave them little choice but to fight the insurgent-Democratic coalition.[66] Just before the close of the 60th Congress, Cannon sought to consolidate his support by sponsoring the creation of Calendar Wednesday, which the House approved, 168–163. Democrats and insurgents opposed the move, which they correctly realized was an effort to win over a handful of reluctant reformers (Hechler 1940, 47–48). Yet even after Cannon had won back the votes of these members, he still faced the prospect of defeat in the 61st Congress, where Democrats would hold eight more seats than in the 60th Congress.

So in the days before the 61st Congress opened, Cannon and his lieutenants feverishly negotiated a series of agreements with Democrats. The GOP leaders offered tariff favors to a handful of Georgia, Louisiana, and Tammany Hall Democrats (Hechler 1940; Cooper 1990). Cannon also promised to place several Democratic rebels on top House committees, thereby appealing to their personal power interests (Barfield 1970). Still needing more support, Cannon agreed to several changes worked out by Tammany Democrat Fitzgerald and Republican Regular James Mann of Illinois. Fitzgerald insisted on the motion to recommit for the minority and on a provision to require a two-thirds vote (rather than a majority vote) to set aside Calendar Wednesday. Mann advocated the consent calendar, which had also been part of earlier Democratic proposals (Marguiles 1996, 15; Mayhill 1942, 129). Sixteen Democrats defected to help defeat the insurgent-Democratic proposal; twenty-three then joined the Regular Republicans to enact the Fitzgerald substitute. Cannon appears to have targeted Democrats with relatively conservative voting records: in general, the Democratic defectors were to the right of their fellow partisans as measured by their first-dimension NOMINATE scores ($p < .01$). Fitzgerald, in particular, was considered sympathetic to the conservative cause (Marguiles 1996, 14–15). Cannon's ability to win over these dissident Democrats averted a serious blow to the GOP leadership.

Still, the 1909 reforms constituted at least a partial victory for the reformers. Most notably, the guarantee of a motion to recommit proved a valuable resource for the minority party. Tiefer (1989, 454) refers to it as one of the minority's "most important formal procedural prerogatives," and as a "safety valve" because it affords the minority a recorded vote on its alternative version of proposed legislation. It is intriguing that the motion to recommit was not part of the insurgent-Democratic proposal and came about only through Regular Republicans' efforts to co-opt opposition members. A focus simply on Republicans' or Democrats' partisan interests, therefore, could not make sense of this (or other) facets of the 1909 changes.

The 1909 reforms also served rank-and-file members' power goals, though to a lesser extent than reformers had hoped. Fitzgerald's amended version of Calendar Wednesday turned out to be only a slight improvement over the original rule; it was awkward to use and vulnerable to obstruction (Cooper 1988).

By comparison, the consent calendar was a significant success. Before its adoption, members needed the Speaker's recognition to pass legislation by unanimous consent. Although any member could object to such a request, the Speaker's role as a gatekeeper gave him added leverage (Peters 1990). The consent calendar rule deprived the Speaker of any special role in processing such legislation. The Democrats further refined the procedure when they became the majority in 1911, and in 1924 a cross-party coalition of Democrats and insurgents amended the rule again to enhance its effectiveness (see chapter 3). The consent calendar constituted a clear-cut procedure for handling noncontroversial legislation that provided important benefits for individual members.

Each of the three elements of the Fitzgerald reforms constrained the Speaker's recognition power, but Cannon retained control of committee assignments and influence over the Rules Committee. As a result, the 1909 revolt did not really improve the prospects for progressive legislation in the 61st Congress (Mowry 1958). Calendar Wednesday proved inadequate for major legislation, and Cannon still used the Rules Committee to bottle up bills he opposed.[67] Insurgents disagreed about whether significant progress had been made, with conservatives like Gardner more positive than such radicals as Victor Murdock of Kansas (Gwinn 1957, 175).

Both observers and participants believed that the 1909 reforms would end rules agitation in the 61st Congress (Atkinson 1911, 99). But Cannon provoked further anger by demoting several insurgents from their committee posts shortly after the Payne-Aldrich tariff passed in August

1909. His actions—and President William Howard Taft's threats to with-hold the insurgents' patronage—turned the rebels into martyrs, inadvertently making opposition to party leaders more politically lucrative (Gwinn 1957, 184). Insurgents "became intent upon launching their [next] attack at the first opportunity" (Peters 1990, 83). Ironically, despite its shortcomings, Calendar Wednesday furnished such an opportunity in March 1910.

Rules Reforms, 1910

Just as the 1890–1910 period began with the revolutionary Reed rules, it ended with a counterrevolution that overthrew the party government of Reed and Cannon. The 1910 reforms barred the Speaker from the Rules Committee, doubled the committee's membership from five to ten, and provided that Rules members would be elected by the House. These changes weakened the speakership and inhibited majority party control in the House.[68]

As in 1909, reform gained support from progressives in both parties. However, the perfect Democratic support for the 1910 changes—including both progressive and more conservative party members—suggests that minority party interests also played a role (see appendix B.1). Models 3–5 of table 2.3 use logit to analyze members' votes on final passage of the 1910 reforms. Since party is a perfect predictor of Democrats' votes, the analysis is restricted to Republicans. Among Republicans, first-dimension NOMINATE scores are a strong predictor of votes on behalf of reform, with progressives more likely to vote in favor. The estimates for the second-dimension NOMINATE scores are less robust than in 1909, but this appears to stem in part from the limited number of cases.[69] The estimate for committee portfolio values is also smaller than in 1909 and is no longer statistically significant, though it is correctly signed. Nonetheless, there are indications from the roll call data that members with poorer committee assignments were more likely to support reform.[70]

The most interesting questions raised by the 1910 changes are why and how the insurgent-Democratic coalition succeeded after nearly everyone had given up on the possibility of reform in the 61st Congress. This time around, the insurgent-Democratic coalition garnered the votes of fourteen Republicans and all twenty-three Democrats who had backed Cannon in 1909. Two major forces contributed to this increase in support: the rising tide of public opinion against Cannon, which became increasingly salient as the 1910 election approached, and Democratic leaders, who solidified their party's ranks.

Midwestern and Democratic newspapers had been critical of Cannon before the March 1909 rules fight, but press criticism of the Speaker became more intense and widespread in the months that followed. The unpopular Payne-Aldrich tariff of 1909 especially irritated the press, who widely condemned the GOP for reneging on a promise to reduce tariff rates.[71] After the bill passed, even some press outlets allied with the Regular Republicans began criticizing Cannon (Bolles 1951). By January 1910, Republican papers were divided into those advocating Cannon's resignation and those remaining ominously silent (Atkinson 1911, 75–76).

Cannon's mounting unpopularity helped the insurgents win over numerous Republicans with no history of progressivism or reform (Brown 1922, 144). For example, midwestern conservative Charles Townsend (R-Mich.) allied with the insurgents after his constituents attacked him for supporting Cannon in 1909 (*Morning Patriot*, Jackson, Michigan, November 25, 1909). Another conservative, Ohio's Paul Howland (R-Ohio), countered attacks on his vote for the tariff bill by making his role in the 1910 anti-Cannon insurgency the focus of his reelection campaign (Baker 1973). More generally, the mean first-dimension NOMINATE score of the fourteen new insurgents is .36, well to the right of those Republicans who consistently opposed Cannon (mean = .22; $p < .01$).[72] Another indicator of this ideological gap is that 50 percent of the insurgents who fought Cannon in both 1909 and 1910 had voted against the Payne-Aldrich tariff, while just 7 percent of the newcomers had done so. Moreover, these apparent converts did not suddenly become committed progressives. In fact, only two of the fourteen joined the National Progressive Republican League or ran as Progressives in 1912, whereas half of the original insurgents qualified as progressives on at least one of those criteria.[73] The insurgent victory, then, owed much to progressive Republicans' aligning their own ideological interests with more conservative Republicans' position-taking interests.[74]

The increase in Democratic support for the insurgents likely derived from both position-taking and partisan interests. The twenty-three Democrats who voted for the Fitzgerald compromise in 1909 suffered considerable press criticism (Barfield 1970, 311) and probably did not want to be on the "wrong" side of the Cannonism issue a second time. But the perfect Democratic unity on the votes taken during the March 1910 rules fight likely also derived from party-based interests and behavior. The Democrats had responded to the Fitzgerald-led insurrection by making caucus votes binding when two-thirds of party members agreed (Barfield 1970). Furthermore, as their 1910 electoral prospects continued to improve, the Democrats became more cohesive and willing to compromise their differences (Marguiles 1996, 17). Party members had castigated Fitzgerald and his fellow traitors for their disloyalty in March 1909 and had intimated that such behavior would be punished in the future (*Post*, March 17, 1909, 1).[75] The prospect of a Democratic majority in 1911 made it risky for party members to oppose their fellow Democrats.

At the same time, the impending Democratic victory could have under-mined Democratic leaders' commitment to reform. Fitzgerald, for one, argued that Clark would soon become Speaker and thus should not weaken his own powers (Dunn 1922, 2:118). Clark himself understood that Cannon "is our most valuable asset in the impending campaign," and that a successful battle against "czar rule," particularly if it culminated in election of a new Speaker before the 1910 election, risked saving Republi-cans from their biggest liability (Bolles 1951, 219). But the Democrats had promised to fight Cannon and thus could not credibly campaign on the issue if they failed to help Norris once his proposed rules changes reached the floor. Baker (1973, 683) concludes that these constraints led Democrats to strive "to redeem their 1908 pledge to end Cannonism as cheaply as possible."

The Democrats achieved this by convincing Norris to eliminate those rule changes that threatened the flexibility of the future majority party. For example, Norris had proposed a geographically representative, fifteen-member Rules Committee, but Norris agreed on a ten-member commit-tee without geographic representation after Clark persuaded him that he would not otherwise gain unanimous Democratic backing (Hechler 1940). The resulting proposal safeguarded party influence over assign-ments to the committee and left it a relatively small body more amenable to central control. Once again, two groups backed a single change for different reasons: Democrats wanted a limited decentralization (compati-ble with their campaign promises, their expectation of majority status in the 62nd Congress, and some party members' belief that power had be-come too centralized under Cannon), while the hard-core insurgents wanted influence dispersed more extensively. Although the 1910 reforms served both constituencies, Democrats' changing interests as an incipient majority compromised the insurgents' decentralizing thrust.

Norris's entrepreneurial role was particularly important considering Democrats' ambivalence and the presence of several insurgents more inter-ested in posturing for constituents than genuine reform. Norris, however, took advantage of members' position-taking interests to bring about a direct vote.[76] On March 16, 1910, Cannon tried to displace the normal proceedings under Calendar Wednesday by claiming that a census bill was in order because of its constitutional privilege.[77] Norris recalled that the Constitution also provides that each House "may determine the rules of its proceedings." Accordingly, the next day he claimed constitutional priv-ilege for his motion to change the rules. Cannon ordinarily would have denied Norris recognition, but the constitutional claim caught him off-guard, allowing Norris to present his resolution. Once the resolution reached the floor, members who wanted to go on record as favoring reform had little choice but to support it. The rules issue had such a high profile that even procedural motions relating to the Norris proposal would be easy for voters to interpret (see Brown 1922, 155).[78] Norris's successful manipulation of members' position-taking interests shows again how the interplay of multiple interests typically drives processes of change.[79]

The 1910 reforms had far less pronounced effects on policy than one might expect given the immense attention paid to the insurgents' battle against Cannon. The Rules Committee elected after the March 1910 revolt included no insurgent Republicans and instead had a solid conservative majority (Hechler 1940). This is further evidence that the reforms were not the simple product of a cross-party, progressive ideological coalition. Once the provision for geographic representation on Rules had been dropped, the insurgents made no organized bid to gain a seat on the committee (*NYT*, March 21, 1910). Insurgent James Davidson (R-Wis.) reflected progressives' reluctance to become too closely tied to the Democrats when he confided that it was safer "to keep the responsibility on the old crowd" than to risk a permanent cross-party alliance (Holt 1967, 23). While insurgents and Democrats could agree on the 1910 reforms, they were motivated by potentially conflicting interests and thus did not act on substantive policy issues or assume actual control of the reconstituted Rules Committee (Jones 1970).

Much of the short-term impact of the revolt was symbolic and electoral. The events of 1910 gave insurgents the prestige and legitimacy that they had lacked in an era characterized by strong norms of party loyalty. Norris himself wrote two years later that the revolt had helped create "a new atmosphere in the House of Representatives. There is more independence than there ever has been" (quoted in Holt 1967, 19).

Furthermore, the insurgent-Democratic victory likely contributed to success at the polls. Democrats, who won a sizable majority in the 1910 elections, had the best of both worlds: since Cannon remained Speaker for the rest of the 61st Congress, they could attack "Cannonism" and share the credit for having taken away one of the Speaker's main powers. Insurgents also used their votes against Cannon to considerable effect in the campaign. Wolf (1981, 415) points out that while only 54 percent of all Republicans were reelected in 1910, 81 percent of the Republicans who supported the reform agenda throughout 1909 and 1910 were reelected, as were 70 percent of all Republicans who voted against Cannon in March 1910. While hard-core insurgent Republicans were disappointed with the revolt's impact—the failure to secure consideration for progressive policies, the election of a Democratic majority in 1910, the growing importance of the Rules Committee (see below)—they at least could take comfort in the electoral dividends that they shared with their erstwhile Democratic allies.

Beyond its short-term political impact, the revolt against Cannon had lasting effects on House operations. Galloway and Wise (1976, 133) write that the Norris-led rebellion "dethroned the Speaker from his post of power," and Bolling (1968, 75) adds that "the Speaker would never again be as powerful." The new Democratic majority further diminished the speakership in 1911 by taking away the Speaker's power to appoint House committees. Thus, the regime of Speaker-led party government launched by Reed had come to an ignominious end. By the 1920s, it was commonplace to argue that "leadership in the House is in commission" (Chiu 1928, 315; Luce 1926, 117–19). Party leaders, committee chairmen, the Rules Committee, and rank-and-file members competed for influence, so that no single officer or group was as powerful as the Speaker had been in the Reed-Cannon era.

The emergence of the Rules Committee as a competitor for power is a particularly important legacy of the 1910 changes. Before 1910, the Rules Committee had been little more than the agent of the Speaker. But soon after the Norris reforms, the committee emerged as a significant presence in its own right, as its scope of operations expanded substantially. During the four Congresses in which Cannon served as Speaker, Rules had reported just 58 special orders. But it reported twice as many in the four Democratic Congresses that followed, and 181 special orders in the four Republican Congresses from 1919–27 (Chiu 1928, 155).[80] Cooper (1988, 162) argues that before the 1910 revolt, Rules had been "an emergency committee" that only stepped in to rescue the majority party when "cumbersome" House procedures threatened to derail important legislation. After the Norris reforms, Rules became, among other things, a traffic cop that "dealt with all aspects and all areas of the House's business continually."

This was by no means what insurgents seeking to disperse power throughout the committee system had intended. But the Rules Committee was well positioned to take on a critical role because the 1909–10 reforms left in place earlier changes, such as the Reed rules and the powers granted to the Rules Committee in 1892–95, that had made the House a majority-rule institution and had given the Rules Committee important agenda-setting privileges. The Norris resolution loosened the Speaker's influence over Rules without directly challenging the committee's powers. Furthermore, those elements of the 1909–10 reforms that insurgents hoped would provide a way around party leaders and the Rules Committee—in particular, Calendar Wednesday and the June 1910 discharge rule—proved ineffective, allowing the Rules Committee to gain pervasive control over scheduling.

Whom the committee would serve remained an open question. Although it often cooperated with majority party leaders, the Rules Committee could also potentially serve as an important power base for cross-party coalitions opposed to the majority party leadership. Indeed, for the sixty-five years after 1910 in which the Speaker did not control appointments to Rules, conflicts over the committee's role in the House centered on whether it should serve the majority party or cross-party floor majorities (Van Hollen 1951; Oppenheimer 1977).

CONCLUSIONS

Several conclusions emerge from this analysis of congressional development in 1890–1910. First, I offer a much-revised view of an important period in congressional history. Contrary to prevailing accounts (Brady and Althoff 1974; Sinclair 1990), I have shown that the 1890–1910 era does not qualify as a case of sustained, coherent party government. The paralyzed Democratic majorities of 1891–95, the fragmented GOP majorities under Henderson in 1899–1903, the Senate Appropriations decentralization of 1899, and the strife-ridden Republicans of 1909–10 belie the interpretation that strong party leaders imposed order on the Congress for this twenty-year period. Instead, the majority party had to contend with coalitions rooted in members' policy and power base interests, in addition to coalitions that derived support from minority party interests. These competing coalitions precluded the consolidation of party government in the House and Senate.

Second, the evidence from this period suggests that intersections among multiple member interests drive processes of change. The potential for institutional changes to serve as common carriers puts a premium on entrepreneurial members' ability to align multiple interests behind a specific reform. Examples of this entrepreneurial activity include Reed's filibustering to force Democrats to accede to antifilibustering rules in 1894; Cannon's attacking Senate dominance to garner bipartisan support for his revitalization of the speakership in 1903; and Norris and his fellow insurgents' success in framing a reform package in 1909–10 that appealed to progressives' ideological interests, Democrats' partisan interests, and individual members' power base interests. These three instances demonstrate that entrepreneurial members can translate members' potentially contradictory goals into concrete institutional changes. Models that emphasize a single member interest miss the important intersections among multiple goals.

The 1890–1910 period also illustrates how members' multiple interests generate institutions that are full of tensions and contradictions. With few exceptions, each individual change derived from several potentially competing purposes. Furthermore, congressional institutions developed through a layering of innovations on top of preexisting institutions intended to serve other goals. For example, the 1909–10 rules changes did not repeal most of the reforms adopted in the 1890s but rather added new devices, such as the consent and discharge calendars, providing protections to the minority and to individual members. Thus, the reforms superimposed new mechanisms for effective action by cross-party coalitions on top of a structure that still provided significant strategic advantages for the majority party. The broader point is: reformers rarely have the opportunity to build institutions from scratch. As noted in chapter 1, preexisting institutions create constituencies dedicated to the preservation of existing power bases. Those seeking change therefore often find it easier to add to the existing structure than to dismantle and replace it. This results in legislative institutions that embody conflicting purposes.

Perhaps most importantly, we see in 1890–1910 that institutions develop through a pattern of innovation and response, in which the successful pursuit of a narrow set of interests provokes a reaction in which members organize to promote competing interests. The selection of the figurehead Speaker Henderson, Cannon's reinvigoration of the speakership in 1903, and the revolt against Cannon in 1909–10 illustrate this oscillatory motion. The decision to elect Henderson is especially telling: where conditional party government theory leads one to expect increasing centralization as Republican homogeneity and party polarization peaked soon following the 1896 realignment, House members instead demanded decentralization. The parallel developments in the Senate—as junior members stripped Allison's Appropriations Committee of much of its jurisdiction just two years after the Iowa senator had seemingly consolidated his power—likewise suggests that arrangements that empower majority party leaders tend to be unstable, even when the majority party is homogeneous. This is so because changes that centralize power in the hands of party leaders threaten members' other interests, such as their goal of exercising power as individuals, and thus generate pressure to fragment power.[81] The result is not some stable, effective compromise that is reasonably satisfactory for all members. Indeed, based on the history of this era, it is doubtful that a stable compromise exists that can simultaneously satisfy members' multiple interests.

Institutional Development, 1919–1932: Cross-Party Coalitions, Bloc Government, and Republican Rule

THE INSURGENT Republican rebellion of 1910 presaged some of the difficulties that GOP leaders would face in the 1919–32 period. In 1919, Republicans regained control of both houses of Congress for the first time since the revolt against Cannon but still faced a substantial faction of midwestern and western progressives who disagreed with important elements of the party's agenda. Prior to the 1920 election, the common goal of defeating Woodrow Wilson and his League of Nations united the Republicans. But soon after Warren Harding became president in 1921, sectoral and ideological fissures began to test GOP unity.

The tension between GOP leaders' efforts to maintain working control of Congress and bids by cross-party coalitions to empower individual members and enhance the opportunities for bipartisan coalitions to shape policy outcomes drove institutional development in this period. While cross-party coalitions were not as successful as they would be in 1937–52, when the conservative coalition dramatically reshaped congressional institutions, even in this earlier period progressive Republicans and Democrats managed to impose severe constraints on the GOP's party-building efforts. Senate Republican leaders had particular difficulty limiting the influence of progressive Republicans and their Democratic allies.

Applying the criteria for case selection from chapter 1 generates a list of ten significant institutional changes in 1919–32:

1. House Republicans' forming a Steering Committee in 1919
2. Separating the House majority leader's position from the committee system in 1919
3. Recentralizing jurisdiction over appropriations in the House and Senate
4. Consolidating the Senate committee system in 1920, with the elimination of forty standing committees
5. The formation of the Senate "farm bloc" in 1921
6. Liberalizing the House rules in January 1924
7. Repealing the 1924 discharge rule in December 1925

8. The revitalization of the speakership by House Speaker Nicholas Longworth (R-Ohio)

9. Punishing the dozen House Republicans who had supported the Progressive party's Robert La Follette for president in 1924

10. Reforming the House rules in 1931, including passage of a liberalized discharge rule

Appendix B.2 summarizes the floor votes that directly related to these ten changes, while table 3.1 identifies the member interests and effects associated with each change.

The institutional changes adopted in 1919–32 support the argument that disjointed pluralism characterizes congressional development. First, multiple member interests played a significant role in eight of the ten changes (see table 3.1). In several cases, the interactions among coalitions promoting contradictory interests produced compromises that undermined the effectiveness of the changes in question. Thus, individual members' power base interests seriously compromised the recentralization of Senate appropriations. In other cases, changes gained passage by serving as common carriers for multiple interests. For example, the 1924 and 1931 House rules reforms each passed by appealing simultaneously to rank-and-file members' power base goals and to progressives' policy interests.

Second, entrepreneurial members repeatedly capitalized on the multiplicity of member goals by devising innovations that tapped diverse bases of support. A noteworthy example is the Republican Longworth's successful appeal to Democratic leaders' power interests as he moved to reinvigorate the speakership. Longworth worked with Democratic leader John Nance Garner (D-Tex.) to form a bipartisan leadership alliance that successfully countered rank-and-file pressures to fragment power.

The 1919–32 period also supports the claim that congressional institutions develop through a tense accumulation of innovations rooted in competing motivations. In 1919, still traumatized by the explosion of discontent that brought down Cannon, the incoming House GOP majority responded to demands to disperse power by electing a figurehead Speaker, depriving the floor leader of an important House committee chairmanship, and vesting considerable influence in the hands of a Steering Committee. These moves furthered the decentralization originating in the revolt against Cannon. But dissatisfaction with the limited effectiveness of this new mode of organization led to Longworth's aggressive 1925 bid to recentralize power in the speakership. At the same time, some of the earlier, fragmenting changes, such as removal of the floor leader from House committees, remained in place. The result was a mixed system that included protections for individual members (such as an improved consent calendar process and a strong—though not impermeable—seniority system), along with new leadership instruments designed to empower party leaders in this

TABLE 3.1 Summary of Collective Interests Associated with Institutional Changes, 1919–1932

Case	Primary Interest	Common Carrier for Other Interests?	Compromised by Other Interests?	Coalition Shaping Change	Main Effects of Change
GOP Steering Committee, 1919	Individual power bases	Majority party (effectiveness)	Committee made too large to be effective (sectoral interests)	Majority party	Helped build party programs, but committee made less effective due to enlargement
Separation of floor leader from legislative committees	Individual power bases	Majority party (effectiveness)		Majority party	Made floor leader specialized office; severed link between party and committee elites
Appropriations recentralization	Congressional capacity and power	Policy (conservatives)	Legislative committees given ex officio status on Senate Appropriations Committee (individual power bases)	Bipartisan reformist	Added degree of centralization, particularly in House

TABLE 3.1 Summary of Collective Interests Associated with Institutional Changes, 1919–1932 (cont.)

Case	Primary Interest	Common Carrier for Other Interests?	Compromised by Other Interests?	Coalition Shaping Change	Main Effects of Change
Senate committee consolidation, 1920	Senate capacity	Majority party (reputation)		Universalistic	Made more orderly committee system
Senate farm bloc	Policy (sectoral)			Cross-party sectoral	Hurt GOP program; started bloc activism
House Rules changes, 1924	Policy (progressives)	Minority party; individual power bases	Mangled discharge rule (majority party) interests)	Cross-party ideological	Boosted individual member prerogatives
Discharge rule repeal, 1925	Majority party (effectiveness)	Policy (conservatives)		Majority party	Made discharge rule ineffective
Longworth's revival of speakership	Majority party (effectiveness)	Democratic leaders' power		Party based, but element of bipartisan cooperation	Increased Speaker power; established bipartisan leadership alliance
Punishment of presidential election defectors, 1925	Majority party			Partisan	Strengthened party discipline in House
House rules reforms, 1931	Individual power bases	Policy (progressives, issue-specific blocs); majority party (reputation)		Cross-party reformist (antileadership)	Attacked committee chair power; helped "special interests" force floor votes

more diffuse context. Congressional development in the 1920s is characterized by the disjunction between the dispersive pressures generated by GOP factionalism and rank-and-file individualism, and the drive, particularly in the House, to recover a significant role for the majority party.

Support for the fourth claim, that changes that push congressional organization far in a single direction tend to provoke contradictory changes that promote competing interests, is less noteworthy in the 1920s than in 1890–1910. It is true that Longworth's reinvigoration of the speakership was a response to earlier changes that had fragmented power. But, on the whole, there was no dramatic push toward a single coherent model of organization in the 1920s; as a result, the need to defend competing interests from a single dominant interest was less pressing.

In this chapter, I first discuss two cases that primarily involved broadly based moves to bolster congressional capacity. I then turn to cases in which cross-party coalitions united to fragment power in the Congress. Consideration of these cases is followed by an analysis of two bursts of changes undertaken by Republicans: the first, adopted in 1919, enhanced decentralization, while the second, adopted in 1925, moved back toward stronger central leadership. I conclude by comparing the GOP's experiences in the 1920s to the party's 1890–1910 experiment in party government.

CONGRESSIONAL CAPACITY AND POWER

The specter of an all-powerful executive branch in the wake of a major war has repeatedly generated waves of congressional introspection and reform. Just as Roosevelt's dominance during World War II gave rise to the Legislative Reorganization Act of 1946, and Nixon's encroachments during the Vietnam War era contributed to many of the notable changes adopted in the 1970s, World War I provoked Congress to make important changes in its committee system. President Wilson had "excluded Congress from a major share in planning war policy," creating resentment among "Democrats as well as Republicans [who] believed that the legislature should have a larger part" in policymaking (Clements 1992, 160–61). To justify such a role, members of Congress made a concerted effort to put their house in order.

Recentralizing Appropriations

In June 1920, the House returned exclusive jurisdiction over spending bills to its Appropriations Committee. This reversed a series of decisions made in 1879–85 that had distributed control over appropriations among seven different committees. Under the system in use from 1885 to 1920 in the House and from 1899 to 1922 in the Senate, several legislative committees had the power to report appropriations for programs within their jurisdictions.[1]

Recentralizing appropriations reduced the jurisdictions of House committees with 146 members and of Senate committees with 66 members and empowered two committees with far fewer members.[2] As one would expect from studies documenting members' proclivity to defend their committees' jurisdictions (King 1997), power base interests shaped members' voting behavior on this reform: members of committees losing jurisdiction voted 71–38 against taking up the appropriations recentralization in the House, while members of the House Appropriations Committee voted 19–0 in favor. The effects of committee membership on support for the recentralization are robust when controls are added for party, ideology, seniority, and region (see the coefficient estimates for "Gain Turf" and "Lose Turf" in table 3.2).

The puzzle is how reformers passed a measure that redistributed jurisdiction from the many to the few. The answer is rooted in the multiple interests served by legislative institutions: personal power motivations are but one of several interests that determine decisions about legislative organization. In this case, widely shared concerns about congressional capacity and power interacted with ideological motivations to overwhelm members who stood to lose jurisdiction.

Several specialized studies of the appropriations reforms have emphasized the role of member concerns about congressional capacity and power (Wander 1982; Damon 1971; see also Cooper 1988). William Willoughby, an outside expert who helped Congress frame its budget reforms, diligently worked to convince members that recentralizing appropriations would strengthen the Congress (Stewart 1989). Members had become increasingly suspicious of executive agencies, which often capitalized on Congress's fragmented authority by playing committees off one another. Appropriations Chairman James Good (R-Iowa) remarked on the floor that "great trouble lies in this divided authority . . . we see great departments going to one committee for an appropriation, and if the funds are not granted they go to another, and not infrequently they succeed" (CR, June 1, 1920, 8117). Binkley (1962, 266–67) points to Congress's frustrations with mounting executive power and concludes that the 1920 rules change showed that House members "would maintain intact their ancient guardianship of the public purse against executive usurpation" (270).

But even as Congress resisted executive leadership,[3] fiscal exigencies and electoral pressures encouraged members to allow the president a more central role in budgeting. The House approved what eventually became the Budget and Accounting Act of 1921 just days before it recentralized

TABLE 3.2 Logit Analysis of Roll Call Vote on Special
Rule Providing for Consideration of Appropriations
Recentralization in House, 1920 (SE in parentheses)

Independent Variable	Model 1	Model 2
Gain Turf	1.07*	1.05*
	(.46)	(.46)
Lose Turf	−1.30**	−1.30**
	(.28)	(.28)
First-dimension	1.90*	2.49**
NOMINATE score	(1.06)	(.41)
Republican	.42	
	(.71)	
Terms	−.05	−.04
	(.05)	(.05)
West	−.65*	−.62*
	(.34)	(.33)
Constant	.36	.54
	(.39)	(.23)
Proportional Reduction in Error	.26	.25
N	313	313

Note: The same pattern of results is obtained when the roll call on final
passage of the rules change is analyzed. I focus on the vote on the special rule
because it was the most closely contested roll call. "Gain Turf" is a dummy
variable for members who either served on Appropriations prior to the vote or
were appointed to the committee in its immediate aftermath. The results are
unchanged if this variable is recoded so that only those serving on Appropriations prior to the vote are scored as gaining jurisdiction. "Lose Turf" is a
dummy variable for members of the committees that lost jurisdiction (members who also served on HAC are coded 0 for this variable). Adding a dummy
variable for the South produces an insignificant coefficient estimate and does
not affect the remaining estimates.
    $*p < .05.$ $**p < .01.$

appropriations.[4] The new budget system gave the president the authority
to review departmental requests and to submit an annual budget to Congress in consultation with the newly created Bureau of the Budget. This
move to enhance the president's say in the budget process led members
to develop new congressional machinery so that the legislative branch
could keep pace. In his detailed study of budgetary reforms, Stewart
(1989, 184) argues that the "logic of the national budget system required
Congress to match the president in institutional centralization." Proponents of the appropriations change emphasized that successful budget
reform required both the executive and the legislative branches to adopt
more centralized procedures (CR, June 1, 1920, 8103, 8116). For example, Democrat R. Walton Moore of Virginia noted that absent the recen-

tralization of appropriations, "we will have an imperfect and incongruous budget system" (CR, 8114). Republicans Good, Simeon Fess of Ohio, and Walter Magee of New York made similar arguments about the imperative to match the new executive budget with parallel legislative machinery (CR, 8103, 8106, 8116). Members thus understood that only recentralizing appropriations would prevent the new budget system from adding to the president's already growing influence and further undercutting congressional power.

Fiscal conservatives' interest in reducing government spending also fostered support for budget reform. Many authors argue that members' desire to restrain spending in response to the large wartime deficits motivated the appropriations change (Brady and Morgan 1987; Wander 1982, 32, 35; Wolf 1981, 482–87). Although several defenders of the existing system denied that the Appropriations Committee was a more effective guardian of the Treasury than the legislative committees, most members seemed to share the assumption that recentralizing appropriations would help curb spending (CR, June 1, 1920, 8103–17). An analysis of the key House vote on the appropriations recentralization shows that conservative ideology—as measured by members' first-dimension D-NOMINATE scores—significantly increased support for the change (see table 3.2).[5]

Rising public concern about spending forced even some conservatives who stood to lose jurisdiction under the recentralization to support it. As noted above, 38 of 109 members serving on committees slated to lose jurisdiction voted in favor of recentralization. The 38 supporters had a mean first-dimension NOMINATE score of .21, as compared to a mean score of −.01 for the 71 opponents (difference-in-means test, $p < .01$). Interestingly, Bovitz (1999) shows that among this group of "jurisdiction losers," conservative ideology had a significantly greater impact on the votes of electorally vulnerable members than on the votes of members with safe seats. The need to maintain a fiscally responsible image forced vulnerable conservative members to vote for reform even as it undermined their committee power bases.

A final interest that may have been relevant to the change is party. Republicans had gained a majority in the 1918 elections on a platform emphasizing the need for governmental reform and retrenchment (Stewart 1989, 199, 224; Kiewiet and McCubbins 1991, 172). Moreover, as the majority party in Congress, Republicans were more likely both to gain credit for passage of needed reforms and to be blamed if the reforms were stymied. As a result, GOP leaders were among the main advocates of the appropriations recentralization (see Stewart 1989). Nonetheless, the change was largely a bipartisan matter. The recentralization had been endorsed by President Wilson and was part of the 1916 Democratic platform (House Select Committee on the Budget 1919, 8). Most Democrats had apparently favored reform of the spending process in previous years, but party members could not agree on a specific proposal (Stewart 1989, 194–96). Former Democratic Speaker Champ Clark (D-Mo.) sponsored the 1919 resolution creating the special committee that ultimately recommended the rules changes. The House adopted Clark's resolution on a voice vote (CR, July 31, 1919, 3431). Finally, passing the appropriations changes required the votes of many Democrats, including several prominent party leaders. Therefore, there is insufficient evidence to conclude that party played a significant role in this case.[6]

The Senate's decision in 1922 to recentralize appropriations in the upper chamber arose from many of the same factors as the earlier House move. An additional source of pressure in the Senate was that the House Appropriations Committee had changed the titles and contents of the spending bills once it had regained control of all appropriations. The changes made jurisdiction over a few of the bills ambiguous and threatened to leave the Senate Appropriations Committee (SAC) with almost no jurisdiction (CR, January 18, 1922, 1320–22, March 1, 1922, 3203). This additional source of pressure was crucial because recentralization faced more difficult obstacles in the Senate than in the House. These obstacles included stronger committee-based objections: 69 percent of senators, as opposed to 34 percent of representatives, were on committees that would lose jurisdiction under the new system. Moreover, key Senate Republican leaders, such as Henry Cabot Lodge of Massachusetts, opposed recentralization, although they voted for the compromise ultimately adopted (CR, March 6, 1922, 3425). Finally, George Norris (R-Nebr.) and other insurgent Republicans had much leverage in the Senate at this time and likely could have blocked any reform they believed would empower conservative Republicans.

In response to these obstacles, the Senate adopted a reform plan that included major concessions to the foes of centralization. When appropriations for programs within a particular legislative committee's jurisdiction came under consideration, that committee (if it formerly had the power to report appropriations) could choose three of its members to act as ex officio members of SAC; when the bill went to conference, the legislative committee could place one representative on the conference committee. The Senate also restricted the ability of SAC to add legislation to spending bills, mandating that an entire bill would be subject to a point of order if the Appropriations Committee had added any amendments that contained new or general legislation. The former proposal was intended to mitigate the opposition of members of the committees losing jurisdiction (Fenno 1966, 518; CR, March 2, 1922, 3287). The latter helped convince insurgents such as Norris that the reforms would not unduly centralize power (CR, March 1, 1922, 3202).[7] The resulting package drew the strong support of Democratic leaders Oscar Underwood of Alabama and Joseph Robinson of Arkansas, as well as leading progressive Republicans such as Norris.[8] It passed with relative ease, although some Democrats and Republicans, most notably Pat Harrison (D-Miss.) and George Moses (R-N.H.), continued to object that the change would give the Appropriations Committee too much power.

The provisions intended to placate foes of the 1922 reforms had a major impact on the subsequent evolution of appropriations politics. The ex officio membership rule gave the Senate's appropriations process an important element of decentralization. This element fits in with the general resistance to strong leadership characterizing the Senate throughout the 1920s. Fenno (1966, 518) observes that House leaders gained support for recentralization in part by enlarging the Appropriations Committee and appointing a few members of legislative committees to these new slots, while the Senate provided the legislative committees with permanent representation on SAC. Fenno argues that "the House solution made possible an exclusive, differentiated Appropriations Committee, whereas the Senate solution perpetuated a direct substantive committee influence in the appropriations process" (518). Therefore, the Senate reforms had been deeply compromised by the tension between individual members' power base interests and senators' shared interest in enhancing congressional capacity.

This differentiated House committee quickly regained its former status as a key institutional power base, and once again the chairman of Appropriations became one of the most influential House leaders (Brown 1922, 240–41; Binkley 1962, 271). A powerful Appropriations Committee provided an element of centralization in a House otherwise characterized by a diffuse leadership structure in the early 1920s (Galloway and Wise 1976, 318; MacNeil 1963, 395). Furthermore, the committee once again became the place where executive requests for funding received their most serious scrutiny and alteration (Fenno 1966).[9]

In addition to strengthening the Appropriations Committee, the 1920–22 reforms probably helped reduce spending in the 1920s (Rogers 1926, 193–94; Brady and Morgan 1987, 232). Stewart (1989, 211) argues persuasively that the reforms "served as potent symbolic foci for retrenchment. Some retrenchment would have come without reform, but the reforms provided new mechanisms to effect it." It is intriguing that prior to passage of the Appropriations recentralization, House Republicans had used their new Steering Committee to encourage spending reductions (CR, July 31, 1919, 3433; January 24, 1920, 1997; June 1, 1920, 8110). The switch to reliance on the Appropriations Committee—with its more bipartisan tradition relative to other prestige committees, such as Ways and Means (Luce 1926, 92–93; Fenno 1966)—perhaps made it more likely that spending cuts could be effected without immense partisan strife.

Senate Committee Consolidation of 1920

The same concern with economy and efficiency that drove reformers to seek budget system changes following World War I led them to criticize the large number of congressional committees that seldom, if ever, met. In response, the Senate passed a resolution in May 1920 eliminating forty minor committees and reducing the size of the remaining committees. Philander Knox (R-Pa.), the chairman of the Rules Committee, proposed the consolidation. The Rules Committee acted on the proposal rapidly and with unanimity. The measure gained floor approval without objection on a voice vote, and the changes took effect at the opening of the 67th Congress in 1921.[10]

The brevity of the Senate's discussion of this reform and the absence of roll call votes on its passage requires that conclusions about its motivations be somewhat tentative. Nonetheless, the committee changes appear to have primarily served members' shared stake in the Senate's capacity. Republicans' interest in fostering an image of economy and efficiency amid rising public concerns about excessive spending also seems to have played a significant role in encouraging the reform.

World War I had severely tested Congress's institutional capacity, leading members of both parties to acknowledge major flaws in how the House and Senate conducted business. Reformers sought to eliminate committees that served no legislative purpose and to make the remaining committees more compact and thus better able to function effectively. Democratic leader Underwood, an advocate of the consolidation, complained that "with the size of the committees and their number, we all must be assigned to several more or less important committees," resulting in poor attendance, difficulties in obtaining a quorum, and inadequate attention to legislation (CR, June, 18, 1918, 7707; see similar statements of support from Republicans Knox and Wesley Jones of Washington, CR, May 27, 1920, 7715–16, and from Nebraska Democrat Gilbert Hitchcock, CR, April 13, 1921, 207). The reduction in committee size was intended to ameliorate these attendance problems, making it easier for committees to gain a quorum and perhaps improving the quality of committee work.

Yet a justification based on broad, institutional interests begs the question of why the reform was not approved until 1920. Members had long resisted reducing the number of committees because even inactive committees provided their chairmen with office space, a printing allowance, and a modest staff. Minority party members were given the chairmanships of many of these minor committees, generating a bipartisan constituency for the status quo. Haynes (1938, 284) argues that the timing of the 1920 change depended on the opening of the Senate office building, which provided much improved office space for all senators. This eliminated the primary justification for the so-called sinecure committees.

But the opening of the Senate office building is an incomplete explanation. After all, the building opened in 1909, eleven years before the 1920 reform. Elmer Burkett (R-Nebr.) had proposed then that the Senate do away with thirty-six committees; instead, senators voted to add nine new ones (CQ 1982, 253; Robinson 1954). It took World War I to demonstrate the need to streamline congressional organization in order to compete with the executive (Byrd 1988, 2:243–44). Furthermore, the gigantic wartime deficits directed public attention to waste and inefficiency and made committee reform a possible source of electoral benefits for members.

Knox and his fellow GOP leaders initiated the change, apparently in the hopes of capturing a disproportionate share of these electoral benefits for Republicans. GOP efforts to claim credit for the consolidation were at least somewhat effective. The Republican-allied *Washington Post*, in particular, did a front-page story on the reform that credited the Republicans with fostering a "far more compact and responsible legislative body" that would result in "a considerable savings in the expense of the Senate" (April 2, 1921, 1). Republican leaders had managed to align all members' interest in improving the Senate's capacity with their partisan interest in creating a reputation for efficiency.

But even as GOP leaders initiated the consolidation, it is critical to note that Democrats also backed the change. Indeed, Democratic leaders Underwood and Robinson fought back against GOP efforts to credit-claim by making a point of going on record in strong support of the consolidation (CR, May 27, 1920, 7715–16).[11] Though Republicans' interest in a good party reputation gave their leaders reason to instigate the reform, the coalition that adopted it was a universalistic one evidently grounded in all members' shared interest in enhancing the Senate's ability to respond to the daunting challenges it faced in the aftermath of the war and the concomitant growth of the executive branch.

The 1920 reforms inaugurated a period of consolidation in the committee systems of both chambers. The number of committees had grown tremendously since the Civil War, as the Senate went from twenty-two standing committees in 1862 to forty-two by 1889 and to seventy-four in 1919. The House went from thirty-nine standing committees in 1862 to sixty-three in 1919. The 1920 Senate reform was followed by the recentralization of appropriations in 1920 and 1922, the 1927 elimination of eleven minor House committees, and the Legislative Reorganization Act of 1946, which reduced the number of committees in each chamber even further (see chapter 4). Very few new committees were created during this period. Instead, as new issues emerged, the jurisdiction of the existing committees expanded to incorporate them. This process meant that roughly ten committees with extensive jurisdictions became increasingly prominent in the legislative process.

Kravitz (1974, 35) argues that the 1920 reforms also had important unintended effects on committee assignment processes. Prior to 1920, seniority often was based on a member's length of time in the Senate rather than his tenure on a specific committee. As a result, members were on occasion appointed to chair committees that they had not served on in the past. The reduction in committees eliminated this practice, and "length of service on a particular committee, rather than in the Senate, became the invariable usage" in appointing chairmen (Kravitz 1974, 35). Although Kravitz does not elaborate on the implications of this change in custom, it likely strengthened the committee system because longer committee tenures improved both individual and committee expertise.

Though, as noted above, GOP leaders initiated the consolidation, it did not increase the Republican majority's influence over the committee system. Republicans had spoken of establishing an "interlocking directorate" (*Post*, April 2, 1921, 1), but the committee consolidation took place shortly after the party limited members to positions on two major committees (Robinson 1954, 305; Luce 1922, 129). This 1919 change—instigated by Norris on behalf of progressives and junior members concerned about Old Guard domination—forced a handful of conservative Republicans each to surrender one slot on an important committee (Brady and Epstein 1995). Furthermore, the operation of the seniority principle gave western senators, many of whom were at odds with the majority of their party, the opportunity to chair important committees. Party dissidents such as William Borah of Idaho and Norris used their chairmanships as power bases to pursue their policy priorities. The Republican Old Guard simply lacked control of many key Senate committees throughout the 1920s.

A final point about the 1920 consolidation is that while it ended the proliferation of standing committees, it ultimately failed to reduce the size of committees. The GOP's enlargement of ten committees in 1921 began a reverse trend. Republicans did this in part to ensure Regulars' control of committees, although they had only mixed success.[12] Subsequent increases lacked such a clear majority-party cast. For example, the Senate increased the size of committees in December 1927 "as a concession to the progressive faction and the minority," following GOP losses in the 1926 elections (MacMahon 1928, 653). The willingness of both parties to increase the size of committees shows that members' interest in committee power bases generally counts for more than does the abstract institutional interest in committees of manageable size. Only on rare occasions, when concern for institutional efficiency is particularly salient (and holds the potential for electoral benefits), will members countenance reforms that cost some senators their committee places.

The Republican majority promoted both the appropriations centralization and Senate committee consolidation, as party leaders sought to align their party's interest in a reputation for effective governance with all members' stake in congressional capacity and power. But neither change is best viewed primarily in partisan terms. Each enjoyed considerable bipartisan support, owing substantially to members' commitment to a strong Congress. At the same time, individual members' power base interests also produced compromises that undercut the effectiveness of the changes, especially in the case of the Senate appropriations recentralization. As a result, these cases illustrate not only that institutional changes can serve as common carriers for multiple member interests, but also that tensions among competing interests often lead to changes that do not effectively promote any specific interest.

CROSS-PARTY COALITION CHANGES

As the 67th Congress convened in April 1921, Republicans had good reason for optimism: fresh from a sweeping election victory, they enjoyed augmented majorities in both the House and Senate, along with control of the presidency. Yet by July 1921 Republican control of the legislative process had come unglued, and for the rest of the 67th Congress dissidents in both parties effectively challenged GOP leaders. Republicans passed a reasonable amount of legislation but failed to create a popular record to campaign on and thus suffered a severe setback in the 1922 election (Murray 1973, 77–80).

The GOP's troubles derived from the vitality of cross-party coalitions that united Democrats with dissident Republicans. Three institutional changes in this period—the formation of the Senate farm bloc in 1921 and the House rules changes adopted in 1924 and 1931—primarily involved cross-party coalitions. In each case, rank-and-file members challenged leaders' partisan goals. These three changes together helped to forge a more fragmented, open congressional authority structure.

Senate Farm Bloc

The agricultural crisis following the war led to the formation of the farm bloc in the spring of 1921. The Senate farm bloc was an alliance of some twenty senators, drawn in approximately equal numbers from both parties, who met together regularly, planned legislative strategy, elected their own leaders, publicized their activities, and worked closely with the American Farm Bureau Federation to mobilize constituent pressure. Unlike the more fluid and undisciplined House version of the bloc, the Senate group was formally organized and for a time fulfilled a role akin to both a legislative committee and a party steering committee (Welliver 1922, 160; Bradley 1925; Winters 1970, 74). As a result, the Senate farm bloc warrants consideration as an *institutional* change.[13]

Formation of the Senate farm bloc is the clearest case in any of the four periods of an institutional change that advanced a sector's policy interests. The bloc overcame traditional sectional and party lines dividing southern Democrats from midwestern Republicans in order to ameliorate the agricultural sector's postwar crisis. Senators' policy interests evidently are sufficient to explain this change: farm-state senators faced extremely strong constituency pressure to adopt new policies, and there is little evidence that other interests played a significant role.[14]

Senator William Kenyon (R-Iowa), who initiated the Senate bloc's formation in May 1921, became its first chairman. Kenyon quickly gained a reputation as a skilled floor leader (Winters 1970, 89), an important characteristic given that the farm bloc was comprised of "individualists who had never worked with any organization and had no experience in doing so" (Barnes 1922, 56). In his first move as chairman, Kenyon pushed for a consensus program of agricultural legislation. To design a program, the bloc held meetings with farm experts, top cabinet officials, economists, and representatives from farm organizations (Bradley 1925, 715; Anderson 1921, 3; Welliver 1922). The farm bloc also formed committees to gather information on specific issues and to devise proposals that its members could unanimously support (Welliver 1922; "Farmers' Party" 1921). The bloc used its committees to "crystallize individual opinion among congressmen and focus attention upon some specific action" (Anderson 1921, 4). Indeed, the bloc acted similarly to a legislative committee, albeit one representing only a single interest.

In addition to studying issues and formulating programs, the Senate farm bloc planned floor strategy as a party steering committee would. Barnes (1922, 57) observes that, in anticipation of the bloc's first floor vote, "the plans were carefully laid at a meeting of the bloc the night before—as they have been for nearly every vote since—and they worked like clockwork the next day." While defending the bloc against charges of seeking special favors, Arthur Capper (R-Kans.) claimed that "we simply try, like a big steering committee, to get cooperation in support of measures of common interest" (Welliver 1922, 165). Commentators on the 67th Congress noted that the farm bloc had taken away much of the floor planning role from party leaders. Brown (1922, 269) writes that "the leadership which had been intended for the Steering Committee was lodged in the 'Agricultural Bloc' " (see also Widenor 1991, 55). This steering function proved important because floor success often required winning a series of votes and responding to Republican leadership tactics intended to divide the coalition. For example, in July 1921, GOP leaders sought to adjourn the Senate in order to block various measures opposed by the Harding administration. Farm bloc members defeated the motion to adjourn and forced the Senate to meet until six of the bloc's bills had passed. The farm bloc ensured that all its members understood that defeating the adjournment motion would enable passage of a specific list of bills. This coordination function is often performed by party leaders and also brings to mind the work of the Progressive bloc in the fight over the House rules during the 68th Congress (see below).

These efforts resulted in a series of successful farm bills and significantly less attention to Harding's and Old Guard Republicans' priorities. Republican leaders were not eager to help the farmer (Barnes 1922; Rogers 1922, 48–49). The Harding "normalcy" program emphasized tax and spending cuts, tariff increases, a strong merchant marine, and a gradual scaling back of government (Murray 1973, 46–48; Hicks 1960). These goals were not compatible with farmers' calls for government aid.[15] But the farm bloc overcame GOP leaders' resistance. Widenor (1991, 55) notes that the "bloc's influence in the Senate was evident in the vast array of farm legislation that it passed, even in the face of frequent opposition from the president and the regular Republican leadership" (see also Leuchtenberg 1993, 101–2). Although Republican leaders dropped their opposition to many of these measures prior to their passage, there is little doubt that the leadership was troubled by the farm bloc's efforts (Hicks 1960, 55; Brown 1922, 268–69). In his authoritative study of the Harding administration, Murray (1973, 44–45) argues that "with the farm bloc in the picture, the Republican majorities indicated by the congressional election results in 1920 appeared rather meaningless . . . this farm group created havoc in Republican ranks," while Jones (1970, 70) observes that the farm bloc was "a major cause of inaction and dissension among the majority Republicans" (see also Shideler 1957, 164).[16]

The farm bloc's successes prompted fears that "party government had given way to bloc government" (Ripley 1969a, 93). These concerns led GOP leaders to defend party responsibility against special-interest blocs. In his annual message to Congress in December 1921, Harding argued "there is vastly greater security, immensely more of the national viewpoint, much larger and prompter accomplishment, where our divisions are along party lines, in the broad and loftier sense, than to divide geographically, or according to pursuits, or personal following" (*NYT*, December 7, 1921, 8). The president made an even more direct reference to the farm bloc when he addressed a special conference on agriculture in January 1922. Harding claimed that agriculture is "truly a national interest, and not entitled to be regarded as primarily the concern of either a class or section—or bloc" (*NYT*, January 24, 1922, 1).

The farm bloc maintained this level of importance for only a short time. On January 31, 1922, Harding offered Kenyon a coveted position on the Circuit Court of Appeals in a transparent maneuver to take away the bloc's leader (Murray 1973, 63). Chairing the farm bloc had enhanced Kenyon's power and public profile. Nevertheless the Iowa senator left the group when his own goal of individual advancement conflicted with his Senate role. Arthur Capper succeeded Kenyon but proved a poor floor leader, and the farm bloc soon became little more than an informal discussion group (Hansen 1987, 198). The bloc met on occasion in the succeeding 68th Congress to promote farm legislation, and the press referred to Capper as the "chairman" or "spokesman" for the farm bloc throughout the 1920s (see, e.g., *Post*, January 13, 1924, 5). But the bloc ceased to be a major force in the legislative process after the 67th Congress. The farm bloc also lost strength because of divisions over future policy directions (Winters 1970, 89) and because of bloc members' perception that farm relief issues might not recur often enough to warrant a permanent bipartisan organization (Hansen 1991).

The farm bloc's decline by no means spelled the demise of cross-party coalitions that pursued programs contrary to those of party leaders. In fact, another major reason for the farm bloc's decline was the rise of the so-called Progressive bloc, led by Robert La Follette Sr., which posed even more of a threat to Regular Republicans. The 1922 elections brought in numerous insurgent Republicans who were dissatisfied with the farm bloc's piecemeal approach and preferred a broader set of progressive policy innovations (Bradley 1925, 717; Winters 1970, 90). According to the *Times*, "the role of 'chief trouble maker' has slipped from the leader of the farm bloc and landed upon the leader of the insurgent group" (May 18, 1924, section 7, 20).

Indeed, the farm bloc—with its unusual willingness to work in a formally organized, public manner independent of party leaders (Rogers 1926, 97; Bradley 1925, 714; "Farmers' Party" 1921)—apparently encouraged the formation of the Progressive bloc, as well as several other dissident groups that became prominent in the 1920s. Robertson (1983, 307) notes that the farm bloc "was a fortunate precedent for the establishment of the Progressive Bloc." In commenting in 1924 on the farm bloc's apparent decline, the *Times* argued that "the significant thing to realize is that the lessons of the [farm] bloc have been well learned by men who will be in the next Congress, and who will undoubtedly use them" (May 18, 1924, section 7, 20).

The farm bloc set the tone for a decade of repeated bursts of more-or-less organized, open, cross-party cooperation to promote programs that undermined the agenda control of majority party leaders. In addition to the Progressive bloc, these cases include the antiprohibition group formed in the 69th Congress (Hasbrouck 1927, 33), the "Coalition" in the Senate in 1929–30 (Warren 1959, 60–61; Haynes 1938, 448–53, 469), and Fiorello La Guardia's (R-N.Y.) "Allied Progressives" in the House in 1931–33 (Schwarz 1970, 119–22; Warren 1959, 161).[17] In the midst of this activity, Black (1928, 405) concluded that "the blocs have written most of the domestic political history of the past three Congresses, and have made largely negative the role of the chief executive of the nation." Coolidge and Hoover's repeated vetoes of the McNary-Haugen farm relief bill are critical examples of the GOP's persistent troubles in managing its internal divisions.

Since the farm bloc was a move by a faction, rather than a change approved on the floor or by either party, the formation and activities of this cross-party coalition do not constitute evidence against partisan theories of legislative organization. It is inappropriate to expect a partisan model to account for all organized activity among legislators. The farm bloc does, however, underscore the ability of cross-party coalitions to organize themselves in ways that greatly complicate party managers' tasks and thus highlights an aspect of legislative politics that typically is missing from party government models. Individual members pursued sectorally based policy goals by forming an organization that displaced the agenda put forward by majority party leaders with its own favored list of priorities.

House Rules Reforms of 1924

While the House farm bloc was less effective than its Senate counterpart, cross-party coalition activity in the House increased noticeably following Republican losses in the 1922 elections. When the 68th Congress convened in December 1923, a group of approximately twenty progressive Republicans held the balance of power in the House and worked with Democrats to pass a package of reforms in January 1924.[18]

Three elements of the 1924 changes have been identified by both contemporary accounts and secondary sources as important: liberalization of the discharge rule for bringing measures bottled up in committee to the floor; a ban on "pocket vetoes" by the Rules Committee chairman; and loosening the germaneness restriction on revenue bills (Rogers 1925, 764; "Record of Political Events" 1925, 66–68; Haines 1924, 16; Damon 1971). The old discharge rule had widely been considered unworkable. The new rule introduced the concept of a discharge petition and provided that when a petition gained 150 signatures, it would go on the discharge calendar, which would be the first order of business two Mondays per month.[19] The pocket vetoes ban arose because Rules Committee chairman Philip Campbell (R-Kans.) had repeatedly blocked floor consideration of special orders for measures that he opposed. The germaneness change repealed the so-called Underwood rule of 1911, which had made it extremely difficult to amend tariff or tax bills on the floor. The 1924 reforms also banned floor consideration of special orders from the Rules Committee on the same day that they were presented, unless approved by a two-thirds vote.[20] Finally, the new rules amended the consent calendar process to require three objections instead of one to defeat a measure called up for a second time under the procedure.

The 1924 reforms derived from a confluence of progressives' policy interests, minority Democrats' partisan goals, and junior members' interest in a broader distribution of power. The resulting bipartisan reformist coalition succeeded in undermining the agenda control of majority party leaders and committee elites, but Old Guard Republicans also managed to weaken the reform package.

Evidence for the existence of a cross-party coalition is compelling. The key votes on the discharge and germaneness changes united progressive Republicans and Democrats against the majority of the Republicans (see appendix B.2). The pocket vetoes ban, though not the subject of a direct vote on the floor, resulted from Democratic and progressive anger at the Republican leadership's keeping popular matters from reaching the floor. As Congress convened, Democratic leaders listed all three of these changes as priority measures, and the progressive Republican group listed the discharge and pocket veto changes as priorities (*Post*, December 5, 1923, 1, 4; Haines 1923, 12). A Democrat, R. Walton Moore of Virginia, also initiated the rule requiring one day's notice before a vote on a special order from the Rules Committee. Several GOP leaders opposed that change, too, but it passed on a teller vote by a 141 to 104 margin (CR, January 18, 1924, 1139–41).[21]

Policy interests played a key role in generating the coalition for reform. As table 3.3 shows, first-dimension NOMINATE scores are a powerful predictor of votes on the discharge rule and germaneness changes, with members on the left of the ideological spectrum favoring reform and conservatives opposing the changes.[22] Members viewed loosening the discharge rule as a way to get progressive legislation to the floor in the face of opposition from conservative committee and party leaders (*Post*, December 1, 1923, 1). Similarly, Democrats and their progressive Republican allies hoped that repealing the highly restrictive Underwood germaneness rule would facilitate amendments to make the expected GOP tax bill less favorable to the wealthy (CR, January 14, 1924, 958).

But an ideological explanation for the 1924 reforms is incomplete. First, minority party interests also mattered. While the high correlation between the NOMINATE scores and partisanship (r = .89) makes it virtually impossible to disentangle the effects of ideology and party statistically, there are several indications that both variables affected adoption of the 1924 reforms. With respect to ideology, the Progressive Republicans who initiated the discharge rule changes were clearly well to the left of their antireform Republican counterparts.[23] The importance of party, on the other hand, appears most clearly in the move to delete the germaneness requirement, which gained the support of all 178 voting Democrats, notwithstanding the substantial policy divisions between progressive and conservative party members (see Murray 1973; Schwarz 1970; and Hicks 1960, 102, for evidence on Democratic policy divisions).[24] Many relatively conservative Democrats also backed the discharge rule changes despite their skepticism about the progressives' substantive agenda. For these members, partisan considerations were central: Democrats saw the rules changes as providing a means to create problems for the Republican majority (see Cooper 1988, 170; Galloway and Wise 1976, 176). The goal of allowing floor majorities, rather than the majority party, to control the agenda united Progressive Republicans and Democrats, even in the case of Democrats whose ideological proclivities were otherwise more similar to those of Regular Republicans.[25]

Second, the power base motivations of junior representatives also played a role. As table 3.3 shows, controlling for ideology and party, members who served fewer terms in the House were significantly more likely to support a liberalized discharge rule.[26] An example suggests that the size of this effect was far from trivial: setting the ideology variable at the floor median, a Republican in his sixth term would have an expected probability of just .24 of voting for the most liberal version of the discharge rule (the Crisp motion to require just one hundred signatures on discharge petitions), while a first-term Republican with the same ideological location would have a .45 probability of voting for the proposal. Therefore, as was the case with the Senate appropriations decentralization of 1899, junior members again emerged as advocates of decentralized agenda control. In this case, rank-and-file representatives had become increasingly disgruntled because committee and party leaders frequently obstructed popular measures that did not necessarily have much ideological or partisan content. For example, the fight in the 67th Congress over New York Regular Republican Hamilton Fish's bill to fund attendants for disabled veterans strengthened members' desire to reform the discharge process (Hasbrouck 1927, 149–51; see also House Committee on Rules 1924, 32–33; Bolling 1968, 111). It may well be that as member careerism increased in the early twentieth century (Price 1975), there was more de-

TABLE 3.3 Logit Analysis of Rules Reform Votes, 1924 and 1925 (SE in parentheses)

Independent Variable	Vote on Graham Amendment to Require 218 Signatures on Discharge Petitions, 1924	Vote on Crisp Amendment to Require 100 Signatures on Discharge Petitions, 1924	Final Passage of New Discharge Rule, 1924	Vote on Garrett Amendment to Ease Germaneness Rule, 1924 (Republicans only)	Final Passage of Tightened Discharge Rule, 1925 (Republicans only)
First-dimension NOMINATEs	-7.46** (1.14)	-6.88** (1.13)	-7.05** (1.15)	-18.77** (3.41)	-14.21** (2.73)
Republican	.57 (.64)	.15 (.61)	1.25 (.75)	n/a	n/a
Terms	-.18** (.06)	-.19** (.06)	-.19** (.06)	.10 (.12)	.06 (.13)
West	1.27** (.39)	.10 (.43)	.60* (.36)	.33 (.64)	.47 (.63)
Constant	.49 (.35)	.04 (.34)	1.47 (.41)	2.08 (.78)	.87 (.81)
Proportional Reduction in Error	.65	.65	.54	.68	.57
N	408	406	393	221	233

Note: The dependent variable in each case is coded such that a positive score is associated with the proreform position (i.e., support for a more liberal discharge rule and for easing the germaneness rule).

*p < .05 (one-tailed test).   **p < .01 (one-tailed test).

mand for rules changes that empowered individual members.[27] However, since the seniority distribution of House members did not change markedly in the early 1920s, the timing of the change reflects the impetus provided by a dissident ideological faction large enough to control the floor when united with the minority party (see figure 6.1 and discussion in chapter 6).

The ability of reformers to withstand pressure from Republican leaders warrants emphasis. Prior to the opening of the 68th Congress in December 1923, majority leader Longworth publicly stated that the party would make no concessions to any organized group and predicted that the progressives' unity would quickly dissipate during the rules fight. Yet the progressive Republicans held together admirably. They delayed the reelection of Frederick Gillett (R-Mass.) as Speaker, voting against him through nine ballots on the House floor. The insurgents only agreed to vote for Gillett after Republican leaders promised to allow a full debate on rules changes. The agreement specified that the rules of the House would be adopted for thirty days, during which time the Rules Committee would consider various reform proposals. The House as a whole would then have the opportunity to debate the Rules Committee's suggested changes, as well as amendments proposed from the floor, and to have recorded votes on the various proposals. The insurgents achieved some, though not all, of their priorities in the ensuing debate on the rules.

The progressives were able to remain united partly because they caucused repeatedly and had an identifiable leadership (*Post*, December 1, 1923, 1, 5; *NYT*, December 2, 1922, 1, 2; December 30, 1922, 2; Hasbrouck 1927, 19). After the bloc met to plan strategy for the upcoming session, the *Washington Post* reported that "the La Follette insurgents, forming a band of about 25, who declare they will stand by their guns through thick and thin, issued an ultimatum to the Regular Republicans after a long session yesterday. They formulated an elaborate platform, and say they will not permit the election of a Speaker or the organization of the House until their demands have been met" (December 1, 1923, 1). Particularly interesting is insurgent leader John Nelson's (R-Wis.) statement quoted in the *Post:* "the purpose of this conference is to give every progressive the opportunity to know his fellow progressives, to cement progressive forces into a harmonious fellowship . . . we are going to be tried as gold in a furnace. All real progressives will be put to the acid test" (5).[28] The existence of something approaching a formal organization among the progressive Republicans enabled them to stay together through the long series of roll calls on the speakership, and to select leaders to negotiate a settlement with Longworth. The need for coordination was pressing because passing a series of rules changes required that members stand against the majority of Republicans on numerous roll calls, where it was not always certain what threats or accommodations would be attempted by GOP leaders to pull apart the rebellious Republicans and their Democratic allies.

The Rules Committee proposal for rules changes, which was presented to the membership on January 12, 1924, met several progressive Republican demands, such as the ban on pocket vetoes and a liberalized discharge rule. The proposal did not include Democratic leader Finis Garrett's (D-Tenn.) proposal to strike the strict germaneness restriction for amendments to revenue bills. But 26 Republicans joined with the Democrats to eliminate this restriction (see appendix B.2). The Rules Committee compromise on the discharge process satisfied some progressive Republicans, but not the core group of approximately twenty who had held up Speaker Gillett's election. The main floor battle on discharge focused on the number of signatures to require on discharge petitions. The Rules Committee proposed 150. The Regular Republicans moved to increase this number to 218, so that only a majority of the House could force an issue to the floor. Though 27 Democrats defected from their party to back this motion, 44 Republicans bucked their leaders, joining with the great majority of Democrats to defeat the amendment. Democrat Charles R. Crisp of Georgia (son of the former Speaker, Charles Crisp) then sponsored an amendment to reduce the discharge requirement to 100. This was backed by the Democratic leadership and by 19 insurgent Republicans. But this time 44 Democrats joined 180 Republicans in turning back further liberalization of the rule. These Democratic defectors tended to be more senior than their party colleagues who voted to set the requirement at 100, again suggesting a junior-senior cleavage.[29] The floor statements by the Democratic defectors suggested that their seniority had generated a greater commitment to defending committees from floor attacks. For example, future Speaker Sam Rayburn of Texas, then the second ranking Democrat on the Commerce Committee, stated, "I would not support this rule if my party were in power. I shall not support it when my party is not in power. I do not support this rule because I do not believe in half-baked legislation. If you are going to adopt this rule and say that it is wise to work under it, why not abolish all committees of the House and let us have a riot" (CR, January 15, 1924, 999). Therefore, it appears that a handful of relatively senior Democrats' commitment to an effective committee process combined with Regular Republicans' partisan interests to adopt a discharge rule that fell short of progressives' objectives.

In spite of the bipartisan reformers' floor victory on the germaneness rule and the partial victory on the discharge fight, the effects of the 1924 rules changes were not as dramatic as the progressives or their Democratic allies had hoped. The discharge change remained in effect only for a single Congress and, even in the 68th Congress, proved a disappointment. The

rule had been framed by a Rules Committee on which neither conservatives nor progressives had a clear majority. As a result, "the new rule embodied concessions to both sides" (Damon 1971, 221). For example, the
rule did not prevent minority obstruction on the floor. This shortcoming
allowed a filibuster engineered by GOP leaders to defeat the Barkley-How-
ell railway disputes bill, the one measure to reach the floor through the
discharge process (Hasbrouck 1927, 155–62).

The germaneness change had more of an impact on House operations.
After the Democrat-insurgent coalition passed this reform, Ways and
Means chairman William Green (R-Iowa) warned that a flood of amend-
ments would result, delaying passage of the major tax cut proposed by
Secretary of the Treasury Andrew Mellon (*Post*, January 15, 1924, 1).
When the bill came up for consideration in February 1924, progressive
Republicans and Democrats passed a variety of amendments to the bill,
including a substantially greater surtax on high incomes than Regular Republicans favored. Although it is difficult to say whether the repeal of the
germaneness rule was necessary for these amendments to receive consideration, the change does appear to have made the Democrats' and progressive Republicans' task somewhat easier.[30] The tax bill ultimately enacted
in 1924 disappointed Mellon and his conservative Republican followers.
In the long term, easing the germaneness restriction made sponsors of
revenue legislation more reliant on the Rules Committee for restrictive
rules that limited floor amendments.

The ban on pocket vetoes checked the ability of the Rules Committee
chairman to hold up legislation supported by the committee (Damon
1971, 124–25). This may have helped progressives and Democrats in the
68th Congress because the Regular Republicans lacked control of the committee at that time.[31] But the Regulars regained firm control of the Rules
Committee in the 69th Congress. The other rules changes, such as the
improved consent calendar process and the one-day waiting period for
votes on special rules, provided resources for individual members to pursue
legislation of interest to their constituents and to protect themselves from
surprise moves by party or committee leaders.

Indeed, the long-term significance of the 1924 reforms had less to do
with progressive policy innovation than with increasing rank-and-file
members' influence. While progressives did set much of the agenda for
the 68th Congress and emerged victorious on several significant matters,
including the numerous amendments that "mutilated" the Mellon tax bill
(Rogers 1925; Blakey and Blakey 1940, 223–46; Murray 1973, 132–33),
the House progressive bloc largely faded after the GOP's big gains in the
1924 elections. However, even as GOP leaders repealed the liberalized
discharge rule in 1925, the changes to the consent calendar, ban on pocket
vetoes, and waiting period for special rules remained in effect and were

strengthened by the reforms adopted in 1931. The 1924 rules changes had constituted the first major move since the Cannon revolt to protect individual members from obstruction by party leaders and committee chairs. As Hard (1925, 370) observes, Longworth had allowed the rules to change in a "direction toward less control of the House by chairmen of committees and toward more control by the rank-and-file members." Just as in 1909–10, a dissident faction of progressive Republicans had united with minority party Democrats to promote changes that ultimately did more to empower individual members than promote progressive policy innovation. Again, this suggests how the interactions among coalitions promoting multiple member interests shape institutional development.

House Rules Reforms of 1931

Republican gains in the 1924 election allowed the party to repeal the discharge rule adopted earlier that year. The House stayed under relatively firm Republican control for the rest of the 1920s: the majorities there were safer than those in the Senate, and Longworth, who took over as Speaker in 1925, often succeeded in defending party priorities from progressive challenges. In the 1930 election, however, the GOP margin fell to just a handful of seats. During the intervening thirteen months before the 72nd Congress convened, both parties promised to revise the discharge rule in an effort to woo dissident members who would likely hold the balance of power. In the meantime, GOP losses in special elections actually produced a slim Democratic majority when the new Congress finally met in December 1931. Upon convening, the House approved a package of rules changes, the most important of which greatly liberalized the discharge process. The new version of the rule required a mere 145 signatures to place a petition on the discharge calendar, and it shielded discharged measures from obstruction.[32]

Although the lopsided 407–7 vote makes it infeasible to analyze the adoption of the changes statistically, it appears that the reforms found their inspiration in the same progressive reformism and rank-and-file discontent that motivated the 1924 reforms.[33] Progressives' and antiprohibition members' belief that a liberalized discharge rule would favor their respective policy priorities intersected with rank-and-file members' desire for greater influence in committee and floor deliberations to produce a large-scale reform. Democratic and GOP leaders, though reluctant to accept rules that undercut their prerogatives, nonetheless went along with the changes, both to win the support of progressives and to bolster their respective party's popular image.

Rank-and-file concern that committees—and particularly committee chairmen—unduly influenced the course of legislation predated the 72nd Congress. In addition to the limited checks on Rules Committee abuses adopted in 1924, the House passed the Ramseyer rule in 1929, requiring committees reporting bills that amended existing law to provide information about the text of these laws (CR, January 28, 1929, 2371–74; Damon 1971, 82). But the 1931 changes went beyond these mild protections for rank-and-file members by providing that a majority of committee members could force a committee meeting to consider legislation, by specifying that the rules of the House applied to its committees, and by providing that House conferees, typically senior committee members, could be discharged from their conference without recourse to a special rule from the Rules Committee. Damon (1971, 83) emphasizes that these changes aimed to defend "the prerogatives of individual members vis-a-vis the standing committees" (see Cooper 1988, 172–73 for a similar assessment). Progressive Republican John Nelson of Wisconsin declared that the changes battled the "fundamental evil of our system—the concentration of power . . . in a few leaders, with corresponding loss of power to the individual Member" (CR, December 8, 1931, 77). Democrat Adolph Sabath of Illinois added that the proposed rules would protect the rights of individual members, who in the past were "at the mercy of the Speaker . . . and of the various chairmen of the committees" (CR, December 8, 1931, 82). The 1931 revisions thus furthered the broad effort dating back to the revolt against Cannon to give rank-and-file members more power.

But individual members' power base interests were not the sole motivation for the 1931 changes. The onset of the Great Depression led many members of both parties to favor major policy departures and to view rules reform, especially a liberalized discharge rule, as a means to this end. These members recognized that the Democratic leaders poised to take over the House shared their conservative Republican predecessors' resistance to substantial policy changes (*New York Herald Tribune*, November 23, 1931, 8). Many members regarded incoming Speaker John Nance Garner (D-Tex.), in particular, as too conservative (Bolling 1968, 150). Following the 1930 election, Garner and Senate Democratic floor leader Joseph Robinson had joined five other prominent Democratic leaders in "a pledge of cooperation" with the Hoover administration (Schwarz 1970, 33). Such gestures angered Democrats and progressive Republicans who were eager to respond aggressively to the depression. The perception that party and committee leaders did not share their desire for policy change exacerbated representatives' concerns about defending their prerogatives as individual members.[34]

However, it is a dramatic oversimplification to reduce this rank-and-file unease to a single ideological dimension. The depression inspired a wide variety of policy proposals supported by very different groups and interests. There simply was no clear "liberal" or "left-wing" program in the House in December 1931 (Schwarz 1970, 71–74). But representatives were nonetheless challenging existing policies with increasing vigor, and those advocating rules reform hoped to aid these challenges. Herring (1932, 849) observes that the new discharge rule "provided a means whereby blocs dissatisfied with the leadership of the House could bring forward questions for consideration." The "bloc" most concerned with amending the discharge rule was the antiprohibition group. These "wets" believed a liberal discharge rule would allow a test vote on prohibition repeal, a proposal that the relevant committee chairmen and most Democratic and Republican leaders opposed. Newspaper accounts of the discharge reform emphasized the prohibition issue's influence. The *Times* noted that "the wet group, to force a record vote, are strongly backing the rules liberalization program" (December 2, 1931, 1; see also *Post*, December 2, 1931, 1). The wets sought a discharge number below 218 because they knew they lacked the support of a majority of members. Notwithstanding their certain floor defeat, the wets wanted a test vote on prohibition before the 1932 election in order "to smoke out those who have been straddling up until now" (*Post*, December 3, 1931, 1). As will be noted below, the wets were not the only special interest to take advantage of the discharge process.

Partisan interests also played a role in the 1931 reforms. It is noteworthy that the floor debate surrounding the reforms had a distinctly partisan cast. Democrats and Republicans proposed competing but similar packages of reforms, although the Democratic plan included a slightly more effective discharge process. The partisan tenor of the floor debate was rooted not in the substance of the reforms—which members of both parties claimed to support—but in each party's desire to appear the more ardent reformer. In the narrowly divided House, both party's leaders fought for the allegiance of Democratic and Republican insurgents who had been seeking rules reforms for years with limited success.

Several months before the 72nd Congress convened, MacMahon (1931, 934) predicted that no matter which party turned out to be the majority, "dissident elements would be in a position in the new Congress to bargain for changes in the House rules." Republican leaders, expecting to retain a narrow majority in the 72nd Congress, suggested early in 1931 that they would make concessions on rules to accommodate party insurgents. These signals initiated floor discussions of the discharge rule in January 1931 (MacMahon 1931, 934). At the Republicans' February 1931 caucus, which considered organizational matters for the upcoming Congress, party members instructed Rules Committee Republicans to prepare amendments to the House rules. The *Washington Post* noted that "this paves the way for a liberalization of the House rules, which will come by virtue of the close alignment in the next Congress, whether any direct action comes from the caucus resolution or not" (February 27, 1931, 2).

Democrat Charles Crisp, who had been advocating for reform since 1924, renewed his proposal for a liberal discharge rule in January 1931, when it still appeared the Democrats would be in the minority. Democratic leaders backed Crisp but became less enthusiastic about reforming the discharge rule once they actually won majority status. Indeed, the *Post* reported in December 1931 that leading Democrats "are opposed to liberalizing the rules. Having suffered under them while a huge Republican majority was in control, they now would like to retain them and thus strengthen their grip" (December 3, 1931, 1). But Democratic leaders could not afford to alienate Crisp and his allies: as the *Post* noted, "there are independents, or liberals, among the Democrats as well as among the Republicans, and it is difficult to see how Jack Garner can head off a new set of rules" (1). The sole change that Democratic leaders made to weaken Crisp's January proposal was to raise the number of signatures required from 100 to 145.[35] This took place after Democratic and Republican leaders held "unofficial conferences" so that the two parties could agree on the same number of signatures (*Post*, December 6, 1931, 1).

Despite this bipartisan leadership collusion, it is essential to note that the small group of insurgents did not simply allow the parties to set the reform agenda. Fiorello La Guardia, now a Republican after his earlier flirtation with the Socialist party, led a band of about nineteen progressives that pressed both parties for a commitment on rules reforms before the majority party of the 72nd Congress had been determined (*NYT*, February 26, 1931, 4; March 4, 1931, 8; October 25, 1931, 3; *Post*, October 29, 1931, 8). La Guardia's band was primarily composed of Republicans but also included a few Democrats, giving it considerable leverage in the narrowly Democratic 72nd Congress (Mann 1959, 299, 301; *Post*, December 5, 1931, 4; CR, December 8, 1931, 75).[36] La Guardia later recalled that when it appeared the GOP would retain majority status but "would require every vote," he "opened negotiations" with Republicans on the Rules Committee (CR, December 8, 1931, 75). La Guardia and his allies "were then given absolute assurance that these amendments would be acceptable." When conditions changed so that the Democrats appeared to have a majority, Crisp gave La Guardia similar assurances. La Guardia concluded from these events that credit for the reforms belonged to "the small group of determined Members on both sides of the House who have been fighting for these amendments for the past 10 years, and have really forced both sides to bring them in. . . . I say also that this pill is as bitter to swallow to some Members on the Democratic side as it is to some of the older Members on the other side" (75).

Beyond their desire to placate insurgents, both parties also wanted to create a favorable public image by supporting reform. Although House rules typically attract little popular concern, the discharge change received front-page coverage in major national newspapers in December 1931. Herring (1932, 850) observes that "both parties sought credit for the change in the rules." Democrats accused Republicans of switching sides on the discharge issue simply because they were now in the minority. The Democrat Sabath remarked that Republicans "will not succeed in deceiving the country" about their interest in reform (CR, December 8, 1931, 82). Republicans responded that they had favored reform even when they still thought they would be in the majority (CR, December 8, 1931, 74). But Democrats had the better argument: they had pushed for a more liberal discharge rule for several years while the Republicans came out for reform only when their majority was in jeopardy. At the same time, the Democrats' commitment to liberalized rules while in the minority made it difficult to reverse themselves now that the party was in the majority. Republicans, insurgents in both parties, and the press would have jumped on the new majority party for such a clear inconsistency.

Although it is difficult to trace the effects of the 1931 rules restricting committee chairmen (see Damon 1971, 84, 229, and Cooper 1988, 171–72, for conflicting interpretations), there is little doubt that the discharge changes had substantial implications for House operations. The new rule provided the first effective means to discharge bills from House committees since the Civil War era, when motions to discharge lost their privileged status (Galloway and Wise 1976, 104).

From the start, members used the new discharge rule to force votes on popular programs that party leaders wished to ignore. In his review essay on the first session of the 72nd Congress, Herring (1932, 853) notes that the discharge rule had been invoked to bring to the floor "matters initiated largely by certain sectional or group interests." In particular, it helped pass the soldiers' bonus, despite the opposition of the Ways and Means Committee and party leaders, and it forced votes on prohibition repeal and on an expensive bill for western irrigation (Herring 1932, 850–53).[37]

Because of its usefulness for alleged special interests, the discharge rule quickly "became an incumbrance and source of embarrassment to the Democratic leaders" (Cooper 1988, 171). As a result, party leaders sought to roll back the 1931 rule in succeeding Congresses. Despite their newly mammoth House majority after the 1932 election, Democratic leaders could not obtain the necessary support to tighten the rule in 1933 because roughly one-third of the party's members vowed to fight the change on the floor (Schickler and Rich 1997a). But in 1935, the once-more augmented Democratic majority succeeded in increasing the number of signatures required to 218, preventing the use of the rule without the support of a committed majority.

Norms also limited use of the discharge process. Many members were apparently reluctant to sign discharge petitions, even for measures they claimed to support. Damon (1971, 224–25) argues that reciprocity often deterred use of the discharge process: "all members had a stake in protecting the position of the committee to which they belonged; few would be willing to jeopardize the one source of special advantage accruing to them in the House." It appears that more than a few members adopted a standing decision never to sign discharge petitions (Galloway and Wise 1976, 106). Speaker Garner's 1932 ruling that the names of signatories would remain secret unless the petition gained the necessary number of signatures made it easier for members not to sign even for popular measures.[38]

The evolution of the discharge rule illustrates how disjointed pluralism characterizes institutional change. The 1924 and 1931 rules revisions each drew support from a confluence of multiple interests. In both cases, the proximate cause for reform was the combination of a narrow floor majority and an organized dissident faction seeking policy change. But rank-and-file power base concerns provided a critical backdrop of support for the reforms. In the long-term, the 1924 and 1931 changes enhanced these individual member prerogatives more than they promoted a specific ideological agenda.

More broadly, the discharge process exemplifies how institutions come to embody conflicting purposes as they develop through successive innovations. The 1931 rule not only created a low threshold for discharge petitions, but also included provisions designed by Crisp to shield the discharge process from filibusters (Beth 1994). Thus, the 1931 revisions made the discharge rule a flexible outlet for groups dissatisfied with committee obstruction. But Garner's 1932 ruling that the signatories of discharge petitions would be kept secret and the Democrats' 1935 change increasing the number of signatures to 218 made it far more difficult to use the discharge process. These later changes reconciled the discharge rule with a strong committee system and a degree of majority party agenda control—exactly the two obstacles to floor consideration that galvanized proponents of the 1931 discharge rule.[39] Ultimately, the discharge process included features that served a range of partially incompatible purposes.

The activities of the farm bloc and the House rules changes adopted in 1924 and 1931 pose difficulties for partisan theories of legislative organization because they underscore that cross-party coalitions can create institutions that challenge majority leaders' agenda control. In each of these cases, dissidents had access to an identifiable organization independent of the two major parties. The farm bloc, the progressive bloc of 1923–24, and La Guardia's band of insurgents each possessed a degree of organization that enabled their members to coordinate their actions and their leaders to negotiate with party leaders. The result of each of these changes was that dissident majority party members and their allies in the minority could push items onto the legislative agenda that party leaders hoped to shut out: the farm bloc transformed the agenda of the 67th Congress, notwithstanding GOP leaders' goal of submerging the divisive farm issue; progressive Republicans and Democrats capitalized on repeal of the Underwood rule in 1924 by introducing numerous amendments that watered down the GOP's top priority, a major tax cut; and in the 72nd Congress of 1931–33, several blocs used the liberalized discharge rule to force popular programs to the floor, despite opposition from majority leaders. Whereas party government models maintain that majority leaders use their agenda control to block measures that hurt their party (Cox and McCubbins 1993), these cases suggest that cross-party coalitions can use institutional innovations to force such items to the floor.

The 1924 and 1931 rules reforms also illustrate that the conjunction of multiple interests can facilitate cross-party collaboration. In both cases, members' interest in greater rank-and-file influence fused with progressives' policy interests. Members agreed to support the 1924 and 1931 reforms in spite of their different objectives. An approach that focuses on a single member interest misses how institutional changes gain approval by serving as common carriers for multiple interests.

PARTY-BASED CHANGES, PART 1: DECENTRALIZATION

Not all the institution building in the 1920s featured bipartisan coalitions. There were two bursts of institutional changes adopted by majority party Republicans in the 1919–32 period, both in the House. The first occurred in 1919 when the House GOP created a Steering Committee and developed a differentiated floor leadership. These new institutions provided Republicans with a much more decentralized leadership structure than the party had when it last enjoyed majority status, in the 61st Congress of 1909–11. The Speaker was no longer to be a czarlike figure in the GOP, giving way to a decentralized mode of operations that empowered the floor leader.

Although the 1919 changes were party based in the sense of being adopted internally by the Republicans, the interests that gave rise to these innovations were not simply partisan. Instead, the changes derived from an intriguing conjunction of interests. Members' personal power goals sparked demands for more inclusive policymaking than had prevailed in the days of Reed and Cannon. Progressive Republicans, who continued to distrust their party's conservative leadership, added to the pressure to fragment power. But even in the midst of these centrifugal tendencies, GOP leaders sought new mechanisms to influence House action. The Steering Committee and floor leadership changes reflect efforts to accommodate member demands for fragmentation and Republicans' shared stake in their party's effectiveness. These efforts proved only partially successful, leading to the second wave of party-based changes discussed below, which were more explicitly geared toward enhancing GOP control of House deliberations.

The Republican Steering Committee

At the outset of the 66th Congress (1919–21), the new Republican majority in the House created a Steering Committee to guide scheduling and policy decisions. In sharp contrast to institutional arrangements under Reed and Cannon, the GOP barred the Speaker and the chairmen of the principal House committees from the new committee. Instead, floor leader Frank Mondell (R-Wyo.) chaired the panel.[40]

While the absence of roll call votes and of detailed studies of this change provide a thin evidence base, the creation of the Steering Committee appears to have most directly reflected rank-and-file demands to disperse power within the GOP. This urge to decentralize derived partly from ideological divisions between progressive and Regular Republicans that had persisted since Theodore Roosevelt's presidency. Brown (1922, 212) argues that "the dread of arousing another insurgency" led party leaders to decentralize. Progressive and moderate Republicans emphasized that a return to anything resembling the Cannon regime would lead to another disastrous party split. Longworth vividly expressed this fear after the GOP's Committee on Committees selected members allied with conservative James Mann (R-Ill.) for nearly all key leadership positions. The future Speaker angrily condemned Mann's control of the party apparatus as "the most complete sort of triumph for reactionism. If it had been deliberately planned to restore the conditions existing in the House ten years ago, as a result of which the Republican majority became a minority, the plan could not have been more successfully consummated" (*Post*, March 14, 1919, 1).

Yet the GOP's ideological divisions do not fully explain Longworth's complaints. After all, the Ohio Republican had conservative views similar to Mann's (Gilfond 1927; Hard 1924).[41] Instead, Longworth and other rank-and-file Republicans hoped to use the Steering Committee and other devices to augment their own access to power. The decision to bar the Speaker and important committee chairmen from Steering certainly indicates an intention to diffuse power (Brown 1922, 211–12; Cooper 1988, 165). Hasbrouck (1927, 92) concludes that the role accorded to the Steering Committee was part of a more general movement "to broaden the basis of support by distributing the chief positions among more members of the party." Thus, members' individual power goals and the GOP's factional divisions helped create a broad, inclusive Steering Committee.

Ironically, however, the Steering Committee's initial composition favored Mann's faction of senior, conservative members. Frederick Gillett had defeated Mann in the speakership election, due to concerns that Mann's questionable financial dealings and his initial skepticism about American involvement in the World War I would hurt the GOP's image.[42] But most party members apparently had more confidence in Mann than in Gillett, and thus Mann emerged victorious from the intraparty power struggles that followed Gillett's election as Speaker. Gillett proved a lackluster Speaker, while the true party leaders were Mann (until his death in 1922) and his ally Mondell (Peters 1990, 100–101; Hasbrouck 1927, 17; Chiu 1928, 320–21). The most important of the 1919 intraparty struggles gave Mann control of the GOP Committee on Committees, which appointed Mondell floor leader—after Mann turned down the job—and provided Mann's faction with a solid majority on the Steering Committee (*NYT*, March 31, 1919, 7; *Post*, March 14, 1919, 1, 3). Indeed, only one Gillett supporter, Longworth, won a slot on Steering. Longworth led an effort in May 1919 to add western and agricultural representatives to the committee but lacked sufficient conference support to overturn the Committee on Committees (*NYT*, May 17, 1919, 12; May 18, 1919, 19).[43]

Notwithstanding Longworth's complaints about the Steering Committee's composition (*Post*, March 14, 1919, 1, 3; May 17, 1919, 1), the committee initially succeeded in developing party programs that were widely acceptable. In spring 1919, Steering presented the GOP conference with a program for the special session convened by President Wilson. The conference adopted this program, which among other things provided for an early return of phone and telegraph lines to private hands, the constitutional amendment guaranteeing women's suffrage, merchant marine legislation, and tax cuts (*Post*, May 18, 1919, 1). The Steering Committee also played a direct role in encouraging spending reductions by House committees. Republican Gilbert Haugen of Iowa observed in June 1920 that Steering had in the current session reviewed "the estimates submitted [by executive agencies] and . . . recommended large decreases" (CR, June 1, 1920, 8110; see also CR, July 31, 1919, 3433; January 24, 1920, 1997). Haugen went on to observe that the various appropriations committees carried out these recommended cuts.

In sum, the Steering Committee provided a leadership instrument for the GOP and formulated party positions that Republicans on House com-

mittees were then encouraged to implement. Mondell acknowledged that
Steering "frequently" met with Republicans on House standing committees to form common positions on pending matters (CR, January 24,
1920, 1999). Ripley (1967, 77) also notes that Steering members "were
recognized as agents of the leadership and hence could bargain with or
apply pressure on other Republicans."

But members' power base and sectoral interests soon began to undermine the Steering Committee's effectiveness. In 1921 the GOP conference enlarged Steering in response to dissident members' demands for
inclusiveness. The decision to add representatives from California and
Minnesota followed "considerable debate and dissension in the caucus"
(Ripley 1969a, 91). Brown (1922, 213) observed at the time that the
change disclosed "the inherent fear in the Republican party of the groups
into which their party had shown a tendency to break up." John Nolan
(R-Calif.) and Sydney Anderson (R-Minn.), the members added to the
committee, were viewed as representatives of organized labor and agriculture respectively, and as such the move "was indicative of an increasing
tendency in the House toward the disintegration of party and the growth
of the special class" (Brown 1922, 216). Steering remained prominent for
a few more years, but the committee continued to increase in size so that
by December 1927 it had ten official members, in addition to the Speaker,
Rules Committee chairman, and whip, each of whom also often attended
its sessions (Cooper 1988, 378). Cooper (1988, 165) argues that the increases in size during the 1920s "crippled [the committee's] capacity to
serve as a basis for coherent leadership with the result that by 1929 it
seldom met and had instead been replaced by an inner conclave of leaders"
(see Chiu 1928, 335–36 for a similar assessment). The Steering Committee therefore demonstrates how an institution comes to embody conflicting member interests. A combination of partisan, power base, and sectoral
interests produced an unwieldy committee that ultimately proved poorly
suited to achieving any of its designers' purposes.

Separating the Floor Leader from the Legislative Committees

In another sharp break with prior practice, Republicans decided in 1919
to relieve floor leader Mondell of his responsibilities on legislative committees. Previously, the majority leader had chaired either Ways and Means
or Appropriations. When the Democrats regained majority status in 1931,
they followed the Republican example and also kept their floor leader off
of major committees.[44]

The floor leadership change appears to have derived from member concerns about respecting seniority and limiting centralization of power, and

from Republicans' desire to safeguard the effectiveness of party leaders despite these concerns. This explanation is tentative because there is scant work on the 1919 change and because primary sources yield little information.[45] While scholars have discussed the importance of the floor leadership shift, they have not generally cited primary sources or other evidence that might explain the motivations behind the change.

Comparing the 1919 decision with an earlier, related change suggests the relevance of the emerging seniority system and of Republicans' interest in vigorous leadership on the floor. In 1911 incoming minority leader Mann broke with precedent, announcing he would not serve on any committees. In the past, the minority leader had been the ranking member of Ways and Means. But Sereno Payne (R-N.Y.), rather than Mann, was the senior Republican on Ways and Means. Mann appears to have been reluctant to displace Payne for fear of being accused of an abuse of power (*Post*, April 9, 1911, 8). This fear was especially salient because Cannon had alienated many party members by violating seniority a few years earlier. At the same time, members hailed Mann's decision because they believed it would "give him a less hampered opportunity to arrange a militant campaign against the Democrats on the floor" (*Post*, April 9, 1911, 8; April 12, 1911, 4).

Mann's decision might well have been the precursor to the 1919 change. Still, the GOP decision to deprive the majority leader of an important committee chairmanship seems surprising since Democrats' successfully used this dual-leadership model under floor leader Oscar Underwood in 1911–15 (Ripley 1967, 95–98; Peters 1990, 97). But, as in 1911, membership devotion to committee seniority may have played a critical role. Mann's faction, which controlled GOP committee assignments in the 66th Congress, believed strongly in seniority (*NYT*, February 28, 1919, 1, 4; March 1, 1919, 13). It would have violated seniority to promote Mondell, who was only entitled to the second ranking slot on Appropriations, to the chairmanship of either Ways and Means or Appropriations. An alternative consistent with the seniority system would have been to appoint as floor leader the senior Republican on either committee. But Democrats' experience with Claude Kitchin (D-N.C.)—a foe of Wilson's policies who became Ways and Means chairman and thus floor leader in 1915 because of his seniority—demonstrated the costs of allowing committee seniority to dictate the party floor leader. Indeed, Polsby (1968, 157–58) argues that as seniority became more automatic, it proved "cumbersome and impractical" for the floor leader to acquire his position by virtue of chairing Ways and Means or Appropriations.

A second factor behind the change was the Republican effort to make their leadership effective despite a figurehead Speaker who lacked the support of the party caucus. Republicans compensated for Gillett's weakness by providing the floor leader with new party responsibilities, making him chairman of the Steering Committee and Committee on Committees (Chiu 1928, 320–21). These time-consuming duties would have reduced Mondell's ability serve in an important committee chairmanship.

Furthermore, members' power base interests most likely would have militated against a system that allowed the Ways and Means chairman to serve as floor leader and as chairman of two important party committees. Pressures for decentralization in the Republican party were quite strong in 1919 (Peters 1990, 99–101; Cooper 1988, 164–65). Indeed, as noted above, the caucus rule setting up the Steering Committee barred the chairmen of important committees from Steering. This rule suggests that rank-and-file members would not tolerate the concentration of power implied by allowing the chairman of Ways and Means also to serve as a top party leader.

The 1919 move therefore appears to have emerged from a confluence of several interests. Individual members would not allow the floor leader to hold too many reins of power and may also have hoped to prevent unnecessary seniority violations. At the same time, the 1919 change promised Republicans a more focused, and perhaps effective, floor leader.

Indeed, the lasting effect of the 1919 change is that it transformed the majority leadership into a differentiated office responsible for scheduling business and managing the floor on behalf of the majority party. The floor leader could specialize, serving as a clearly identifiable party leader rather than a part-time leader with committee duties competing for his attention (Polsby 1968, 158; Peabody 1976, 34). Nelson (1976, 17) observes that "in 1919, the functional autonomy of the office was assured when [Mondell] abandoned his seat on Appropriations to become the Republican majority leader." As MacNeil (1963, 96–97) emphasizes, the floor leader finally emerged as a leader of "independent rank" who could devote his "entire time to managing the floor business of the House." It is probably no coincidence that the Congressional Directory first recognized the floor leader as a House officer just two years after the 1919 change. In addition, on May 27, 1919, the House passed a resolution providing staff assistance for the majority floor leader (CR, 278). This appears to have been the first time that the House explicitly allocated staff to that office.

Mondell used his position as majority leader aggressively. Through the Steering Committee, he helped to craft GOP positions on matters still pending in legislative committees (Ripley 1969a, 98–99). Mondell also testified before several standing committees, advising them on policy (Ripley 1969a, 99). This gave Mondell influence across a range of issues. In addition, Mondell strengthened the floor leader's role as an information source for members. Mondell initiated the practice of providing rank-and-file Republicans with a weekly bulletin outlining the tentative program for the following week (Hasbrouck 1927, 110). Before then, "it had often been difficult for members to know what business was scheduled to come before the House" (Ripley 1969a, 99). The majority leader's informational role accentuated the perception that the floor leader had become "the general manager of his party in the House" (Brown 1922, 224).[46]

Two caveats must be added to this story of increasing floor leader influence. First, Mondell's prominence in GOP politics stemmed from the unusual situation of a Speaker explicitly elected as a figurehead. Subsequent floor leaders have typically been the Speaker's lieutenants (Ripley 1967, 27).[47] Even the floor leader's position as chairman of the Steering Committee became far less important after Speaker Longworth weakened the committee in 1925.

A second caveat is that differentiating the floor leader's position came at a cost for Republicans. Separating the floor leadership from the chairmanship of Ways and Means severed an important institutional linkage between party leaders and the committee system, further fragmenting power in the House (Cooper 1988, 165; CQ 1982, 134–35). Smith and Deering (1990, 37) list a series of changes adopted by the Republicans— separating the floor leadership from the chairmanship of a major committee, barring the chairmen of major committees from serving on the Steering Committee or on Rules, and increasing adherence to the seniority principle—and conclude that "these changes formally divorced the leadership from the committee system, allowing committee chairs to become independent powers within the jurisdiction of their committees. Party leadership became a somewhat more fluid group of elected leaders and selected lieutenants, who were now more dependent upon personal skills than formal powers to shape House decision making."

Therefore, a differentiated majority leadership helped the GOP by providing a full-time floor manager who could assist the Speaker in strategic decision-making and in bargaining with and informing rank-and-file members. But it also contributed to the Republican shift away from the "interlocking directorate" approach of the past, in which key party leaders also held major committee posts that provided crucial resources for their leadership (Cooper and Brady 1981, 413). The relatively divided and individualistic Republican rank and file militated against a return to this older approach to party government. A separate, identifiable party leadership emerged that supplemented, but did not supplant, the leadership from within the committee system (see Truman 1959b, 688). The 1919 change is thus an important moment in the development of a bifurcated leadership structure in which party leaders both competed and collaborated with increasingly independent committee chairmen. Along with the revolt against Cannon, it emerges as one of the harbingers of what would eventually be called the "textbook Congress" (see Shepsle 1989).

PARTY-BASED CHANGES, PART 2:
A RETURN TO SPEAKER-LED GOVERNANCE?

Though the 1919 changes foreshadowed the feudal organization that took hold under the Democrats in 1937–52, the path toward fragmented authority was by no means linear and uninterrupted. Instead, dissatisfaction with the decentralized mode of operations adopted in 1919 enabled Nicholas Longworth to gain support for several changes in the mid-1920s that empowered party leaders. Longworth enhanced the speakership and encouraged Republicans to close off the discharge process and to punish party members who had supported La Follette in the 1924 presidential campaign. These changes strengthened Regular Republicans in their ongoing quarrels with party dissidents.

But Longworth could not simply overturn all of the decentralizing changes that had been made since 1909. For one, he had to accommodate the entrenched seniority system. He therefore made clear when he punished La Follette's supporters that the resulting seniority violations were an exception brought on by extreme circumstances. They did not constitute a broad attack on the seniority system. Furthermore, to a much greater extent than Reed or Cannon, Longworth relied on alliances with Democratic leaders to withstand the centrifugal pressures emanating from rank-and-file members' personal power goals and from the GOP's continuing factional divisions. Longworth's leadership added a degree of centralization, albeit on a more bipartisan basis than in the past, to the decentralized structure that had taken shape in the first decades of the twentieth century.

Longworth's Revival of the Speakership

The immediate successors to Joseph Cannon, Champ Clark and Frederick Gillett, had been lackluster Speakers. Majority party leadership had shifted from "the chair" (as the speakership is often called) to the majority leader and, after 1919, the Steering Committee. On succeeding Gillett, who left the House in 1925 to become a senator, Nicholas Longworth immediately began to return the speakership to a central place in House deliberations. He replaced the decentralized leadership approach represented by the Steering Committee with a far more personalized and centralized mode of operations.[48]

Acting as an entrepreneur, Longworth capitalized on the pluralism of member interests by aligning Republicans' interest in more effective party leadership with Democratic leaders' desire for more influence over House deliberations. Democratic leaders gained influence that they had lacked when the Republican Steering Committee was the GOP's primary leadership instrument; in exchange, they cooperated with Longworth. The resulting bipartisan leadership may appear anomalous in light of the hostility between Democratic and GOP House leaders since the mid-1980s, but it operated effectively throughout Longworth's six-year tenure as Speaker and persisted as late as the 1940s and 1950s, when Rayburn and his close friend Republican Joe Martin of Massachusetts led the House.

Shortly after taking office, Longworth wrote to his sister that he had been "able to take the majority leadership from the Floor to the Chair, which most Speakers in recent years, except Reed and Cannon, were not able to do" (Chambrun 1933, 294). Longworth's contemporaries attributed much of the new Speaker's influence to his charm and flashy personality (Hard 1925). But Longworth's revival of the speakership also resulted from his changes to the institutions of leadership. Longworth displaced the Steering Committee, on which the Speaker had only ambiguous status, and instead relied on his own mechanisms: an informal coterie of men who became known as his "lieutenants" and the bipartisan Bureau of Education (Peters 1990, 103–6; MacNeil 1963, 81–82). In the wake of the weak leadership of Speakers Clark and Gillett from 1911 through 1925, concrete changes in leadership instruments were necessary to return the Speaker to prominence.

Longworth's maneuvers had a sharp partisan element. A month before his election as Speaker, the Ohio Republican stated his belief in "responsible party government. That's what we are going to have in the next Congress. We had a taste of bloc government in the last Congress" (*NYT*, November 3, 1925, 6). In his inaugural address, Longworth asserted that the Speaker has the duty "standing squarely on the platform of his party, to assist in so far as he properly can the enactment of legislation in accordance with the declared principles and policies of his party" (CR, December 7, 1925, 382). MacNeil (1963, 33) argues that through his pronouncements Longworth "candidly announced he would be the political leader of the House, not its moderator, and instituted a new concept of the Speakership." Longworth personally took the lead in punishing the twelve Republicans who had backed La Follette for president, and in repealing the 1924 discharge rule. These moves signaled the Republicans' renewed commitment to party government.

Very soon after Longworth became Speaker, contemporary observers began to note the leadership changes. Arthur MacMahon wrote in 1927 (299) that "there was evidence of a little dissatisfaction on the ground, especially, that the role of the Steering Committee was being unduly usurped by an inner group of four persons—Speaker Longworth, floor leader Tilson, Chairman Snell of Rules, and Representative [James]

Begg."[49] The Steering Committee had been superseded by a smaller, more flexible group that put the Speaker at the center of party deliberations. Most members recognized the Steering Committee's shortcomings, and so the party caucus reelecting Longworth in 1927 turned out to be harmonious (Ripley 1967, 101; MacMahon 1927, 299). Republicans appreciated Longworth's ability to make their party and the House an effective and prestigious partner in government (see Gilfond 1927; Page 1928).

A conditional party government explanation for Longworth's centralization would point to his party's large majorities and the dampening of GOP divisions following progressives' disappointing showing in the 1924 election. But the speakership had been a minor position amid important variations in majority size and homogeneity in 1911–25. Although Longworth enjoyed fairly comfortable majorities (with the exception of the 70th Congress of 1927–29), he never had a majority as substantial as Gillett enjoyed in the 67th Congress of 1921–23. Furthermore, Republicans still faced important divisions, particularly on farm policy, during Longworth's tenure (Murray 1973, 144; Jones 1970, 50, 59; McCoy 1967, 193). Indeed, an examination of the distribution of Republicans' first-dimension NOMINATE scores suggests that Republican homogeneity did not increase during the Longworth years: the standard deviations of Republicans' scores in the two Congresses preceding Longworth's speakership were .12 and .17, while the standard deviation ranged from .16 to .17 during Longworth's six years as Speaker.[50]

Instead, it seems likely that Longworth had greater freedom to centralize because of his unusual position within the party: he was a "Regular" with some progressive predispositions and insurgent roots (Hard 1924, 88–89; Brown 1922). On the one hand, Longworth had first achieved prominence by attacking Mann, the Old Guard's candidate for Speaker, and by fighting the arch-conservatives' control of the Committee on Committees and Steering Committee (*NYT*, March 12, 1919, 1; *Post*, March 14, 1919, 1, 3; March 17, 1919, 2; May 15, 1919, 1). At the same time, Longworth supported the Regulars' policy agenda and did not tolerate the extreme disloyalty of certain progressive Republicans. Simply put, a wide range of members were comfortable with Longworth's leadership.

But perhaps more importantly, Longworth did not rely solely on GOP support. His approach featured far more bipartisanship than the Reed-Cannon model of Speaker-led party government. Confronted with a party that still harbored significant factional divisions and considerable distrust of assertive leadership, Longworth worked with his friend, Democratic leader Garner, to form a bipartisan leadership alliance.[51] Longworth and Garner instituted the Bureau (or Board) of Education to oversee the House in a cooperative fashion. Toward the end of each day, Garner and Longworth, along with handpicked members from both parties, including Rayburn, Snell, and John McDuffie (D-Ala.), typically adjourned to the Speaker's hideaway office for drinks and discussions. MacNeil (1963, 81–82) argues that the Bureau of Education was so named "not so much because Longworth and Garner were educating young members there in parliamentary strategy and practice as because they used it to learn what was going on in the House." By placing the Speaker at the center of House information networks, these sessions "enormously helped the Speakers— Longworth, Garner, and Rayburn—to reestablish the old prestige of their office" (83). The sessions also helped build bipartisan comity and allowed the leaders of both parties to direct the unwieldy House membership (MacNeil 1963, 82; Hardeman and Bacon 1987, 115). Peters (1990, 105) concludes that "the 'Board' enabled the leaders of the two parties to reach a working accord." MacNeil (1963, 82) agrees that "Longworth and Garner frequently reached agreements on the legislation coming before the House. . . . They opposed each other on controversial bills, but even on the controversial measures there were areas where accommodations were possible." Finding areas of agreement was not terribly difficult because Garner and Longworth were both relatively conservative.[52]

Longworth's efforts to reach out to Democratic leaders annoyed some members of both parties. Timmons (1948, 122) observes that "some Republicans thought that Garner got the best of Longworth [in the Board of Education]. On the other hand, some Democrats felt that Longworth got the best of Garner." An example of disgruntlement with this bipartisanship came at the opening of the 69th Congress in December 1925, when "a non-partisan tax bill was laid before the members, the result of an unprecedented tete-a-tete between the Speaker and [Garner]" (Gilfond 1927, 452). Progressive Republicans and their Democratic allies bitterly attacked Garner for "surrendering" to Longworth (CR, December 9, 1925, 548–49; December 10, 1925, 653–54). But Garner's support had come at the price of Longworth allowing the minority leader to help shape the bill—a change from past practice with respect to tax legislation (Blakey and Blakey 1940, 255–61).

Longworth's close relations with Democratic leaders paid dividends for him personally and for the Republican leadership as a whole. Schwarz (1970, 65), in his study of the Hoover administration, argues that Democratic leaders had by 1929 become "accustomed to enhancing their power by collaboration with the majority. Their dissent tended to be perfunctory." Similarly, journalists Robert Allen and Drew Pearson (1931, 243) claimed that Garner's interactions with Longworth on the floor were a mere "sham battle" (see also Gilfond 1927, 453).

The lasting impact of Longworth's speakership was this bipartisan leadership coalition, rather than reestablishment of a Reed-style party machine. Peters (1990, 98) notes that "it was during the Republican hege-

mony of the Roaring Twenties that the seeds of the bipartisan stability
that would later characterize the feudal period were planted." Longworth
and Garner upheld conservative policies and restrained populist pressures
from rank-and-file members. Schwarz's (1970) account of the 72nd Congress (1931–33)—Garner's only as Speaker and the first following Longworth's death—suggests that Democratic and GOP leaders worked hard
to head off policy changes favored by backbenchers in both parties. The
1931 move to liberalize the discharge rule was thus a reaction to this
ongoing bipartisan leadership.

Therefore, while Longworth strengthened the speakership as a party
institution, he also fostered bipartisanship in ways that contradict a simple
partisan interpretation. Just as the party-based institutional changes of
1937–52 proved quite limited, the partisan reforms of the 1920s took
account of a House in which cross-party coalitions competed seriously for
influence. Longworth's approach encouraged Garner and other Democratic leaders to work with the Regular Republicans rather than with progressive Republicans, as they had done during the 1924 rules fight. Democratic leaders gained influence over House deliberations, while the GOP
benefited from reduced partisan hostility and improved manageability.

Repeal of the Discharge Rule

Longworth's leadership was by no means strictly bipartisan, of course. In
one of his first moves as Speaker, he successfully pushed for repeal of the
discharge rule passed by the Democratic–progressive Republican coalition
in January 1924. Under the new rule adopted in December 1925, the
discharge process essentially became a dead letter for the next six years.
The rule required the support of 218 members at three separate stages of
the legislative process and included devices that made it extremely difficult
to gain high participation at some of these stages (Beth 1994, 10; Hasbrouck 1927, 163–64).[53]

The roll calls on this change suggest that it was motivated by Republicans' partisan interest in strengthening their agenda control and conservatives' policy interests. Consistent with a partisan interpretation, all 168
Democrats, including those with conservative records, voted against the
change, while 90 percent of Republicans voted in favor. As discussed
below, the unanimous support of Republican freshmen and the vote-switches by several Republicans who had favored a more liberal discharge
rule in the past also suggest the importance of party-based interests and
behavior. At the same time, the last column of table 3.3 shows that ideology is still a strong predictor of Republicans' votes on this issue: conservatives backed repeal, while progressive Republicans tended to oppose it.[54]

For conservative Republicans, tightening the discharge rule was attractive not only because it promised to enhance their party's effectiveness, but also because it would help keep progressive legislation off of the floor.

Contemporary commentators and secondary sources concur that GOP leaders fought for the change in order to protect the party's dominant conservative wing. *Political Science Quarterly* asserted in 1926 ("Record of Political Events" 51–52) that "the Republican leaders forced through [the change], which will keep the control of the House securely in the hands of the leaders." Hasbrouck (1927, 163–64) and Chiu (1928, 279–82) agree that the change was enacted to block progressive measures opposed by party leaders. Democrat Garrett charged more specifically that the Republicans wanted to block a vote on tariff reductions (CR, December 16, 1925, 934).

The underlying factor allowing GOP leaders to replace the discharge rule was the party's twenty-two-seat gain in the 1924 election, which provided a working majority for the Regular Republicans. The GOP's new, sixty-four-seat advantage over the Democrats (247–183) enabled it to triumph in a close 207–196 vote despite the defection of twenty-two insurgents (see appendix B.2). Hicks (1960, 102) writes that "the balance-of-power status that had given the irregulars so much standing in the preceding Congress was now a thing of the past, and Republican conservatives, with an occasional assist when necessary from like-minded Democrats, were in complete control."

But the Republicans also benefited from the votes of several party members who had supported the insurgents in 1924. Seventeen of the thirty-eight Republicans returning to the House who had voted against the leadership's January 1924 amendment to require 218 signatures on discharge petitions switched sides and now voted to curtail the discharge process. Given Republicans' narrow margin of victory, these vote switches were crucial. The members who now voted with the leadership—men such as Royal Johnson (R-S.Dak.), Frank Clague (R-Minn.), and Harold Knutson (R-Minn.)—were moderately progressive Republicans not too closely identified with either the Regulars or the hard-core insurgents. Indeed, the mean ideology score for the switchers (.24, SE = .02) placed them well to the left of those Republicans who had voted with the party in both 1924 and 1925 (.42, SE = .01), but to the right of those Republicans who defected in both years (.03, SE = .04).[55]

A plausible explanation for these switches is that, unlike in 1924, the Republican leadership could now pressure wavering members. The increased GOP majority meant that progressives lacked the leverage they had enjoyed in the 68th Congress. Longworth declared that defectors in the 1924 presidential election would be punished unless they voted for the new discharge rule and backed the party nominee for Speaker (Galloway and Wise 1976, 177). Garrett also claimed that Republicans were threatening punishment to secure the votes of party members who had voted for the 1924 rule (CR, December 7, 1925, 389). Still, the pressure on incumbent members should not be exaggerated. Schickler and Rich (1997a) show that GOP leaders did not use the discharge rule vote as a basis for punishing disloyal members; instead, the other two tests announced by Longworth—support for Coolidge for president in 1924 and for the Republican nominee for Speaker—were applied (see also CR, December 16, 1925, 935).[56]

The main effect of party pressure may have been to intimidate the fifty-seven freshmen Republicans, none of whom voted against the leadership on the discharge change. Hasbrouck (1927, 36–37) argues that Longworth waited to make most committee assignments in order to maximize his leverage with the freshmen. Controlling for ideology and region, freshmen Republicans apparently were more likely to support the change than were their more senior colleagues—a reversal of the typical pattern in which junior members tend to support decentralized agenda control.[57]

Though the new rule made GOP leaders less subject to discharge efforts, it was no panacea for the Republicans.[58] Murray (1973, 144) observes that even after 1924, "dissident farm elements continued to disrupt Republican party harmony by joining with the Democratic minority to attack the administration on such matters as public power and farm policy." The Regulars' continuing troubles in the Senate, in particular, limited the impact of Longworth's innovations. Indeed, Ripley's (1969a, 107) assessment of the 69th Congress suggests that the legislative product pleasing to the president and Republican congressional leaders "was not large . . . but several legislative developments displeased Republican leaders." These included the McNary-Haugen agriculture bill (which Coolidge vetoed) and the defeat of several administration priorities.

Nonetheless, the 1925 discharge rule emerges as a Republican leadership success, though one that depended very much on the size of the party's majority in the House. Such a rule had been impossible in the 68th Congress, when the GOP enjoyed only a slim majority, and Republican leaders were forced to admit before the 72nd Congress in 1931 that even if the party retained a slim majority, the discharge rule of 1925 would have to be sacrificed to placate party insurgents. The 1924–1925–1931 discharge changes therefore underscore the importance of the ideological balance of power on the floor as a determinant of institutional rules (Schickler 2000). Members' policy interests proved a substantial constraint on the majority party's ability to dictate the contours of the discharge process. Republican leaders required a substantial majority to overcome progressive Republicans' interest in cooperating with Democrats to loosen the majority party's agenda control.

Punishing the 1924 Presidential Election Defectors

As noted above, one of Longworth's first actions as Speaker was to sanction party members who had backed La Follette for president in 1924. Twelve House Republicans and four Senate Republicans supported La Follette's third-party bid, instead of the Republican party nominee, Calvin Coolidge.[59] After Coolidge's victory and Republican congressional gains that promised the party a safe majority in the 69th Congress (1925–27), Republicans in both chambers decided to punish the defectors for their disloyalty. In the Senate, the GOP barred insurgents Edwin Ladd and Lynn Frazier of North Dakota, Smith Brookhart of Iowa, and La Follette from the party conference. The Senate GOP also stripped the defectors of their seniority.[60] House leaders excluded the progressives from their organizational caucus of February 1925, where party officers were selected for the 69th Congress. Before that Congress convened in December, Republican leaders removed defectors John Nelson from the Rules Committee and James Frear (R-Wis.) from Ways and Means. The rest of the defectors were purged from their committees after they refused to vote for Longworth as Speaker. The sole exception was Oscar Keller (R-Minn.); GOP leaders spared him from sanctions after he voted for Longworth.[61] The punishments qualify as an institutional change because they clarified the criteria used for committee assignments and at least in the House were part of a more general strengthening of party control.[62]

Republicans' decision to punish the La Follette supporters is a relatively straightforward instance of a party-based change intended to discourage disloyal behavior and to strengthen party control of legislative committees. The specific partisan interest upheld in this case appears more directly electoral than legislative. Regular Republicans were clearly concerned that party members who actively campaigned against party nominees could do electoral damage. Walter Edge (R-N.J.), one of the leaders of the Senate movement to punish the defectors, expressed this concern: "La Follette came to New Jersey during the campaign and spoke on behalf of my opponent. . . . It must be obvious that a Senator cannot make every effort to defeat and destroy a party and at the same time participate in its conference" (*NYT*, November 29, 1924, 1).

Notwithstanding the Regular Republicans' anger, a necessary precondition for punishing the dissidents was the party's working majority in both chambers during the incoming 69th Congress. Insurgents in both houses had strayed extremely far from the party path in the 68th Congress, yet only the GOP's 1924 gains "opened the way for party leaders to discipline" these members (CQ 1982, 136). Longworth, in defending the decision to punish the defectors, noted that "the Republican Party has a substantial majority with or without them. Ought we to have acceded to their demand [for treatment as Republicans]?" (quoted in Bolling 1968, 114). In the Senate, a few western Republicans forced floor votes to overturn the punishment. However, Regular Republicans defeated this effort easily, and most Democrats did not even vote on the matter. This Democratic behavior contrasts sharply to their willingness in the 68th Congress—when the Republican majority had been smaller—to cooperate with GOP progressives to elect a Democratic chairman of the Commerce Committee. Haynes (1938, 292) notes that "for the first time in two years the Republicans had a working majority. The Democrats, accordingly, chose to keep out of this 'family dispute.' "

Despite the apparent similarity in how punishment transpired in the House and Senate, there were substantial differences between the two chambers. First, House Republicans imposed more severe sanctions. The Senate GOP dropped its insurgents to the bottom of their committees but did not remove them. With the exceptions of Keller and Henry Cooper (R-Wis.), the House insurgents were removed from all significant committees.[63] Second, rank-and-file members initiated the Senate sanctions, while party leaders played a more prominent role in the House. At a Senate Republican conference held on November 28, 1924, Senators Edge, David Reed of Pennsylvania, Selden Spencer of Missouri, and Richard Ernst of Kentucky led the drive to punish the defectors. The conference passed Reed's proposal to bar La Follette's supporters from the conference and to forbid them from filling party vacancies on committees.[64] The *Times* noted that the "action of the conference came as a complete surprise" because party leaders had said that no decision about the defectors would be made until the start of the 69th Congress (November 29, 1924, 1). By contrast, in the House, Longworth took the lead in sanctioning the defectors (*NYT*, November 29, 1924, 2; Ripley 1967, 22).

These House-Senate differences reflect Republicans' tenuous hold on the upper chamber and their weak party leadership in the Senate. It should be little surprise, therefore, that the punishment of the Senate defectors had less significant effects. Progressive Republicans in the Senate remained influential throughout the rest of the 1920s, often allying with Democrats to frustrate the Regulars' plans (Mayer 1964, 400–402; Olssen 1980). McCoy (1967, 267) notes that Republican leaders "had the power to discipline progressives but not to dictate their votes." Even this power to punish proved fragile. The 1926 elections left the GOP with a bare majority in the Senate, one dependent on the votes of Frazier and Brookhart. As a result, the Republicans invited both men back into the conference and made Frazier chairman of the Indian Affairs Committee, "which he particularly desired," while "Brookhart was similarly reassigned as a Republican to his previous committees or to better ones" (Berdahl 1949,

497). Allen and Pearson (1931, 203) write that the Republican leaders had shown themselves "ready to make peace on the Insurgents' terms."[65] The 1925 punishments not only were short-lived but also did not signal a party determination to sanction future defectors. Three Republican senators campaigned for Democrat Al Smith in the 1928 presidential race, yet "they were not formally disciplined and their excellent committee assignments were continued" (Berdahl 1949, 505). This pattern continued into the next decade. Berdahl (1949, 504) contrasts House Republicans' punishment of a handful of disloyal members during the 1930s to Senate Republicans' "liberal treatment" of defectors. Decades later, Senate Republicans still adhered to the seniority system more strongly than the other three congressional parties (Smith and Deering 1990, 71–72). In sum, the GOP's ongoing inability to rein in members' individualism and the party's fragile floor majority seriously compromised the impact of the Senate punishments.

In contrast, the punishment of the House Republican defectors underscored the revival of party leadership under new Speaker Longworth. Peters (1990, 104) observes that the punishments helped Longworth establish a reputation for toughness: "having dealt decisively with the insurgents at the outset, [Longworth] faced little opposition within the party" (see also Ripley 1967, 191–92; Josephy 1979, 311). While Longworth did allow the progressives back into the party in 1927, it was on his own terms: the insurgents voted for Longworth as Speaker at the opening of the new Congress.[66] Though the insurgents denied they would submit to party dictates, the organized insurgent revolt in the House was essentially over (Berdahl 1949, 503). The Wisconsin insurgents became less unified in the years following La Follette's death and less bold in challenging party leaders (Allen and Pearson 1931, 237–39).

Although the punishment of the House insurgents furthered Longworth's restoration of a form of party government, the punishments did not supersede the constraints imposed on party leaders by the seniority system that had emerged in the early twentieth century. Rather, the 1925 change was layered on top of the seniority system, serving to clarify and refine it rather than displace it. Individual members wanted clear criteria for maintaining their committee assignments. As a result, House GOP leaders made it explicit that members would lose their committee assignments only in the case of extreme disloyalty. In effect, the leaders allowed a wide range of dissident activities. Unlike Cannon, when he punished dissidents in 1907–9, House leaders made it clear why members were being punished and what criteria would be used to judge members' party standing in the future. These criteria were far from stringent, allowing members to defect on important matters without fear of substantial punishment (Schickler and Rich 1997a, 1997b).

In 1925, the Republicans punished members only for defection in the presidential election and in the election of the Speaker; members who refused to back the new discharge rule but stayed loyal in the campaign were not sanctioned. Following the punishment of the insurgent Republicans in 1925, support for the party's presidential candidate and nominee for Speaker became the primary criteria for good party standing. There are very few instances of seniority violations for other reasons during the fifty-year period spanning 1925–75 (Berdahl 1949; Schickler and Rich 1997a; Ripley 1967, 53).[67] Prior to 1925, there had been no accepted definition of what constitutes a good party member. But soon thereafter, Hasbrouck (1927, 35–36) wrote that "the vote on the caucus nominee for Speaker has come to be the critical test of party allegiance." In 1937, Hamilton Fish (R-N.Y.) stated on the floor that a "bona-fide Republican . . . is one who supports his party's candidate for the presidency" (CR, February 17, 1937, 1314–15). Berdahl (1949, 504), referring to Fish's remark, concludes that "perhaps that criterion fits the realities as closely as any, so far as the Republican party in the House is concerned."

Making presidential election loyalty a key criterion for party standing is consistent with Cox and McCubbins's (1993) emphasis on parties' shared electoral bond as one basis for partisan behavior in the House. But this case (and subsequent events) is in tension with another central aspect of Cox and McCubbins's party cartel model: the idea that parties are procedural coalitions that enforce unity on House rules votes by threatening sanctions. Sanctioning members for dissent in the presidential election does not help the majority party exercise control of House procedures. Republicans who defected on the 1924 and 1925 House rules votes, but remained loyal in the presidential election, were not punished. In addition, the Republicans' willingness to make concessions to party dissidents on the rules when it appeared the party would enjoy only a slim majority in the 72nd Congress (1931–33) suggests that intimidating dissidents could not protect Republican control of the rules in a narrowly divided House.

CONCLUSIONS

The major changes in congressional institutions in the 1919–32 period did not produce a coherent authority structure well suited to achieving a specific set of interests. Rather, institutional development once again took on a disjointed, pluralistic cast as the interactions among coalitions promoting an array of interests produced changes that pushed in multiple, partially incompatible directions.

Both chambers adopted innovations in the years following World War I to improve congressional capacity and power. Nevertheless, the appropriations recentralization approved by both chambers and the committee consolidation adopted by the Senate were more than functional responses to institutional needs. The appropriations changes derived from a confluence of all members' institutional interests and conservatives' policy interests, while the committee consolidation was driven both by institutional and partisan calculations. At the same time, the reforms, most notably the Senate appropriations changes, were compromised by provisions that safeguarded rank-and-file members' access to committee power bases. These cases demonstrate both that specific changes can serve as common carriers for multiple interests and that changes often are compromised by conflicts among competing interests.

Similarly, multiple interests shaped the House rules changes of 1924 and 1931. Dissident Republicans and Democrats aligned their common policy objectives with rank-and-file concerns about access to power. These cases illustrate that cross-party coalitions can capitalize on the multiplicity of member interests to promote institutional changes that threaten the agenda control of party elites. This potential hinders the development of a well-functioning majority party cartel.

But the majority party contested such cross-party coalition efforts. House Republicans undertook two separate sets of innovations to make their party more effective. The first reforms, adopted in 1919, made the floor leader a more specialized party officer and created a Steering Committee that provided a forum for Republicans to unite on a common program. Nevertheless, these two changes also had decentralizing features that cut against the goal of enhancing the majority party's effectiveness. The caucus rules barring the Speaker and important committee chairmen from the Steering Committee, and subsequent decisions to expand this committee, reflected rank-and-file members' interest in dispersing power and limited the effectiveness of Steering. The separation of committee and party leadership embodied in relieving the floor leader of his committee responsibilities also reflected rank-and-file resistance to centralization. This latter move struck a significant blow to the interlocking directorate model that the GOP had employed in the Reed and Cannon years, and that Democrats had continued during Underwood's tenure as majority leader. Thus, the GOP's party-building innovations of 1919 were also compromised by tensions among competing member goals.

While the second set of party-based changes more effectively empowered Republican leaders, it by no means signaled a return to the vigorous party government of Reed and Cannon. Longworth resuscitated the speakership, but he did so in part through a bipartisan alliance with Democratic leader Garner. Longworth and Garner's cooperative use of the Bureau of Education makes little sense from the perspective of majority party cartel theories. Instead, an approach that emphasizes the diverse coalition-building possibilities rooted in multiple member interests is necessary to understand this and other changes adopted in 1919–32.

At a general level, institutional development in the 1920s reflected an uneasy combination of the features of the two very different eras before and after: the strong party government institutions of the 1890–1910 period and the decentralized, committee-based system that took root after 1937. Changes in the House resembled more the earlier period: notwithstanding the limitations on the GOP's party building, Republican leaders often managed effectively the lower chamber's agenda and passed policies favored by most party members. The House GOP's periodic difficulties, especially in 1924 and in the months leading up to the 72nd Congress in December 1931, reflected the same factors as in 1909–10: a relatively slim (or even vanishing) majority and a sizable progressive faction. The main difference between the two periods is that rank-and-file members' power base interests had become a more pronounced source of pressure for decentralization by the 1920s. The emergence of the seniority system and the separation of party and committee leadership fragmented the House authority structure.

Both rank-and-file pressures toward fragmentation and the GOP's factional divisions played an even greater role in the Senate, severely undermining the majority party there. Senate Republican leadership suffered throughout the 1920s. Lodge's prestige declined markedly during Harding's first year in office (Paxson 1948, 270), and his successor as floor leader, Charles Curtis (R-Kans.), was "little more than a party hack" (McCoy 1967, 197). Just as Democratic leaders in both houses had to contend with many hostile southern committee chairmen after 1937, Senate GOP leaders faced numerous committee leaders hostile to Regular Republicans' conservative priorities. Norris, Borah, Gerald Nye of North Dakota, Peter Norbeck of South Dakota, Charles McNary of Oregon, Hiram Johnson of California, and James Couzens of Michigan were all progressives who headed standing committees in the 70th Congress (1927–29). MacMahon (1928, 653) commented in 1928 that "perhaps the only committee assuredly under strictly regular control was Privileges and Elections, and even it had been forced to share its power" with a Democrat-led special committee investigating election fundraising abuses.

Furthermore, senators eager to promote their personal power, their electoral prospects, and the interests of their ideological allies, repeatedly created new institutions that threatened the Republican majority's electoral and policy interests. Kenyon helped form the farm bloc in 1921, and, a year later, La Follette founded what became its successor, the progressive bloc. In an even more direct preview of southern Democrats' strategies in the 1937–52 period, dissident Senate Republicans also conducted investigations to boost their individual careers while inflicting serious damage on the GOP.[68]

With its farm bloc, progressive-controlled standing committees, weak party leadership, and antiexecutive investigations, the Senate of the 1920s brings to mind the conservative coalition Congresses of the 1937–52 period and bears almost no resemblance to the party "machine" that Aldrich, Allison, and other GOP leaders had constructed in the 1890s. While House Republicans governed more effectively as a majority, members' power-base motivations and the recurrent strength of cross-party coalitions constrained the GOP in the lower chamber. Institutional development in 1919–32 reflected the diversity of member interests, resulting in a structure that increasingly came to embody conflicting imperatives.

Institutional Development, 1937–1952: The Conservative Coalition, Congress against the Executive, and Committee Government

THE DIFFICULTIES confronting Democratic leaders in 1937–52 easily surpassed Republicans' earlier troubles with progressive insurgency. In January 1937, the liberal coalition led by Franklin Roosevelt, fresh from a sweeping election victory, appeared in firm control of the Congress and the country. Yet by the end of the year, the Democrats were in disarray and conservatism was on the rise in Congress and nationally. This dramatic turnabout began with Roosevelt's ill-advised court-packing plan but had roots in broader trends: rising labor militancy, southern trepidation about African-Americans' entry into the Democratic coalition, and a severe recession each challenged Democratic unity (Patterson 1967). The conservative revival—almost unimaginable so soon after the 1936 election—inaugurated a long period in which conflict between liberal northern Democrats and a cross-party coalition of Republicans and southern Democrats dominated congressional politics.

During the fifteen years between 1937 and 1952, when the conservative coalition shaped policies under Democratic presidents, Congress adopted a number of institutional changes in response to the new power balance. Applying the methodology described in chapter 1, I identified nine important institutional innovations in this period:

1. Changing the mode of operations of the Rules Committee in 1937 so that it became a power base for the conservative coalition

2. Tightening the relationship between party leaders and the president in 1937 through regular weekly meetings at the White House

3. Launching loyalty investigations in 1938, with the creation of Martin Dies's (D-Tex.) Special Committee on Un-American Activities

4. Streamlining the committee system under the Legislative Reorganization Act of 1946

5. Increasing committee staff following the Legislative Reorganization Act

6. Expanding legislative oversight of the executive during and after World War II, and systematizing it under the Legislative Reorganization Act

7. Creating party policy committees in the Senate, and in particular Senator Robert Taft's (R-Ohio) use of the Republican Policy Committee as a power base

8. Creating the Joint Committee on Atomic Energy in 1946

9. Adopting the 21-day rule to allow bypassing of the Rules Committee in the 81st Congress (1949–50)

Appendix B.3 presents the floor votes that directly related to these changes, and table 4.1 summarizes the collective interests important in each case.

The 1937–52 period provides further evidence that disjointed pluralism characterizes congressional development. Multiple collective interests played an important role in six of nine changes (see table 4.1). Furthermore, entrepreneurs repeatedly promoted changes that served as common carriers. For example, reformers seeking to strengthen congressional capacity and power by streamlining the committee system attracted additional support for the Legislative Reorganization Act by including new perks for individual members. Multiple interests also shaped reform in more conflictual ways. Indeed, excepting the creation of the Joint Committee on Atomic Energy, each attempt to reinforce Congress's institutional position faced competing goals that ultimately undermined reform.

The 1937–52 period also supports the claim that new institutional arrangements are often superimposed on preexisting structures intended to serve different purposes. The Rules Committee is an excellent example. Changes adopted in 1890–1910 had left the committee with responsibility for protecting the majority party from legislation opposed by its leaders and protecting the chamber as a whole from ill-advised, special-interest bills. Conservatives' takeover of the committee in 1937 made it an unreliable agent of the majority party but left in place its other traditional role as a control committee protecting the House. When liberals added the 21-day rule to subvert the conservatives' control, they also limited Rules' ability to serve as a control committee. This, in turn, created opportunities for members to push special-interest bills opposed by Democratic and GOP leaders alike. A series of innovations, each seeking to promote a different set of objectives, had combined to create a process that failed to serve any given interest particularly well.

As in the 1920s, there is only limited support for the claim that a series of innovations that push congressional organization far in a single direction will provoke countervailing changes. While Democrats' 21-day rule was a response to conservative successes in shaping institutions, there was

TABLE 4.1 Summary of Collective Interests Associated with Institutional Changes, 1937–1952

Case	Primary Interest	Common Carrier for Other Interests?	Compromised by Other Interests?	Coalition Shaping Change	Main Effects of Change
Rules Committee change, 1937	Policy (conservatives)			Cross-party ideological	Weakened Democratic leaders; built conservative power base
Weekly leadership meetings	Majority party (effectiveness)			Majority party	Added to ambiguity surrounding leaders' position
Dies committee	Policy (conservatives)	Individual power bases		Cross-party ideological	Added new conservative power base; created entrepreneurial outlet
Committee consolidation, 1946	Congressional capacity and power	Individual power bases; member perks (pay raise, pension)	Integrative devices deleted (individual power bases)	Bipartisan reformist	Reinforced position of committees and chairs; weakened party leaders
Committee staffing expansion, 1946	Congressional capacity and power	Reelection; individual power bases	Personnel director deleted (individual power bases)	Bipartisan reformist	Strengthened committees and chairmen

TABLE 4.1 Summary of Collective Interests Associated with Institutional Changes, 1937–1952 (cont.)

Case	Primary Interest	Common Carrier for Other Interests?	Compromised by Other Interests?	Coalition Shaping Change	Main Effects of Change
Investigations explosion	Congressional power and policy (conservatives)	Individual power bases (entrepreneurial opportunities)	Congressional prestige threatened by excesses of individual entrepreneurs	Cross-party ideological or broad bipartisan (varied by case)	Strengthened committee; generated entreprenurial opportunities; made trouble for Democratic executive branch
Senate policy committees	Partisan (minority party, primarily)	Policy; congressional power		Bipartisan	Provided resources for Taft's leadership
Joint Committee on Atomic Energy	Congressional capacity and power			Bipartisan	Added strong committee that dominated congressional nuclear policy
21-day rule	Policy (liberals)	Majority party	Compromises over party leaders vs. committee chair control of process	Majority party, but cross-party ideological element	Temporarily assaulted conservative Rules Committee; bolstered committee chairs

no major push toward a single coherent model of organization in 1937–52. Therefore, there was less need for members to organize to defend competing interests. However, if one extends the time frame slightly, there is more support for this claim: several changes in 1937–52 were a reaction against the big movement toward president-led party government that had taken place during FDR's first term.

On the whole, the most important feature of the 1937–52 period is that the dynamics of institutional change were propelled by bipartisan reformist coalitions concerned about a perceived decline in congressional power, and by cross-party ideological coalitions hostile to most majority party members. Party-based coalitions played a surprisingly limited role. The success of cross-party coalitions offers an important counterpoint to models that privilege parties as determinants of legislative organization (Cox and McCubbins 1993). In analyzing the conservative coalition changes, I focus on the question of how and why this cross-party coalition could shape congressional institutions.

By contrast, weak political parties, strong cross-party coalitions, and concerted efforts to improve congressional policymaking capacity are each consistent with Krehbiel's (1991) nonpartisan, informational model of legislative organization. In the concluding section of this chapter, I consider the strengths and limitations of this perspective when applied to the 1937–52 period. But first I analyze the individual changes, beginning with the changes intended to bolster congressional capacity and power. I then turn to the cases primarily involving conservatives' ideological goals, followed by those involving partisan interests.

CONGRESSIONAL CAPACITY AND POWER

The growing power of the executive branch during the Great Depression and World War II heightened congressional sensitivity to the declining position of the legislature. In the wake of Roosevelt's commanding performance, members, as well as critics in the press and academia, believed that Congress could not recapture its coequal status without dramatically increasing its policymaking and oversight capacity. Three changes derived primarily from concerns about congressional capacity and power: the committee consolidation under the Legislative Reorganization Act of 1946, the expansion in committee staffing brought about by the act, and the creation of the Joint Committee on Atomic Energy. The reformist coalitions in these cases were broad and inclusive, as most members shared the goal of defending congressional prerogatives. Partisan and ideological interests exerted little force. A fourth institutional change, the boom in investigations, differs from the first three in that conservatives' policy interests and concerns about congressional power had roughly equal force. These four changes also provided new resources for ambitious members, thus serving their electoral and power interests.

Legislative Reorganization Act: Committee Consolidation

The streamlining of the committee system has long been regarded as the cornerstone of the Legislative Reorganization Act (see, e.g., Galloway 1953, 591).[1] It reduced the number of committees dramatically: from forty-eight to nineteen in the House, and from thirty-three to fifteen in the Senate (Galloway 1953, 592). Furthermore, the Reorganization Act for the first time defined committee jurisdictions in specific terms and made these jurisdictions more systematic and comprehensive.[2]

The Reorganization Act was adopted by a bipartisan coalition seeking to improve congressional operations and thereby resist presidential encroachments. The bill passed the Senate by a 49–16 vote. Thirteen of the dissenters were majority Democrats. The House passed the bill on a division vote, 229–61. Most members who opposed the measure cited the pay raise and pension benefits that it provided as their reason, although several were senior southern Democrats who did not want to eliminate committees that provided chairmanships for the party. As Theodore Bilbo (D-Miss.) declared, "I love the Republicans, but I do not like to surrender so many chairmanships while the Democratic Party is in power" (CR, June 10, 1946, 6566). A logit analysis of the vote on Senate passage shows that committee chairmen and southern Democrats were less likely to support the measure than were other senators.[3] Nonetheless, there was considerable support for reorganization even among the southern chairmen: six voted in favor, five against, and three did not vote.

Notwithstanding the hesitation of a few senior Democrats, a striking bipartisanship characterized the Reorganization Act. Its progenitors included Democrats, such as Jerry Voorhis of California and Mike Monroney of Oklahoma, Republicans, such as Everett Dirksen of Illinois and Wallace White of Maine, and the Independent Robert La Follette Jr. of Wisconsin. The La Follette–Monroney committee, which devised the reorganization proposal, consisted of six Democrats, five Republicans, and La Follette. The committee reported the proposal unanimously, although three Democrats dissented from specific sections.[4] House leaders did insist on some significant changes before sending the proposal to the floor, but members of both parties consulted closely on these modifications, and Republican leaders strongly supported the revised measure (see CR, July 25, 1946, 10041, 10049). Monroney and Dirksen managed the bill jointly on the House floor and worked as a team to ward off hostile amendments (see, e.g., CR, July 25, 1946, 10039–41, 10085, 10094–95). In the Senate, La Follette managed the bill, while Republican White, among others, helped fight amendments (see, e.g., CR, June 8, 1946, 6529–30).

Davidson and Oleszek (1977), like most scholars, argue that the growth of executive power was by far the strongest motivating force behind the act (see CQ 1982, 264; Cooper 1988; and King 1997 for similar assessments). They note that rising executive influence during the depression and World War II "led reformers to view a reorganized Congress as a way to redress the imbalance of power that had developed between the branches" (1977, 14).

Members' statements underscore their concerns about congressional capacity and power. Conservative Republican Styles Bridges of New Hampshire, in endorsing the bill, claimed that Congress had "relatively stood still" as the executive branch had expanded tremendously (CR, June 10, 1946, 6558) and argued the Reorganization Act promised to "to equalize the difference between the executive, the legislative, and the judicial branches of government" (6561). In a similar vein, Taft, La Follette, and Monroney praised the Reorganization Act for helping Congress to meet modern-day governing challenges (CR, June 5, 1946, 6344–45; June 6, 1946, 6375). Monroney noted that "we simply cannot struggle along under this type of workload unless we equip ourselves to answer the challenge that the Constitution's framers intended the Congress to carry" (CR, July 25, 1946, 10039).

Liberals and conservatives from both parties testified before the La Follette–Monroney committee that reform was necessary for Congress to compete effectively with the executive branch. When the liberal Jerry Voorhis (D-Calif.) attacked Congress's recent failure to put "forward any alternative constructive program of its own," conservative Eugene Cox (D-Ga.) commended Voorhis for his "magnificent statement" and added that "you have been classified as an ultra-progressive and I as a mossback reactionary, and still there is not the slightest difference between my views and the statement you make" (Joint Committee 1945, 41). Several Republicans also weighed in at the hearings about the importance of reorganization. For example, Owen Brewster of Maine testified that Congress must streamline the committee system "if we are to retain any semblance of the ancient division of functions under our Constitution" (Joint Committee 1945, 230). Edward Rees (R-Kans.) summed up the attitude of many members when he argued that "the time has come when the Congress should no longer be satisfied with the role of a rubber stamp" (Joint Committee 1945, 237).[5] The remarkably consistent message from Democrats and Republicans across the ideological spectrum was that Congress had become institutionally crippled and that reorganization was essential for its rehabilitation.

Concern about congressional prestige also contributed to reformist sentiment. Press and radio criticism of congressional performance had become particularly harsh during World War II (Cooper 1988, 187; King 1997), and members of both parties believed reorganization could improve Congress's tattered reputation. In endorsing the reorganization bill, Senate Republican leader White remarked that "we should restore . . . the legislative branch of the Government to the place of authority, dignity, and respect which it once held in the minds of the people of the United States, but which day by day it is now forfeiting" (CR, June 8, 1946, 6531). Dirksen added that improvements in congressional operations are "some little thing we can do to retrieve the esteem in which this body ought to be regarded by the people" (CR, July 25, 1946, 10049; see also a similar statement by Massachusetts Democrat Thomas Lane, CR, July 25, 1946, 10055). The bipartisan commitment to congressional prestige is particularly striking in contrast to the 1980s and early 1990s, when Republicans sought majority status by attacking Congress for its alleged corruption and ineffectiveness.

However, interest in congressional capacity, power, and prestige was not sufficient to pass the Reorganization Act. Davidson (1990) emphasizes the role of procedural entrepreneurs, such as La Follette, Monroney, Dirksen, Voorhis, and Estes Kefauver (D-Tenn.), in devising specific proposals and in encouraging support for the reorganization program as a whole. Davidson argues that an unusual number of members in the 1940s cultivated an interest in congressional operations—both to improve their own individual position in the legislature and out of a genuine concern for institutional maintenance.[6] The efforts of entrepreneurs were important because the reform measure had to overcome the opposition of members who would lose their personal power bases because the act eliminated so many committees. Reformers worked before and after passage of the act to compensate these members with good assignments on the consolidated committees, thus tempering their resistance to reform (Ripley 1969b).

Reformers also included a pay raise and a pension system in the act in order to elicit support from potential foes. Members understood that public reaction against the raise would be mitigated since it was part of a major bipartisan reorganization bill supported by the press and outside experts (see CR, June 8, 1946, 6533; CR, June 10, 1946, 6560). La Follette noted that he had pushed to have the pay raise, pension system, and committee consolidation "wrapped up in one package" for just this reason: members would be more willing to sacrifice some committee power bases if doing so would lead to a better salary (CR, June 8, 1946, 6533). This again illustrates that institutional reform can be facilitated by the interactions among multiple interests: reformers harnessed individual members' desire for increased pay and perquisites to enact a reorganization plan that primarily served broad institutional interests. Monroney liked to point out that the 1946 act had been approved partly because of its "ice cream" provisions, which made its "spinach" more palatable (CR, July 25, 1946, 10045; see also Bibby and Davidson 1972, 253).[7]

Furthermore, interactions among multiple interests helped pass the Reorganization Act in that committee consolidation promised not only to improve congressional functioning, but also to provide members more widespread access to important committees. James Wadsworth (R-N.Y.), the main architect of the House consolidation plan, claimed that the present system of forty-eight committees "dooms an undue proportion" of members "to service on committees whose work does not attract their interest, for the simple reason that they haven't much work of any importance to do" (Joint Committee 1945, 88). One of his primary goals in eliminating minor committees was to ensure that "every committee of the House shall be important, and that every member of the House, be he a newcomer or an oldster, shall be on an important committee" (CR, July 25, 1946, 10042; see also Goodwin 1970, 67). To help disperse committee power bases, the Reorganization Act also limited each senator to two committees and each representative to one major assignment.[8]

The committee consolidation was thus a common carrier for broad institutional interests as well as individual members' interest in pay, perks, and power bases. By contrast, majority party interests played little role. As noted above, Wadsworth, a member of the minority party, devised the plan that served as the basis for the changes in House jurisdictions (Joint Committee 1946, 4; Davidson and Oleszek 1977, 8). The La Follette–Monroney committee modified the Wadsworth plan only slightly and reported it with all but Eugene Cox in support. La Follette, an Independent, framed the Senate changes, which passed the La Follette–Monroney committee without dissent. When the Reorganization Act reached the floor, very little discussion in either chamber focused on the jurisdictional changes. The only floor change in the jurisdictions occurred in the Senate, where Finance Committee chairman Walter George (D-Ga.) objected to the proposed Veterans Affairs Committee, which would infringe on Finance's turf. George's amendment to eliminate the Veterans Committee passed on a voice vote.

One reason that the 1946 changes generated little opposition was their scope. The consolidation was less ambitious than the number of committees eliminated would suggest. As Davidson and Oleszek (1977, 10) point out, the 1946 act "was confined principally to consolidating or abolishing generally minor committees rather than shifting jurisdiction from one committee to another" (see also Groseclose and Stewart 1998). Committees that were merged usually had closely related jurisdictions and shared several members in common (King 1997). Moreover, many of the eliminated committees reemerged soon thereafter as subcommittees. Indeed, Kravitz (1974) and Smith and Deering (1990, 42) argue that the Reorganization Act spawned an increase in the number of subcommittees, particularly in the Senate.

Still, the importance of the committee reshuffling should not be discounted, even if one rejects the more optimistic assessments of the reformers themselves. The committee streamlining profoundly affected the congressional authority structure by reinforcing the already-strong system of powerful standing committees and committee chairmen. By reducing the number of committees and expanding their jurisdictions, the Reorganization Act made each committee a more potent power base for its members and chairman. The new subcommittees did not weaken the influence of full committee chairmen, at least in the years immediately following passage of the Reorganization Act, because subcommittees in this era typically were not power centers and depended on the committee chairman for staffing and bill referrals. Smith and Deering (1990, 39), like Kravitz (1974) and Davidson (1990), conclude that the Reorganization Act "had the effect of further increasing the power of chairs of standing committees. . . . The act helped to guarantee that committee chairs would dominate congressional policy making for the foreseeable future."

The La Follette–Monroney committee sought to offset these effects by including procedural restrictions on the chairmen and new integrative mechanisms to coordinate committee activities. But the restrictions on the chairmen were difficult to enforce and often ignored in practice (Kofmehl 1977, 32–33; Cooper 1988). Efforts at promoting better coordination proved even less successful. Reformers sought two integrative devices: a revamped budget process that would provide simultaneous consideration of spending and revenue matters, and stronger political parties, which would give Congress more energetic leadership to compete with the president. The proposed budget process encountered strident opposition, especially from senior members of the House Appropriations Committee, who believed the proposed reforms were unworkable and would undercut the influence of their committee. Enforcement provisions for the new budget process were removed from the Reorganization bill before it even reached the House floor, and resistance from the Appropriations Committee ensured that the process was never implemented (Davidson 1990, 369; Fenno 1966).

The La Follette–Monroney committee proposed to strengthen the parties by creating party policy committees and a joint legislative-executive council. Reformers hoped these new institutions would help coordinate and plan the legislative program. But both of these features were dropped from the bill at the insistence of House Speaker Sam Rayburn of Texas, who believed that party committees would reduce his ability to manage the House through informal contacts (Cooper 1988, 242; CQ Almanac 1946, 531). Thus, party and committee leader resistance scuttled the only provisions of the bill that threatened the prerogatives of committee elites. Dodd (1977, 286) writes that "in their attempt to protect fundamental personal prerogatives, members of Congress failed to take the really difficult steps that might have helped resolve structural problems within Congress."

Therefore, the tension between broad institutional goals and narrower individual and committee-based objectives compromised the success of the Reorganization Act. Members' desire to preserve their committee power bases precluded coordination devices that might otherwise have enhanced congressional capacity. In the absence of any integrative mechanisms, the committee consolidation not only strengthened the position of committee leaders, but also reduced party leaders' influence. Before the Reorganization Act, the sheer number of committees had given party leaders more flexibility in doling out committee assignments to members, and the overlapping and ambiguous committee jurisdictions had accorded leaders more opportunities to affect bill referrals (Goodwin 1970, 38; Davidson 1990, 367). Cooper (1988, 295) concludes that "consolidation of the committee system made it a much less flexible instrument, a flexibility that in the past had been used to hurdle the limitations imposed by seniority and entrenched committee minorities." Contrary to the hopes of many of the authors of the Reorganization Act, it made the position of party leaders even more difficult.

Legislative Reorganization Act: Committee Staffing

The increase in committee staff is the Reorganization Act's other main legacy. Prior to 1946, professional committee staffs were uncommon in Congress. The Appropriations Committees and the Joint Committee on Internal Revenue had fairly large staffs, but the vast majority of committees employed only a few clerks and no professional staffers (Kofmehl 1977, 3–4; Ripley 1983, 268).[9] The Reorganization Act authorized each standing committee to appoint four professional and six clerical staff members. The act authorized the Appropriations Committees to hire as many professional staffers as they deemed necessary; other committees could request additional staff from their chamber. Most committees quickly took advantage of the new staffing authorization. Congressional committees nearly doubled their staffs in the first four years after the act took effect; in 1946, committees had employed 356 staffers—few of them professionals—while in 1950, they employed a total of 673 staffers, 286 of whom were professionals (Galloway 1953, 606).[10]

Much like the committee consolidation, members intended the increase in professional staff to reinforce congressional power by improving the policymaking capacity of committees. Members believed committees' dependence on executive officials for expert information undermined Congress's ability to craft policies that departed from executive priorities (Cooper 1988, 216; Goodwin 1970, 143; Kammerer 1951b). The drive for improved staff had begun with separate proposals by Dirksen, Voorhis, and Clifton Woodrum (D-Va.) in 1939–41. Dirksen declared in 1942 that Congress "must be able to challenge the information presented by government functionaries with expert information assembled by its own expert staffs" (CR, October 1, 1942, 7945). But this idea received serious attention only when the La Follette–Monroney committee was established in 1945. Members from both parties testified before the committee that more staff were necessary to compete with the executive. Republican Styles Bridges argued, "I personally am opposed to the loaning of experts by departments downtown for use up here. I feel that we should have a staff on our committees and we should do away with the downtown-loaned experts, who are always biased individuals" (Joint Committee 1945, 283). Texas Democrat William Poage noted that the lack of expert committee staff meant that "we rely upon the people that we seek to direct to tell us how to direct them. The result is that Congress does not direct, and that the executive branch of the Government becomes stronger and stronger" (Joint Committee 1945, 307).[11] Once again, it is striking that several liberals, including Voorhis and Lane, called for improved staffing to reduce dependence on the executive branch, which was, after all, in the hands of liberal Democrats (CR, January 18, 1945, 349; CR, July 25, 1946, 10054).

The staff increase also served as a common carrier for electoral and personal power interests by enhancing members' ability to respond to constituent demands and to utilize committee power bases. Democrat E. C. Gathings of Arkansas underscored the relevance of electoral goals when he testified that inadequate committee and personal staffing prevented members from keeping in contact with and responding to their constituents (Joint Committee 1945, 261–62; see also CR, June 10, 1946, 6533). Similarly, John Phillips, a junior Republican from California, referred to increased personal and committee staff as the type of "help which makes a good Congressman, both here and at home" (Joint Committee 1945, 995–96). In his review essay evaluating the Reorganization Act, Davidson (1990, 372) concludes that "by laying foundations for professionalized Capitol Hill staffs, the act itself provided resources of potential use to lawmakers of all types." Therefore, it should be little surprise that improved staffing enjoyed broad, bipartisan support (Robinson 1954, 382–83; Fox and Hammond 1977, 14, 21–22).

The sole point of contention was this: who would select and control the staffers? The La Follette–Monroney committee proposed to make the professional staff permanent employees of Congress, appointed on the basis of merit and not subject to dismissal for political reasons. Although committees would appoint their own staff, a central director of personnel would determine the necessary qualifications for appointment to each committee, thereby undercutting patronage-minded chairmen (CR, June 8, 1946, 6518; Cooper 1988, 222–23). But several Senate committee chairmen strongly objected to the personnel director position, charging that it would create a modern-day "czar." The post was deleted on a voice vote after La Follette realized that the reorganization plan would otherwise face a prolonged filibuster. Davidson (1990, 369) argues that this decision was a "serious blow to the goal of upgrading and regularizing personnel standards" (see also Galloway 1953, 414–15). It exemplifies how members' interest in preserving the independence of committee power bases limited attempts to enhance congressional capacity.

Thus, the Reorganization Act empowered committees to select their own staff, though with instructions to appoint them without regard to political affiliation. Some authors have argued that this arrangement essentially left chairmen with control over staff selection (Ripley 1969b, 201). However, each full committee could overturn its chairman's staffing decisions. Some committees created special personnel subcommittees to oversee staffing (Kofmehl 1977, 70–71). In other cases, the chairman delegated authority to appoint certain staffers to the ranking minority member. Still, committee members were often reluctant to challenge the chairman's staff selections for fear of reprisals and perhaps because they saw staff selection as the prerogative of the chair (Kammerer 1951b, 1127; Cochrane 1964, 347). As a result, staff quality varied widely across committees and was prone to change with each new chairman (Cooper 1988; Galloway 1953, 414–15; Kammerer 1951b).

Therefore, the conflict between members' interest in a competent professional staff and senior members' interest in protecting their prerogatives as committee leaders came to an ambiguous resolution: there was no clear, widely accepted policy on who should select and control staff (Kofmehl 1977, 54–61, 70–80). The implications of the staffing provisions for the congressional authority structure were thus quite complex. These provisions undoubtedly strengthened many committees as policymaking centers. But the absence of accepted quality standards meant that several committees lacked effective staffs for years after the Reorganization Act's passage, presumably undermining these committees' influence and performance (see Galloway 1951; Kammerer 1951a; Ripley 1969b, 143). Within the committees themselves, Smith and Deering (1990, 45) point out that the new crop of professional staffers was generally loyal to the committee chairmen, enhancing the already substantial influence of the committee leaders. Still, there have been some cases of revolts against chairmen who made particularly egregious staffing decisions (Kofmehl 1977).

The implications of committee staffing for party strength in Congress were also mixed. It is interesting that Congress did not consider giving the party caucuses or party leaders control over committee staff. Such an arrangement would have made it easier for the majority party to make committee operations conform to an integrated party agenda. But no one proposed centralized party control in 1946.[12] Committee members' desire for autonomy and reformers' commitment to expert staffing free of patronage precluded central party direction. This contrasts with staffing practices in several state legislatures today, such as Illinois, Michigan, and Pennsylvania, in which most staffers remain responsible to the party leadership even as they are assigned to serve party members on legislative committees (Rosenthal 1981, 214). In comparison to this form of party control, which is what one might expect in a system of strong majority party government, the arrangements adopted by Congress in 1946 accorded committees considerable freedom from external interference.

Nevertheless, since the majority party selected the chairman and a majority of members on each committee, committee staffing had the potential to promote party aims, and at times it did. For example, in 1949, majority Democrats on the Senate Labor and Public Welfare Committee replaced the committee's chief staffer because he supported the antilabor Taft-Hartley Act of 1947. The Democrats replaced him with someone described as a "Democratic expert" (Kampelman 1954). Scholars studying professional staff turnover when party control of Congress changed (as in 1949 and 1953) argue that turnover tended to be highest on committees dealing with highly partisan issues, as one would expect based on theories of conditional party government (Kammerer 1951b; Kampelman 1954; see Rohde 1994).

But it is a dramatic oversimplification to argue that the improved staffing was a boon to the majority party. Goodwin (1970, 151) argues that even when the Democrats controlled Congress, which remained the norm after 1946, the staffs generally were "tipped in the direction of the conservative position, a fact that satisfies most of the seniority leaders and most of the staff members, and that disturbs the 'young turks.'" Conservative southern Democrats chaired several key congressional committees and retained after 1948 many staff members hired by their Republican predecessors in 1947 (Kammerer 1951b, 1129). Moreover, these chairmen used their influence over hiring to promote their conservative agendas. For example, when the conservative Graham Barden (D-N.C.) succeeded Democratic regular John Lesinski (D-Mich.) as chairman of

House Education and Labor in 1950, Barden replaced the bulk of the majority professional staffers and reorganized staff operations to promote closer working relationships between minority and majority staffers (Kofmehl 1977, 60–61). As late as 1965, Democratic senators interviewed by Ripley (1969b, 205) agreed that the control of committee staff by conservative chairmen posed a genuine problem for party members.

Therefore, notwithstanding the paucity of staff members formally designated by the minority party (Cochrane 1964), the staffing provisions of the Reorganization Act were not a cartelistic move by the majority party. Indeed, to approach the matter from one relevant vantage point, it was not until the 1960s that minority party members began to push seriously for improved minority staffing, and even then they had to overcome the resistance of several ranking minority members who were satisfied with the staffing arrangements on their own committees (Cochrane 1964, 344–45). Although committee staffing did provide disproportionate benefits to the majority party on some committees, for the most part improved post-1946 staffing is best understood as a change that empowered committees and their chairmen, with mixed implications for the majority party.

Notwithstanding the many limitations of the Legislative Reorganization Act of 1946, its provisions for committee consolidation and staffing expansion stand out as among the most important changes shaping the modern committee system. As such, it is particularly troubling for partisan theories that a bipartisan group shaped the LRA, and that a broad, bipartisan majority adopted it. When the Republicans gained majority status in 1947, they did not try to alter the committee jurisdictions or staffing provisions approved the previous year, nor did the Democrats when they regained control of Congress in 1949. It is telling that during floor debate on the Reorganization Act, no Republicans complained that the Democrats were foisting a partisan maneuver upon the Congress. Yet a handful of Democrats did complain about the party's willingness to eliminate committees that provided chairmanships for party members (CR, June 8, 1946, 6529; June 10, 1946, 6566).

The Joint Committee on Atomic Energy

The creation of the Joint Committee on Atomic Energy (JCAE) in 1946 originated in much the same reform currents behind the Legislative Reorganization Act. The committee played a prominent role in U.S. nuclear policymaking for much of the next thirty-one years, until it was abolished in 1977. The Atomic Energy Act of 1946, which created the JCAE, granted the committee unique powers to oversee the new Atomic Energy

Commission (AEC). The committee used these powers to push aggressively for expanded military and civilian uses of atomic energy.[13]

A single interest—members' concern for congressional capacity and power—proved critical in motivating adoption of the JCAE. The idea for a joint committee came from conservative Republican Arthur Vandenberg of Michigan and moderate Democrat Edwin Johnson of Colorado. These two senators each emphasized effective congressional consideration of nuclear issues. Vandenberg first proposed creation of a joint committee to study atomic energy in 1945. In a private letter to House Republican leader Joe Martin of Massachusetts, Vandenberg explained that a new joint committee was needed because otherwise the issue would get bogged down in a turf battle among the many House and Senate committees with a plausible jurisdictional claim. Vandenberg (1952, 222) advised Martin that "this is very dangerous business. . . . My obvious purpose is to concentrate this terrific responsibility in one place." The House initially proved resistant to the joint committee concept, but the Senate nonetheless created a special committee of its own, which framed the Atomic Energy Act of 1946.

Within this Special Committee on Atomic Energy, Johnson noted early on that he had been "struggling" to find a way "to keep the control of atomic energy in the hands of Congress" (Special Committee on Atomic Energy 1946, 202). Johnson complained that the proposed Atomic Energy Commission would be an executive agency immune from congressional control. A few weeks later, Johnson proposed a joint congressional commission to control all aspects of nuclear policymaking. The joint commission would be made up of five members from each chamber, upholding the principle that "Congress ought not to delegate too rapidly its authority" (Special Committee on Atomic Energy 1946, 415). Johnson's proposal violated the separation of powers by giving Congress an executive function and thus seemed a political nonstarter (see Special Committee on Atomic Energy 1946, 414–15). But Vandenberg proposed a compromise that committee members unanimously adopted: Congress would create an Atomic Energy Commission in the executive branch but add the JCAE as a congressional check on the commission (Post, March 13, 1946, 2). Vandenberg noted that the JCAE would have the "right of constant knowledge and information with respect to what the Atomic Energy Commission is doing" (Special Committee on Atomic Energy 1946, 482).

While Vandenberg and Johnson hatched the idea of a joint committee, several liberal Democrats supported the initiative, arguing it would ensure congressional control of the Atomic Energy Commission. The chairman of the Senate Special Committee, Brien McMahon (D-Conn.), argued that "nothing could be so necessary as that Congress should have the means of watching over this new and powerful organization" (CR, June

1, 1946, 6097). Pointing to the JCAE, he added that "this bill preserves the prerogatives and powers of the Congress and provides the means for their wise and effective employment" (6098).[14]

Members of both parties and all ideological factions thus appear to have agreed that a Joint Committee with unusual powers was necessary for Congress to retain influence given the context of important security concerns, severe technical complexity, and heightened member sensitivity to Congress's institutional position (Green and Rosenthal 1963, 266–67). Members made no criticisms or amendments to the JCAE when the proposal came to the floor.[15]

Specialized studies of the Atomic Energy Act agree that concerns about congressional capacity and power played a critical role in the JCAE's creation. Green (1971, 166) argues that the JCAE was an extraordinary committee "created as a legislative counterweight to the exceptional powers granted" to the Atomic Energy Commission. Thomas (1956, 18) notes that members believed that "Congress must place the tightest possible legislative rein on the new agency" (see also Hewlett and Anderson 1962, 1:507). Balogh (1991, 50) concludes that "members at both ends of the ideological spectrum agreed on the need for more congressional control" and hence embraced creation of the JCAE.

Strong congressional influence over nuclear policy depended on mechanisms that would make this influence well informed and constructive. Thomas (1956, 17) observes that "it became evident that if Congress were to obtain more than its customary control over this new administrative agency, it must do so by changing its traditional legislative committee structure." It was no small thing to create a *joint* House-Senate committee; in congressional history these had been rare, though interest in them as a device to improve congressional capacity had risen in the 1940s (Galloway and Wise 1976, 289).

In view of its ambitious mission, Congress granted the JCAE unusual powers that allowed it to become an important institutional power base. Indeed, in an era of powerful committees it stood out as particularly influential (Galloway and Wise 1976, 290). The JCAE was the only joint committee with the power to report legislation, and it was given exclusive jurisdiction over all bills and resolutions relating to atomic energy (Thomas 1956, 19). This meant that Congress would consider only the bills that emerged from the JCAE; there would be no second committee to serve as an appeals court, constructing an alternative bill for Congress to consider (Green and Rosenthal 1963, 271). Joint committee status also facilitated a close relationship with the AEC, which had no alternative body in Congress with whom to maintain contacts (Thomas 1956, 240).

Moreover, the Atomic Energy Act granted the JCAE unprecedented access to AEC decision making. The requirement that the AEC keep the committee "fully and currently informed" gave the JCAE an unusual capacity for surveillance (Thomas 1956, 18–19). Green wrote in 1971 (170) that the JCAE "has aggressively and imaginatively used its right to be kept . . . informed so as to reduce the doctrines of executive privilege and separation of powers—if not to a shambles—to a near nullity in the atomic energy sphere." Congress also authorized the JCAE to hire as large a staff as it deemed necessary and to requisition whatever assistance it needed from the executive branch. The institutional isolation of the AEC in the executive branch further bolstered the JCAE's position. Green and Rosenthal described the JCAE in 1963 (25) as the "apotheosis of the congressional committee, with more abilities and fewer liabilities than other committees."[16]

The committee did not take immediate advantage of its many resources. At first, it focused almost entirely on AEC security and management and did not develop substantive policies (Hewlett and Anderson 1962, vol. 2; Balogh 1991). Starting in 1949, however, the JCAE began to take an active interest in nuclear policymaking. McMahon, who became chairman in 1949, made the committee more activist (Hewlett and Anderson 1962, 2:449; Thomas 1956, 112–13).[17] The Connecticut Democrat had just entered the Senate in 1945, but from the start of his Senate career he had worked diligently to establish himself as Congress's leading expert on atomic energy. As JCAE chairman, he aggressively sought to capitalize on what was clearly "the opportunity of a lifetime" for a junior senator (Hewlett and Anderson 1962, 1:436). Later, the committee served as a power base for Clinton Anderson (D-N.Mex.), who pushed public power projects and repeatedly attacked the AEC for allegedly withholding information from the committee (Green and Rosenthal 1963, 59–60). The ambitions of such JCAE members as McMahon, Anderson, and Republicans Bourke Hickenlooper of Iowa and Sterling Cole of New York energized the committee and encouraged its rise to power (Green and Rosenthal 1963; Thomas 1956).

In thinking about the committee's implications for congressional organization, it is worth noting that the JCAE earned a reputation for nonpartisanship, particularly before the full emergence of the public power issue in the mid-1950s (Thomas 1956, 176; Green and Rosenthal 1963, 54). Party ratios on the JCAE were fixed by law at ten to eight, limiting the majority party's control over the committee. An informal subcommittee with two members from each party selected the panel's staff (Green and Rosenthal 1963, 66). This arrangement underscores the extent to which the committee was organized to address the informational challenges facing the Congress as a whole with respect to nuclear issues. As informational models would predict, noncommittee members generally deferred to this highly specialized, fairly representative committee (Green and Rosenthal 1963; see Krehbiel 1991). Contrary to distributive models, there is little evidence to suggest that the JCAE was stacked in favor of a particular sectoral interest.[18]

Yet the JCAE was more than the mere agent of the Congress. It exercised its most substantial influence through consulting with the AEC rather than through legislating (Green 1971). The absence of competing congressional power centers forced the AEC to respond assiduously to committee pressure, and the JCAE's broad statutory authority and extensive staff resources allowed it to make extraordinary demands on the commission (Green and Rosenthal 1963, 267–71). While the JCAE was not immune to control by floor majorities, the technical complexity of atomic energy issues and the AEC's dependence on the committee impeded floor challenges to JCAE administrative pressure. Moreover, by controlling the information available to members, the JCAE influenced members' perceptions of the relevant issues.

The apparent independent impact of the committee led Dahl and Brown (1951, 21) to argue that "the Committee *is* the Congress when it comes to atomic energy policy," and Green and Rosenthal (1963, 272) to conclude that the JCAE took away far more power from the executive than it gave back to Congress (see also Balogh 1991, 52). These claims likely overestimate the committee's independence from latent floor majorities.[19] Still, the JCAE was an extremely influential committee that added another element to the feudal power structure in the Congress. A conjunction of events—heightened congressional concern about executive power, a surge in member interest in joint committees as tools to oversee the executive, and the emergence of a critically important, technically complex new issue that crosscut existing jurisdictional boundaries—had shaped the creation and development of an institutional power base that would play a central role for three decades. Green and Rosenthal (1963, 266) conclude that "had the Congress chosen to deal with atomic energy through conventional congressional committees, the history of the atomic-energy program would have been quite different."[20]

There can be little doubt, therefore, that creation of the JCAE, along with the committee consolidation and staffing increase under the Reorganization Act, were designed primarily to enhance congressional capacity and influence during an era of immense executive power. It is noteworthy that reformers believed the most feasible way to strengthen the institution was to strengthen the committee system (see Davidson and Oleszek 1977, 7). In the context of a deeply divided majority party and an already-decentralized authority structure, it makes sense that reformers would focus on committees, rather than party leadership instruments (notwithstanding the preferences then of many political scientists).

Still, a nagging question remains: Did these changes do more to empower *individual* committees and committee leaders than to increase the effectiveness of the committee system as a whole? In the case of the Reorganization Act, at key moments members' interest in their committee power bases trumped their interest in congressional capacity and power. Removing coordination mechanisms and the personnel director from the Reorganization Act meant that individual committees would not face new external controls to correspond to their enhanced resources. The absence of integrative mechanisms hindered developing broad policy responses to difficult problems that crosscut committee jurisdictions. Individual committees had increased capacity and resources, but the committee system as a whole became a more fragmented and less flexible instrument.

Unlike the Reorganization Act and most of the other cases discussed in this book, the JCAE is a rare instance of a significant change shaped by only a single interest. Thus, the difficulties posed by tensions among competing interests are less salient in this case, and the JCAE successfully achieved its creators' primary goal of enhancing congressional capacity and power. But the irony is this: in order to compete for control over nuclear policy with the executive, Congress granted the JCAE such unusual and extensive tools that the committee's status as an agent of the Congress became somewhat ambiguous.

The Investigative Explosion

The rash of special investigative committees during World War II, and the increased oversight by standing committees in the aftermath of the Reorganization Act, also targeted the power imbalance between Congress and the executive branch. Greater congressional concern with executive abuses had emerged by 1939, with the high-profile House investigations of the National Labor Relations Board and the Work Projects Administration. The boom in investigations gathered steam during World War II, when Congress created an unusually large number of special committees to supervise executive administration of the war. Some of the more prominent investigations during the war years included the Truman committee (the Senate Special Committee to Investigate the National Defense Program, created in 1941), Howard Smith's (D-Va.) Committee to Investigate Acts of Executive Agencies Beyond the Scope of their Authority (created in 1943), and Harry Byrd's (D-Va.) Joint Committee for the Reduction of Nonessential Federal Expenditures (created in 1941).[21]

After World War II, the Reorganization Act encouraged and systematized this increase in oversight. Streamlining the committee system and providing professional staffs helped standing committees carry out oversight, thus obviating the need for special committees (Cooper 1988, 190, 206–8; Galloway 1953, 306; Riddick 1949, 152). Moreover, the act instructed each standing committee to exercise "continuous watchfulness" over the agencies in its jurisdiction. Standing committees conducted the vast majority of investigations after 1946.[22] My discussion encompasses the creation of influential new committee units and the change in the mode of operations of existing standing committees as they became more focused on oversight.[23]

The explosion in investigative activity promoted a variety of collective interests, but most directly reflected broadly based member unease about growing executive power during the New Deal and World War II, and conservatives' more specific goal of undermining the liberal Roosevelt and Truman administrations. Thus, it no surprise that appendix B.3, which summarizes the floor votes on prominent investigations during this period, shows that several were approved almost unanimously, while several others pitted a majority of Republicans and southern Democrats against a majority of nonsouthern Democrats. Few passed on party line votes uniting the Democrats against the GOP.

Many members came to view investigations as a potent way to defend congressional power (Cooper 1988, 201–4; Damon 1971, 257; Josephy 1979, 343). Robinson (1954, 369) observes that "after 1937 the Senate's investigations were basically for the purpose of controlling the executive." With the war in Europe, Congress had little choice but to delegate substantial power to the president, and "once these powers were granted the Senate tried to hold the executive responsible through the process of investigation" (369).

Although one might expect this motivation to have been strongest among Republicans, it is striking how many liberal Democrats wanted to defend congressional power through vigorous investigations. Monroney claimed that sharpened oversight is needed "to keep [agencies] in line with the intent of Congress" (CR, July 25, 1946, 10040). The progressive La Follette declared that a "grave constitutional crisis exists," as "public affairs are now handled by a host of administrative agencies headed by nonelected officials, with only casual oversight by Congress" (CR, June 5, 1946, 6344). Liberal Democrat Jerry Voorhis took the lead in advocating more concerted oversight (Cooper 1988, 203–5). Voorhis initiated the Reorganization Act's provision assigning increased investigative responsibilities to each standing committee, arguing that "Congress should know from day to day whether powers granted by it are being properly used" (Joint Committee 1945, 40). Voorhis testified before the La Follette–Monroney committee that "conservative and progressive Members alike" agreed on the need for closer scrutiny of executive actions (1945, 25). The subsequent testimony of Republicans Edward Rees and Homer Capehart and conservative Democrat William Poage echoed Voorhis's arguments about the need for better oversight (Joint Committee 1945, 259–60, 308–9, 326–29). Given such bipartisan support, the Reorganization

Act's oversight provisions were adopted without controversy. This case thus supports the hypothesis that members of Congress will generally respond to major advances in executive power by moving to defend Congress's role. Democratic whip Robert Ramspeck (D-Ga.) summed up this idea when he noted that "we are trying to keep up with this great, colossal executive government that we have expanded all over this country" (Joint Committee 1945, 304).

Nonetheless, the investigative boom also derived support from conservatives' policy interests. As appendix B.3 shows, conservative coalition votes approved Howard Smith's investigation into the National Labor Relations Board in 1939 (Dierenfield 1987; Patterson 1967; Latham 1966), the Smith probe of executive agencies in 1943 (Dierenfield 1987), the inquiry in 1944 into Roosevelt's decision to seize Montgomery Ward (Young 1956), and the creation of the House Un-American Activities Committee as a standing committee in 1945. A logit analysis of each of these roll calls shows that first-dimension NOMINATE scores, which tap into the economic left-right dimension, are a powerful predictor of members' votes: in each case, conservatives were more likely to vote for the investigation than were liberals (see table 4.2). Second-dimension NOMINATE scores, which in this era reflect the north-south cleavage over civil rights and civil liberties issues, are also significant in each case: conservatives on this dimension were more likely to vote for each investigation.[24]

Even in some cases where liberals did not fight an investigation on the floor, there is reason to believe conservative interests were still at work. For example, Democratic leaders hoped to block Woodrum's 1939 investigation of corruption in the WPA (Porter 1980, 79–80). New Deal foe Eugene Cox introduced the resolution to fund the investigation, which gained approval from the Rules Committee in a 7–4 vote pitting Republicans and conservative Democrats against the administration's defenders (*Post*, March 23, 1939, 2). Democratic leaders then dropped their opposition, knowing they had little chance of prevailing on the floor. Woodrum's investigation went on to disclose "malpractices and abuses within the New Deal agency" (Porter 1980, 80). In subsequent years, the conservative majority on Rules pushed other investigations opposed by Democratic leaders. For example, the committee reported the resolutions authorizing Smith's executive agencies probe and the Montgomery Ward inquiry over the opposition of chairman Adolph Sabath (D-Ill.) and Democratic leaders (*Post*, February 4, 1943, 1; April 29, 1944, 1, 3; May 1, 1944, 1; May 2, 1944, p.1, 2).

These inquiries illustrate that conservatives successfully used investigative committees as a cross-party power base from which to attack Democratic presidents and to undermine the national Democratic party

TABLE 4.2 Logit Analysis of Votes to Authorize Selected Investigations (SE in parentheses)

Independent Variable	NLRB Investigation, 1939	Executive Agencies Investigation, 1943 (Democrats only)	Montgomery Ward Inquiry, 1944	Un-American Activities, 1945
First-dimension NOMINATE score	12.72** (2.04)	9.03** (2.58)	12.80** (2.93)	13.06** (1.99)
Second-dimension NOMINATE score	9.67** (1.36)	4.34** (1.43)	4.68** (1.54)	3.17** (1.09)
Democrat	2.38* (1.09)	n/a	.18 (1.57)	3.74** (1.17)
Constant	.03 (.68)	4.11 (.83)	4.60 (1.35)	-2.32 (.70)
Proportional Reduction in Error	.76	.65	.81	.73
N	401	190	368	392

Note: Each roll call was on the vote to authorize the investigation in question, except for Un-American Activities, where the roll call was on the Rankin amendment to make HUAC a standing committee. The logit analysis of the vote on the Smith executive agencies investigation excludes Republicans because they unanimously voted for the resolution, making party a perfect predictor of their votes. This results in an infinite coefficient and standard error for the party variable.

*p < .05.   **p < .01.

(Josephy 1979; Barone 1990; Taylor 1954).[25] Conservatives' reliance on investigations led Speaker Joe Martin (R-Mass.) to quip as the 80th Congress began that he would "start each day with a prayer and end it with an investigation" (as quoted in Goodwin 1970, 15).

The contrasting circumstances surrounding the Truman committee in the Senate and the Smith committee in the House, the two leading investigators of executive performance during World War II, suggests the range of motivations that led to each individual inquiry, as well as the investigative explosion more generally. The Truman committee was created in 1941 when Cox proposed investigating the defense program. To forestall this move, Roosevelt ally Senator James Byrnes (D-S.C.) arranged to have loyal Democrat Harry Truman appointed to head a Senate committee with a similar mandate (Barone 1990, 150; Wilson 1975b). Truman himself was eager to undertake the inquiry because he saw an opportunity to promote sectoral and sectional interests important to his state: Truman had earlier proposed an investigation to redress "geographical and economic injustices" in the distribution of war contracts (as quoted in Wilson 1975b). According to Truman, big eastern corporations received a disproportionate share of contracts. Truman committee members earned positive publicity for uncovering poor administrative practices and encouraging a fairer distribution of the economic benefits from the wartime mobilization (Riddle 1964; Wilson 1975b). Therefore, the Truman committee served as a common carrier for members' interest in congressional power, for narrower sectoral and sectional interests, and for members' interest in securing power bases from which to make a record and gain favorable attention.

By contrast, the Smith committee originated in late 1942 when conservatives Cox, Woodrum, and Martin selected Howard Smith "to impugn bureaucratic excesses" (Dierenfield 1987, 102). Smith soon drafted a resolution so broad that it "would throw open to inquiry any action, rule, procedure, regulation, order or directive taken or issued by any department or agency" (*Time*, February 22, 1943, 22). Republicans unanimously voted to establish the Smith committee, as did ninety-two of ninety-seven southern Democrats, while northern Democrats were evenly divided on the proposal. As noted above, a logit analysis of the roll call reinforces the importance of conservatives' ideological interests: conservatives were much more likely to support the investigation than were liberals (see table 4.2).

However, ideological interests were not the sole motivation. The deep split among northern Democrats reflected the widespread desire, even among liberals, to defend congressional power. That liberals such as Voorhis voted for the Smith inquiry shows it served members' broad institutional interests in addition to the ideological pursuits of congressional conservatives. Voorhis announced, "I am going to vote for the resolution because . . . I believe Congress has the duty not only to pass laws but also to see that they are administered and carried out in accord with congressional intent" (CR, February 11, 1943, 878).

From the beginning, the Smith committee sought to show that executive agencies routinely abused their power and ignored the wishes of Congress (Harris 1964). The committee conducted several damaging investigations, especially of the Office of Price Administration, which conservatives disliked because it limited profits and was unsympathetic to rural interests (Dierenfield 1987, 103–4). Young (1956, 107) argues that "it was not always clear whether the [Smith committee] investigators wished only to improve OPA procedures by exposing delinquencies or whether they wished also to undermine confidence in the agency so that it might be the more readily scuttled."[26]

More generally, the poor record of majority party Democrats in avoiding troublesome investigations is striking. The only two examples are a resolution in 1937 to investigate that year's sit-down strikes in the automobile industry, and Republican efforts, beginning in early 1942, to investigate the bombing of Pearl Harbor. Even so, although Democrats defeated the strike investigation in 1937, this did not prevent the Dies committee from conducting a damaging probe of the strikes in time for the 1938 election (Goodman 1968). The Democrats did delay the Pearl Harbor investigation for three years and then proceeded to conduct an inquiry helpful to the administration, although generally regarded as impartial (Ritchie 1991).

While several prominent investigations at once served the distinctive interests of conservatives in both parties and traduced liberal Democratic and White House interests, very few inquiries suited the majority Democrats' interests. The Truman committee can be viewed as a majority party instrument to only an extremely limited extent. Truman conducted his committee's deliberations in an impartial, nonpartisan manner, and thus its work received considerable praise from members of both parties (Wilson 1975b; Riddle 1964, 51, 159–60). In much the same way, Richard Russell's (D-Ga.) inquiry in 1951 into President Truman's dismissal of General MacArthur was noted for its nonpartisanship and restraint (Barone 1990). Russell's conduct earned "plaudits from Old Guardsmen and spokesmen of the Truman administration alike" (Wiltz 1975, 418). After 1937, it was quite an achievement for the Democratic White House to receive a "fair shake" from a congressional inquiry.

Millard Tydings's (D-Md.) investigation in 1950 of Joseph McCarthy's initial flurry of charges against the State Department is the most important example of a majority party–driven investigation. The resolution authorizing the investigation passed on a voice vote after Democrats accepted three Republican-sponsored amendments concerning the powers and operations of the committee. But the committee's deliberations were sharply partisan, with the Democratic majority undertaking to discredit McCarthy (Latham 1966). In the end, however, the Tydings investigation was a disaster for the Democrats: McCarthy dominated the proceedings, and Tydings's efforts to discredit McCarthy contributed to his own defeat in the 1950 election (Grantham 1976). Although Democrats won a series of floor votes to accept the Tydings committee's report, there is little doubt that Tydings and other Democrats had suffered more damage than McCarthy and the Republicans.

In addition to advancing broad institutional and ideological interests, the investigations boom was also a common carrier for individual members' personal power and electoral interests. The rise in investigative activity was fueled (and molded) by entrepreneurial members seeking potential political benefits. Numerous authors have noted that investigations enhanced investigators' careers (Taylor 1954; Marx 1951; Josephy 1979, 344). By funding hundreds of investigations, Congress provided many outlets for ambitious members to gain publicity and please the home audience and other attentive publics.

With very few exceptions after the 1920s, majority party members chaired investigative committees. These members thus gained disproportionate career benefits from investigative entrepreneurship in the 1940s and 1950s. However, many conducted their inquiries with little regard for the interests of their party as a whole. This is not just the case for conservative Democrats who explicitly targeted liberal and administration interests. Moderate Democrat William Fulbright from Arkansas was perhaps the most aggressive investigator of corruption in the Truman administration (Barone 1990). Another Senate entrepreneur, liberal Democrat Estes Kefauver of Tennessee—who, like Fulbright, was a "temperamental outsider" (Barone 1990, 227)—in 1950 conducted an investigation of organized crime that inflicted serious damage on some big-city Democratic leaders (Wilson 1975a).[27]

These entrepreneurs were, of course, somewhat constrained by contextual factors such as the level of conservative strength on the floor. For example, conservatives won more support for their investigations in 1943, just after the Republicans had made substantial midterm electoral gains in both chambers (Young 1956). But conservative Democrats gained approval for investigations throughout this period, even when conservatives lacked a clear floor majority (e.g. 1938–42, 1945–46). This suggests that amid such deep concern about rising executive power, the conditions were consistently favorable for entrepreneurial members proposing investigations.

The net effect of these investigations was not necessarily a set of institutional power bases well designed for promoting Congress's institutional standing. Each individual investigation, while due in part to frustration with executive encroachments, was motivated as well by some combination of ideological, electoral, and personal power interests. Although the Reorganization Act improved the efficiency and effectiveness of legislative oversight by shifting the bulk of investigative activity from ad hoc special committees to standing committees (Griffith 1967), it did not ease the tensions among these multiple interests.

These tensions are particularly apparent when one considers whether standing committees should have the power to undertake investigations without party or floor approval. The Reorganization Act granted all Senate standing committees extensive subpoena power so that they could conduct investigations within their jurisdiction without a vote on the floor. This made it more difficult for party leaders and floor majorities to control committee investigators (Taylor 1954) and therefore contributed to the decentralized authority structure of the 1937–52 era. Robinson (1954, 393–94) writes, somewhat melodramatically, that each Senate committee "was thus given the power to weaken party responsibility although the [Reorganization] Act had as one of its purposes the strengthening of party responsibility."

The La Follette–Monroney committee had proposed extending this same power to all House committees, but Rayburn and Martin insisted on limiting it to the Appropriations, Expenditures in the Executive Departments, and Un-American Activities Committees (Taylor 1954, 233). Emanuel Celler (D-N.Y.) sponsored an amendment to give all House committees the same powers as Senate committees, but it was rejected on a voice vote after Monroney reminded members that an agreement had been reached with the leadership of both parties (CR, July 25, 1946, 10074). Rayburn's and Martin's ability to modify the Reorganization proposal suggests that even in the 1940s, party leaders were better able to clamp down on entrepreneurial pressures in the House than in the Senate. This is a case of party leaders' acting in a distinctly nonpartisan manner to protect the institution from perceived dangers rooted in members' individual interests (Taylor 1954, 233, 259; see Mayhew 1974). As subsequent experience in the Senate would prove, members' interest in congressional prestige conflicted with their interest in maximum entrepreneurial opportunities.

Following the Reorganization Act, the Senate conducted most of the prominent congressional investigations, as it had done prior to the rise of the Dies committee and other House special committees in the late 1930s and 1940s (Taylor 1954). The autonomy granted to Senate committees encouraged entrepreneurial members to undertake many investigations that enhanced the Senate's influence. But without central control over investigators, the Senate could not ensure that only "responsible" members led the inquiries (Marx 1951; Taylor 1954).[28] In the end, congressional investigators' excesses created a backlash that undermined the credibility of congressional investigations and damaged the reputation of Congress as a whole (White 1957, 264; McGreary 1951, 438–39).[29] As a result, while congressional investigations proved an effective weapon for curbing the executive, it is not at all clear that they substantially improved Congress's institutional standing. Byrd (1988, 1:581) notes that McCarthy's antics in particular "made the public suspicious of congressional investigations as a threat to civil liberties, a suspicion that lingered for two decades until erased by the stellar work of the Watergate Committee." Members had chosen, particularly in the Senate, to battle the executive branch in a manner that also promoted maximum individual entrepreneurial opportunities. But this method of challenging executive power damaged Congress's reputation.

CROSS-PARTY COALITION INSTITUTIONAL CHANGES

Two institutional changes during this period were attempts to develop power bases in the committee system to promote cross-party conservative causes. These are the change in the operations of the Rules Committee in 1937 and the onset of loyalty investigations starting with the Dies committee. In these two cases, as opposed to the expansion in investigations discussed above, conservatives' ideological interests played a greater role than members' concern about executive power. Roll calls relating to these changes typically divided members sharply, with most Republicans and southern Democrats opposing a majority of nonsouthern Democrats. In exploring the Rules Committee changes and the loyalty investigations, it is worth considering whether these developments simply reflected the policy preferences of floor majorities. The analysis presented below suggests that though floor majorities were important, they cannot fully explain these institutional power bases.

House Rules Committee, 1937

The Rules Committee was transformed in the late 1930s from a generally reliable tool of majority party leaders into the principal institutional power base in the House for the cross-party conservative coalition. Led by Democrats Eugene Cox and Howard Smith and Republican Charlie Halleck of Indiana, the conservative coalition on the Rules Committee held up liberal initiatives; made substantive alterations in bills a condition for access to the floor (Lapham 1954; CQ 1982); provided favorable terms for the consideration of conservative floor amendments (Lapham 1954); forwarded many resolutions that initiated politically damaging investigations of Democratic administrations (CQ 1982; Van Hollen 1951); and denied roll call votes for amendments sought by Democratic leaders (House Committee on Rules 1983, 142–43, 148; Lapham 1954, 128–29; CR, March 11, 1943, 1862).[30]

The Rules Committee change can be explained in terms of a single collective interest: the policy goals of conservatives. It has often been observed that conservatives lacked a formal organization during the supposed era of conservative coalition rule (Brady and Bullock 1980). Yet with the Rules Committee securely controlled by conservative Democrats and Republicans who consulted with one another regularly, there was little need for a formal, extrapartisan organization to coordinate coalition activities. By providing favorable terms of consideration for conservative substitutes and amendments, and denying such favorable terms for liberal measures, the Rules Committee facilitated conservative unity on the floor.[31]

How did a cross-party coalition put into effect this institutional change? Enabling factors include the revolt against Speaker Joseph Cannon in 1910, which reduced party leaders' direct domination of the Rules Committee. In addition, the seniority system made purging recalcitrant committee members extremely costly and thereby made Rules members somewhat independent. Declining floor and popular support for President Roosevelt's liberal programs also played a key role.

Beyond these background factors, a series of soon-regretted committee assignments by Democratic leaders critically influenced the Rules Committee. By the time that the liberal-conservative split in the Democratic party became apparent in 1937, archconservatives Cox, Smith, and Dies had already been appointed to Rules. Cox had been appointed to the committee in 1931. At the time, he apparently was slightly to the *left* of the average House Democrat.[32] Smith had been placed on the committee in 1933 as a concession to Rayburn, after his faction's defeat in a party leadership contest. "The liberal Democratic leadership," Smith's biographer Bruce Dierenfield (1987, 74) explains, "unwittingly had given [Smith] the position on Rules that assured his power for more than three decades." Smith had only been in Congress two years then and appeared a New Deal supporter, though he was a bit to the right of the average Democrat.[33] Two years later, in 1935, Dies was placed on the committee. At the time, Dies stood out as a prairie populist suspicious of big business and, based on the NOMINATE measure, ranked as one of the more liberal Democrats.[34] In that same year, Smith became one of the first southerners to break openly with the Roosevelt administration, opposing his party on several measures that a majority of southerners supported. It was not long before Dies also began attacking Roosevelt and other leading Democrats. By 1939, Cox, Smith, and Dies ranked among the very most conservative Democrats. Further buttressing conservative strength, William Colmer

(D-Miss.) was appointed to one of a handful of openings on the committee in 1939. Because he supported the recently passed Wages and Hours bill, Colmer was then regarded as a relatively loyal New Dealer (Van Hollen 1951). He quickly established himself as one of the most conservative members of the House.[35] The net result of these appointments was that from 1939 on, the Rules Committee consistently included three to five Democrats who scored among the most conservative 10 to 20 percent of party members.[36] The southerners on Rules, who always comprised at least half of the committee's Democrats in this period, tended to be among the most conservative, least loyal southern Democrats.[37]

The presence of conservative Democrats on Rules was not sufficient to make the committee an instrument of opposition to the majority party. It was critical that conservative Democrats on the committee—including 1938 purge victim John O'Connor of New York, who chaired Rules when it first began to resist majority party leaders—were willing to alter the accepted role of the committee and to cooperate with Republicans in doing so. Prior to 1937, Rules Committee Democrats had voted to report several important bills that they personally opposed, arguing that the Rules Committee should support majority party policies (Lapham 1954, 93; House Committee on Rules 1983).[38] Van Hollen (1951, 82) observes that prior to the late 1930s "it was assumed that committee members would support the leadership." O'Connor, who in 1933 had stated that the committee was and should be an agent of the majority party and of the president, reversed himself in 1937 and asserted that the committee should serve the House and its committees (Lapham 1954, 89). Under the leadership of O'Connor, Cox, and Smith, Rules abandoned "its traditional role as party agent; it was embarking instead on a thirty-year period as an agent of opposition" (Dierenfield 1987, 59).

For the Dixiecrats, success depended on forging good working relationships with committee Republicans. Cox and Smith accordingly developed close personal ties with Martin, who served on Rules during the pivotal 75th Congress (1937–38), when the committee first became a conservative tool, and Halleck, who joined the committee when Martin departed to become minority leader in 1939 (Patterson 1966, 1967). Smith described how these relationships fostered cooperation: "[Martin] and Cox worked together on many issues. Our group . . . did not meet publicly. The meetings were not formal. Our group met in one building and the conservative Republicans in another, on different issues. Then Eugene Cox, Bill Colmer or I would go over to speak with the Republicans, or the Republican leaders might come to see us. It was very informal. . . . A coalition did exist in legislation. But we met in small groups. There were no joint meetings of conservative Republicans and southern Democrats" (quoted in Dierenfield 1987, 114). The presence of Cox, Smith, and

Halleck on the Rules Committee meant that a small group of conservative leaders could implement strategies agreed upon through these informal contacts.[39] It also helped that the Rules Committee was a small, informal committee, with only twelve to fourteen members. Because many southern Democrats were wary of a formal coalition with Republicans, it was important to avoid public signs of an alliance that would scare them off (Dierenfield 1987, 102; Patterson 1966, 1967). The Rules Committee was ideally suited for quiet negotiations that avoided the glare of publicity on the floor.

That the Rules Committee was an institutional power base for a cross-party ideological coalition does not mean that the committee typically failed to represent the policy positions of a majority of members on the floor. Nor should it be forgotten that committee decisions were overturned on a handful of occasions when its actions were drastically out of step with most members.[40] Yet the relevant preferences of a majority of members were not unambiguously exogenous. The reality was complicated. The Rules Committee reported rules that affected the visibility of votes on amendments and substitutes (Lapham 1954; Van Hollen 1951). As a result, the committee could manipulate how much members had to modify their own personal preferences to cater to constituency preferences (Schickler 1994). The committee's sponsorship of investigations that targeted liberal causes also shaped members' positions. Dies's investigation, among others, depended in part on conservative floor strength, but its adoption reinforced that strength by discrediting many executive officials and liberal interest groups (Taylor 1954; Patterson 1967, 317–18, 327).

My assessment of the Rules Committee differs considerably from Cox and McCubbins's (1993, 270–71) view that the conservative majority on Rules actually benefited the Democratic party. Cox and McCubbins argue that by providing southerners with a partial veto on liberal legislation, the Rules Committee helped keep the deeply divided party from falling apart. There is something to this view: the committee's influence did enable southerners to block legislation that just might have driven them from the party. In this sense, the Republicans' decision to cooperate with the southerners in blocking liberal legislation emerges as an important strategic move. The minority party chose to pursue policy interests instead of a partisan interest in highlighting issues that would exacerbate the opposition party's internal divisions.

But the Rules Committee did not simply block legislation; it also actively promoted conservative priorities. Cox and McCubbins (1993, 240–41, 271) mistakenly suggest that the Rules Committee rarely forced consideration of matters opposed by Democratic leaders. Lapham (1954, 125) counts "about a dozen occasions" in just the 78th Congress of 1943–44 when the Rules Committee reported a rule that "was unwanted or deficient in some respect from the point of view of [Chairman] Sabath and presumably the majority leadership" (see, e.g., *Post*, February 4, 1943, 1; May 1, 1944, 1). In that Congress and on several other occasions, Rules promoted investigations that undermined the electoral interests of non-southern Democrats. The committee targeted labor interests in particular—both through investigations and restrictive legislation—thereby hurting a constituency essential to nonsouthern Democrats (Van Hollen 1951, 202). It is not at all clear that Democratic leaders thought these costs were worth the benefits provided by the Rules Committee's restraining influence on liberal legislation. At the very least, Cox's, Smith's, Dies's, and Colmer's extreme conservatism—which placed them to the right of most *southern* Democrats—rendered them far from ideal guardians of the party's interests. Indeed, Sam Rayburn, apparently recalling his role in arranging Smith's promotion to Rules in 1933, wrote to a colleague in November 1948 that he intended "not [to] make mistakes this time" by placing disloyal Democrats on Rules (as quoted in Dierenfield 1987, 124).

While the transformation of the Rules Committee into an institutional power base for conservatives derived from only a single collective interest, this case had major consequences for other interests: it made Democratic party leaders' task much more difficult by depriving them of what had been a major leadership instrument. Legislative committee leaders thus became more independent of party leaders, reinforcing the decentralized House committee system. Furthermore, Republicans' alliance with the southern Democrats complicated their pursuit of majority status since party members could less easily construct policy alternatives that would distinguish them from Democrats. Decades later, in the 1960s, Gerald Ford (R-Mich.) led aggressive young Republicans in calling for a shift away from cooperation with the southerners and toward single-minded pursuit of a partisan agenda promoting majority status (Manley 1973).

Furthermore, although a single interest shaped the 1937 change, the Rules Committee continued to embody several purposes. As I argue in chapter 1, key congressional institutions often develop through an accumulation of innovations inspired by different interests. The Rules Committee's evolution prior to 1937 had been shaped by a series of innovations, dating back to the middle of the nineteenth century, which had made it both an agent of the majority party, giving it disproportionate control over the House agenda, and an agent of the House as a whole, shielding members from votes on popular but unwise legislation. The committee's new, post-1937 role as an agent of a cross-party coalition jettisoned the committee's serviceability as a majority party agent. But this new rule did not displace the committee's other traditional role, as a control committee protecting House members from excesses attributable to electoral pressures. Thus, Rules continued to block special-interest leg-islation that members would have had trouble voting against but that the leaders of both parties opposed (Lapham 1954, 111; Van Hollen 1951). As the case of the 21-day rule illustrates (see discussion below), it proved difficult to dislodge the Rules Committee's post-1937 role as a conserva-tive power base while still preserving its older role as a gatekeeper serving the entire House.

Dies Committee on Un-American Activities

Conservative control of the Rules Committee was not the only institu-tional change of the late 1930s that posed difficulties for Democratic party leaders. The creation of committee units to investigate the loyalty of left-leaning federal workers, activists, union organizers, and celebrities began in 1938 with the Dies Special Committee on Un-American Activities. Martin Dies molded his committee into a potent weapon for attacking liberal causes by associating the New Deal and its supporters with commu-nism. The Dies committee was not the first congressional investigation into subversion, but its systematic interrogation of reluctant witnesses and its ability to garner headlines were new. As Schneier (1963) observes, "whether or not Martin Dies was the first to sense the almost boundless possibilities opened by this tactic, it was he who set the pattern." A new mode of operations had entered the scene (Taylor 1954, 70–71).[41]

After Dies departed the House in 1944, most observers expected his committee to dissolve. However, John Rankin (D-Miss.) revived the com-mittee through a surprise floor amendment to the rules, creating the per-manent House Un-American Activities Committee. HUAC conducted several influential inquiries, most notably its investigation of Alger Hiss in 1948. Indeed, the Dies committee began a series of loyalty investigations that continued into the early 1950s and that included the Senate Judiciary Committee's investigation of U.S. China policy (conducted by its Internal Security Subcommittee and chaired by Democrat Pat McCarran of Ne-vada) and Joseph McCarthy's (R-Wis.) investigative forays as chairman of the Senate Government Operations Committee in 1953–54.

Much like the House Rules Committee, the Dies committee and the loyalty investigations that followed it after World War II served as institu-tional power bases for the cross-party conservative coalition. In addition, the inquiries provided an outlet for individualistic entrepreneurship. The leading loyalty investigators were scarcely team players in the Sam Rayburn "to get along, go along" mode. Dies, McCarthy, McCarran, and Richard Nixon (R-Calif.) skillfully used the press to gain attention for themselves and for their causes. Dies's ambition is suggested by his sponsorship of numerous unsuccessful resolutions in the 1930s proposing investigations of a wide variety of targets, including lobbying by international bankers and the alleged shackling of the press by the administration (Gellerman 1944). When he finally succeeded in gaining approval for an investigation, he used it to impress his constituents as well as a national audience and to carve out a powerful niche for himself (Saunders 1939). Similarly, McCarthy and Nixon used their investigative activism to enhance their personal power and electoral standing (see Mayhew 1974, 69, on McCarthy and Goodman 1968 on Nixon). As such, the loyalty investigations were a common carrier for political entrepreneurs' electoral and power base interests and for an ideological faction.

Members initially supported Dies because he promised to investigate both fascist sympathizers and groups with communist ties. New Dealer Samuel Dickstein (D-N.Y.) had repeatedly sought an investigation into Nazi activities in the United States and enthusiastically backed Dies's proposal in 1938 for a special committee on "un-American" activities. Dies's proposal thus attracted support from members wanting to attack either the extreme right or the far left (CR, April 27, 1938, 5881–82; May 26, 1938, 7583–84; *Time,* June 20, 1938, 12). Although a few Democrats expressed concern that Dies would simply attack liberals, the resolution to create the committee passed on a division vote, 191–41.

It was not long, however, before this concern proved correct. Leuchtenberg (1963, 280–81) writes that the Dies committee "largely ignored the Nazis, although much of the pressure for the inquiry had come from antifascist congressmen, and made itself a forum for allegations of communist infiltration." Given the overwhelming Democratic majority in the 75th Congress (1937–38), Dies needed to enlist urban liberals and moderates concerned about fascism. But the resurgence of conservatism nationally and in Congress in the late 1930s, and the positive publicity generated by Dies's indefatigable efforts to expose communists, quickly protected the committee from political attacks even though Dies had effectively dropped fascists as a target. In this case, an institutional change adopted to serve members with various ideological viewpoints ended up serving conservatives alone. By early 1939, Dickstein had changed sides, vehemently attacking the Dies committee's work (CR, January 24, 1939, 733–35).

The seven-year success record of the Dies committee is difficult to square with theories claiming that the majority party controls the institutional power bases of the House. From the start, the Dies committee attacked liberal Democrats. Indeed, in the 1938 election the committee was widely credited with defeating the Democratic governor of Michigan and Democratic candidates in Minnesota and California (CR, February 3, 1939, 1109; Alexander 1955; Goodman 1968). Dies deliberately timed committee hearings to coincide with that election, defeating the committee's two loyal New Dealers who had sought to postpone the investigation until after the election (CR, February 3, 1939, 1110; Saunders 1939, 235). Dies promised not to undertake similar hearings during the 1940 election campaign, but he nonetheless published his book, *The Trojan Horse in America*, right before the election. The book attempted to link the New Deal and its leaders to the communist "menace" (Ogden 1944; Wreszin 1975). In the weeks leading up to the 1944 election, the committee published a report attacking the CIO's newly prominent Political Action Committee for its alleged communist sympathies. The CIO-PAC had been actively campaigning for Roosevelt and other liberal Democrats (Goodman 1968; Wreszin 1975).

Throughout the Dies committee's history, Republicans and conservative Democrats on the committee cooperated to discredit liberal causes and administration officials. Saunders (1939, 231) notes that a "division of labor" quickly developed among conservative members, with each tackling a particular bastion of alleged subversion. Surveying the Dies committee's record from 1938 to 1944, Alexander (1955, 116) credits Dies with the "development of a congressional committee into a form of opposition within the party." Taylor (1954, xvi) adds that conservatives used the Dies committee to saddle "Democratic-liberal groups with the onus of Communist advances."

Although Dies made it clear by the end of 1938 that he was determined to undermine liberal Democrats and New Deal programs, party leaders were nonetheless unable to stop him or his successors. The severe divisions within the party and the popularity of the committee's work hampered party leaders. Democratic divisions were so fierce starting in Roosevelt's second term that many conservative southerners became more devoted to their regionally based faction than to the party itself.[42] Polls demonstrated the popularity of the loyalty investigations: 74 percent of those Americans who had heard of the Dies committee approved of its work (Brett and Menefee 1939). Thus, when Roosevelt urged Democratic leaders not to renew the Dies committee in January 1939, they responded that such an action would be "politically dangerous" (Ogden 1944, 109). Rayburn even joked that Martin Dies could beat him in his own district (Barkley 1939).

As appendix B.3 shows, Republicans and southern Democrats overwhelmingly supported the Dies committee. Although many northern Democrats disapproved of Dies's work from the start, political considerations made them reluctant to oppose Dies publicly (Ogden 1944; Brett and Menefee 1939). Not until January 1943 did a substantial number of members go on record against renewing the committee's mandate. In that vote, and in the 1945 vote on Rankin's bid to make the Dies committee a standing committee, a clear majority of nonsouthern Democrats voted to terminate the investigation. But the GOP and southern Democrats defeated the liberals in each case. In both 1943 and 1945, conservatives, as measured by first- and second-dimension NOMINATE scores, were significantly more likely to vote in favor of continuing the investigation than were liberals (see table 4.2 for the 1945 results).[43]

Speaker Rayburn did tame the Un-American Activities Committee somewhat through caucus changes adopted in 1949 (Cox and McCubbins 1993). But the committee continued to plague the Democratic Left for some time to come (Goodman 1968). Perhaps more importantly, the major loyalty investigations shifted to the Senate in the late 1940s, where party leaders were unable to restrain Senators McCarran, McCarthy, and William Jenner (R-Ind.). These senators launched various investigations damaging to the Truman and then Eisenhower administrations (Taylor 1954; Goodman 1968). McCarran's Internal Security Subcommittee, for example, sought to prove that State Department communists had engineered the "loss" of China to the Communists (Latham 1966, 15).

Since partisan theories clearly fail to explain the loyalty investigations, it seems plausible that Krehbiel's (1991) majoritarian, informational theory could. Recall that Krehbiel (1991) argues that committees are agents of floor majorities. In this view, committees typically are representative of the chamber as a whole and provide noncommittee members with information about the relationship between proposed policies and outcomes. But this case does not fit comfortably into such a model either. While conservative majorities protected the loyalty investigations for much of this period, the Dies committee was far more than an instrument of the floor. Instead, it helped to define members' policy preferences and issue understandings. After promising in May 1938 that his committee would complete its work in seven months, Dies worked to make the committee so popular that it would be impossible to abolish (Goodman 1968). His committee did much to set the terms of debate surrounding subversion and to define the communist "threat" broadly enough to encompass left-leaning New Dealers and labor union leaders who often were not communists. Dies began to do this *before* conservatives made their significant gains in the 1938 election. By shaping public opinion, the Dies committee virtually determined members' public, or constituency-induced, preferences. Furthermore, by defining subversion for members of Congress themselves, Dies arguably affected members' own views.

The imperfect correspondence between members' "public" and private preferences was demonstrated by the series of votes on Rankin's proposal for a permanent Un-American Activities Committee. Rankin was actually defeated on the initial tally, a teller vote in which individual representatives' votes were secret. However, Rankin knew that many members

would be reluctant to oppose the investigation publicly (Taylor 1954, 75).
When he called for a record vote, his amendment carried. *Time* reported
that "a score of members complained that they wanted to vote against the
amendment but could not afford to stand up and be counted. Their reason: so many of their constituents believed in the value of Dies's committee" (*Time,* January 15, 1945, 21). Thus, investigators manipulated procedure to play upon members' electoral interests (see Alexander 1955;
Goodman 1968).

Beyond this question of the exogeneity of member preferences, informational theories also fall short because the Dies committee was widely
recognized as extremely biased. It never attempted to determine the genuine extent of the communist "threat," a critical (and difficult to answer)
question for members in these years (Saunders 1939; Wreszin 1975). With
a few notable exceptions, such as the Alger Hiss probe, the information
provided by the committee was virtually useless, yet members still relied
upon it to define the subversion issue. By encouraging the public perception that communism posed a serious danger to American institutions,
the committee virtually guaranteed its own perpetuation and funding,
regardless of the quality of the information it provided.

Therefore, the "loyalty regime," of which the Dies committee was an
integral part, resulted from strategic innovations by ambitious members
such as Dies and Rankin, who were promoting their own careers while
also benefiting the conservative coalition. To establish his committee, Dies
promised to investigate the right wing as well as the left. If Dies had kept
his promise, the partisan impact of his work would have been minimal.
But Dies quickly discovered that he could generate enough publicity from
sensational disclosures so that impartiality would not be necessary for the
committee's perpetuation. Journalist Kenneth Crawford (1939, 112) declared that the "amazing success" of the Dies committee's first hearings
"as an experiment in publicity . . . awakened Dies and his associates to a
full realization of the . . . political gold mine they had struck. From [then]
on it was catch as catch can with no holds barred."

Although Democratic leaders might well have expected Dies to attack
left-wing interests, Dies's meager legislative record did not inspire much
trepidation (Barkley 1939; Goodman 1968). Had Democratic leaders anticipated Dies's tactics and success, they might have sought, like Byrnes in
1941, to stave off his inquiry by having a moderate but loyal Democrat
sponsor a resolution for a similar investigation. Under the control of
someone like John McCormack (D-Mass.), who had chaired an earlier,
more restrained inquiry into subversion, the 1938 investigation would
likely have been more balanced and would not have created so much concern about communist subversion. This alternative, however, would have

been difficult to implement both because of conservatives' control of the Rules Committee, which had jurisdiction over resolutions for investigations, and because leading a responsible inquiry into subversion promised mainstream Democrats little in the way of a career boost and much potential trouble. Indeed, for many years, Democratic leaders had considerable difficulty convincing liberals and moderates to serve on the Un-American Activities Committee (Goodman 1968). In sum, it is probably not correct to view the loyalty investigations as inevitable products of the membership's policy preferences. The investigators' success derived instead from a handful of ambitious conservatives' aggressive efforts to define subversion as a threat from the left, and to make this issue salient to reelection-conscious members.

The 1937 Rules Committee change and the Dies committee were both triumphs for the cross-party conservative coalition. In both cases, southern Democrats and Republicans shaped House institutions in ways that promoted conservative interests. Like the changes that sought to augment congressional capacity and power, these changes built upon the committee system, further fragmenting an authority structure in which many committees served as member power bases and in which majority party leaders enjoyed few tools to influence outcomes.

But the conservative coalition changes pose more of a challenge to partisan theories because these innovations not only served members of both parties—as was the case in the changes seeking to bolster congressional power—but also imposed significant costs on nonsouthern Democrats, who typically made up a majority of the majority party. This makes the question of *how* cross-party coalitions could pursue their interests particularly important. In the case of the Rules Committee, the committee's small size and the fortuitous appointments of leading Democratic conservatives facilitated cross-party cooperation.

The Dies committee and the loyalty regime, by contrast, were rooted more directly in interactions among multiple interests. The confluence of urban liberals' interest in investigating Nazis and conservatives' interest in investigating communists helped create the Dies committee. Perhaps more importantly, the loyalty investigations were fueled by members' interest in individual entrepreneurship. A conservative organization was not required to obtain the potential benefits from these investigations because individual conservatives had sufficient incentives to sponsor inquiries that would promote their own careers at the same time as they benefited the conservative cause. The freewheeling investigations led by Dies, McCarran, McCarthy, and Jenner maximized the publicity obtained by individual members, while attacking liberal causes in a forceful manner. Although the loyalty investigations were, in general, an effective conservative tool, this reliance on entrepreneurship made the investigations somewhat disorganized and allowed excesses, such as those perpetrated by McCarthy, that ultimately embarrassed conservatives.

PARTY-BASED INSTITUTIONAL CHANGES

Three of the institutional changes adopted in this period were largely concerned with partisan interests: the 21-day rule, the Senate Republican Policy Committee, and the weekly leadership conferences at the White House. However, party-based interests were not the only collective goods involved in these cases, which together illustrate the limited strength of the majority party in this period. These changes by no means seriously undermined elements of congressional organization that weakened party influence.

The 21-Day Rule

The Rules Committee's new mode of operations generated prolonged and heated controversy. This controversy culminated, for a short while, in adoption of the 21-day rule in 1949. Under the new rule, the chairman of a committee reporting a bill and requesting a special rule for its consideration "could request recognition for the purpose of calling it up if it had been adversely reported by the Rules Committee or if that committee had failed to report the rule for twenty-one calendar days after reference" (Galloway and Wise 1976, 185). Members used the rule eight times in the 81st Congress (1949–50) to force floor consideration of bills blocked in the Rules Committee (CQ 1982, 161).[44] In addition, the threat of the use of this rule likely led the Rules Committee to report several other significant measures, including a major housing bill and legislation expanding the social security program (Lapham 1954, 211–14; Bolling 1968, 179; Barone 1990, 223).[45]

A confluence of Democrats' partisan interests and liberals' ideological interests motivated the 21-day rule. The evidence for policy interests is particularly compelling. Liberals wanted to undermine the conservative coalition's Rules Committee power base and thus to pave the way for liberal legislation. A logit analysis of the roll call to approve the rule shows the influence of policy preferences. The strong, negative coefficient for first-dimension NOMINATE scores shows that liberals were far more likely to favor the 21-day rule than were conservatives (see model 1 of table 4.3). Second-dimension NOMINATE scores, which as noted above reflected the north-south split over civil rights, fall a bit short of statistical significance (p = .10), though these scores are stronger predictors of subsequent votes on the 21-day rule (see discussion below).[46] First-dimension NOMINATEs continue to be significant when the votes of Democrats and Republicans are analyzed separately.

The evidence for partisan interests is less compelling, but nonetheless is fairly strong. Model 1 shows that party has no effect when included alongside first- and second-dimension NOMINATE scores. One difficulty, however, is that first-dimension NOMINATE scores are highly correlated with party (r = .83).[47] Though ADA scores are also highly correlated with party, it is intriguing that when ADA scores are substituted for first-dimension NOMINATE scores, both party and ADA scores are significant predictors of members' votes: liberals and Democrats are most likely to support the 21-day rule (see model 2 of table 4.3).[48]

Despite the equivocal statistical results, the Democrats' handling of the rules change suggests its importance to the party. Following the 1948 election, most observers believed that the success of the Truman administration's program depended on subverting conservative control of the Rules Committee (Truman 1959b; Goodwin 1970, 212–13). This program would in turn benefit most Democrats by demonstrating that the national party keeps its promises and governs effectively.

Rank-and-file Democrats initiated the 21-day rule. Herman Eberharter, a liberal Democrat from Pennsylvania, organized a steering committee to lobby for his proposal to curb the Rules Committee and persuaded Speaker Rayburn to endorse the change. Democrats then held a caucus to discuss the rule and, in an extremely rare move, voted 176 to 46 to "bind" all party members to vote for the change on the floor.[49] Days later, the full House adopted the rule on a 275 to 142 vote. The party-based explanation is buttressed by the striking support of southern Democrats, 73 percent of whom voted for the new rule (see appendix B.3). In the wake of the surprising Democratic victory in November 1948, many southerners were apparently willing to identify their interests with those of their party and its leadership. Even such noted conservatives as Edward Hebert (D-La.) and Otto Passman (D-La.) backed the change.

Nevertheless, compromises adopted en route to passage of the 21-day rule benefited legislative committees and, more specifically, their often-conservative chairmen, instead of party legislation. To gain Rayburn's support, Eberharter agreed to authorize only committee chairmen, rather than committee majorities, to invoke the rule. Rayburn apparently believed that chairmen would use the rule more "responsibly" (Van Hollen 1951). Thus, the 21-day rule enhanced the position of the already-powerful committee leaders (Bolling 1968, 180; Galloway and Wise 1976, 146). In addition, Rayburn insisted that he not have clear discretion over whom to recognize under the rule, since he wanted to avoid any difficult political

TABLE 4.3 Logit Analysis of Votes on 21-Day Rule, 1949–1951 (SE in parentheses)

Independent Variable	Passage of 21-Day Rule, 1949		Vote on Revoking 21-day rule, 1950	Vote on Revoking 21-day rule, 1951
	Model 1	Model 2	Model 3	Model 4
First-dimension NOMINATE score	-11.27** (1.85)		-12.87** (1.94)	-12.24** (1.93)
Second-dimension NOMINATE score	-1.63 (1.26)	-6.22** (1.18)	-6.38** (1.25)	-6.12** (1.25)
Democrat	-1.33 (1.17)	3.64** (.93)	-3.51** (1.19)	-1.74 (1.14)
ADA Score, 1948		.04** (.01)		
Constant	2.38 (.72)	-2.51 (.36)	2.77 (.71)	.95 (.66)
Proportional Reduction in Error	.69	.56	.75	.77
N	416	295	423	419

Note: Votes are coded so that a vote in favor of adopting or retaining the 21-day rule is scored 1 and a vote against the rule is coded as 0. The vote analyzed in 1951 is Cox's proposal to delete the 21-day rule. The results are unchanged if the vote on the previous question motion (which would have blocked Cox's proposal) is analyzed.

*p < .05.   **p < .01, one-tailed.

choices, given his relatively conservative home district. This further empowered committee chairmen (Lapham 1954). These provisions likely attracted the support of committee leaders and others with a stake in the committee-based power structure.[50] Nonetheless, the impetus for the change had clearly come from liberals, not committee leaders, and it is interesting that the liberals' achievement reinforced the position of certain conservative committee chairmen, such as Rankin of Veterans Affairs, Barden of Education and Labor, and William Whittington (D-Miss.) of Public Works.

Under the rule, Rayburn had discretion over whom to recognize only when two or more chairmen sought recognition at the same time. He used this discretion on a handful of occasions to hold off action on measures that he deemed inadvisable. But three of the eight measures brought up under the 21-day rule were special-interest bills opposed by the leadership (Lapham 1954). One of these, a rivers and harbors bill, became law, and another, a veterans' hospitals bill, passed the House but died in the Senate. The veterans' bill was brought to the floor by Rankin, a fiery foe of the 21-day rule, who was delighted to use the rule to pass a bill he supported while at the same time undermining party leaders' faith in the rule's wisdom (Van Hollen 1951).

Cox led an effort in January 1950 to overturn the 21-day rule and garnered the votes of eighty-five Democrats. Cox's bid fell short because the Democratic leadership secured sixty-four Republican votes (see appendix B.3). The increase in southern defections and in Republican support for the rule are each largely attributable to Cox's linking the rule with an upcoming civil rights measure, a bill to create a permanent Fair Employment Practices Commission (Van Hollen 1951). Indeed, the dramatic increase in the size of the coefficient for second-dimension NOMINATE scores reflects the increased salience of racial politics at the time of the 1950 vote (see model 3 of table 4.3). Cox did succeed in repealing the rule at the beginning of the next Congress in January 1951, after Republican gains in the midterm elections increased conservatives' voting strength (though Democrats still enjoyed majority status). Repeal of the rule fully restored the Rules Committee as a power base for conservatives (Galloway and Wise 1976, 146).[51] Once again, first- and second-dimension NOMINATE scores are significant predictors of members' votes (see model 4 of table 4.3).

The shift in outcomes from 1949 to 1951 illustrates how floor majorities can shape House institutions and contradicts the view that the majority party is able to block rules changes that a majority of its members oppose. The ideological power balance on the floor instead appears critical (Schickler 2000). The floor median, which had been .20 closer to the Democratic median than to the GOP median in 1949, shifted to the right in 1951, so that it was .07 closer to the Republican median than to the Democratic median. But this conclusion about the influence of the median voter merits an important caveat: Eberharter and his liberal colleagues might have been able to adopt a different strategy that would have had a more lasting impact on the committee. For example, had liberals sought to increase the size of the committee, as was done later in 1961, they might have turned the committee in a more liberal direction.[52] Although conservatives could have negated such a change following the 1950 election, this would likely have proven difficult for the cross-party coalition.[53] In 1949, Rules chairman Sabath favored enlarging the committee because he did not want it to lose influence, even though he was generally outvoted there on controversial matters. Reformers opposed this idea, however, because they believed a rules change would provide a firmer guarantee that the Rules Committee would never again block legislation favored on the floor (Van Hollen 1951).[54]

The most important aspect of this case is that the 21-day rule's boost to the majority party proved both short-lived and limited. The rule further empowered committee chairmen regardless of whether they supported the party. Thus, the 21-day rule assaulted one element of the committee-centered authority structure—the Rules Committee—only to reinforce other elements of that same structure.

The effectiveness of the 21-day rule was also compromised because it was layered on top of a preexisting structure that served competing interests. The rule added a new mechanism to circumvent Rules Committee obstruction, but it by no means erased the strategic advantages that the 1937 change in the Rules Committee's role provided to conservatives. Instead, the process governing special rules in the 81st Congress amounted to a hybrid, combining features from the changes in 1937 and 1949, as well as earlier innovations. On the one hand, the threat of the 21-day rule forced the Rules Committee to report rules for bills that a majority on the committee opposed. At the same time, on several occasions the Rules Committee shaped the content of these rules in ways that favored conservatives (Lapham 1954, 211–30).[55] The 21-day rule thus created a complex process in which liberals had more opportunities to force measures to the floor, but conservatives retained an advantageous position to determine the terms of bill consideration.

While this hybrid process may sound like a reasonable compromise, it had important shortcomings. The 21-day rule created new openings not only for liberals promoting Democratic programs, but also for members pushing special-interest legislation opposed by the leaders of *both* parties. By (temporarily) taking away the Rules Committee's power of obstruction, the 21-day rule limited the committee's ability to perform its long-standing role as a control committee, protecting members from popular but ill-advised bills. The accumulation of innovations over time resulted in a process that no longer served any given collective interest particularly well.

Senate Republican Policy Committee

The La Follette–Monroney committee included party policy committees for each chamber in its reorganization proposal in 1946. But House leaders—in particular, Speaker Rayburn—opposed this innovation because they feared these committees would reduce their flexibility (Bone 1968, 168). As a result, Rayburn forced the removal of policy committees from the Reorganization Act.

Nonetheless, reformers won a partial victory a few weeks later when the Senate formally created and funded policy committees under a provision of the Legislative Branch Appropriations Act of 1946 (CR, August 1, 1946, 10602). The provision passed on a voice vote with no controversy. The resulting Senate Democratic Policy Committee, which was chaired by the party floor leader, varied in importance over the years but was not very consequential during this period.[56] However, the Senate Republican Policy Committee did play an important role as a leadership instrument, particularly from 1946 to 1952, when it was chaired by Robert Taft, who used the committee to develop Republican alternatives to the Democrats' domestic programs.[57]

In this case, a single innovation served as a common carrier for Taft's desire to build up the Senate GOP as well as his own career, for liberal Democrats' interest in improving the programmatic coherence of their party, and for reformers' concerns about congressional power. In practice, the policy committees did little for the Democrats in 1946–52 but did help Republicans challenge the president, at least while Taft led the committee during the Truman administration.

The initial impetus for party policy committees came from reformers in both parties who believed the committees would strengthen Congress. Policy committees would help Congress frame a coordinated agenda of its own, rather than relying upon executive initiatives. For example, Voorhis argued that Congress has "largely abdicated its most essential function, namely, that of devising on its own motion long-range legislative programs" (Joint Committee 1945, 29). Asserting that reversing this abdication was the "key to the future position of the Congress in our scheme of government," Voorhis claimed policy committees would finally allow Congress to devise "broad legislative programs, with the whole overall national picture in view" (28). Similarly, Claude Pepper (D-Fla.) noted that policy committees would "fix more authority for the determination of party policy in the Congress" as opposed to the White House (Joint Committee 1945, 848). Robert Heller of the nonpartisan National Planning Association—the author of a report entitled *Strengthening the Congress* that received much favorable attention from reformers (Robinson 1954)—testified that policy committees would provide "coordination and planning," allowing Congress to "formulate [policy] effectively and get something done" (Joint Committee 1945, 849). Heller labeled policy committees "the capstone" of his plan for strengthening the legislative branch (844).

In addition to promoting congressional power, policy committees also promised to serve liberals' ideological interests. With the Rules Committee and several other legislative committees in the hands of the conservative coalition, policy committees offered a mechanism for the national Democratic party, which was largely controlled by liberals, to impose some discipline on conservative party members. Thus, liberal Democrats Voorhis, Kefauver, and Albert Gore Sr. of Tennessee were among the leading advocates of policy committees (Cooper 1988, 238–40). Liberal advocacy groups, such as the Union for Democratic Action (which in 1947 became Americans for Democratic Action), also endorsed policy committees as a means to "fix the locus of party responsibility for legislative action on a national level" (Joint Committee 1945, 931). The fear that policy committees would promote a liberal agenda likely explains why conservative Eugene Cox objected so heatedly to their creation. Cox expressed the fear that a majority party policy committee would become a "supercommittee" that would put other "committees in a strait-jacket" (Joint Committee 1945, 846). Cox understood that liberals' calls for strengthened parties threatened his collaboration with Republicans against liberal policy initiatives.

Reformist desire to strengthen congressional parties coincided with Taft's interest in developing a well-funded, active power base from which he could frame a Republican program. The story of the GOP Policy Committee actually goes back to 1944, when the Republicans revived their long-dormant Steering Committee. When Senate Republican floor leader Charles McNary of Oregon died in February 1944, Taft was a logical candidate for floor leader. But Taft did not want the post and instead successfully pressed for a Steering Committee that would develop Republican policies (Drury 1963; Patterson 1972).

The mere existence of a steering committee did not necessarily portend much action. The Senate Democratic Steering Committee was inactive throughout this period, and the Senate Republican Steering Committee of the 1920s did not play a significant legislative role (Jewell and Patterson 1966, 191). From the start, however, Taft used the Steering Committee "to shape a party image far more aggressive than it had been under the mild-mannered McNary" (Patterson 1972, 267). Taft hired a well-regarded political scientist, George Smith, as executive secretary and asked fellow Republicans to submit topics for discussion. The committee debated policy issues and formulated Republican legislative proposals (Joint Committee 1945, 361). For example, in 1946 Taft persuaded the Steering Committee to recommend six amendments to Truman's proposal requesting authority to draft strikers. Although the president's request had passed the House 306 to 13, Taft successfully convinced the Senate to substitute a much modified bill (*Post*, May 29, 1946, 1; May 30, 1946, 1; Patterson 1972, 307).

Acting as an entrepreneur, Taft drew upon the reformist ferment of 1945–46 to obtain more staff for the GOP Steering Committee. Testifying before the La Follette–Monroney committee, he emphasized improving the central research staff for the Senate GOP as opposed to seeking minority staff on the standing committees. When told that House Republicans wanted minority clerks for all major committees, Taft replied that "in the House it may be better to do it that way. In the Senate, I think it is better to have the minority conference have a research staff" (Joint Committee 1945, 226; see also 376–77). Senator Owen Brewster (R-Maine), who testified after Taft, disputed this point, arguing, "I am not at all as enthusiastic about exactly the way [Taft's] proposal has worked out, or would be likely to work out. . . . I believe the minority in the various committees should be the ones to whom the collective minority should look" (230). As in other cases discussed in this chapter, rank-and-file concern for enhancing committees conflicted with more purely partisan interests. But in this instance, the settlement provided staffing both for committees and for the Senate parties.[58]

After the Senate approved the policy committees, Republicans converted their Steering Committee into a new, better-funded Policy Committee. During Taft's chairmanship, the Policy Committee met weekly and discussed a wide variety of issues. After each of its meetings, Taft would announce "his 'impression' that this or that had been 'the general view' of the session" (White 1954, 60–61). The committee did not make decisions that were binding on party members; instead, it sought positions on issues where Republican divisions were not terribly serious. These positions were then transmitted to all Senate Republicans. However, the record of the committee in enlisting members behind its positions was mixed. Patterson (1972, 348) argues that the Policy Committee was "the chief source of [Taft's] power and the fount of most official positions taken by Senate Republicans during his tenure." Similarly, Lester (1969, 100) maintains that Taft "dominated the committee and through it dominated the policies of the congressional Republicans." Jewell and Patterson

(1966, 196) are more circumspect: during Taft's years as chairman (1944–52), there were "instances of Republican senators giving unanimous or virtually unanimous support to a recommendation of the Policy Committee concerning a measure that would not normally generate such unity; in a few cases its recommendations were ignored."[59]

The Policy Committee was significant for the institutional structure of the Senate because it provided Taft with important resources for party leadership in a decentralized, committee-centered era. Unlike Democratic leaders Alben Barkley of Kentucky and Sam Rayburn, Taft's leadership was not based on close personal ties with members. Instead, it depended on his expertise on issues and on his forceful advocacy of his positions (Patterson 1972). This approach required the sort of staff assistance that was plentiful in the executive branch but that simply was not available to party leaders in either chamber before 1946. By building a high-quality, central research staff—something that the Democrats neglected to do with their policy committee funding (Kammerer 1951a, 55–56; Bone 1968, 177)—Taft strengthened party influence over members, who otherwise would have depended on committee staffs for information.

Moreover, the GOP Policy Committee served as a forum where leading party members could find grounds for agreement. This was particularly important because Taft recognized that, when his party gained a majority in the Senate in 1947, "it needed an organized program with which to confront the Truman administration. He decided that the Policy Committee could provide the leadership and the staff to achieve this goal" (Jewell 1959, 968). The presence of a liberal Democrat in the White House helps explain why the Policy Committee was deemed essential to Republican legislative (and in turn electoral) success. Following Eisenhower's election in 1952, Taft remarked to a friend that he did not mind abandoning the Policy Committee chairmanship to serve as floor leader, because "when our party controls the White House most of the Republican policy is made there anyhow" (quoted in White 1954, 215).

Therefore, the GOP Policy Committee provided an element of coordinated party influence in a Senate otherwise lacking in formal party devices. Taft had capitalized on a conjunction of diverse factors to make this institutional innovation possible: reformist desire to strengthen congressional parties, the presence of a Democrat in the White House, and a Senate Republican party with important but manageable divisions. Taft used the committee to push a program through the Senate in the 80th Congress (1947–48) that could have helped both the party's image and his own reputation. Unfortunately for Taft and the Senate Republicans, House Republicans deemed key elements of this program too liberal. Had the House Republicans accepted Taft's aid-to-education and housing bills in anticipation of the 1948 campaign, Truman's accusation that the 80th Congress was a "do-nothing" Congress might not have rung true (Patterson 1972). The problem, of course, is that the success of a Senate party-building device depends in part on House members who might have very different plans for constructing a beneficial party image.

Weekly Leadership Meetings with the President

The onset of weekly leadership meetings at the White House was also a party-based change. Starting in 1937, Democratic leaders in the House and Senate met on a weekly basis with Presidents Roosevelt and then Truman to plan their party's program. Republicans continued the regular meetings when Eisenhower became president, and the Democrats followed suit after retaking the White House in 1960 (Ripley 1983, 232; Lester 1969). This was an informal innovation that did not involve a majority vote on the floor or in either party's caucus. Nonetheless, it constituted an important change in leadership instruments. As discussed below, the meetings brought congressional party leaders into closer consultation with the president, helping to institutionalize a new understanding of the leaders' responsibilities.[60]

The leadership meetings served a single interest: protecting the president's party, which for all but two years of this period meant, on the congressional side, majority party Democrats. The Democrats' reputation had suffered during Roosevelt's second term because FDR had insistently pushed his policies on a recalcitrant Congress and its deeply divided Democratic majority (Barone 1990; CQ 1982). The leadership meetings marked a shift in Roosevelt's relations with Democratic leaders: in the past, he had dictated to party leaders, rather than consulting with them, and at times even surprised them with his proposals. This lack of coordination became intolerable as the administration's strength in Congress waned amid the conservative resurgence of 1937 (Lester 1969). In November 1937, recently elected majority leader Sam Rayburn initiated the weekly meetings after several embarrassing episodes in which FDR's surprise announcements had made Speaker Bankhead "look a fool" (Alsop and Kintner 1941; Riddick 1946, 161–62).[61]

In recent years, political scientists have downplayed the possibility that congressional leaders would consider themselves responsible to the president; after all, the membership, not the president, selects the leaders (Sinclair 1990, 134). Nonetheless, Roosevelt was firmly in control during his first term as the White House shaped legislative strategies and tactics for the Democratic party (Ripley 1967; Barone 1990). Roosevelt's significant role in the 1937 selection of Rayburn and Barkley as party floor leaders underscores Democratic leaders' partial responsibility to the president (*Time*, December 14, 1936, 15, August 2, 1937, 10; MacNeil 1963).

There is much evidence that the leaders themselves were coming to view their role as largely one of aiding the president, and that party leaders were increasingly evaluated based on the fate of presidential programs (MacNeil 1963, 34–35; Huitt 1961, 336; Peters 1990, 124).[62] Voorhis complained in 1944 (648) that in recent years "strong" presidents had come "to expect majority party leaders in Congress to function principally as agents of the White House on Capitol Hill, rather than leaders of Congress developing and pushing through congressional legislative programs. . . . In consequence the Congress has been to a degree deprived of independent leadership." In 1959, David Truman (1959b, 298) argued that there was no "categorical" answer to the question of whether the party leaders of the 1930s to 1950s had been principally loyal to the rank and file or to the president.

As long as the vast majority of congressional Democrats supported the president's goals, there was little potential for conflict between legislative leaders' long-established role as party leaders and their newer role as presidential lieutenants. Roosevelt's first-term successes had translated into stunning election victories for House and Senate Democrats. Moreover, Roosevelt's popularity made dissident Democrats reluctant to oppose him publicly. By the end of 1937, however, the changed conditions noted at the opening of this chapter encouraged many Democrats to oppose the president openly (Patterson 1967). Democratic House and Senate leaders now had to mediate between two very different conceptions of the image that the Democratic party should cultivate. The weekly meetings helped to manage this conflict. Party leaders Rayburn and Barkley, who took part in these meetings from the beginning, demonstrated that legislative leaders could be presidential lieutenants even in this difficult situation.

But amid fierce congressional-executive tensions, the role of presidential lieutenant both elevated and undermined the party leaders in Congress. The leadership meetings elevated party leaders by placing them at the center of communications with the president, thereby forcing both the congressional membership and the president to rely on them to transmit and interpret information across the branches. Truman (1959b, 296) argues that "the mere fact of the meetings, uniquely composed as they are and normally conducted without even the presence of staff, presumptively gives the congressional participants 'inside' intelligence concerning both the President and the other chamber that . . . can be a source of influence." Moreover, the meetings enhanced leaders' national status because they became identified as the Democratic party's legislative spokesmen (Truman 1959a, 690; Lester 1969). Thus, the *New York Times*, discussing the resumption of the meetings in January 1949 after a hiatus during the Republican-controlled 80th Congress, commented that "this renewal of a custom long cherished by the Democrats in Congress pleased [the leadership] immensely" (January 1, 1949, 2).

At the same time, the weekly meetings reinforced the leaders' dependence on the president (Truman 1959b, 257). The low congressional standing of Presidents Roosevelt and Truman for much of the 1937–52 period meant that being a presidential spokesman often forced leaders into unwelcome adventures for which the leverage provided by presidential support was inadequate. This problem was less severe for Rayburn than for Barkley. Even as Rayburn did much to "establish the tradition of legislative deference to the presidency" (Peters 1990, 124), his strong ties with senior committee leaders meant that his authority did not solely depend on the president. Barkley lacked such ties and was regarded by his colleagues (and by himself) as "the president's man" (Ritchie 1991; Patterson 1967, 148). His very selection as leader would have been impossible if not for Roosevelt's support, and thus his colleagues viewed him as "an exalted White House errand boy" (Patterson 1967, 148). While Rayburn and majority leader McCormack were considered reasonably effective leaders despite their severely divided party, Barkley was the first in a series of three Democratic floor leaders in the Senate who lacked influence and were therefore widely regarded as weak and ineffective (Ritchie 1991; Huitt 1961).[63] The position of Senate Democratic floor leader did not regain respectability until Lyndon Johnson took the post at the start of the Eisenhower administration (Evans and Novak 1966; Huitt 1961). The weekly leadership conferences did not cause Barkley's low stature in the Senate; however, they did contribute to the ambiguity surrounding his position as a leader.[64]

The weekly meetings were a major step institutionalizing party leaders' developing role as agents of the president. Designed to prevent surprises from the White House, the meetings tied party leaders ever closer to the president. But this did not displace leaders' traditional role as agents of the rank and file (Truman 1959a). Members continued to expect party leaders to act as their agents and not simply to represent the president. The effectiveness of the weekly leadership meetings in promoting Democratic party interests depended on whether the leaders could use this new institution to reconcile the competing demands of congressional and presidential party leadership. Rayburn was relatively successful in negotiating the contradictions inherent in his dual responsibility, but Barkley allowed his perceived responsibilities to the president to engulf his leadership.

The three party-based changes adopted in this period do not alter the basic picture of a congressional authority structure that had been reshaped to fight the executive and to bolster the cross-party conservative coalition, often with substantial costs for majority party Democrats. One of the three changes, the creation of Senate party policy committees, primarily bene-fited the Republicans, who were in the minority throughout most of this period. A second change, the 21-day rule, was repealed by the cross-party conservative coalition after a mere two years and even while in force still left the conservative-controlled Rules Committee with substantial power. Finally, the weekly leadership meetings helped party leaders maintain a measure of influence as communication focal points, but the meetings also heightened the tension surrounding Democratic leaders' position as agents of both rank-and-file party members and the president.

CONCLUSIONS

The conservative coalition wrought major institutional changes in 1937–52. But it was by no means alone in shaping congressional development. On several occasions, liberals worked with conservatives to pass important innovations designed to boost congressional power. Partisan coalitions also enjoyed a few significant, though limited, successes.

Not only were different interests important in different cases, but multi-ple collective interests typically drove each individual change. These case studies once again show that the potential for a single change to serve multiple member interests has critical implications for institutional devel-opment. Among other things, this potential facilitates institutional changes that benefit coalitions that lack the advantages of a party organiza-tion. Several cases illustrate that entrepreneurs can often harness individual members' "narrow" interests in reelection, improved perks, and personal power to bring about institutional changes that also serve the interests of broad, cross-party coalitions. Institutional innovations serve as common carriers in part because entrepreneurs deliberately design changes that ad-vance a range of collective interests. Thus, reformers included a pay raise in the Legislative Reorganization Act of 1946 to appease members threat-ened by the committee consolidation. Similarly, the new investigative committees gained support because of both the substantive policies they promoted and members' interest in molding an authority structure that provided them with numerous entrepreneurial opportunities.

Entrepreneurs themselves are often willing to expend the energy and resources necessary to establish these new power bases in part because they stand to obtain special benefits from their creation. For example, Martin Dies and his colleagues on the Dies committee promoted their own ca-reers while forging an institutional power base benefiting congressional conservatives. Similarly, Taft simultaneously gained personal power and promoted the GOP's partisan goals through the Senate Policy Committee. Even in the case of the JCAE, which I argue is less clearly a common carrier for multiple interests, the ambitions of such committee members as Brien McMahon and Clinton Anderson pushed the committee to capitalize fully on its potential (Green and Rosenthal 1963; Thomas 1956).

These cases not only highlight the pluralism of member goals but also the disjointed character of institutional development. Conflicts among competing interests often compromise changes and build tensions into specific institutions. Thus, members' interest in defending the prerogatives of standing committees led them to delete important features of the Reorganization Act that had been intended to improve congressional capacity by imposing quality controls on the committees (e.g., the personnel director) and by better coordinating committee efforts (e.g., the legislative budget, policy committees, and legislative-executive council).[65] Although the Senate Republican Policy Committee did provide some coordination under Taft, the GOP was in the minority for most of this period, and the lack of cooperation between House and Senate Republicans when the GOP was briefly in the majority undermined the success of the Senate experiment with policy committees. Tensions among competing interests are also important in the development of specific institutions over time: these case studies show that party leaders' roles and the regime governing special rules each embodied contradictions because innovations were layered on top of preexisting institutions intended to serve different goals.

The pervasive tendency for multiple collective interests to influence institutional development means that specific institutions rarely constitute coherent solutions to a specific collective goods problem. This in turn limits the power of theories that use a single collective interest to explain key features of legislative organization. As noted above, Krehbiel's nonpartisan, informational theory fares better than partisan or distributive accounts in this period. There is plentiful evidence that the majority party had only weak influence on institutional design in 1937–52. Furthermore, the sectoral interests identified by distributive theorists, while relevant to the Truman committee, did not play a significant role in the other changes. By contrast, the committee consolidation and staffing increase under the Reorganization Act and the creation of the JCAE are clearly related to the informational concerns identified by Krehbiel, and conservative successes with the Rules Committee, repeal of the 21-day rule, and various investigations each reflect the importance of floor majorities.

Yet a narrow focus on informational concerns and the policy preferences of floor majorities deflects attention from other key features of institutional development in this period. Most notably, members' interest in plentiful institutional power bases both contributed to and compromised efforts to increase congressional capacity and power. Entrepreneurial members' electoral and power interests provided much of the impetus behind the investigations boom, which simultaneously promised to help re-store Congress as a coequal branch of government. In the short term, the investigations successfully fought executive encroachments. But the failure of the House, and especially the Senate, to exert effective control over its ambitious members allowed excesses that ultimately undermined the credibility of these investigations and damaged congressional prestige.

More generally, the changes intended to improve Congress's institutional position reinforced an authority structure that dispersed power among a decentralized collection of standing committees. Individual committees gained resources to check the executive, but the ability of party leaders, and even floor majorities, to channel the energies of the committees did not keep pace. The result was a series of success stories in controlling the executive—numerous investigations, the Joint Committee on Atomic Energy, reduced reliance on the executive for staff assistance—but also a widespread perception that Congress as a whole lacked the leadership to compete consistently with the president and bureaucracy.

A focus on the tensions among multiple collective interests helps to make sense of patterns of institutional development that other theories simply do not encompass. Krehbiel's informational model, like Cox and McCubbins's partisan theory, does not grapple with the possibility that Congress will, at times, lose considerable power and prestige to the executive branch. Nor do these theories lead us to anticipate the difficulties that confront would-be reformers seeking to improve Congress's institutional position in response to these periodic declines. Yet the loss of congressional power and prestige is a recurring theme driving key episodes of institutional reform over the past two hundred years of congressional history. Furthermore, these episodes of reform typically involve competing interests beyond Congress's institutional position, such that the solutions devised by members often have ambiguous implications for congressional capacity, power, and prestige.

Institutional Development, 1970–1989: A Return to Party Government or the Triumph of Individualism?

THE 1970–89 PERIOD began with the conservative coalition still a potent force in congressional politics. Nixon's recent election had generated considerable speculation that conservative Democrats and their Republican allies would speedily recover from the policy setbacks they had suffered at the hands of Lyndon Johnson in the mid-1960s. Even more ominous for liberals, majority party Democrats suffered from weak and aging leadership. John McCormack (D-Mass.), who served as Speaker until January 1971, was widely criticized for haphazard scheduling and poor strategic planning (Bibby and Davidson 1972). McCormack and his leadership team also supported the Vietnam War, estranging them from a growing number of Democrats. Senate leader Mike Mansfield (D-Mont.), though a foe of the war, eschewed personal power and fostered an environment in which the individual senator was sovereign (Baker 1991). The prospect of Democrats' unifying behind strong leadership to combat a Republican president seemed remote at best.

Yet less than two decades later, during the 100th Congress (1987–88), Speaker Jim Wright (D-Tex.) and the Democrats scored an impressive array of victories over Ronald Reagan. The Speaker's forceful leadership reminded commentators of not only Wright's own hero, Sam Rayburn, but also of "czars" Thomas Reed and Joseph Cannon (Barry 1989; Peters 1990).

This chapter explores the immense changes that reshaped the congressional landscape after 1970. I identified thirteen significant institutional changes during 1970–1989:

1. Adopting the Legislative Reorganization Act of 1970
2. Opening up the committee process in the House and Senate through the 1973 and 1975 rules changes requiring committees to meet in public
3. Augmenting the resources of House subcommittees, particularly the Democratic caucus's adopting the subcommittee "bill of rights" in January 1973
4. Creating a new budget process under the Congressional Budget and Impoundment Control Act of 1974

5. Authorizing the Speaker to refer bills to multiple House committees

6. Enhancing the Speaker's role in making committee assignments through House Democratic caucus reforms in December 1974

7. Overthrowing seniority in the House, most prominently by deposing three committee chairmen in January 1975

8. Granting additional committee staff to junior senators in 1975

9. Restructuring the Senate committee system through the 1977 Stevenson committee reforms

10. The boom in Senate obstruction, as manifested in rising numbers of filibusters, the development of the postcloture filibuster, and the institutionalization of "holds"[1]

11. Increasing use of restrictive special rules that limited amending opportunities in the House after 1979

12. The resurgence of the speakership after 1983, particularly with Wright's leadership in 1987–88

13. Creation of the Conservative Opportunity Society in 1983 by militant House Republicans led by Newt Gingrich (R-Ga.)

Appendix B.4 summarizes the votes that directly related to these changes, and table 5.1 identifies the member interests and effects associated with each change.

The 1970–89 period provides further evidence that disjointed pluralism characterizes congressional development. As in the other periods examined, multiple collective interests typically shaped each institutional change. For example, the rise in subcommittee power in the House served as a common carrier for junior members' interest in a broader distribution of power and liberal Democrats' interest in undermining conservative committee chairmen. Once again, entrepreneurs played a critical role in devising such common carriers: in this case, liberal Democrats garnered support for their attack on the chairmen by appealing to subcommittee leaders' power base goals.

In several other cases, the tensions among competing interests forced compromises that undercut the success of institutional changes. Thus, the Budget Act of 1974, though initiated by members concerned about improving congressional capacity in the wake of Nixon's challenges to the legislative branch, included concessions to liberals fearful of spending cuts and to authorization committees protective of their power. These concessions undermined the new budget committees' ability to coordinate Congress's fiscal policy.

The Budget Act also illustrates the third claim about disjointed pluralism, namely that institutions develop through superimposing new arrangements on top of preexisting structures designed to serve different

TABLE 5.1 Summary of Collective Interests Associated with Institutional Changes, 1970–1989

Case	Primary Interest	Common Carrier for Other Interests?	Compromised by Other Interests?	Control Coalition Shaping Change	Main Effects of Change
Legislative Reorganization Act of 1970	Individual power bases (junior members)	Congressional capacity and power; policy (liberals); minority party	Some concessions made to chairmen	Bipartisan reformist	Made legislative process more open; increased floor amendments
Open committee meetings, 1973, 1975	Congressional prestige	Individual power bases; reelection (position-taking platforms)		Bipartisan reformist	Opened committee process; helped disperse power
Empowering of House subcommittees	Individual power bases (junior Democrats)	Policy (liberals); majority party		Majority party (liberal Democrats)	Undermined chair influence; dispersed power
Budget Act of 1974	Congressional capacity and power	Majority party (Democrats' opposition to impoundments)	Existing committee jurisdictions preserved (individual power bases)	Universalistic	Created centralizing potential, not realized until 1980s
Multiple referrals, 1974	Congressional capacity and power	Majority party; individual power bases		Universalistic	By 1980s, combined with other changes to boost majority leaders
Democratic committee assignment shift, 1974	Majority party (effectiveness)	Liberal interests	Large, diverse committee to do assignments (individual power bases)	Majority party (liberal Democrats)	Increased party leader role

Case	Primary Interest	Common Carrier for Other Interests?	Compromised by Other Interests?	Control Coalition Shaping Change	Main Effects of Change
Deposing of chairmen, 1975	Majority party (effectiveness)	Liberal interests; individual power bases (junior members)		Majority party (liberal Democrats)	Significantly reduced chairmen's power
Senate staffing, 1975	Individual power bases (junior senators)	Minority party; Senate capacity and power		Bipartisan reformist (junior senators)	Dispersed power in Senate; boosted individual entrepreneurship
Stevenson Committee reforms, 1977	Senate capacity and power	Individual power bases (junior senators); minority party (staffing)	Several committees preserved (electoral and power base interests)	Bipartisan reformist (junior senators)	Made more orderly comm. system; added to junior member resources
Boom in Senate obstruction	Individual power bases/reelection	Minority party	Statutory debate limits; cloture changes (congressional capacity)	Universalistic	Made Senate harder to manage; dispersed power
Rise of restrictive rules in House	Majority party	Policy (liberals); Congressional capacity		Majority party	Increased majority party agenda control
Revitalization of speakership	Majority party	Policy (liberals)		Majority party	Significantly increased centralization, leadership influence
Conservative Opportunity Society	Minority party	Conservative interests; individual power bases (junior Republicans)		Junior minority members	Promoted guerrilla tactics; tarnished House and Democrats

purposes. The budget reforms of 1974 did not dismantle the preexisting system of authorization, appropriations, and revenue committees. Rather, the reforms left those standing committees intact and added budget committees, annual budget resolutions, and the reconciliation process to the mix (Rieselbach 1994, 67). For the budget committees to coordinate effectively the government's fiscal policy, incursions into the jurisdictions of these turf-conscious committees would inevitably be required (Schick 1980a). The result has been recurrent jurisdictional conflict. The Budget Act did not settle how Congress would handle budgeting; rather, it created new rules to structure the battle for control and new actors to take part in that battle.

The 1970–89 period also provides support for the fourth claim about disjointed pluralism: innovations designed to serve one set of member interests repeatedly provoked coalitions with competing interests to enact changes of their own. The reforms that began with the Legislative Reorganization Act of 1970 further fragmented power in the already decentralized Congress. The resulting difficulties stirred a dramatic response in the House, where Democrats enacted a series of institutional changes to reverse course. But individual members' commitment to their power bases precluded eliminating the earlier decentralizing changes. Instead, Democrats added new mechanisms for party control to this fragmented authority structure. Even as Wright raised the speakership to new heights, he and his successors continually struggled against the individualistic assumptions that had become embedded in House institutions. Furthermore, the Democrats' successes in reviving party government led to a GOP reaction similar to the Democrats' response to "czar" rule in 1909–10: devastating attacks by Gingrich and his Conservative Opportunity Society on the House and its majority party. Indeed, this pattern of innovation and response resembles the 1890–1910 period, in which majority party bids to centralize power engendered changes that safeguarded individual members' influence (see chapter 2). The evidence from 1970 to 1989 therefore reinforces my argument that members' multiple interests give congressional development a disjointed, pluralistic cast.

On the whole, three quite different clusters of member interests drove institutional development in 1970–89. Liberal Democrats' partisan and ideological interests formed one cluster, motivating such changes as the increased use of restrictive rules and the revitalized speakership. David Rohde and John Aldrich have argued that these changes helped bring about a new era of vibrant party government, one that recalls the earlier GOP experiment with strong party government in 1890–1910 (Rohde 1991; Aldrich and Rohde 1995). But other changes partially offset the Democrats' partisan reforms. In particular, individual members' interest in a broader allocation of influence contributed to several changes that dispersed power, such as the Reorganization Act of 1970. Furthermore, members' interest in congressional capacity, power, and prestige motivated still other changes, including the Budget Act of 1974. These three reformist thrusts, though at times compatible, generated innovations that in important ways were contradictory.

In this chapter, I first analyze the changes intended to strengthen congressional capacity and power. I then consider the changes motivated by members' personal power goals, followed by House Democrats' party-building moves and the GOP response. I show that while the majority party, particularly in the House, gained a much more significant role in steering the legislative process, the limitations of the Democrats' flirtation with party government are equally noteworthy.

CONGRESSIONAL CAPACITY, POWER, AND PRESTIGE

Among other things, the 1970s were a time of congressional resurgence (Sundquist 1981). Prior to these reforms, it had become commonplace to bemoan the decline in congressional power. Members appeared unable to influence U.S. policy in Southeast Asia and unwilling to stop Nixon's use of impoundments to chip away at their power of the purse. In January 1973, *Time* magazine even made the "Crisis in Congress" its cover story, arguing that the legislative branch "has been forfeiting its powers for years. . . . It no longer effectively checks the President" (January 15, 1973, 12). *Time* interviewed current members, scholars, and civic leaders, who generally agreed that restoring Congress's institutional standing required major changes. Amid such concerns, members undertook a concerted effort to reassert congressional prerogatives. Just as the dramatic increase in presidential power under Franklin Roosevelt had spurred a congressional call-to-arms, Lyndon Johnson's and Richard Nixon's challenges to congressional authority provoked a similar response.

Congress-centered interests motivated four institutional changes in the 1970s. Members adopted the Budget Act, the multiple referral rule, and the Stevenson committee reforms in order to improve Congress's policymaking capacity, which members believed critical for safeguarding congressional power.[2] A fourth case, rules requiring open committee meetings, aimed primarily to improve Congress's sagging prestige. As in 1937–52, in each case members of both parties worked together to defend Congress's institutional standing.

Nonetheless, these changes did not simply serve institutional interests. The Budget Act and multiple referral rule had significant partisan overtones, while the Stevenson reforms and the open meetings rules garnered support from junior members eager to disperse power. The long-term impact of these changes depended on the compatibility of these other interests with congressional capacity, power, and prestige.

Budget Act of 1974

Conflicts with Richard Nixon over fiscal policy and his extensive use of impoundments to limit spending provoked Congress to adopt the Budget Act of 1974. The act created budget committees in the House and Senate and charged them with proposing budget resolutions that set spending and revenue totals. These budget resolutions would not require the signature of the president. Annual reconciliation bills would then enact the specific tax and spending changes required to meet the budget resolution targets. The Budget Act also limited the power of the president to impound funds and created the Congressional Budget Office as a source of independent expertise for the House and Senate.[3]

Most specialized studies of the Budget Act have emphasized concerns about congressional capacity and power (Ellwood 1985; LeLoup 1989; Palazzolo 1992; see also Fischer 1977). Before 1974, Congress had no institutional mechanism for coordinating revenue and spending decisions. Economic troubles, rising deficits, and increased levels of "backdoor" and "uncontrollable" spending led many members to view this inability "to take an overview of the budget . . . as a fundamental flaw" (LeLoup 1989, 276).[4] Nixon exacerbated this sentiment by repeatedly attacking Congress for its fiscal irresponsibility and by drastically expanding the use of impoundments. LeLoup (1989, 276) notes that, faced with such presidential defiance, the "vast majority of senators and representatives agreed in principle that a new budget process was essential if Congress was to retain a meaningful role in making fiscal and budget policy." During floor debate on the reform bill, members of both parties and all ideological factions repeatedly returned to the theme of congressional capacity and power. GOP conference chairman John Anderson (R-Ill.) declared that "this will prove to be one of the most monumental reassertions of congressional prerogatives in this century" (CR, December 4, 1973, 39344). His more conservative colleague, David Martin (R-Nebr.), noted that he too supported the bill "because it provides a mechanism by which Congress can play a more responsible role in the budget process" (CR, July 18, 1974, 19676). Similarly, liberal Democrat Al Ullman of Oregon proclaimed that the new budget process would make Congress "a more respected institution and a more effective partner in government" (CR, December 4, 1973, 39348).

Nixon's public attacks on the Democratic-controlled Congress linked Democrats' partisan interests to bipartisan concerns about congressional capacity. As the majority party, Democrats feared that they would be blamed for Congress's lack of a fiscal policy. They also viewed budget reform as a weapon against Nixon's impoundment of funds for social programs. Many Republicans, by contrast, believed that impoundments should be allowed under some circumstances to supplement congressional controls on spending. Thus, the most sharply partisan element of the reform battle concerned impoundments. Southern and nonsouthern Democrats united to adopt strong anti-impoundment provisions over the opposition of a narrow majority of Republicans (see appendix B.4). A logit analysis of the House vote on Martin's unsuccessful amendment to delete impoundment control from the budget bill shows that Democrats were significantly more likely to vote to retain the anti-impoundment provisions than were Republicans (b = −1.91, SE = .87), even controlling for first-dimension NOMINATE scores and region. First-dimension NOMINATE scores were also significant (b = 9.44; SE = 1.81), suggesting that the policy goals of liberals reinforced Democrats' partisan interests.[5]

Nonetheless, partisan interests by no means dominated the budget reform fight.[6] As appendix B.4 shows, excepting impoundment control, most of the key votes on the budget bill were not party votes. Indeed, Democrats were seriously divided on many specific issues, and Republicans provided much support for the act as a whole (see below). Liberal Democrats were reluctant to support budget reform because they feared it might lead to reduced domestic spending. That same assumption engendered considerable bipartisan conservative support for reform. Following liberal successes in using backdoor spending to evade the appropriations process, the Budget Act "can be regarded as an attempt to establish new controls [on spending] in place of the older ones" (Schick 1980a, 311; see also Ellwood and Thurber 1981, 250). The Joint Study Committee—a panel dominated by tax and appropriations committee members from both chambers—tailored the initial reform proposal to conservatives' objectives. The JSC proposal assigned two-thirds of the seats on the newly created budget committees to members of the predominately conservative money committees; it also included provisions that made it harder to increase spending (Schick 1980b).

Needless to say, liberals resisted reforms biased against high spending. They were helped by a confluence of interest with legislative committee members who wanted to protect their power bases and thus opposed centralizing power in the money committees. By guaranteeing that the already powerful tax and appropriations committees would dominate the new budget committees, the JSC proposal cut against the drive to disperse influence in Congress. The Senate responded to these objections by eliminating the requirement that the Senate Budget Committee include members of Appropriations and Finance. The House Rules Committee reduced the money committees' share of seats on the House Budget Committee from two-thirds to less than half, and also provided a unique rotating membership feature: members could serve on the committee for no more than four years out of any ten.[7] This limitation was intended to "preclude the development of entrenched power within the committee. No one was going to make a legislative career out of service on the Budget Committee, and consequently, there would be no burning interest among members to increase greatly the committee's power" (Wander 1984, 22). The term limit provision undermined the effectiveness of the House Budget Committee, but it addressed members' interest in dispersing power and liberals' goal of checking conservative dominance. As the product of competing interests, the new budget process embodied conflicting imperatives: coordinate congressional consideration of spending and revenue decisions, but do not allow a small group of individuals to direct fiscal decisions.

The House Rules Committee made a handful of other changes designed to win over liberals. It dropped most of the provisions that placed special burdens on spending advocates. As alluded to above, the Rules version also appealed to liberals by combining legislation to limit presidential impoundments with the budget reform bill. Liberal Democrats still "really preferred no bill at all, primarily because the programs they favored would probably fare much worse at the hands of a centralized, coordinated budget system. . . . Nevertheless, blocking budget reform entirely appeared to be impossible" (Wander 1984, 20). So they settled for a process that did not overtly discriminate against spending programs and that provided much-sought-after limits on impoundments.

While liberal Democrats worked actively to amend the JSC proposal, Republicans were also involved at each stage of the process. Indeed, the bipartisan Joint Study Committee reported its proposal unanimously (Schick 1980b). When the House Rules Committee revised the measure, its chairman, Richard Bolling (D-Mo.), worked with Appropriations chairman George Mahon (D-Tex.), liberal Democrats, and Republican leader John Rhodes of Arizona to craft a new version (Wander 1984, 20).[8] On the floor, only one minor amendment was adopted, and the resulting bill passed with all but three Republicans and 206 of 226 Democrats voting in favor.

The bill then went to the Senate, where the most important action took place in the Rules and Administration Committee. Rules member and Democratic whip Robert Byrd of West Virginia oversaw delicate negotiations involving staff members from ten Senate committees and the House Appropriations Committee. Byrd sought to make the new process as workable as possible, even inserting a provision that shielded budget resolutions and reconciliation bills from filibusters (Binder and Smith 1997). At the same time, Byrd made changes to defuse fears that the budget committees would infringe on other committees' jurisdictions (Schick 1980b). The resulting bill was approved unanimously by the Rules and Administration Committee. The full Senate adopted the bill on an 80–0 vote, after approving a few conservative amendments that strengthened the controls on spending (Wander 1984). The conference report reconciling the House and Senate versions also gained approval by an overwhelming margin in each chamber, amid praise from members of both parties (see CR, June 18, 1974, 19676; June 21, 1974, 20475).

The rules committees had effectively fashioned a compromise that appealed to a wide range of members and that apparently did little to threaten existing power bases. While the underlying pressure for reform came from members' stake in congressional capacity and power, the bill had to be reconciled with other goals. As Schick (1980b, 80) concludes, Congress accommodated "diverse interests in the Budget Act." But this resulted in an "ambiguous and permissive process" that left much up to future implementation.

The new budget process had a major impact. First, and perhaps most importantly, it created a new set of committees and procedures that were superimposed on the existing structure of authorization, appropriations, and revenue committees. To avoid fierce opposition, the framers of the act respected existing committee power bases, adding a new framework to "the existing decision-making processes, with minimum disruption to established methods and procedures" (CQ Almanac 1974, 146). But the resulting need to gain the cooperation of these entrenched committees made the budget committees' task much more difficult. Schick (1980a, 289) argues that the "coexistence of the old and new centers of power has generated fresh opportunities for strife." The budget committees have repeatedly fought with the appropriations and authorization committees over spending priorities, and with the revenue committees over tax policy and entitlements (Ripley 1983, 431; Schick 1980a). While some inter-committee conflict is inevitable, there is little doubt that had Congress designed a new budget process from scratch, it would not have created so many separate decision-making stages (Sundquist 1981, 438; Rieselbach 1994). But legislative institutions are rarely created de novo; instead, Congress typically must reconcile innovations that address new challenges with members' stake in existing power bases. In this case, Congress added an element of centralization to an otherwise incremental and fragmented process, creating an uneasy amalgamation.

The budget process that has played out since 1974 exemplifies this tension between fragmentation and centralization. Ironically, the greatest triumph for centralization occurred in 1981, when President Reagan, on the advice of former GOP congressman David Stockman, seized upon the budget process to reorder spending priorities. Taking advantage of a precedent set by the House in 1980, Stockman moved to include reconciliation instructions in the first, as opposed to second, budget resolution. This allowed Reagan to package his domestic spending cuts and defense increases early in the process, capitalizing on the momentum from his election victory and "setting the terms of the budget debate entirely to [his] liking" (Rieselbach 1994, 117). Thus, the congressional budget process allowed Republicans and conservative Democrats to impose their priorities on congressional committees while avoiding direct votes on specific spending reductions. Senate Republican leader Howard Baker of Tennessee observed that Reagan's early use of reconciliation produced a budget "that would have been impossible to achieve" through the normal committee process (as quoted in Oleszek 1996, 73).

Beyond Reagan's success in 1981, the new budget process had complex implications for the degree of centralization and partisanship in Congress. In the Senate, bipartisan cooperation characterized the budget process, at least initially. The Senate Budget Committee's first chairman, Edmund Muskie (D-Maine), worked closely with ranking Republican Henry Bellmon of Oklahoma to develop ambitious budget resolutions that could pass on the floor and that would establish the committee as an important player. In the House, bipartisan cooperation proved almost nonexistent. House Republicans appointed archconservatives to the Budget Committee, and Democrats responded in subsequent years by selecting hard-core liberals (Ellwood and Thurber 1981). Furthermore, the term limits placed on House members reduced their incentive to seek the bipartisan cooperation that might have enhanced the committee's independence (Fischer 1977).

The highly partisan votes on House budget resolutions have led some observers to argue that the new budget process strengthened the chamber's party leaders (Davidson 1992). The Democrats have, from the start, linked the budget committee closely to the party's leadership and at times succeeded in using the budget process to help establish their spending priorities (Sinclair 1995b; Kiewiet and McCubbins 1991). But even leaving aside the Democrats' devastating defeat at the hands of Reagan in 1981 —which constitutes the most consequential use of the budget process to date (see Barone 1990; Rieselbach 1994)—the new procedures imposed heavy burdens on majority party Democrats.

Before gaining majority status in 1995, House Republicans rarely took part in shaping budget resolutions and provided few votes to assist their passage. This stemmed in part from the Democrats' partisan approach to the budget process, but it also derived from Republicans' calculation, as Trent Lott (R-Miss.) put it, that "you do not ever get into trouble for those budgets which you vote against" (quoted in Price 1992, 94). The GOP's strategy meant that Democratic leaders had to expend tremendous resources to pass budget bills solely with Democratic votes. Budget resolutions and reconciliation bills require that members cast an explicit vote for or against a specific level of spending, taxes, and deficits. It should not be surprising, then, that in a time of mounting deficits, budget resolutions often presented House Democrats with difficult political problems (Sinclair 1995b, 109). Sundquist (1981, 231) argues that "the congressional budget process created new tensions within each house and intensified divisions within the majority party." Particularly in the House, majority leaders and Budget Committee Democrats "underwent an annual ordeal to frame a resolution acceptable to enough Democrats to win . . . approval." On more than one occasion, leaders had to beg members to vote for distasteful budgets simply to prevent the process from falling apart completely (Sundquist 1981; Barry 1989).

As Reagan's innovative use of reconciliation in 1981 illustrates, the budget process has been far from static since 1974. The Gramm-Rudman Act of 1985, the Budget Enforcement Act of 1990, and the rise of legislative-executive summits have continued to reshape this process. The lasting significance of the 1974 act is that, during an era of democratization and dispersal of power, it added centralizing mechanisms to the fragmented, uncoordinated congressional budget process. But the new coordinating devices were grafted onto the preexisting decentralized structure without removing any of the centrifugal forces that would frustrate budget-makers' efforts. The bipartisan leadership of Muskie and Bellmon allowed the Senate Budget Committee to compete effectively with other committees. But in the House, majority party Democrats gained only a tenuous hold on the process, which gave the party new tools to assert its priorities, while also generating expectations that the party could not always meet.

Multiple Referrals

Less than four months after Congress enacted the Budget Act, the House empowered the Speaker to refer bills to multiple committees. This change was one of several reforms emanating from the Democratic caucus's Committee on Organization, Study, and Review, chaired by Julia Hansen of Washington. Scholars generally do not treat the Hansen committee package as an important change: it amounted to a much-watered-down version of changes initially drafted by Richard Bolling's Select Committee on Committees (see CQ 1982, 184, and Deering and Smith 1997, 38, on the Hansen reforms). But one element of the Hansen reforms, the multiple referral rule, has had substantial implications for House operations.[9]

Supporters of multiple referrals hoped to enhance Congress's capacity to deal with policy problems that encompassed several committees' jurisdictions. The change also served Democrats' partisan interest in strengthening the speakership, though this was less salient than concerns about congressional capacity. In addition, multiple referrals responded to members' power base interests by delegating major legislation to more committees and thus to more members. While these origins made multiple referrals relatively noncontroversial, by the mid-1980s the new procedure had become an important tool in majority party leaders' arsenal.

Member concerns about the adequacy of the committee system led the Bolling committee to include multiple referrals in a wide-ranging package of procedural and jurisdictional changes presented in April 1974. In their detailed study of multiple referrals, Davidson, Oleszek, and Kephart (1988, 5) conclude that the procedure was "intended to bring the wisdom and perspective of several different committees to bear upon complex public issues, to make the committee system more flexible in considering policies that cut across jurisdictional boundaries, and to encourage inter-committee cooperation and contain jurisdictional conflicts." Collie and Cooper (1989, 262) add that reformers believed multiple referrals would enhance lateral connections across committees. In an increasingly dynamic environment, such lateral relations permit "expertise to be brought to bear more flexibly" and effectively (see also Oleszek 1996, 103).[10] Consistent with an emphasis on congressional capacity, Lloyd Meeds (D-Wash.) claimed on the floor that the absence of multiple referrals is one of the "greatest deterrents to this Congress [*sic*] meeting its modern jurisdictional requirements" and asserted that the change would do more than any other Bolling committee proposal "to make the House function properly" (CR, October 8, 1974, 34406). David Martin, the ranking Republican on the Bolling committee, agreed that the new process would "alleviate the difficulties that we get into of jurisdictional disputes between committees" (CR, October 8, 1974, 34454).

Partisan motivations also contributed to the change in 1974. Bolling, who had long favored expanding the Speaker's power, played a major role in drafting the multiple referral rule (House Select Committee on Committees 1973, 287–92). According to a longtime aide, Bolling sought multiple referrals in large part because he believed they "would strengthen the Speaker's hand" (cited in King 1997, 100; see also Davidson, Oleszek, and Kephart 1988, 5). To Bolling, expanding the Speaker's power was instrumental to developing a stronger, more effective majority party (see Bolling 1968).

But the partisan element of this change was fairly limited. Since Republicans had equal representation on the Bolling committee, they could have easily kept the new rule out of the committee's package of proposed changes. But few members appear to have foreseen that the rule would ultimately benefit majority party leaders. Instead, the Bolling committee's deliberations suggest that the multiple referrals provision was not controversial (House Select Committee on Committees 1973, 279–95, 428–35; CR, October 8, 1974, 34454). The sole criticism on the floor came from conservative Republican Robert Bauman of Maryland, who moved to strike what he called "these new and unprecedented powers" for the Speaker (CR, October 8, 1974, 34406). Bauman's opposition supports a partisan or ideological explanation for the change, but no other Republicans spoke for the Bauman amendment, which was defeated on a voice vote (CR, October 8, 1974, 34407). It is also noteworthy that both the Hansen committee's substitute and Nebraska Republican David Martin's alternative proposal included language on multiple referrals similar to the Bolling committee's.[11] This again suggests a broad, bipartisan consensus that the House needed multiple referrals.

Members' power base interests also likely played a significant role in this case. The Bolling committee's hearings suggest that some members believed multiple referrals would broaden their jurisdictional claims. For example, Foreign Affairs chairman Thomas Morgan (D-Pa.) and ranking Republican William Mailliard of California endorsed a "coreferral" system to ensure that their committee would have a say over more legislation (House Select Committee on Committees 1973, 428–35, 659–60). Representatives especially hoped to force Ways and Means, with its wide jurisdiction, to share more of its legislation (Ornstein and Rohde 1978). Along these lines, Davidson, Oleszek, and Kephart (1988) contend that the change was part of the 1970s trend toward diffusing power, since the rule gave members and committees another procedural window to influence legislation. Multiple referrals thus promised to spread influence among more committees and more members.[12]

While few members opposed multiple referrals, the Bolling committee's other proposals drew considerable fire from members who stood to lose jurisdiction under the reform plan.[13] Defeat of the jurisdictional changes had an important impact on the subsequent development of multiple referrals. The Bolling committee had expected that multiple referrals would be rare, serving only as a limited supplement to jurisdictional consolidation. But the failure to realign jurisdictions left in place many overlaps that necessitated frequent multiple referrals.[14] Thus, a relatively noncontroversial change that received little attention at the time acquired more importance than anticipated.

While the framing and adoption of the multiple referral rule was bipartisan, subsequent developments had a more partisan tenor. In January 1977, House Democrats passed a package of House rules changes that included a provision to expand the Speaker's authority to set deadlines on multiply referred measures. Republicans strongly objected to several elements of the Democratic package, but not to the change to the multiple referral rule (CR, January 4, 1977, 53–70). This suggests that the rule had not yet acquired a partisan reputation.

Indeed, the lack of GOP opposition perhaps reflected the general belief at the time that the referral rule had shown little promise as a leadership tool. The scholarly consensus—and the view of many members—up through the early 1980s was that multiple referrals enhanced member opportunities to participate but created new hurdles for legislation (Davidson 1980a; Sheppard 1985). Many members complained that "by increasing the number of actors with delaying or vetoing powers, multiple referrals erect new obstacles to policy making" (Davidson 1980a, 122).

But in the late 1980s, a new view of multiple referrals began to take shape (Davidson, Oleszek, and Kephart 1988; Collie and Cooper 1989). By that time, the number of multiply referred measures had grown to nearly one-third of all important bills, and the success rate of such measures had improved significantly (Sinclair 1995a). It slowly became apparent that multiple referrals had combined with other changes to empower party leaders. For example, the Speaker's increased control over the Rules Committee reinforced the impact of multiple referrals on leadership power. When majority party leaders would negotiate intercommittee compromises on multiply referred bills, they had the added leverage of being able to offer a restrictive rule to protect the resulting measure. Speaker Wright, in particular, used multiple referrals aggressively to force committee action on his priorities. Wright not only set tight deadlines for committees but also became personally involved in working out intercommittee disputes over the substance of multiply referred bills and in framing the special rules governing their consideration on the floor (Rohde 1991).

While multiple referrals contributed to the influence of majority party leaders, a few caveats are in order. Speakers of the House have generally hesitated to set deadlines for multiply referred measures. Most multiple referrals have been joint referrals with no time limit.[15] Even when a bill is referred sequentially to multiple committees, typically a time limit is set only on committees besides the first one given jurisdiction. Sinclair (1995a, 2) notes that decision rules slowly developed that made the specific type of referral a "relatively automatic" decision. Furthermore, Wright's successor, Tom Foley (D-Wash.), shunned deadlines and rarely pressured committees to reconcile their differences on multiply referred measures (Young and Cooper 1993).

The GOP's 1995 decision to abolish joint referrals underscores their limitations. Republicans had long argued that such referrals "mired Democratic Speakers in intramural turf fights" (Evans and Oleszek 1997, 90). The GOP instead required the Speaker to designate a primary committee for each multiply referred bill, thereby providing more committee accountability. This suggests that while multiple referrals facilitated Democratic party programs in the 1980s, individual members' power base interests had compromised the procedure. Multiple referrals created opportunities for leaders to coordinate committee decision making, but they also expanded committee members' ability to claim new jurisdiction, enmeshing the majority party in ever more divisive turf disputes. The multiple referrals change had promised to serve members' institutional, partisan, and power base interests, but these goals pulled in partially opposing directions.

Stevenson Committee Reforms, 1977

While House reformers failed to make major changes in committee jurisdictions in 1974, just three years later the Senate altered jurisdictions and committee procedures significantly. A bipartisan special committee chaired by Adlai Stevenson III (D-Ill.) proposed these changes. After some modifications on the floor, the final version created a new Energy Committee, eliminated three minor committees, rearranged the jurisdictions of several others, restricted the number of committees and subcommittees on which a member could serve, and limited the number of chairmanships a member could hold.[16]

A bipartisan coalition spearheaded by junior members enacted the 1977 reforms. The Stevenson committee reported its proposal with only one dissenting vote, and the Rules Committee unanimously sent its revised version to the floor. Enacted on an 89–1 floor vote, the reforms served as a common carrier for senators' stake in congressional capacity and power, junior members' interest in improved access to committee power bases, and minority party Republicans' interest in increased staff assistance. However, tensions between senators' personal power goals and broader institutional interests forced important compromises. The resulting reforms created nearly as many problems as solutions.

The 1977 changes derived from the widespread belief among Democrats and Republicans that the Senate committee system could not meet modern governing challenges. Republican William Brock of Tennessee, co-chairman of the Stevenson committee, declared that the "committee system is the crucial element in any serious effort to strengthen Congress" (*Congressional Quarterly Weekly Review* [*CQWR*], March 15, 1975, 542). Stevenson complained that overlapping jurisdictions meant "we sometimes end up reinventing the wheel simultaneously in different subcommittees. And we often end up dealing with parts of an issue with no mechanism to put the parts together" (CR, March 31, 1976, 8844). Judith

Parris (1979, 319–20), a staffer for the Stevenson committee, later recalled that senators had increasingly found their institution "less effective
than they thought possible . . . [as] the congressional workload spiraled
continuously upward." Senators turned to committee reform "to
strengthen their capacity to act as effective representatives and national
policy makers."

Independent observers agree that concerns about the Senate's capacity
were critical (Davidson 1980b; Deering and Smith 1997; Malbin 1977).
In a detailed study of the 1977 changes, Davidson (1980b, 15) characterizes the Stevenson reforms as an effort "to tidy up [the Senate's] deterio-
rating committee system" (16). Malbin (1977, 106) adds that while no
one wanted to lose helpful committee assignments, "a number of senators
have indicated that they are willing to yield important personal power
bases for the sake of helping the Senate put its business in better order."

At the same time, many junior senators believed that subcommittee
assignments and leadership posts were inequitably distributed. In another
example of entrepreneurial members' capitalizing on multiple goals, Stevenson and Brock sparked interest in committee changes by linking these
changes with junior members' power goals (Davidson 1980b). Stevenson
characterized the battle as "a contest of power. The numbers in the Senate
have changed. . . . The membership is younger and juniors are more numerous. . . . The juniors are no longer on their knees. We're not asking,
we're demanding. We're organizing and using power" (*CQWR*, December 13, 1975, 2717). Stevenson's and Brock's agitation led to the formation of the Stevenson committee in 1976. Junior senators were overrepresented on that panel.[17]

The junior-senior cleavage is apparent when one examines the decision
to cosponsor the resolution creating the Stevenson committee. The bivariate correlation between length of service and the decision to cosponsor is
a healthy $-.58$.[18] This relationship holds up in a multivariate logit model:
controlling for party, ideology (as measured by first-dimension NOMI-
NATE scores), and region, junior members were significantly more likely
to cosponsor the resolution than were their more senior colleagues (b =
$-.48$; SE = .12). In addition, committee chairmen were significantly less
likely to cosponsor the resolution (b = -2.07; SE = 1.23; $p < .05$), again
suggesting a power struggle between the haves and have-nots.

Junior senators benefited from several provisions of the resulting reform
package. The original Stevenson committee proposal limited the number
of committee and subcommittee chairmanships that each member could
hold. Junior senator Dick Clark (D-Iowa) sponsored a successful floor
amendment that tightened these limitations, allowing full committee
chairmen to head only two subcommittees, instead of the three subcommittee chairmanships allowed to other members. The Clark amendment

TABLE 5.2   Logit Analysis of Selected Senate Votes on Institutional
Changes, 1973–1977 (SE in parentheses)

Independent Variable	Stevenson Reforms [a] (Clark Amendment)	Open Committee Meetings [b]	Senate Staffing Change [c]
Length of Service	−.19*	−.70**	−.14*
(# of two-year terms)	(.08)	(.17)	(.07)
Committee Chairman	−8.23	.39	−1.32*
	(n/a)	(1.32)	(.89)
First-dimension	−2.33	−8.73**	−1.32
NOMINATE score	(1.32)	(2.22)	(1.31)
Democrat	−1.08	−2.85*	−1.41
	(.89)	(1.16)	(.92)
South	−1.15	.53	−1.24*
	(.73)	(.90)	(.70)
Constant	2.09	4.20	2.48
	(.68)	(1.05)	(.68)
Proportional			
Reduction in Error	.47	.68	.39
N	89	97	99

Note: A vote in favor of reform is scored as 1 and a vote against reform is scored as 0.
[a] Table Clark amendment barring chairmen from heading more than two subcommittees (Feb. 1977).
[b] Roth amendment requiring a public vote to close a committee meeting (Mar. 1973).
[c] Table Gravel resolution for increased staffing (June 1975).
*p < .05.   **p < .01. One-tailed tests, except for the ideology and party variables (for which there are no clear expectations, and therefore two-tailed tests are appropriate).

"was seen as a major victory for younger members over the committee chairmen, all of whom opposed it" (*CQWR*, February 12, 1977, 281).

Table 5.2 presents a logit analysis of the vote on the Clark amendment, along with analyses of the votes on open committee meetings and improved staffing for junior senators. In each reform, seniority more than party or ideology defined Senate voting. The analysis of the Clark amendment shows that junior members and nonchairmen were more likely to support the change than were senior senators and chairmen.[19] By contrast, party, region, and first-dimension NOMINATE scores are insignificant.[20]

The Rules Committee also approved another Clark amendment stating the sense of the Senate that "all senators receive one subcommittee assignment on a committee before any senator received a second" (Parris 1979, 328).[21] These two amendments ensured that the reforms dispersed desirable committee power bases among more members, thus fulfilling a major goal of junior reformers.[22]

Minority party Republicans capitalized on committee reform as well, increasing their access to committee staff. Facing resistance from Democratic committee chairmen, reformers needed solid Republican support to pass a strong reform bill. The composition of the Stevenson committee—with six members from each party—ensured that GOP concerns would receive attention. Republicans also took part in Rules Committee negotiations over how to modify the select committee's proposal. Some key Republicans, including Rules member Robert Griffin (R-Mich.), threatened to withhold support unless they were guaranteed more committee staff. Griffin believed that staff support was "politically more vital to [Republicans] than committee reorganization" (Malbin 1977, 111). On a 5–4 vote, the Rules Committee approved Griffin's amendment, which mandated staff allocations in proportion to the size of each party's committee delegation. The amendment specifically guaranteed that the minority party would control at least one-third of staff funds on each committee. While earlier reforms, such as the 1970 Reorganization Act, had promised increased minority staffing, those provisions had not always been enforced. The changes in 1977, however, were enforced and made a genuine difference (Senate Committee on Rules and Administration 1988, 18–22).

In addition to securing the support of Republicans and junior members, reformers also made numerous concessions to those who stood to lose from reorganization. Senate reformers believed that Bolling's refusal to compromise provoked the House to reject his plan and adopt the much weaker Hansen substitute. Stevenson was willing to make significant concessions as long as these concessions still left major reforms in place. The Rules Committee restored five committees slated for abolition under the Stevenson proposal: Veterans, Small Business, Ethics, Joint Taxation, and the Joint Economic Committee. Rules also reversed a few other jurisdictional changes that had aroused intense opposition. A lopsided floor vote restored the Select Aging Committee, though Stevenson did win a reduction in the committee's size.

Some of these concessions reflected members' electoral interest in catering to powerful constituencies. Groups representing veterans, small business, and the elderly successfully lobbied to save their committees. Other concessions, such as allowing Commerce chairman Warren Magnuson (D-Wash.) to retain jurisdiction over oceans, were more directly tied to the personal power interests of the senators involved (Parris 1979). A mix of reelection-oriented particularism and members' power base interests thus watered down the Stevenson changes. By the time that the committee reforms passed, "provisions that damaged vital interests of preeminent actors in particular subsystems had been deleted" (Parris 1979, 330).

The final key to the Stevenson reforms was electoral. The chairmen of the three full committees slated for abolition were defeated in the 1976 election. That election also brought to Washington an extremely large freshman class of eighteen senators, meaning a majority of senators had now arrived since 1970. As a result, the upper chamber was more than ever "a Senate of juniors with much to gain and little to lose" from committee changes (Stevenson, as quoted in Malbin 1975, 651). The numerical strength of junior members led then-Democratic whip Robert Byrd to become a supporter of committee reform. Though generally suspicious of reform, Byrd realized that he might need the support of junior Democrats to get elected majority leader after Mike Mansfield's imminent retirement (Davidson 1980b). In 1976, Byrd rescued the resolution creating the Stevenson committee from the Rules Committee, which had held it up for more than a year. After the Stevenson committee reported its proposal, Byrd agreed to schedule a vote on the reforms when the new Congress convened in January 1977. Byrd also helped negotiate key compromises that ensured the measure's passage. Thus, junior members' restiveness and Byrd's personal ambitions intersected in 1976–77 to assist Stevenson's bipartisan reformist coalition.

Despite the many compromises made en route to passage, the Stevenson changes nonetheless had a substantial impact on the Senate committee system. The Senate eliminated three standing committees, along with five select and joint committees. Members also made significant changes in the jurisdictions of the remaining committees. For example, the Senate created a single Energy and Natural Resources Committee with authority over most energy legislation. Perhaps most importantly, the number of subcommittees fell from 174 to 110, and the average number of committee and subcommittee assignments per member fell from 18 to 10.5 (Ornstein, Peabody, and Rohde 1997, 23).[23] Davidson (1980b, 29–30) concludes that the changes "reduced jurisdictional overlap and competition . . . [and] made the Senate a more viable work environment for the bulk of its members."[24]

The reforms' other major impact was to empower junior senators. The new procedures giving junior members better subcommittee assignments and limiting the number of committees that a chairman could lead dispersed power among more senators (Davidson 1980b; Bailey 1988). Stevenson triumphantly declared that the reform "democratizes the Senate" (*CQWR*, February 12, 1977, 280). Yet the gains for junior members made the Senate an even more fragmented institution and undermined its policymaking capacity. By the mid-1980s, many members complained of disarray and ineffectiveness, some of them blaming the democratizing reforms of the 1970s (*NYT*, November 25, 1984, 40). Members' interest in boosting the Senate's capacity through streamlining the committee system had been momentarily reconciled with junior members' power base interests in 1977. But the diffusion of power bases reduced party leaders' leverage and made it increasingly difficult to coordinate the semi-independent operators who comprise the contemporary Senate (Bailey 1988; Davidson 1989). Thus, the Stevenson reforms illustrate how tensions among competing member interests can lead a reform primarily initiated to serve broad institutional concerns to have long-term effects inconsistent with that objective.

Opening Up the Committee Process, 1973–1975

In March 1973, the House forced its committees to hold all of their sessions in public, unless they first voted publicly to close that day's meeting. Two years later, the House also required that conference committees meet in public. The Senate followed on both counts in November 1975.[25]

The open meeting rules differ somewhat from the other cases discussed in this section in that concern about congressional prestige, rather than congressional capacity or power, primarily motivated change. But much like the Stevenson reforms, junior members' interest in undermining committee chairmen also played a critical role. The sunshine rules also promised to make committees more prominent platforms for position taking. However, these goals proved incompatible, as members' posturing for constituents often hindered compromise and policymaking, thereby further undermining public confidence in Congress.

Scholars have repeatedly pointed out that Congress's low public standing led members to embrace open meeting rules (Bullock 1978; Rieselbach 1995; Sundquist 1981). Amid the Watergate scandal and growing citizen demands for "sunshine," members came to view open meetings as a means to regain public confidence (see Cooper 1981; *CQWR*, November 11, 1972, 2975). One of the sponsors of the Senate reforms, Lawton Chiles (D-Fla.), claimed that Florida's experience with open meetings showed they increase public confidence in government (*CQWR*, November 11, 1972, 2975). Republican Matthew Rinaldo of New Jersey asserted that "confidence in our government can only come about when the people are able to observe and participate directly in the deliberative process" (CR, March 7, 1973, 6713). Supporters of the sunshine changes continually returned to this theme. For example, Senate reformers argued in November 1975 that the Rules Committee's much-watered-down substitute proposal would "reinforce the public image of Congress . . . as a closed, secretive body" (*CQWR*, November 8, 1975, 2414).

Regard for the institution's well-being was not, however, the sole motivation for reform. Sinclair (1995b, 35) points out that open committee sessions allowed "members to use those forums for grandstanding." The reforms offered members increased opportunities to put themselves on display for constituents and attentive publics. Members themselves were well aware of these possibilities. A critic of the change, David Dennis (R-Ind.), commented that the proposal would allow members "to make their little speeches for the headlines," while hindering the give-and-take essential to legislating (CR, March 7, 1973, 6712). But most members welcomed additional position-taking platforms (cf. Mayhew 1974).

Junior members in particular believed open meetings would enhance their participation and visibility. Open meetings would loosen committee chairmen's influence by making committee members more accountable instead to their constituents and outside groups (CQWR, March 10, 1973, 501–2; Ornstein 1975). As a result, the battle over the sunshine reforms, particularly in the Senate, was divided along seniority lines just as in the fights over the Stevenson reforms and committee staffing (see table 5.2 and discussion below).[26]

The path to adoption of the sunshine reforms differed somewhat in the House and Senate. In the House, the Democratic Study Group and Democratic caucus actively promoted the change. Democrats Dante Fascell of Florida and Bob Eckhardt of Texas were the lead sponsors of the reforms, which the Democratic caucus endorsed on an 83–37 vote. But it would be wrong to interpret these reforms in partisan terms. Republican John Anderson had sponsored a similar resolution and stated on the floor that he was "totally in agreement" with the Fascell-Eckhardt proposition (CR, March 7, 1973, 6702). Meanwhile, Democratic leaders were reluctant to support the reforms, though they ended up endorsing them (CQWR, December 23, 1972, 3206; January 20, 1973, 72). Finally, reformers were confident that they had sufficient Republican support to survive a rumored revolt by senior southern Democrats (CQWR, January 20, 1973, 71–72). The reforms passed by an overwhelming 371 to 27 margin, with a higher proportion of Democrats than Republicans in opposition (see appendix B.4).[27]

While Democrats played the most active role in the House, the Senate reforms were handled on a more thoroughly bipartisan basis. Leading sponsors included stalwart Republicans such as William Roth (R-Del.) and Brock, along with Democrats Chiles and Stevenson. In 1973, when reformers were stymied in their first major effort to open committee sessions, the key vote on Roth's proposal pitted junior members against their more senior colleagues. The correlation between length of service and voting for open meetings was −.55. By contrast, nearly identical proportions of Democrats (twenty-one of forty-six) and Republicans (seventeen of thirty-nine) backed the Roth amendment. As table 5.2 shows, the strong impact for seniority holds up in a multivariate logit analysis.[28]

By 1975, following the well-received Ervin hearings on the Watergate scandal, support for open meetings had grown considerably. Thirty-one senators cosponsored the 1975 proposal for open committee meetings.[29] Once again, sponsors came predominately from the ranks of junior senators: nineteen of thirty-five members who had entered since the 1970 elections cosponsored the change, as compared to just four of thirty who had entered before 1960. Both parties approved the reforms at their organizational meetings. The open meetings provision passed on a voice vote in each caucus, while the Democrats approved the open conference committee feature by a 22–17 vote, and the GOP by an 18–7 vote. When the proposals reached the floor in November 1975, senior members could muster only sixteen votes for the weaker Rules Committee substitute. Those sixteen dissenters came equally from both parties. A logit analysis of the vote shows that, as in 1973, length of service had a significant impact on members' votes ($b = -.18$; SE = .08). Neither party nor ideology had a significant effect. The open meetings reforms, therefore, stand out as another example of a bipartisan change based on broad, institutional objectives as well as individual-based interests. Once again, junior members spearheaded reforms that undermined committee chairmen and spread influence to more members (see Davidson 1980b).

The rules changes immediately led to a big jump in open meetings. In 1972, the year before the House reforms, 44 percent of committee meetings were closed. A year later, only 10 percent were closed, and this figure continued to fall over the next few years (Dodd and Oppenheimer 1977). A similarly steep decline occurred in the Senate (Sinclair 1989, 105). Furthermore, the provisions requiring open conference committee meetings made one of the most secretive elements of the legislative process more visible and accessible to attentive publics (*CQWR,* February 8, 1975, 290–94).

The sunshine reforms contributed to the wide-open, fragmented, and unpredictable legislative process that developed in the 1970s. More members came to appreciate the rewards for committee activism as the audience for such behavior widened (Sinclair 1989, 105). Committee chairmen lost influence as members sensitive to public scrutiny resisted their quiet lobbying (Bailey 1989; Ornstein 1975). Open meetings also encouraged members to posture for outside audiences, impeding conflict resolution (*CQWR,* September 4, 1982, 2177; Oleszek 1996, 115–16). Sinclair (1989, 105) notes that "with the press and lobbyists watching, compromise may be more difficult, and grandstanding may be encouraged." Indeed, as the incentives for quiet accommodation diminished, the tasks facing committee and party leaders became more difficult.

Many observers have argued that the sunshine reforms also increased the influence of organized interests (Arnold 1990; Schneier and Gross 1993). One Ways and Means Democrat conceded that "the open meeting is not as fruitful as I thought it would be. . . . The public's not there but the interests are" (quoted in Rudder 1977, 124). Another noted that "with the open meetings a member has to play to his special interest" (Rudder 1977, 125).

Dissatisfaction with open meetings led some committees to vote to close their sessions when considering major legislation. In the early 1980s, Dan Rostenkowski (D-Ill.) turned to closed meetings to consolidate his control over Ways and Means and to facilitate that committee's handling of politically sensitive tax issues (Strahan 1990). Similarly, the Senate Finance Committee closed its meetings in 1986 after numerous amendments offered in open sessions threatened to unravel tax reform (Arnold 1990, 221). But the vast majority of committee sessions continue to be public. Although many members have become convinced that open meetings damage the policymaking process (see *CQWR*, September 4, 1982, 2177; Maass 1983), revoking the sunshine reforms would require politically unpopular votes in favor of secrecy.

In any case, open meetings continue to provide members with much-desired position-taking opportunities. The 1973 and 1975 changes derived from a confluence of members' interest in congressional prestige and narrower, individual goals. But in the long term, members' use of the new rules for position taking and individual entrepreneurship has produced a more tortuous and conflictual legislative process that has sapped public confidence in Congress. Davidson (1992, 7–8) concludes that the openness reforms "made it possible for more members to participate in shaping legislation, but it also jeopardized orderly processing of the legislative work load."

The Budget Act of 1974, the multiple referrals change, the Stevenson committee reforms, and the open meeting rules each were adopted by bipartisan coalitions seeking to improve the institutional position of the Congress. While partisan interests were relevant to the Budget Act and the multiple referral rule, the bipartisanship generally characterizing these changes is striking. As in 1937–52, Republicans and Democrats both sensed that they had a stake in maintaining congressional power and prestige in the 1970s. However, this bipartisan commitment unraveled in the 1980s as the Democrats tightened their grip on the House, making Republicans doubt the value of their personal stake in Congress's institutional standing.

INDIVIDUAL POWER BASES

Bipartisanship also generally characterized a second set of institutional changes adopted in the 1970s. The Legislative Reorganization Act of 1970, the expansion in Senate committee staff, the boom in Senate obstruction, and the increased influence of House subcommittees each primarily fostered individual activism. The Reorganization Act and committee staff expansion also derived support from members' concerns about congressional capacity and power. In both cases, junior Democrats and Republicans designed reforms that not only capitalized on members' interest in competing effectively with the executive, but that also devolved power to more members. The House subcommittee changes differ somewhat in that liberal Democrats' policy and partisan interests played an important role in these reforms. Nonetheless, the subcommittee reforms also promoted members' individual power base interests. Together, these changes gave junior members much greater influence and many more outlets for activism. But the resulting fragmentation hindered the majority party's ability to govern effectively.

The Legislative Reorganization Act of 1970

The Legislative Reorganization Act of 1970 made important changes in congressional rules and procedures. It weakened committee chairmen by requiring committees to adopt written rules and helping committee majorities force meetings opposed by the chairman. The act also included sunshine reforms requiring that all committee roll call votes be made public, encouraging open committee hearings, and providing for recorded teller votes in the House. The latter change ended the secrecy surrounding members' votes on floor amendments. Beyond these changes, the Reorganization Act strengthened certain minority rights. For example, it guaranteed minority members of a committee at least one day to call their own witnesses during hearings on a measure or topic. At the same time, the act limited opportunities to obstruct House business, promising a more efficient legislative process (Kravitz 1990). Finally, the reform improved staff resources for committees and created the Congressional Research Service to undertake studies for members and committees.[30]

Much like the first Reorganization Act of 1946, the 1970 act was approved by wide, bipartisan majorities in both the House and Senate (see appendix B.4). As in 1946, the initial impetus for reform came from members of both parties seeking to bolster congressional capacity and power amid fears of presidential aggrandizement. In addition, junior members eager to disperse power pushed for reorganization. Liberal Democrats also seized on the reform effort to promote their policy interests and in doing so formed a coalition with junior Republicans to strengthen the final version of the bill. The ambiguous legacy of the Reorganization Act cannot be understood apart from these diverse interests.

Member concerns about congressional capacity and power were apparent from the start of the Reorganization Act's long odyssey to adoption.

Oklahoma Democrat Mike Monroney, who had cochaired the Joint Committee on the Organization of Congress in 1945–46, sponsored a resolution that created another joint committee in March 1965. Like its predecessor, this committee had equal numbers of members from both parties and reported the bulk of its proposals unanimously (Bibby and Davidson 1972, 254). Several committee members emphasized the need to strengthen Congress so that it could better compete with the executive branch. Republican Senator Karl Mundt argued that "it is high time that we shore up our fences and increase the effectiveness of the Congress in dealing with the tremendously diversified and complex issues with which it is faced, and the growing power of the executive branch" (Joint Committee 1965, 7). Democratic representative Ken Hechler (D-W.Va.) struck a similar tone: "The question is: How can we organize Congress and its committees to restore to Congress and the individual Congressman the primary function of legislating?" (Joint Committee 1965, 13; see also the statement of New Jersey Republican Clifford Case, Joint Committee 1965, 10). In subsequent floor debates on the Reorganization Act, members of both parties repeatedly emphasized congressional capacity and power. Monroney argued that "embarrassing questions are being asked of us. . . . Are we still a viable, creative legislative force or are we . . . mere ornamental trappings to legitimize the legislative program of an increasingly powerful Federal Government?" (CR, January 25, 1967, 1558). H. Allen Smith of California, who as the ranking Republican on the Rules Committee helped shape the bill that finally reached the House floor in 1970, claimed that the proposal "provides a number of mechanisms" to solve the problem that Congress "does not have sufficient information available to it in order to deal effectively with the myriad of legislative problems we face" (CR, July 13, 1970, 23905; see also statement by Missouri Republican Durward Hall, CR, July 13, 1970, 23925–26).

Congressional scholars have also emphasized the importance of congressional capacity and power (Josephy 1979; Sundquist 1981). Evans and Oleszek (1997, 19) note that the "climate of concern about Congress's effectiveness" stimulated the reorganization effort and point out that the resulting act included several moves to strengthen Congress's decision-making capacity. Such changes as the staffing increase mandated by the Reorganization Act promised simultaneously to promote congressional capacity and to give members more resources to pursue their individual goals.

Yet even as concerns about congressional capacity and power encouraged reform, several groups with narrower agendas promulgated specific elements of the Reorganization Act. Junior members were particularly active in promoting their power base interests (Bibby and Davidson 1972). They won numerous victories: in addition to the rules empowering committee majorities against recalcitrant chairmen, the reforms made

Senate committee assignments more egalitarian, codifying and extending party rules limiting senior members' monopoly of the best committee slots. Most importantly, the provision for recorded votes on floor amendments in the House made the floor a much more effective arena for rank-and-file participation while curbing the influence of chairmen. Republican reformer Charles Whalen (1982, 22) of Ohio summed up the power base concerns of junior members when he noted that procedural reform "provided them the chance to construct a leadership bus with more seats."

Liberal Democrats' policy interests also exerted an important influence on the Reorganization Act. In particular, the liberal Democratic Study Group (DSG) pushed the adoption of recorded votes on amendments, a provision that had been omitted from the Joint Committee's proposal. The DSG believed that recorded votes would help pass liberal amendments opposed by conservative committee chairmen. The DSG even undertook a study showing the dismal attendance of northern Democrats on nonrecorded votes and indicating that roll call votes on amendments would produce better liberal attendance and more liberal victories (Ornstein and Rohde 1974).

Yet liberals understood that they lacked the votes to pass such a change on their own, given the opposition of party and committee leaders. As a result, the DSG's Donald Fraser (D-Minn.) and Sam Gibbons (D-Fla.) began meeting with "Young Turk" Republicans, led by New York's Barber Conable (*National Journal*, July 25, 1970, 1611). The two groups first agreed to construct a bipartisan package rather than simply posturing politically. Early on, Republicans had painted the Democratic party as hostile to reform. But Republicans soon chose a different tack: Conable recalled that "we decided we couldn't make this a political issue because we'd lose the reforms we sought" (Bibby and Davidson 1972, 264).

The reformers' strategic maneuvers illustrate how entrepreneurial members can harness diverse interests to support institutional change. The DSG and the junior Republicans negotiated a package of ten amendments that strengthened the reorganization bill. Liberals' main priority was the recorded teller provision. Junior Republicans supported this measure because they too believed it would increase their influence. While senior Republicans often had close working relationships with Democratic chairmen and hence tended to resist reform, junior Republicans lacked such access to power and so provided a critical constituency for the reform movement (Sheppard 1985). As an "embattled minority" (Ornstein and Rohde 1978, 282), many Republicans believed they would profit from a more open Congress. The DSG also appealed to the Republicans by agreeing to several additional amendments that particularly benefited the minority party: these included guaranteed time to debate a motion to recommit with instructions and a guarantee that the minority would receive one-third of all committee staff. The resulting package thus appealed to multiple, distinct member interests. On the whole, nine of the ten elements of the bipartisan package were adopted.

Since the recorded teller amendment passed on a voice vote (as senior members dropped their opposition when its passage appeared certain), there is no roll call data on its approval. However, cosponsorship of the amendment provides a reasonable measure of support for the reform and nicely illustrates the importance of multiple interests (see also Ornstein and Rohde 1974). The amendment was cosponsored by 182 representatives. A logit analysis shows that seniority and ideology (as measured by first-dimension NOMINATE scores) are each significant predictors of cosponsorship: junior members and liberals were disproportionately likely to be cosponsors.[31] The estimated effect of terms of service is $-.16$ (SE $= .04$), while the ideology effect is -6.72 (SE $= .90$). The negative coefficient for committee chairmen is also consistent with the power base dynamic, though it falls short of statistical significance (b $= -1.14$; SE $= .83$). Furthermore, although nearly identical proportions of Republicans and Democrats sponsored the amendment, Republicans apparently were more likely to be cosponsors than were Democrats, controlling for ideology and seniority (b $= 2.25$; SE $= .48$).[32] Again, these results suggest that recorded teller votes served as a common carrier for liberal Democrats, Republicans, and junior members in both parties.

The bipartisan package of amendments ensured that the Reorganization Act fulfilled reformers' objective of weakening committee chairmen and dispersing power. Ornstein and Rohde (1978, 282) argue that the act "chipped away at the power of chairmen to control events," while Kravitz (1990, 391) notes that "by denying members the anonymity they previously enjoyed, the new rule encouraged them to vote on amendments as they believed their constituents wanted them to, even if it meant defying committee leaders." Indeed, Smith (1989) argues that the recorded teller change dramatically increased floor amending activity in the 1970s, thus making House deliberations more collegial and floor-centered, in contrast to the earlier committee-dominated system.

In the short term, the recorded teller change also achieved the DSG's objective of furthering liberal policies. In the early 1970s, recorded votes helped liberals pass several floor amendments, most notably one that overturned congressional support for the supersonic transport project (Ornstein 1975). More broadly, the curbs on chairmen's power turned out to be just the first step in liberals' successful bid to shift power from committee chairmen to rank-and-file members.

But many liberals soon realized that the recorded teller change also had created problems for the Democratic party. The sharp rise in Republican amending activity after the recorded teller change far outpaced the modest Democratic increase (Smith 1989, 33–34, 148). This development stemmed partly from Democrats' successes in reining in conservative-dominated committees: Republicans, rather than liberal Democrats, were now the ones dissatisfied with committee products (Rohde 1991). Still, in this new environment, Republicans seized upon the recorded teller change to sponsor numerous politically popular amendments that exposed Democratic vulnerabilities. Republicans became "adept at drafting amendments that confronted Democrats with an unpalatable choice, pitting their policy preferences against their reelection needs" (Sinclair 1995b, 77).[33] In combination with new crosscutting issues, the GOP amendments led to "less cohesiveness among Democrats, and considerably greater difficulty for Democratic leaders in building majority coalitions" (Smith 1989, 33). As the floor became increasingly difficult to manage, Democratic leaders sought rules changes to limit recorded votes. But in 1974, nearly all Republicans joined 43 percent of Democrats to thwart the leadership's plan.[34]

So the Reorganization Act emerges simultaneously as a liberal and a GOP victory, and as the first of several steps increasing fragmentation, openness, and individualized entrepreneurship.[35] Whereas standing committees—and their senior members, in particular—had in the past been the primary shapers of legislation, the floor became an increasingly critical battleground in the 1970s. Recorded teller votes were superimposed on a long-standing decentralized committee system, generating an institutional "order" characterized by considerable unpredictability and turmoil. Smith (1989, 15) concludes that the "tidy decentralized process characterizing the [1950s and 1960s] was transformed into a somewhat strained combination of decentralized and collegial elements." By 1979, Democrats became increasingly convinced that this untidy combination threatened too many partisan and ideological interests. Democrats intended the rise in restrictive rules detailed below to counter some of the more deleterious effects of the earlier reforms.

Senate Staffing, 1975

In 1975, the Senate approved a measure that entitled each member to three staff assistants who would help with committee work. Prior to 1975, committee chairmen and ranking minority members had controlled the lion's share of committee staff, but the new rule quickly dispersed control over this important resource.[36]

A bipartisan bloc of junior senators seeking greater access to committee power bases initiated the staffing change. Senators themselves clearly considered the reform a bid to loosen senior members' hold on institutional power. Mike Gravel (D-Alaska), the lead sponsor, argued that in a democracy, "power is distributed on the basis of knowledge. What we say here in this resolution is that we want the apportionment of knowledge on a more equitable basis" (CR, June 9, 1975, 17849). Another key supporter, Robert Packwood (R-Oreg.), declared that "this is a battle between the haves and the have-nots" (CR, June 9, 1975, 17860), adding that junior senators simply wanted "an equal shot with the senior senators to committee staff" (*CQWR*, June 14, 1975, 1236).[37] Senior committee leaders objected publicly to the reform's cost, but they clearly understood that the resolution aimed to dilute their power (*CQWR*, June 14, 1975, 1235). While thirty-seven of forty-four senators elected since 1968 cosponsored the Gravel resolution, only three of eighteen committee chairmen did so (Malbin 1975, 649).

Floor voting also manifests this junior-senior cleavage (see table 5.2). The key vote was on a motion by Rules and Administration chairman Howard Cannon (D-Nev.) to table the Gravel resolution. The correlation between a dummy variable for committee chairmen and voting to table the Gravel resolution was .44, and the correlation between length of service and tabling the resolution was .36. A logit analysis shows that the seniority and committee chairman variables remain strong predictors of senators' votes controlling for party, ideology, and region (see table 5.2).[38]

Minority party interests also contributed to support for the staffing change. While some ranking Republicans had committee staff, many did not (Malbin 1975). Republicans gave the measure disproportionate support because it promised to increase party members' access to this critical resource. Thirty-three of thirty-eight Senate Republicans cosponsored the Gravel resolution, as opposed to just twenty-four of sixty-two Democrats. Floor voting revealed a similar pattern, with 76 percent of Republicans voting against the Cannon bid to table the resolution, as compared to 47 percent of Democrats. As table 5.2 shows, the party effect remains reasonably strong in the multivariate logit, though falling short of statistical significance ($p = .13$, two-tailed). Much like the Legislative Reorganization Act and the Stevenson committee reforms, the staffing change garnered support from Republicans and junior members generally, both of whom were dissatisfied with their access to power.

A final interest likely contributing to the staff increase was members' stake in congressional capacity and power. While it may be no surprise that junior members seeking improved staffing cited this less self-serving interest (see, e.g., CR, February 5, 1975, 2480), it is striking that a handful of senior members who did not stand to gain personally from the staffing resolution also emphasized the need to compete with the executive branch. Hubert Humphrey (D-Minn.), who noted that he had sufficient staff as chairman of the Joint Economic Committee, nonetheless argued that "this Congress has spent a great deal of time talking about the executive branch. We have loaded them with staff. . . . We have a chance here to take care of the legitimate needs of the Senate" (CR, June 11, 1975, 18401). Republican Charles Percy of Illinois, who as ranking member on Government Operations also claimed to have adequate staffing, called the reform "a vital part of the struggle to bring the working machinery of the Senate into the 20th century" (CR, June 11, 1975, 18397). Numerous scholars agree that the increase in congressional staff in the 1970s—of which the 1975 Senate change was a critical part— stemmed from concerns about challenges from the executive branch amid a growing legislative workload (Jones 1995; Bailey 1989, 87; Schneier and Gross 1993; Rieselbach 1994, 70).

Although each of these interests played a role, the impetus for reform unmistakably came from junior members, who stood to gain the most from improved staffing. Facing the resistance of many senior senators, reformers organized to promote their cause. The classes of 1969–75 met regularly in a bipartisan group cochaired by Brock and Texas Democrat Lloyd Bentsen (Malbin 1975). The most active cosponsors of the Gravel resolution were all involved in these meetings, which helped build support for this and other reforms designed to benefit junior members (Malbin 1975). When the Rules and Administration Committee sought to replace Gravel's proposal with a weaker measure that would allow committee chairmen and ranking Republicans to retain influence over the new staff, the bipartisan reformers fought back, passing a measure similar to the initial Gravel resolution.[39]

Junior members' success stemmed both from their coordinated effort and from their increased numbers. By 1975, forty-four senators had fewer than eight years of seniority. Malbin (1975, 649) argues that "junior senators have chafed at their situation for years, but this is the first year they feel strong enough to do something about it." Reform leader Stevenson declared that "we are not here to beg any more; we are here to require" (as quoted in Malbin 1975: 649).

As intended, the 1975 staffing change dispersed influence and facilitated individual entrepreneurship (Sinclair 1989). Lowe (1975: 1235) argues that, by permitting junior members to hire committee staff, the change "struck at the heart of the power of committee chairmen." Similarly, Rieselbach (1994: 55) notes that the staffing changes "effectively reallocated committee power from senior leaders to rank-and-file members." The individualism, egalitarianism, and unrestrained activism of the contemporary Senate stems in part from the 1975 rules change, along with other changes, such as the 1970 Reorganization Act and the 1977 Stevenson reforms, which undermined senior members' monopoly over the best committee positions (Sinclair 1989; Ornstein, Peabody, and Rohde 1997).[40]

The 1975 reform's impact on the Senate's policymaking capacity was more ambiguous. In the year following its adoption, the number of Senate committee staff rose from 948 to 1,277 (Ornstein et al. 1982, 113). Yet the intersection of junior members' power interests and members' stake in congressional capacity had critical implications. By making the staff available to senators as individuals, rather than to broader units such as committees or parties, the staffing increase further fragmented power. Senate parties suffered as individual senators with "more staff, more money, and more power . . . were able to maintain a new degree of independence from party leaders" (CQ 1982, 281; see also Bailey 1988, 9; Rieselbach 1994, 105). This went along with a more general flowering of individual assertion that at times impeded Senate functioning. The *Times* noted in 1984, following a particularly frustrating session, that the "clear consensus among members was that the Senate was out of control; many put the blame on democratization," including the staffing expansion (November 25, 1984, 1, 40). More and more senators had come to believe that "a decade of diffusion of authority has . . . subverted the institution's constitutional purpose and effectiveness." It seems reasonable to conclude, therefore, that while the 1975 change increased the resources of junior senators, it undermined reformers' additional goal of boosting congressional capacity and power. While the staffing change served as a common carrier for different interests, in the end it promoted individual goals while undermining members' broader, institutional interests.

The Boom in Senate Obstruction

The explosion in obstructive tactics in the 1970s and 1980s derived from similar centrifugal pressures. This change encompasses the increasing frequency of filibusters, as well as the emergence of new techniques, such as the postcloture filibuster and the hold (see below). Each of these developments empowered individual senators while also helping minority party members sabotage majority party proposals. The rise in obstruction has accentuated the Senate's individualistic and anarchic tendencies, making agenda management extremely difficult for majority party leaders. But the Senate has also adapted to obstruction, such that a filibuster-proof majority is not always necessary to pass important legislation.

Unlike most of the other cases in this book, this change came about through an accumulation of individual member actions rather than a single decision of the Senate or either party. As a result, the implications of this case for competing theories of legislative organization must be considered cautiously: it is inappropriate to expect partisan or median voter models, for example, to explain such a change. Furthermore, the evidence on what accounts for this change is more indirect than in most of the other cases. Nonetheless, the obstruction boom constitutes a major development in the Senate's *practices* for considering legislation and thus falls within the scope of this study.[41]

While it is difficult to quantify the level of obstruction in any given Congress (see Beth 1995; Krehbiel 1998), Binder and Smith (1997, 10–11) document increasing filibusters in the 1970s and 1980s. They count just twenty-three "manifest filibusters" in the entire nineteenth century, and they find that the typical Congress from the 1940s to the 1960s had about five filibusters. But from 1970 to 1994, there were 191 filibusters. In just the 102nd Congress of 1991–92, there were a record thirty-five filibusters.

These data may underestimate obstruction since they omit such new techniques for blocking legislation as holds. When holds first developed in the 1960s, they ensured that a senator objecting to a measure would have a day's notice before it came to the floor for consideration (Sinclair 1989). But as the time pressures on the Senate grew and as individual members more aggressively defended their prerogatives, holds became a mechanism to block legislation from even reaching the floor. A longtime Senate staffer observed in the 1980s that "four or five years ago it started to mean that if you put a hold on something, it would never come up. It became, in fact, a veto" (as quoted in Binder and Smith 1997, 12). Majority party leaders have periodically tried to crack down on holds by treating them only as requests for notice. But minority leaders, who are less sensitive to the scheduling difficulties that plague the majority leadership, have generally continued to abide by holds.

The boom in obstruction derives most directly from individual members' power base and electoral interests. In the 1960s and 1970s, the incentive to filibuster increased as the Washington policy community expanded in size and diversity (Sinclair 1989; see also Baumgartner and Jones 1993). More groups offered to reward members for activism that often culminated in obstructive tactics. Individual senators, such as James Allen (D-Ala.), Orrin Hatch (R-Utah), Jesse Helms (R-N.C.), and Howard Metzenbaum (D-Ohio), became heroes to particular constituencies through their unrestrained exploitation of filibusters and holds (Smith 1989, 113; Bailey 1988). In their detailed study of the filibuster, Binder and Smith (1997, 17) highlight senators' electoral and power goals, arguing that obstruction provides "a means for individual senators to champion a cause and attract support" (see also Sinclair 1989; Wrighton and

Kanthak 1997). More generally, the right to unlimited debate enhances "the importance of the senator in the larger polity" (Binder and Smith 1996, 31–32).

The time pressures imposed by a burgeoning workload in the 1960s and 1970s also made the filibuster a more viable strategy (Binder and Smith 1997). Senate leaders became more willing to accommodate even small groups of filibustering senators in order to move legislation along. Oppenheimer (1985, 404) writes that "in a highly-time constrained environment . . . a few senators or even a single one could hold the Senate hostage."

In addition to empowering individual senators, the filibuster offers important benefits to the minority party. As partisan conflict has increased in the Senate in recent years, the minority party has more assertively exploited the filibuster (Beth 1995; Binder and Smith 1997). While partisan filibusters are by no means new, obstruction has become more routinely a partisan matter (*CQWR*, September 5, 1987, 2116; Ornstein, Peabody, and Rohde 1997). Thus, when the Democrats regained control of the Senate in 1987, Republicans "responded with a filibuster strategy that blocked most of the majority's priority legislation. . . . The price of movement was often major concessions on policy" (Sinclair 1989, 215). In return, Democrats responded with a series of filibusters in the Republican 104th Congress (1995–96).

These partisan filibusters often had substantial ideological overtones. But ideological minorities do not always correspond to partisan minorities. Much of the initial impetus for the increase in filibusters came from liberals, who despite Democrats' majority status often found themselves in the minority on the floor as they fought Nixon administration proposals (CQ 1972, 354). Later in the 1970s, conservatives again emerged as the preeminent obstructionists, as Allen perfected the postcloture filibuster and a cadre of New Right senators led by Helms took obstruction to new heights. In the 1980s, liberals and conservatives from both parties filibustered repeatedly. The rise in obstruction thus did not benefit one ideological camp over the other; rather, it enhanced the value of a resource that committed ideologues on both sides found useful.

The boom in minority obstruction has provoked numerous efforts to make it easier to limit debate through the cloture process. In 1975, the Senate reduced the number of votes required for cloture from two-thirds of those present and voting to three-fifths of the entire Senate. But not only did the increase in filibusters continue unabated, senators angered by the 1975 change resorted to new tactics to halt business. Allen invented the postcloture filibuster in 1976, violating a long-standing norm that a filibuster ends when cloture has been invoked. The Alabama Senator exploited loopholes in the Senate's rules to force endless roll calls on amendments and procedural motions following cloture (Oleszek 1996, 257). The Senate adopted new rules in 1979 and 1986 that reduced, but did not eliminate, the threat of postcloture filibusters.

The 1975, 1979, and 1986 rules changes sought to improve the Senate's ability to process legislation but had only a modest impact (Oppenheimer 1985; Sinclair 1989; Smith 1993). Instead, senators have adapted to obstruction by embracing strategies that minimize the damage caused by filibusters and by using statutory restrictions to shield specific areas from most delaying tactics.

As Democratic whip in the 1970s, Byrd devised the "track system," which allowed the Senate to consider multiple bills on the floor at the same time. Before this innovation, a filibuster "delayed not only the bill being debated but all other legislation awaiting floor consideration" (Oppenheimer 1985, 406). With the track system, however, legislation on one track can move forward even as a filibuster blocks a bill on a second track. This makes the Senate schedule more predictable and reduces the damage that a filibuster against one measure can inflict on other bills, but it also facilitates filibusters. Senators need to spend less time on the floor making speeches and face less pressure from their colleagues to stop filibustering since they are not interfering with unrelated legislation (Binder and Smith 1997; Oppenheimer 1985). In the context of preexisting rules that allow unlimited debate, efforts to improve the Senate's efficiency have also facilitated obstruction. An innovation adopted to improve the Senate's capacity had much more complex effects when superimposed on entrenched institutions designed for competing ends.

The most effective response to unlimited debate has been debate restrictions imposed by statutes. Binder and Smith (1997) identify more than three dozen instances in recent decades when Congress has enacted legislation requiring the Senate to vote on a future matter under expedited procedures. For example, as noted above, the Budget Act of 1974 limits Senate debate on budget resolutions, reconciliation bills, and resolutions to approve or disapprove of presidential impoundments. These statutory limitations constituted an ad hoc response to the difficulties posed by more frequent filibusters.[42] Senators have proven willing to accept debate limitations when necessary to achieve some other valued end, such as defending congressional power.[43]

The upshot of these statutory provisions has been that, while filibusters can obstruct most of the Senate's work, procedures that more closely resemble majority rule govern important parts of the agenda. One might even argue that these procedures have made minority obstruction more tolerable for the Senate (and for the American public): though filibusters are now more frequent, critical areas of policymaking—such as reconciliation bills—are largely shielded from obstruction. Though it is doubtful that a group of planners would have designed such a bifurcated structure, a series of disjointed adaptations may have, at least in part, accommodated senators' demand for individual assertion with members' shared interest in being able to pass critical legislation.

Empowering House Subcommittees

Much like the other cases in this section, the reforms empowering House subcommittees served individual members' power base interests. But in contrast to the other cases, these reforms occurred largely within the Democratic caucus, and thus had a stronger partisan and ideological tone. The first caucus reform, adopted in January 1971, limited each member to a single subcommittee chairmanship. Two years later, the caucus adopted the subcommittee bill of rights, which transferred the power to appoint subcommittee chairmen from the full committee chair to the committee's majority party members. This committee caucus would also set subcommittee jurisdictions. In addition, the bill of rights guaranteed subcommittees an adequate budget and staff, along with automatic referral of legislation. The House enhanced subcommittee resources again in 1975 by authorizing each subcommittee chairman and ranking member to hire one full-time staff person to handle subcommittee work.[44]

Scholars have consistently argued that members' power base concerns motivated these changes (Bailey 1989; Loomis 1988; Price 1992; Rieselbach 1994). Limiting members to one subcommittee chairmanship opened up at least sixteen chairmanships for junior Democrats. Furthermore, by dramatically reducing committee chairmen's control over subcommittee resources, the subcommittee bill of rights made each subcommittee (and in particular its chairmanship) a more potent power base. Since even the most junior Democrat could reasonably aspire to a subcommittee chairmanship in the not-too-distant future, a diverse group stood to benefit from these changes. Loomis (1988, 243) argues that underlying the House reforms was the principle of giving "most, if not all, legislators a real voice in the proceedings."

Members' statements also point to the centrality of junior members' power interests. Discussing the subcommittee reforms soon after their adoption, Thomas Foley (D-Wash.) argued that "you could call it a generational conflict. It was a case of middle-ranking Democrats . . . versus the senior membership" (CQWR, Nov 8, 1975, 2409). Similarly, Tip O'Neill later recalled that "the object at the time was to take power out of the hands of the few and give it to more people" (US News and World Report, August 11, 1980, 24).

But the subcommittee reforms did not benefit all junior members equally. Liberal Democrats lobbied hardest for the reforms, in part because they believed that strengthening the subcommittees would not only empower them as individual entrepreneurs, but would also weaken conservative committee chairmen who often blocked liberal legislation. The DSG's Frank Thompson (D-N.J.) and Phillip Burton (D-Calif.) initiated the 1971 changes, correctly anticipating that most of the newly empowered subcommittee chairmen would be liberals (Ornstein 1975). They inserted the proposal into a package of caucus reforms emanating from the Hansen Committee on Organization, Study, and Review. Peter Barash, a staffer for Benjamin Rosenthal (D-N.Y.), initiated the 1973 subcommittee reforms.[45] After Barash persuaded the DSG that his proposal would empower liberals, Burton and Thompson again took the lead in advocating the reform (Ornstein 1975). Thus, liberal Democrats' policy goals shaped the subcommittee reforms, even as these changes simultaneously promoted members' personal power interests.

The ideological dimension of the subcommittee changes, though clearly important, was not the entire story. The 1975 reforms also increased the resources of junior Republicans, since each subcommittee's ranking minority member was allotted a professional staff member. More importantly, ideological divisions among nonsouthern Democrats meant that liberals lacked a clear caucus majority, especially when the first key subcommittee reforms were enacted in 1971 (Ornstein 1975; Bibby and Davidson 1972). As a result, Thompson and Burton had to devise reforms that appealed to junior Democrats' power interests as well. They discovered that spreading subcommittee chairmanships was a formula for pursuing liberal goals while maintaining the broadest possible coalition. Ornstein (1975, 96) argues that the "basis of the argument was 'give the younger members a chance,'" and surmises that many Democrats favored subcommittee reform in 1971 "because it seemed to spread the action to younger members, *not* give more power to liberals." Indeed, the opposition of liberals John Moss (D-Calif.) and John Dingell (D-Mich.), who stood to lose subcommittee chairmanships, helped convince conservative Democrats that the reforms were more balanced than they really were (Ornstein and Rohde 1978). Burton played a particularly active role in building this broad coalition, working to allay southerners' (and some liberals') reservations about the proposed reforms (Ornstein 1975). Both the Hansen committee and the full Democratic caucus thus approved the reforms by wide margins.[46]

A memo written by Barash nicely underscores the confluence of policy and power base goals. Barash argued that "too much power rests in the hands of a few men, most notably the committee chairmen. The goal of reform is not accomplished merely by taking autocratic powers from reactionary chairmen (selection by seniority) and giving them to benevolent progressive committee chairmen (elected by their peers)." Instead, "reform reaching down into and democratization of the entire committee structure is essential" (quoted in Sheppard 1985, 99). Barash goes on to recommend that the DSG promote "the right of autonomous action by the various subcommittee chairmen" (Sheppard 1985, 100).

In sum, the subcommittee changes passed because liberal Democrats had policy reasons to undercut conservative committee chairmen and found that they could forge a broad coalition for doing so by simultaneously appealing to representatives' power base interests. After all, there were more than one hundred subcommittee chairmen and just twenty full committee chairmen (Fiorina 1977).[47] As in the LRA of 1970, DSG activists—in particular, Thompson, Burton, and the staffer Barash—had acted as entrepreneurs, linking liberal policy interests with junior members' power goals.

The subcommittee changes contributed to a seismic power shift in the House. Along with the attack on the seniority system (see below), these reforms struck a major blow to the power of full committee chairmen. At the same time, the reforms created a new set of powerful actors. Each subcommittee chairman now had a power base that could be used to launch initiatives, claim credit, and gain press attention. Policy entrepreneurship became an increasingly widespread activity, and subcommittees proved an important source of programmatic innovation (Loomis 1988; Dodd and Oppenheimer 1993, 51). Davidson (1980a) devised the concept of "subcommittee government" to describe the emerging system. While subcommittee influence varied greatly across issue areas, as a general matter subcommittee chairmen and ranking Republicans now had disproportionate access to important resources, such as staff expertise and communication networks (Hall and Evans 1990; Deering and Smith 1985).

As suggested above, the newly empowered subcommittee chairmen tended to be liberal Democrats (Ornstein 1975). But the fusion of liberals' policy goals with members' individual interest in dispersing power turned out to be a mixed blessing for majority party Democrats. On the one hand, many subcommittee chairmen used their newfound influence to push liberal policies (Rohde 1991). At the same time, Dodd and Oppenheimer (1993, 51) argue that the fragmentation of power under subcommittee government "created a crisis of interest aggregation," as more members and decision-making units had to be accommodated in order to pass legislation and committee chairmen proved less able to broker compromises (see also Deering and Smith 1997). As a result, party leaders struggled to build coalitions amid a more unwieldy and unpredictable environment. *Congressional Quarterly* noted in 1975 that "some members, who look at the House from an institutional standpoint, worry that reform has swung too far" toward decentralization (*CQWR*, November 8, 1975, 2412).

Four years later, amid the tribulations of the Carter administration, Cohen (1979, 1326) observed that "many Democrats, including some erstwhile reformers, have expressed second thoughts about these changes" that had undermined full committee chairmen.

In the 1980s, renewed party leadership and centralization partly reversed the fragmentation brought about by the subcommittee reforms. Even so, substantial remnants of subcommittee power caused considerable difficulties for the Democrats, especially in 1993 when unified party control once again made an ambitious party agenda possible. One of Newt Gingrich's first moves as Speaker, therefore, was to bring subcommittees more under the control of full committee chairmen.

The four changes discussed in this section comprised an ambitious movement to democratize the Congress in the 1970s. Junior members of both parties demanded better access to resources and more influence in committees and on the floor. While other member interests were relevant, the thrust of the changes was to disperse power.

In the Senate, junior Democrats and Republicans cooperated with one another on an ongoing basis, succeeding not only in increasing staffing, but also in passing the Stevenson reforms and the rules requiring open committee meetings (see table 5.2). These three changes, along with the rise in obstruction, made the Senate authority structure more egalitarian and more conducive to individual activism. While the House experienced a similar bipartisanship during consideration of the 1970 Reorganization Act, liberal Democrats soon turned to the party caucus to push for democratization. As a result, even changes that dispersed power had a distinct partisan element in the House. Furthermore, the Democratic caucus's growing role presaged a host of other changes that empowered the majority party.

HOUSE DEMOCRATS AND MAJORITY PARTY INTERESTS

Democrats' party-building changes included the December 1974 shift in control over committee assignments, the January 1975 deposal of three committee chairmen, the increase in restrictive special rules after 1979, and the emergence of a revitalized speakership in the 1980s. In each of these cases, liberals' policy interests fused with Democrats' more general interest in their party's effectiveness. Since liberals comprised a clear majority of House Democrats after the 1974 midterm elections, strengthening the majority also benefited liberals.

These changes were in important respects a response to the earlier changes that had fragmented power in the House. In particular, the increase in restrictive rules came about because Democrats were dissatisfied with the wide-open amending process created by the recorded teller provision of the 1970 Reorganization Act. In addition, a stronger speakership helped to offset the centrifugal pressures engendered by the subcommittee reforms. Democrats could not rely upon the uncoordinated actions of more than 120 committee and subcommittee leaders in their battles with Ronald Reagan. So party members agreed to important changes that centralized power in the House. But these changes coexisted uneasily with the earlier decentralizing reforms. The tension between Democrats' interest in coordination under party leaders and members' interest in continuing to use subcommittees and the floor for individual activism plagued the Democrats into the 1990s.

Democratic Committee Assignment Changes

In December 1974, the Democratic caucus changed the party's committee assignment process, voting 146 to 122 to allow the Speaker to nominate Democratic members to the Rules Committee, subject to confirmation by the full caucus. The caucus also transferred control of other committee assignments from Ways and Means Committee Democrats to the recently created Steering and Policy Committee, which was chaired by the Speaker and included several leadership appointees. This change was approved on a 106–65 caucus vote.[48]

Reformers correctly anticipated that these changes would strengthen the majority party and its leaders. The DSG had proposed the Steering and Policy Committee in 1973, arguing that it would reinvigorate the party apparatus (Sheppard 1985, 98). While this committee did little at first, the DSG's Fraser proposed giving it control over committee assignments explicitly to "enhance [its] status. Now it amounts to something" (*CQWR*, December 7, 1974, 3250). Liberal Democrat David Obey of Wisconsin, also of the DSG, declared, "I want members to owe their committee assignments to the leadership, not to the Ways and Means Committee" (*CQWR*, November 16, 1974, 3119). The same week as the caucus approved the Fraser proposal, Richard Bolling won adoption of the provision granting the Speaker control of nominations to the Rules Committee. Rather than allowing Steering and Policy to make these assignments, Bolling sought to tighten the connections between the Speaker and Rules. He declared that his proposal would be the "first thing that would really strengthen [the leadership's] hand" (quoted in Malbin 1974, 1888).

Much of the impetus for empowering Democratic leaders came from liberals who wanted to promote progressive legislation. While the secrecy surrounding caucus votes precludes a quantitative analysis of support for the changes, liberals clearly spearheaded both moves, which were correctly viewed as conservative setbacks (Malbin 1974; CQ 1976, 766–67; Sheppard 1985; Rohde 1991). Since Ways and Means Democrats tended to be more conservative than most other Democrats, the DSG believed that shifting assignments to the Steering and Policy Committee would produce more liberal delegations on key committees.[49] Giving the Speaker direct control over Rules Committee assignments also made sense to liberals given that committee's history as a conservative power base. While Bolling's long-standing commitment to a strengthened speakership led him to initiate the Rules Committee change, he relied on liberals for most of his support (Malbin 1974; Sheppard 1985, 199).

Members' power base concerns both promoted and limited the 1974 reforms. On the one hand, these concerns encouraged transferring control of assignments from Ways and Means to Steering and Policy. Many members believed Ways and Means had too much power, and taking away its control of assignments was part of a broader attack on its influence (Malbin 1974; CQWR, December 7, 1974, 3250–52). Furthermore, freshmen believed they would fare better under the new committee assignment system, since Ways and Means Democrats had shown little interest in accommodating new members (Sheppard 1985, 198).

Yet Democrats' determination that Steering and Policy be a large, inclusive committee limited its effectiveness as a leadership tool. Sinclair (1995b, 89) notes that by including a mix of regionally elected, appointed, and ex officio members, "reformers hoped to strike a balance among a number of not necessarily congruent concerns." While partisan criteria alone might have generated a compact committee selected entirely by the caucus or by the leadership, members' power base concerns militated against such centralization. Instead, members opted for a larger, more diverse committee that would be harder for a single faction to control. The size of the committee made its deliberations more unpredictable and weakened the leadership's ability to shape its decisions (Smith and Ray 1983), which may explain why Speaker Carl Albert (D-Okla.) opposed giving it responsibility for committee assignments.

The Speaker's new authority over Rules Committee assignments quickly transformed Rules into an "arm of the leadership" (Oppenheimer 1977). While membership changes had already made it more responsive to Democratic leaders, the committee nonetheless still showed signs of independence in the early 1970s (CQWR, March 30, 1974, 804–10). But after the 1974 reform, Rules unmistakably became a leadership agent. Even on those occasions when a majority on Rules opposed the Speaker's position, party leaders could generally gain the committee's cooperation. For example, Speaker Tip O'Neill made clear that he would drop members from Rules who opposed him on key issues (Sinclair 1983). Rohde (1991, 25) concludes that the 1974 change gave the Speaker direct control over "what had been one of the most important independent power centers in the House." In doing so, it reversed one of the key changes wrought by the 1910 revolt against Cannon. The emergence of restrictive rules as a majority party tool in the 1980s depended in part on the especially close relationship between party leaders and the Rules Committee institutionalized in 1974.

The impact of shifting control over other assignments to Steering and Policy was less noteworthy. In the short term, one primary effect was to weaken Ways and Means (Rieselbach and Unekis 1981–82). Because party leaders did not, at first, use Steering and Policy extensively to encourage loyalty and shape committee delegations (Waldman 1981; Sundquist 1981), the dispersive effects of weakening Ways and Means were not immediately offset by the centralizing potential of Steering and Policy. But Steering and Policy eventually began to play a more significant role. Starting in 1979, party leaders brought scorecards showing members' party support on key roll calls into Steering and Policy deliberations on committee transfer requests (Sinclair 1995b; Smith and Ray 1983). Over the next several years, the leadership more actively guided assignment decisions. Evidence from interviews with members strongly indicates that liberals made loyalty a criterion for key committee assignments (Rohde 1994, 348). House Democrats now had more incentives to stick with the party on important votes, and delegations to top committees became more likely to reflect party positions than in the past (Sinclair 1995b; Rohde 1991).

But the leadership's new powers should not be exaggerated. Democratic congressman David Price (1992, 88) of North Carolina argues that the limitations on Steering and Policy's ability to encourage loyalty "are at least as impressive as the instances of its exercise." Most members typically are not seeking a transfer to a new committee and thus have little to worry about from Steering and Policy. Furthermore, Democratic leaders have not used their influence over assignments consistently. Price (1992, 88–89) points out that the leadership gave some of the least loyal "boll weevils" better committee assignments in 1981 and on other occasions when the party lacked a solid floor majority. Notwithstanding these limitations, the December 1974 shift in authority over committee assignments contributed to leadership power and constituted a key element in Democrats' bid to build a more party-centered House. In the hands of Speaker Jim Wright, in particular, it loomed as a critical change.

Deposing the Chairmen, 1975

Just one month after the committee assignments change, Democrats made a far more dramatic move to transform the House committee system. Building on a series of earlier caucus reforms that had provided for secret ballot votes on individual committee chairmen, members voted in January 1975 to depose three chairmen, W. R. Poage (D-Tex.) of Agriculture, Wright Patman (D-Tex.) of Banking and Currency, and F. Edward Hebert (D-La.) of Armed Services. The overthrow of these senior southern chairmen ended the virtually automatic reliance on seniority in selecting committee leaders.[50]

Liberal Democrats' closely related policy and partisan goals once again played a critical role in this case. The DSG initiated the challenge to seniority in the late 1960s, seeking in the words of staff director Richard Conlon to "make the committee chairmen responsive to the Caucus" (quoted in Malbin 1974, 1883). The DSG produced studies showing that committee chairmen were disproportionately conservative and often among the least loyal party members. As northern liberals came to constitute a greater proportion of the caucus, they resented the conservative southern committee barons (Davidson 1980a). Conlon declared that "we are trying to unstack the deck which we feel has been stacked against the majority for the last couple of decades" (quoted in Malbin 1974, 1882). Attacking seniority would strengthen the Democratic party by making chairmen accountable to the caucus, while more specifically benefiting the liberals who increasingly controlled caucus machinery (see Rohde 1991 for a similar account).

But ideological and partisan concerns were not the only factors at work. Junior members in both parties were eager to break senior members' hold on power. Reformers were not simply angry at conservative chairmen: the autocratic behavior of such liberals as Government Operations chairman Chet Holifield (D-Calif.) also stirred their ire (*CQWR*, January 20, 1973, 71). Rieselbach (1994, 52) thus notes that junior legislators (along with many liberals) "chafed under the restrictions on their participation and policy influence that the committee-dominated regime imposed" (see also Davidson and Oleszek 1977, 42–43). Relatively high turnover, peaking in 1975, brought large numbers of new members into the House who supported the attack on seniority (Hinckley 1976; Peters 1990). This fits Diermeier's (1995) hypothesis that heightened turnover can erode norms of deference to committee leaders.[51]

Indeed, the seventy-five freshmen Democrats elected in 1974 catalyzed the 1975 purge. The freshmen sought to demonstrate that they expected equal treatment from their senior colleagues and that they would not wait years to exercise power (Loomis 1988). The new members demanded that each would-be chairman appear before them and answer questions. The three chairmen ultimately deposed in 1975 made a poor impression, evading questions and showing a distinct lack of respect for the freshmen (Sheppard 1985; Hinckley 1976). One of the three, Patman, was a liberal populist, but this did not negate concerns about his age and competence.

Beyond their ideology, the three deposed chairmen symbolized an old, seniority-dominated order that stood in the way of the individualistic policy entrepreneurship that defined the class of 1974 and that increasingly came to characterize the Congress as a whole (Loomis 1988; Uslaner 1978).

Junior member hostility to seniority was by no means confined to liberal Democrats. "Young Turk" Republicans also took on their party's adherence to seniority, and the GOP adopted reforms that were quite similar to and often even predated those of the Democrats. In March 1970, one day before the Democrats created the Hansen committee to study seniority, junior Republicans persuaded House GOP leader Gerald Ford (R-Mich.) to appoint a task force on seniority (*National Journal,* March 21, 1970, 640; Sundquist 1981). The House GOP conference eventually accepted the task force's plan for conference votes on individual ranking minority members. Similarly, junior Republicans in the Senate, led by Robert Packwood, Charles Mathias of Maryland, and Robert Taft Jr. of Ohio, succeeded in implementing recorded conference votes on nominees for committee leadership positions. Still, the GOP did not experience an actual purge, suggesting that ousting a specific committee leader likely required additional factors beyond junior members' power interests, such as the Democrats' ideological feud.

Thus, the overthrow of the seniority system drew support from frustrated liberal Democrats and from junior members in both parties. Nearly all of the important action occurred in party committees and caucuses. The House Democratic reforms originated with the Hansen committee. Under pressure from the DSG, the committee recommended in 1971 that any ten members be able to force a separate caucus vote on an individual chairman. The caucus approved this change on a voice vote. The caucus adopted further reforms in 1973 that also originated with the DSG and that the Hansen committee had modified and reported. These rules made the vote on each chairman mandatory and provided that it would be by secret ballot if 20 percent of the members so requested. The secret ballot provision passed on a 117–58 caucus vote (CQ Almanac 1973, 45). While the caucus vote was not public, a December 1972 survey conducted by Common Cause provides information on individual members' positions on the automatic vote on chairmen (Common Cause 1973). A logit analysis of responses to the survey supports the view that liberals' policy preferences and junior members' power interests drove the reform: ideology and seniority are each significant predictors of support for the change.[52]

Although majority leader O'Neill backed the 1973 Hansen reforms, the leadership's position on seniority was ambivalent. Party leaders opposed liberals' unsuccessful effort in 1971 to oust conservative John McMillan

(D-S.C.) as chairman of the District of Columbia Committee. Speaker Albert and majority whip John McFall (D-Calif.) both told Common Cause that they opposed the requirement for an automatic vote on individual chairmen (*CQWR*, January 20, 1973, 71). However, Albert recognized that a caucus majority favored the requirement and did not resist. Two years later, party leaders were simply bystanders as the freshmen ousted the three chairmen. When Steering and Policy met in January 1975, O'Neill moved that that the most senior Democrat on each committee serve as chairman. But several members objected to this, and Steering and Policy narrowly recommended the removal of Patman and Wayne Hays (D-Ohio) of the House Administration Committee. In the end, the caucus saved Hays but added Hebert and Poage to the list of victims.[53] O'Neill (1987, 284) later recalled that "this was one of the few times when I was genuinely caught by surprise" in the House. As Speaker, O'Neill continued the tradition of leadership deference to seniority. In 1979, when liberals challenged Jamie Whitten's (D-Miss.) ascension to Appropriations chair, O'Neill came to Whitten's defense, declaring that a poor party support record was "no reason to turn a man down" (*CQWR*, January 27, 1979, 153).

Though party leaders were unenthusiastic about the 1975 purge, they sent members the clear message that challenging the caucus decision on the floor would not be tolerated. In an uncharacteristically blunt threat, O'Neill even warned that anyone who challenged the caucus decisions "should be expelled from the party" (*National Journal*, January 25, 1975, 132). The threat of a floor appeal, raised by Hebert but quickly retracted, had little chance of success. Members of both parties regarded committee assignments as a caucus matter, and the overwhelming Democratic majority made it particularly unlikely that a coalition of dissident Democrats and Republicans could succeed (Schickler and Rich 1997a). While Cox and McCubbins (1997) argue that increasing Democratic homogeneity was the key to the onset of seniority violations, roll call data suggests that the majority party remained extremely divided into the late 1970s (see Rohde 1991; Young and Cooper 1997; and figure 6.2). Instead, the swollen Democratic majority allowed party liberals to punish a few of their conservative enemies without the threat of a cross-party floor challenge.[54]

While the 1975 seniority violations had only limited effects on the three committees in question (Berg 1978; Ornstein and Rohde 1977; Rieselbach and Unekis 1981–82), they had a profound impact on the House. Along with the subcommittee bill of rights and other reforms, they greatly reduced the influence and independence of committee chairmen (Bailey 1989). As *Congressional Quarterly* (1976, 743) observed, the demotions, "more than any other event, signaled top-ranking committee members that they would be held accountable to their colleagues for their actions and had to be solicitous of those colleagues if they were to win and hold chairmanships."

Reducing committee chairmen's independence had important benefits for Democrats. Barone (1990, 539) writes that "the message was sent to all chairmen that they must be alert and responsive to the wishes of the majority of the Democratic caucus or they might lose their chairs as well." An aide to O'Neill noted that while the 1973 caucus reforms had not led chairmen to cooperate more with party leaders, "the three chairmen being thrown out in 1975 has affected the willingness of chairmen to cooperate with the leadership . . . they got the message" (quoted in Waldman 1981, 379). Crook and Hibbing (1985) and Rohde (1991) present evidence that the seniority changes have increased committee chairmen's loyalty, and Connelly and Pitney (1994) add that the purge made chairmen more re-luctant to work with committee Republicans.

Notwithstanding these benefits to the majority party, the challenge to seniority also posed some problems for Democrats. Though individual committee chairmen were often recalcitrant, they also served as important focal points for coalition building and could often deliver votes for key measures. The decline in chairmen's influence further fragmented power in the House and gave party leaders and whips more of the legislative burden (Davis 1979; Bailey 1988, 110). Chairmen's role in coalition building may help explain party leaders' reluctance to embrace the attack on seniority. Leaders apparently perceived the potential tension between ever-greater decentralization and the Democratic party's effectiveness.

The Rise of Restrictive Rules

The rise of restrictive rules in the House countered the earlier reforms' dispersal of power. The 1970 Reorganization Act's provision for recorded teller votes, when combined with the new electronic voting system in 1973, spawned an explosion in floor amendments that often successfully challenged committee products (Smith 1989). Meanwhile, the seniority and subcommittee reforms of the 1970s left committee chairmen less equipped to resist floor amendments. Inexperienced subcommittee leaders often managed bills on the floor. The chaotic deliberations that resulted troubled majority party Democrats. Rather than repealing these earlier changes, however, the Democrats developed a partial solution: special rules that restricted amendments. By the mid-1980s, restrictive rules had become the House's standard method for handling major legislation. The share of restrictive rules increased from a mere 15 percent of special rules in 1977–78 to nearly one-half in 1987–88, and to 70 percent in the 103rd Congress of 1993–94 (Sinclair 1995a).[55]

Restrictive rules most prominently served Democrats' partisan interest in countering the GOP's aggressive use of floor amendments to unravel Democratic bills and to embarrass the majority party. In August 1979, forty Democrats signed a letter demanding that the leadership devise more restrictive rules (Smith 1989, 40–42). Speaker O'Neill then met with Rules Committee Democrats and urged them to limit floor amendments. The *National Journal*'s Richard Cohen (1979, 1329) commented at the time that "Democrats of many different stripes" were "looking to their leaders and to the Rules Committee to relieve the agony" brought about by amending marathons. Rules member Butler Derrick (D-S.C.) also noted that "House members have sought me out and said we have to do something about the floor situation and this is the Rules Committee's responsibility" (quoted in Cohen 1979, 1330). In the ensuing years, Rules Committee efforts to shape floor deliberations "expanded qualitatively" with the appearance of "novel devices . . . that stack the deck to favor majority-party outcomes" (Davidson 1992, 21). Specialized studies of changes in the amending process agree that Democrats' partisan interests were critical. For example, Smith (1989, 78) argues that Democrats have embraced restrictive rules "in order to protect their party and committees from unpredictable and politically dangerous floor amendments." Supporting this view, Sinclair (1994) finds restrictive rules are more likely when majority party leaders are heavily involved in a bill's consideration and when a bill divides Democrats against Republicans.

As in the case of the other party-based changes in this period, liberals' policy goals complemented Democrats' partisan interests. Democrats often used restrictive rules to provide cover for members to vote for liberal policies when public opinion was more conservative (Sinclair 1995b). By making the key vote on a controversial measure procedural—namely, the vote to approve the special rule—Democratic leaders enabled "members to vote their policy preferences without paying too big a reelection price" (Sinclair 1993, 249). In the 1980s, examples include restrictive rules used to block votes on mandatory AIDS testing and repeal of the national speed limit (Schickler 1994). Liberal Democrats especially benefited from restrictive rules that prevented GOP amendments that might otherwise have won over moderate and conservative Democrats.

But the growth in restrictive rules did not solely reflect Democratic and liberal interests. All members shared a common stake in the House's capacity to legislate. Peters (1990, 269–70) argues that the reforms of the 1970s had "shattered the power structure of the House and made it very difficult for normal business to proceed," and therefore, "a balanced view of [restrictive rules] suggests causes that lay deeper than the partisan motives of an overbearing majority." Amending marathons and chaotic floor proceedings worried thoughtful members of both parties. Thus, former Republican representative Charles Whalen of Ohio endorsed Democrats' call for more debate and amending limitations to help the House efficiently handle its workload (Whalen 1982, 167). Bach and Smith (1988) argue that the trend toward restrictive rules in part reflected members' shared interest in reducing uncertainty and expediting business. Furthermore, Krehbiel (1991) shows that specialized, diverse committees that reflect the composition of the House are more likely to receive restrictive rules, again suggesting that amending limitations often serve the membership at large.[56] The growing number of multiple referrals and omnibus bills also required greater reliance on complex special rules (Young and Cooper 1993).[57]

Although concerns about congressional capacity likely necessitated some limitations on amendments, Democrats' partisan and policy interests determined the form these limitations took. Bolling, an O'Neill ally who served as Rules chairman from 1979 to 1982, developed many of the specific innovations in special rules (Bach and Smith 1988). As noted above, the Missouri Democrat had long advocated stronger party leadership. In this case, he acted as an entrepreneur, linking Democrats' interest in restricting GOP amendments with all members' interest in orderly floor proceedings and with Rules Committee members' stake in strengthening their committee. Bolling gradually persuaded other Rules members that restrictive rules benefited the committee (Cohen 1979, 1330). He also took the lead in designing special rules, often coaching bill managers about what sort of rule they ought to request (Smith 1989, 43–44). Whereas Bolling's predecessors as chairman resisted changing the committee's role, Bolling used his knowledge of House procedures to "develop an innovative repertoire of devices" (Bach and Smith 1988, 74). Bolling also started the practice of having Rules Committee Democrats caucus on their own as they prepared special rules; this no doubt made partisan concerns more salient (Sinclair 1983). Under a conservative Democrat such as Howard Smith of Virginia or Eugene Cox of Georgia, or even a relatively independent moderate such as B. F. Sisk (D-Calif.), restrictive rules likely would have had a more bipartisan cast. Bolling's leadership and O'Neill's control of nominations to Rules ensured a much different outcome. Later in the 1980s, Jim Wright used restrictive rules even more aggressively to structure the amending process in Democrats' favor. Under Wright, the Rules Committee essentially became a branch of the leadership, writing complex rules that satisfied the unusually specific dictates of the Speaker.

The most profound impact of restrictive rules, therefore, has been to empower majority party leaders. Restrictive rules are probably "the single most powerful tool in the leadership's arsenal" (Sinclair 1995b, 72). Democratic leaders used complex rules to maximize the party's unity and promote outcomes favored by party members (Price 1992; Connelly and Pitney 1994). The Rules Committee became a potent centralizing force in an otherwise decentralized chamber.

This use of restrictive rules provoked an angry reaction from Republicans and, at times, from some Democrats. Republican whip Trent Lott of Mississippi complained in 1987 that the Democratic leadership was trying to gain a "stranglehold on this institution" (*CQWR*, October 10, 1987, 2449), while Judd Gregg (R-N.H.) declared that the Democrats "want to use their power to undercut and essentially destroy the participatory process for those of us who are in the minority" (as quoted in Rohde 1991, 112). The Democrats' efforts to shut out politically potent GOP amendments dramatically increased partisan conflict on votes on special rules (Rohde 1991). By the late 1980s, Republicans typically voted as a bloc against special rules for major legislation. Evans and Oleszek (1997, 43) claim that "ironically, by alienating Republican moderates, [the Democrats'] tactics fostered partisan unity for the GOP reform agenda of the 1990s."

The GOP's unified opposition to many restrictive rules forced Democrats to maintain a similar unity in order to prevail. While the Democrats did so with remarkable success, there were recurrent cases in which dissident party members rebelled, defeating or watering down special rules.[58] By the 103rd Congress of 1993–94, moderate and conservative Democrats had become so fed up with amending restrictions that seventeen of them formed the Fair Rules and Openness Group (FROG), which sought to force votes on its members' amendments (*Roll Call*, April 11, 1994). FROG members did not seek to facilitate Republican amendments, but they nonetheless were willing to vote with the GOP when Democratic leaders refused their demands. Democratic leaders were defeated on six votes on special rules in 1993–94, including most spectacularly the vote on the rule for the Democratic crime bill in August 1994. This suggests the limitations of the leadership's reliance on restrictive rules.

While developing this new role for the Rules Committee, Democratic leaders had essentially left in place earlier reforms that had fostered a more open, collegial legislative process (see Smith 1989). Kravitz (1990) points out the irony that the antisecrecy movement that won adoption of recorded teller voting eventually provoked severe amending restrictions— exactly the opposite of what reformers had intended. This case demonstrates how institutional development takes on a disjointed character.

Democratic leaders lacked the support to overturn the 1970 recorded teller provision,[59] but they did capitalize on members' partisan, ideological, and institutional concerns to add new mechanisms that have limited the damage caused by the earlier reform. The resulting authority structure is an amalgam of conflicting elements: standing rules and individualistic assumptions encourage an open, collegial floor environment even as special restrictive rules impose some centralized control.

The Revitalization of the Speakership

The advent of a revived, powerful speakership in the late 1980s represented the culmination of Democrats' party-building reforms. While O'Neill began to revitalize the speakership, Jim Wright's aggressive leadership in the 100th Congress (1987–88) truly made the office an important agenda-setter and policy promoter.[60]

Democrats' partisan interests played a pivotal role in reviving the speakership. Reagan's 1980 election reflected, at least in part, the Democrats' failure to govern as a team during the Carter years (Aldrich 1995; CQ 1982, 188–89). Moreover, Reagan's early triumphs in office owed much to the cooperation of dissident Democrats. Mainstream Democrats had reason to wonder about their party's future. In the context of this serious threat, otherwise individualistic Democrats came to recognize their shared stake in the party's effectiveness (Rieselbach 1995, 19; Price 1992). O'Neill made greater use of party instruments in the final years of his speakership; his "strategy of inclusion" helped to socialize members into working through party mechanisms (Sinclair 1995b). By the time Wright became Speaker in 1987, many Democrats were demanding "a speaker who would take a more forceful hand in shaping a Democratic policy agenda" (Peters 1990, 264). Now that Democrats also controlled the Senate and Reagan was weakened by the Iran-Contra scandal, it seemed possible for party members to build a positive legislative record for the 1988 election (CQWR, July 11, 1987, 1483).

Once again, ideological interests coincided with partisan goals. A combination of electoral trends (such as the decline in the number of conservative southern Democrats) and changes in the legislative agenda (as deficit politics came to the fore) helped ease the divisions that had plagued Democrats in the 1970s and early 1980s (Rohde 1991). As Democrats' policy preferences became more homogeneous and as Reagan threatened programs valued by a substantial majority of Democrats, party members came to see assertive leadership as necessary (Rohde 1991; Sinclair 1995b). Wright's speakership not only showcased the Democrats' ability to govern, but also aimed to reorient national priorities in a more liberal direction (Aldrich and Rohde 1996).

There are some indications that members' interest in congressional power also supported a stronger speakership. Even as early as the mid-1970s, a small circle of members had perceived that excessive decentralization endangered House functioning (*CQWR*, November 8, 1975, 2412). Reforms adopted at the time, such as the multiple referral rule, strengthened the speakership while enhancing congressional capacity. Barry (1989, 66, 114, 446) shows that Wright occasionally won over dissident Democrats by appealing to their shared interest in the power and prestige of the House. Nonetheless, the complete absence of bipartisan support for this change strongly indicates that concerns about congressional power were not significant. Indeed, Wright's unabashed partisanship dissipated any potential Republican support. To the contrary, the Speaker's relentlessness ultimately unleashed forces that undermined the institutional position of the House.

The revival of the speakership came about through a series of actions taken collectively by Democrats and personally by O'Neill and Wright. The 1970s reforms provided the foundation for strong leadership by granting the Speaker an enhanced role in committee assignments and by allowing the Speaker to refer bills to multiple committees.[61] Democrats also expanded the whip system in the 1970s and 1980s, making it an important instrument of persuasion and information exchange for party leaders (Sinclair 1983, 1995b).

Albert did little with his new powers, but rank-and-file members eventually prodded O'Neill into a more aggressive stance. Although O'Neill experienced more setbacks than accomplishments in his first five years as Speaker (CQ 1988, 872; Dodd and Oppenheimer 1993, 551), he confronted the Reagan administration with some success after Democratic gains in the 1982 elections. Deering and Smith (1997, 44) write that "O'Neill began to put his new powers and resources to work," exploiting "the Rules Committee to structure floor debates to Democratic advantage" and relying on the "revitalized Steering and Policy Committee to monitor committee activities." In addition, Republican efforts to make O'Neill a symbol for the outdated, bloated Democratic establishment thrust a more public role upon the Speaker. O'Neill responded by developing "a new conception of the Speaker's role," as he fought Reagan on television by standing visibly for the average American (Peters 1990, 237). Previous Speakers had not had a high public profile, but O'Neill's tenure "elevated the national visibility of the speakership and thus the office's potential to articulate and establish the House's agenda" (Oleszek 1996, 34).

Wright took full advantage of the Speaker's enhanced resources and public visibility. On his election as Speaker, the Texan outlined an ambitious agenda, including major legislation on clean water, highways, trade, welfare reform, aid to the homeless, farm credit assistance, and deficit reduction. The program emphasized issues on which most Democrats agreed (Rohde 1991). In moving these measures through the House, Wright pushed his powers "to their limits in a way no speaker had done since Joe Cannon" (Peters 1990, 267). He did not hesitate to intervene in committee deliberations or to use restrictive rules, committee assignment decisions, and threats of retribution (Barry 1989; Peters 1990). Nine of Wright's ten priorities were enacted, with the sole failure attributable to Reagan's veto of the trade bill. Beyond his legislative activities, Wright staked out a major role for himself in foreign policy, facilitating the Central American peace process that ultimately halted fighting between the Sandinistas and *contras* in Nicaragua (Barry 1989).

Wright's speakership made the House a more centralized and partisan institution. By the end of the 100th Congress, scholars began to note a dramatic shift in House operations as party leaders became newly influential (Davidson 1988; Dodd and Oppenheimer 1989). Where O'Neill had let the House agenda bubble up through the often-bipartisan committee process, intervening only selectively, Wright seized a much more active agenda-setting and power-wielding role (*CQWR*, March 12, 1988, 623; Dodd and Oppenheimer 1993).

In the short term, this strong, centralized leadership worked reasonably well. For the first time since Thomas Reed, the majority party in the House had, acting independently of presidential leadership, initiated and enacted an extensive program of its own.[62] This not only benefited the Democratic party but also enhanced the power and prestige of the House. Aldrich and Rohde (1996, 1) conclude that the 100th Congress, along with Newt Gingrich's 104th Congress, "stand as high-water marks . . . in House leadership of the policy-making process." Liberal Democrat George Miller of California commented in 1988 that Wright's "risk-taking has given the House back some of its pride" (*CQWR*, March 12, 1988, 624).

But Wright's assertive leadership also created serious problems. Most notably, by virtually shutting out House Republicans, Wright provoked their intense hatred and opposition. One of the most damaging episodes occurred on October 29, 1987, when Wright barely won approval of a deficit reduction bill. After initially being defeated by a coalition of dissident Democrats and Republicans, Wright used an obscure parliamentary maneuver to bring up the bill for a second time on the same day.[63] Then, after declaring that time had expired, Wright held open the roll call until a reluctant member could be virtually dragged from the cloakroom to change his vote, producing a one-vote victory for the Democrats (*CQWR*, November 7, 1987, 2712). This incident, along with other episodes of unusually assertive leadership, provoked such Republican fury that minority party members "were as angry at Wright as Democrats had been at

Uncle Joe Cannon" (Peters 1990, 269). Wright's tactics led to procedural protests and strengthened the hand of Gingrich and other young activists advocating an attack on Wright's personal ethics and the House as an institution (Barry 1989, 362).

Democrats' disaffection with Wright's leadership was milder and less widespread than the GOP's, but noteworthy nonetheless. While Democrats agreed with Wright on several of his priorities, there was considerable disagreement on trade, welfare reform, spending levels, taxes, and *contra* aid.[64] Many resented the constant heavy lobbying from the leadership on these and other issues (Barry 1989). Tim Penny (D-Minn.) complained that Wright allowed conservative Democrats only "token amendments" and "strong-armed [us] into going along" (*CQWR*, March 12, 1988, 625). Barry (1989, 409) notes that in the past, party leaders had "left openings for members to balance their voting records. But this leadership was squeezing so many things it was closing off the outlets. The resentment was growing." Democrats repeatedly showed signs of restiveness and discontent in 1987–88. Buddy MacKay (D-Fla.) noted in December 1987, "I've been finessed. Never have I seen as much difference between what I'm being told we've done this year up here—how great it's been, how much we've accomplished—and what my constituents say back home" (quoted in Barry 1989, 544).

Perhaps more important than these issue-based schisms, Wright's highly centralized mode of operations clashed with Democrats' interest in protecting their power as individual members. *Congressional Quarterly* noted in 1988 (872) that while Democrats took pride in Wright's legislative accomplishments, "many resented being excluded from the process of achieving them. The 'Lone Ranger,' as Wright was sometimes dubbed, had a record of springing major decisions without consulting key colleagues." Committee and subcommittee chairmen who had nurtured their own power bases over the years bridled at Wright's domination. Barry (1989, 153) observes that members "knew [O'Neill] would take care of their agendas. Wright had his own agenda." A Democratic enemy of Wright's commented that "Wright doesn't let these guys play. He's got his . . . agenda. That's it. . . . In a democracy you should be allowed amendments on the floor. . . . There's so much unrest it's unbelievable" (quoted in Barry 1989, 545). Democrats eventually realized to their consternation that their leaders were "trying to create a structure which forced members who wanted to play a role to do so under leadership auspices. The leadership . . . ran more things than O'Neill had ever contemplated running. It ran too much" (Barry 1989, 300).

Wright's ultimate downfall at the hands of ethics charges initiated by Gingrich was more than a personal rebuff. First, it shows that closing off opportunities for minority party members to pursue their legislative interests is dangerous because it fosters incentives to attack the House as an institution and its leadership as individuals. Second, it points to the fragility of the regime of party government that Democrats sought to meld with earlier reforms that had dispersed power. This fragility does not imply that it was a mistake for Democrats to strengthen their party. However, to be sustained in the long term, party-building efforts must also take account of competing interests. Wright failed to do so. His experiment with strong, centralized leadership conflicted with individual members' desire to act as entrepreneurs pursuing their own agendas. Wright's downfall highlights the tensions and contradictions facing bids to establish a highly centralized mode of operations in the contemporary House.

MINORITY PARTY INTERESTS: COS AND THE RISE OF THE REPUBLICAN BOMBTHROWERS

The formation of the Conservative Opportunity Society in 1983 by Newt Gingrich and a small band of like-minded colleagues exemplifies how a string of institutional changes that privilege one set of interests can provoke members to defend a competing set of interests. Militant junior Republicans responded to perceived majority party abuses by adopting increasingly confrontational methods. The rise of COS is one important, though unintended, legacy of the Democrats' party building.

COS gave organizational form to the so-called bombthrower wing of the Republican party. It pursued a strategy of all-out attacks on the Democratic-controlled House as a means to gain majority status. COS members used speeches broadcast on C-SPAN to publicize Democratic misdeeds, while employing obstructionist parliamentary tactics to stall business on the floor. Much like the farm bloc of the early 1920s, COS was a factional maneuver, rather than a change approved by the House as a whole or either party. As a result, it is inappropriate to view this case as contrary to party government or median voter models, and its implications for the other theories reviewed in chapter 1 also need to be interpreted cautiously. Nonetheless, this new leadership instrument had a significant impact on House operations.[65]

During their long tenure in the minority, most Republicans had been content to work within the system, settling for marginal adjustments to Democratic proposals instead of constantly obstructing business (Evans and Oleszek 1997). But there had long been House Republicans who believed that a more disruptive approach was necessary to win a majority (Ornstein 1985). This faction gained strength after the 1978 elections, which brought in Gingrich and other young, activist conservatives. Following the GOP's disappointing showing in the 1982 midterm elections, a dozen "bombthrowers" led by Gingrich formed COS. Gingrich played the role of entrepreneur, aligning ideological, partisan, and power base interests behind creation of a new type of congressional power base: an organization explicitly dedicated to shaping public debate and sharpening partisan distinctions rather than directly influencing House outcomes.

Decades of Democratic control had convinced Gingrich that to "succeed you almost had to destroy the system so that you could rebuild it" (Evans and Oleszek 1997, 27). Only by highlighting Democratic abuses and by disparaging Congress could Republicans win a majority. COS members dedicated themselves to this project, meeting once a week to discuss strategy and tactics. As one COS veteran recalled, Gingrich proposed organizing so that "we could act in concert" rather than as "independent agents running out doing our own thing with no coordination" (as quoted in Pitney 1988, 11). The COS demonstrates that a visible, publicity-conscious bloc can be forged quickly and significantly influence congressional politics (Loomis 1988).

Just as a confluence of partisan and ideological goals facilitated the Democratic party-building in this period, the COS owed much to Gingrich's fusing Republicans' interest in majority status with conservatives' ideological convictions. A central tenet of COS was that a vigorous, positive conservative program would be critical to winning a House majority. Peters (1990, 275) writes that the group's "self-proclaimed mission was to win Republican control of the House by pressing a conservative policy agenda." COS members emphasized both policy and partisan goals: Bobbi Fiedler (R-Calif.) commented that the group "will help to build a coalition for conservative ideas throughout the country," while Duncan Hunter (R-Calif.) added that the organization "has the primary goal of bringing the Republican party to majority status in the House" ("Conservative Opportunity Society" 1984, 11).

Rather than seeking electoral success by moderating the GOP's positions (as advocated by the "92 Group," a bloc formed in 1985 to counter COS), Gingrich emphasized making conservatism more popular and differentiating the Republicans from their Democratic foes (Lemann 1985). Gingrich invented the phrase "Conservative Opportunity Society" to help change Republicans' "lexicon from one of dourness and austerity to one of hope and opportunity" (Pitney 1996, 15). The group attracted support mostly from ardent conservatives, including Robert Walker (R-Pa.), Vin Weber (R-Minn.), and Connie Mack (R-Fla.). Through COS, they could simultaneously promote their own conservative convictions and lay the foundation for an eventual GOP takeover of Congress. A logit analysis of membership in COS finds a strong positive effect for first-dimension NOMINATE scores, indicating that conservative Republicans were substantially more likely to join COS than their fellow partisans (b = 5.25; SE = 1.86).[66]

Junior Republicans' power interests also contributed to the group's success. In contrast to senior Republicans who as ranking committee members could still exert some influence, junior Republicans believed they were shut out entirely from the existing House power structure. Controlling for policy preferences and region, junior members (as measured by terms of service) were more likely to join COS than their senior Republican colleagues (b = −.44; SE = .21). There also appears to be a strong relationship between being a ranking member on a standing committee and joining COS: none of the eighteen ranking committee Republicans had joined the group as of 1984. This again supports the idea that the institutional have-nots spearheaded COS.

Indeed, Gingrich showed frustrated junior members that confrontation and obstruction could provide a new kind of power base. Walker pointed out that "if you accept the fact that you won't get the title of party leader, you actually can, by default, get a central leadership role" (as quoted in Smith 1989, 68). The key to leadership, in this view, was television. COS members used the Congress "largely as a prop to frame issues for the media" (Barry 1989, 165). They made coordinated use of one-minute speeches at the start of each day and of longer, special orders speeches in the evenings to attack the Democrats and propagate conservative ideas. Smith (1989, 68) writes that the "attention the Republican 'young Turks' drew as a result of their television antics gave them a voice they would not have had otherwise." Television coverage of the House floor, which had started in 1979, was still in its infancy when COS "realized that C-SPAN provided an extraordinary tool to reach a new audience" (Balz and Brownstein 1996, 119). Walker noted that "we can't stress enough how much television coverage of the House means to the movement. We're communicating beyond the back-slapping, good-old-boy realm of the House" ("Conservative Opportunity Society" 1984, 14). Where members in the past had used floor debate to argue with each other or to insert material into the *Congressional Record*, Gingrich and his allies sought a broader audience.

Many Republicans had qualms about these disruptive tactics, believing that COS members' strategy would actually hurt efforts to win a majority. Conservative Mickey Edwards (R-Okla.) attacked COS in a 1984 letter to his fellow Republicans, arguing that the party needed to focus on "the individual concerns of 435 different constituencies" as opposed to relying on "guerrilla activities" that merely created "ferment and turmoil" (Pitney 1988, 27).[67] GOP leader Robert Michel (R-Ill.) reportedly welcomed Edwards's broadside (*National Journal*, December 15, 1984, 2402).

But in 1989, just five years after the Edwards letter, Gingrich was elected GOP whip. By 1993, the confrontational approach advocated by COS had been embraced by most Republicans. Gingrich's ability to change how

Republicans viewed the political world was key to his group's success. The Democrats played into Gingrich's hands in that regard. Prior to the 1980s, Republicans could carve out reasonably successful House careers as minority party members. But "Gingrich's gospel of rebellion became more and more persuasive" as the Democrats shut out the GOP (Connelly and Pitney 1994, 8). The Democrats' decision in 1985 to seat Robert McCloskey (D-Ind.) instead of the GOP challenger whom state officials certified had won the 1984 election radicalized many Republicans (Balz and Brownstein 1996, 122). Two years later, Wright's aggressiveness inflamed Republicans' passions and seemed to show that cooperation with the majority was a dead end. During Wright's tenure, Barry (1989, 672) reports that "Republicans were moving closer and closer to Gingrich's idea that the best way to take control of the house was to destroy it."

Gingrich and his COS allies actively capitalized on the resentment that Democrats had created. Republicans went along with Gingrich's ethics campaign against Wright because they loathed the Speaker's tactics. The ethics fight showed Republicans that making the House and its Democratic majority look bad could propel the GOP to power. Ethics troubles forced both Wright and Democratic whip Tony Coelho (D-Calif.) to resign in mid-1989. Gingrich and his COS allies turned such ethics problems into a "symbol of Democratic corruption" (CQ 1988, 872). Gingrich also encouraged freshmen Republicans to pursue the House bank scandal of 1991–92. Public confidence in the Congress fell to new lows amid the barrage of accusations and disclosures.

The COS speeches on the floor, along with a series of audiotapes that Gingrich distributed under the auspices of his political action committee, GOPAC, also played an indirect role in shaping Republicans' preferences. The speeches and training tapes helped to "teach a generation of activists how to think and talk about political strategy" (Pitney 1996, 20). Gingrich used COS and GOPAC to reach his party's future elite; many House Republicans of the 1990s came of age watching Gingrich on C-SPAN (Pitney and Connelly 1996). Indeed, elections in the late 1980s and 1990s brought in more and more Republicans committed to the strategies espoused by Gingrich and COS (Evans and Oleszek 1997). By 1989, half of the eight elected Republican leaders were COS veterans, and Michel was soon forced to take a tougher line with the Democrats or risk losing his job as leader (Connelly and Pitney 1994). The bombthrower wing had captured the House GOP.

Not all of these developments can be credited to COS, but it did give the confrontationalists a forum to coordinate their efforts and message. It also was "the first important vehicle Gingrich rode to power" (Balz and Brownstein 1996, 118). Furthermore, its activities heightened partisanship in the House. In addition to their speeches, COS members often sponsored surprise amendments to embarrass the Democrats. This made Democrats all the more determined to use restrictive rules (Smith 1989). These rules in turn provoked more GOP indignation, continuing the cycle of bitterness and recriminations. While Democrats appeared to control the legislative process, COS attacks took their toll on the party. After Wright's downfall, Balz and Brownstein (1996, 125) write, the "House had become an ethics swamp and an institution mired in partisanship." This description remained apt for the remainder of Democrats' tenure in the majority, as recurrent scandals and bitter party conflict continued to plague the House.

CONCLUSIONS

The array of institutional changes adopted in 1970–89 vividly illustrates that disjointed pluralism characterizes congressional development. Multiple interests typically shaped each innovation. Entrepreneurs often played a critical role in aligning potentially competing interests behind specific changes. Innovations intended to serve new purposes were layered on top of preexisting arrangements designed to serve different purposes. Changes that primarily served one interest repeatedly provoked changes that protected competing interests. This last dynamic was especially apparent in the House, where the difficulties created by junior members' dispersing committee power bases led House Democrats to empower majority party leaders in the 1980s. This in turn provoked increasingly fervent GOP attacks on the majority party and the House.

The Senate did not experience a comparable partisan revival in the 1980s. Indeed, more so than in the House, changes in the Senate in this period can be characterized in terms of a single dominant theme. Opening committee meetings, improving staffing for junior members, reorganizing the committee system, and rising obstruction each made the Senate a more open and egalitarian institution and maximized individual senators' opportunities for entrepreneurship and activism. These changes typically served as a common carrier for junior members' power base interests and for minority party senators' interest in enhancing their resources.

There were a few countervailing tendencies in the Senate. The Stevenson reforms augmented the Senate's policymaking capacity by streamlining its committee system. The budget process launched in 1974 contributed a degree of centralization and increased the potential for party leadership. The debate limitations on budget resolutions and reconciliation measures, in particular, have enabled the majority party to pursue its budgetary agenda without a cloture-proof margin. Finally, Bob Dole (R-Kans.) and George Mitchell (D-Maine) were aggressive party leaders, so that by the early 1990s some were even commenting on the surprising strength of Senate leaders compared to their House counterparts, Michel and Foley (Smith 1993).

Still, Dole, Mitchell, and, most recently, Trent Lott, never had access to the leadership instruments available to Jim Wright or Newt Gingrich. While House Democrats developed restrictive rules to regulate floor deliberations, the Senate's amending process remains wide open (Smith 1989). Roll call data confirms that the increase in Senate partisanship in the 1980s was far less striking than that in the House (Young and Cooper 1997). Preexisting institutions help to explain these differences. The supermajority vote needed to overcome filibusters seriously constrains majority party government in the Senate. The more frequent turnover in party control of the Senate also may reduce the incentives for the majority party to curb minority rights. Furthermore, senators in both parties benefit personally from Senate institutions that provide plentiful opportunities for individual assertion. Majority party senators have proven unwilling to surrender their individual prerogatives to help pass party programs.

In the House, liberal Democrats instigated most of the important changes. In championing the early reforms, such as the Legislative Reorganization Act of 1970, the empowerment of subcommittees, and the attack on seniority, liberals broadened their coalition by appealing to members' interest in increased access to power. These interests were compatible in the early 1970s because undermining conservative committee chairmen had the potential both to boost liberal policies and to disperse power to junior members (Rohde 1991).

Nonetheless, the decision to attack the chairmen through changes that fragmented power bore an uncomfortable relationship to another aspect of many liberals' reform agenda: strengthening party leaders so that they could help pass ambitious domestic programs. James O'Hara (D-Mich.), the DSG's chairman at the start of the reform era, acknowledged the tension between reformers who favored strengthened leadership and those who favored democratizing the House. O'Hara recalled that the DSG's strategists "could never agree on exactly which direction" to move, "so we went in both directions at once" (quoted in Sheppard 1985, 96). That is, the Democrats simultaneously granted new powers to their leaders— through such devices as authorizing the Speaker to appoint the majority members on Rules and to refer bills to multiple committees—and used sunshine and subcommittee reforms to disperse power among individual members and subcommittee chairmen (Sheppard 1985, 95–100).

Initially, the fragmenting changes proved more significant than the centralizing ones, creating considerable difficulties for Democrats during the Carter years. After successfully passing Carter's energy program (which unceremoniously fell apart in the Senate), House Democrats quickly began to show signs of disarray. *Congressional Quarterly* (1982, 188) observed that "as the end of the decade neared, the Democratic leadership's position of authority over Democrats in the House had so eroded that many basic majority party functions had become heavy burdens rather than exercises of power." In a single week in September 1979, four major bills went down to floor defeats, embarrassing O'Neill and the Democrats. In commenting on the events of 1979, Peters (1990, 229) claims that "one would have to go back to the days of obstructionism" of the nineteenth century "to find the House so paralyzed on legislative matters." The next year, the majority passed a budget resolution only after resorting to a lame-duck session, reinforcing "the Democrats' image as a faltering and ineffective party" (CQ 1982, 189). Because the House reforms of the 1970s had forged an authority structure characterized by individual entrepreneurship and fragmented power, they had made the House "a more unwieldy place than it used to be" (CQ 1980, 873; see also Cohen 1979). Thus, Speaker O'Neill wondered aloud in 1980 whether "we put power into the hands of too many? You now have 158 House committees and subcommittees, each with a chairman. . . . People are saying, 'We've gone too far; let's retrench' " (*US News*, August 11, 1980, 24).

O'Neill's query proved prescient. In the 1980s, Democrats responded to the difficulties created by the 1970s reforms by adopting major changes that centralized power in the hands of party leaders. But the Democrats superimposed these changes on top of the earlier innovations that had fragmented power. Restrictive rules countered the rise in amending activity that the Legislative Reorganization Act had spawned, yet the need to pass controversial special rules for each piece of major legislation enmeshed leaders in difficult battles that had rarely been necessary prior to 1970. A revitalized speakership brought coordination to a system nearly falling apart, yet the persistence of the subcommittee bill of rights and sunshine reforms underscored the continuing force of rank-and-file Democrats' demands for plentiful outlets for individual activism. The reforms of the 1970s and 1980s had empowered both rank-and-file Democrats and party leaders, creating an uneasy combination of institutions that minority party members invested considerable resources in toppling.

CHAPTER 6

Understanding Congressional Change

THE PRECEDING four chapters demonstrate that disjointed pluralism has characterized congressional development. In this concluding chapter, I sum up the major patterns that emerge over time and consider the evidence concerning the four claims outlined in chapter 1. I then assess how well alternative theories fare in grappling with this evidence and discuss the relationship of these theories to disjointed pluralism. I conclude with thoughts on the broader implications of disjointed pluralism for political institutions.

MULTIPLE INTERESTS PER CHANGE

The evidence from each period provides strong support for the claim that multiple collective interests shape institutional change. In all but six of the forty-two cases examined, more than one member interest played a significant role.

A critical question is whether the importance of multiple interests depends on how I have defined institutional change. In this study, that definition includes rules and procedures, the committee system, and leadership instruments. Changes in any of these three elements of a legislature's authority structure are included, even if adopted by a party or a faction, rather than by the House or Senate as a whole, or if informal in nature.

Twenty-six of the forty-two cases fit a narrower definition of an institutional change: these were formal changes directly approved by the House, Senate, or both chambers.[1] Interestingly, the creation of the Joint Committee on Atomic Energy (JCAE) in 1946 is the only formal, floor-approved change that is explained by a single interest. By contrast, five of the sixteen cases that did not involve direct floor approval can be explained by a single interest: the rise of centralized Senate party leadership in the late 1890s, the Senate farm bloc in 1921–22, House Republicans' punishment in 1925 of party members who had supported Robert La Follette for president, the conservative coalition's transformation of the Rules Committee in 1937, and the onset of weekly leadership meetings between the president and Democratic leaders in the late 1930s.[2]

Thus, support for the multiple interests claim is even stronger if one limits attention to formal, floor-approved changes and excludes informal, intraparty, and factional moves. Indeed, accommodating multiple interests appears more important for formal changes that require floor approval than for changes that can be adopted by a smaller group of legislators. This makes intuitive sense: building a majority floor coalition likely requires broader appeals and greater compromises than does mobilizing a party or faction. However, the advantage of a formal change approved on the floor is that it characteristically binds all members and may prove difficult to reverse. Therefore, we might expect members to pursue formal floor-approved changes when appeals to multiple interests are feasible and do not require big compromises, and when binding other members is critical.[3]

ENTREPRENEURS' ROLE IN DEVISING
COMMON CARRIER CHANGES

The case studies also demonstrate that entrepreneurs play an important role aligning multiple interests behind common carrier changes. The historical record suggests that entrepreneurs were significant in fifteen of forty-two cases:

Reed rules, 1890: Reed manipulated timing to align his and other reformers' interest in congressional capacity with Republicans' partisan interests.

Restoration of quorum rule, 1894: Reed and his allies filibustered to persuade Democrats that reform would protect their partisan interests and promote congressional capacity.

Revival of the speakership, 1903: Cannon appealed to Republicans' partisan interests and to all representatives' interest in their chamber's power.

Rules reforms, 1909: George Norris, John Nelson, and Champ Clark devised a proposal satisfactory to "mild" and "radical" insurgents and to Democrats.[4]

Rules reforms, 1910: Norris manipulated members' position-taking interests to force a vote on reforms intended to benefit progressives and to spread power.

Revival of the speakership, 1925: Longworth fashioned his leadership into a common carrier for Republicans' partisan interests and Democratic leaders' power interests.

Dies committee, 1938: Dies appealed to both conservatives and liberals in gaining approval for his Special Committee on Un-American Activities and subsequently used the committee to promote both the conservative coalition and committee members' careers.

Investigations explosion, 1940s: Individual entrepreneurs used investigations as common carriers to challenge executive primacy, strengthen the conservative coalition, and provide new power bases.

LRA of 1946: Mike Monroney and Robert La Follette Jr. included new perks for individual members (so-called ice cream provisions) to defuse opposition to the committee consolidation, which was intended to strengthen congressional capacity and power (the "spinach").

Policy committees, 1946: Robert Taft capitalized on reformist ferment to gain more resources for his Policy Committee power base.

LRA of 1970: Donald Fraser, Sam Gibbons, Barber Conable, and fellow reformers devised amendments that linked liberals' policy interests, junior members' power interests, and minority party interests.

Empowering House subcommittees, 1971–74: DSG activists (especially Phil Burton, Frank Thompson, and key staffers) broadened the coalition to attack conservative committee chairmen by appealing to junior members' power interests.

Stevenson committee reforms, 1977: Stevenson and Brock sparked interest in reforms to strengthen the Senate committee system by linking these changes with junior members' power interests.

Rise of restrictive rules after 1979: Bolling linked Democrats' interest in restricting GOP amendments with all members' interest in orderly floor proceedings and with Rules Committee members' stake in their committee's power.

Conservative Opportunity Society, 1983: Newt Gingrich aligned conservatives' policy goals, Republicans' partisan interests, and junior Republicans' power interests behind creation of COS.

This list suggests that entrepreneurs are involved in a diverse set of reforms: eleven involved formal action on the floor, while three were informal changes in leadership instruments (the revivals of the speakership under Cannon and Longworth, and the creation of COS) and one—empowering House subcommittees—involved formal changes in party rules.[5] Thus, restricting attention to formal, floor-approved changes does not mitigate support for the second claim.[6]

One noteworthy pattern is that entrepreneurs were involved in nine of the eighteen cases in which Congress-centered (or chamber-centered) interests were either a primary or secondary motivation, as opposed to just five of twenty-four cases that did not promote Congress-centered interests. This again makes sense: most members can perceive the immediate benefits of changes that promote policy, personal power, or partisan goals. But the benefits of Congress-centered changes are typically more distant.

Entrepreneurs can help craft reforms that will also appeal to other, more tangible member interests.

A further observation is that entrepreneurs include both formal party leaders and backbenchers. Party leaders typically are involved in changes that serve their party's interests, suggesting that they at least partly internalize these interests (see Cox and McCubbins 1993). At the same time, backbenchers have actively promoted cross-party coalitions and minority party interests: notable instances include Norris and his allies in 1909–10, Dies and his fellow investigators in the late 1930s and 1940s, and Gingrich's establishing the COS.[7] In each of these cases, backbenchers pursued changes that challenged the majority party while providing a narrower benefit for themselves (i.e., individual power or reelection). Thus, common carriers not only provide a mechanism for party leaders to shape institutions, but also can facilitate backbencher challenges to majority party control.

PATH-DEPENDENT LAYERING

The evidence from the four periods shows that institutional development often involves superimposing new arrangements on top of preexisting structures intended to serve different purposes. Established institutions create constituencies for their preservation, and thus it is typically easier to add new institutions than to dismantle preexisting ones. The effectiveness of institutional change has repeatedly been compromised by the need to accommodate a preexisting authority structure that privileged other interests.

For example, in 1890–1910, Allison and Aldrich attempted to centralize power in the Senate. However, the persistence of unlimited debate and of seniority rights to committee chairmanships limited the success of this experiment with strong party government. In the House, insurgent Republicans and Democrats stripped the Speaker of his control of the Rules Committee in 1910, while leaving in place earlier reforms that had empowered the committee. This allowed Rules to gain pervasive control of scheduling, something that insurgents seeking to disperse power throughout the committee system had clearly not intended.

In the 1920s, changes in Senate appropriations and the House discharge process exhibit similar dynamics. The Senate recentralized appropriations in 1922 but kept an important element of fragmentation by allowing committees losing jurisdiction to have ex officio representatives on the Senate Appropriations Committee. The resulting "mixed" system—which melded reforms from 1899 intended to disperse power with changes in 1922 intended to safeguard control of spending—persisted into the

1970s. The House was more successful in recentralizing appropriations, in part because a smaller proportion of its members stood to lose jurisdiction from the change (see chapter 3). However, House battles concerning the discharge process exemplify the layering of innovations serving competing goals. Reforms adopted in 1924 and 1931 made the discharge rule easier to use, while countervailing moves in 1925 and 1935 (increasing the number of signatures required to 218) and in 1932 (Garner's ruling that the signatories of discharge petitions would be kept secret) made it far more difficult to discharge measures. The changes in 1932 and 1935 helped to reconcile the discharge rule with a strong committee system and a semblance of majority party agenda control—precisely the two obstacles to floor consideration that motivated proponents of the 1924 and 1931 reforms in the first place.

Path-dependent layering also characterized the battles concerning the Rules Committee in 1937–52. The conservative takeover of Rules in 1937 undermined the committee's usefulness as an agent of the majority party. While the 21-day rule of 1949 allowed liberals to circumvent Rules Committee obstruction, conservatives still were well positioned to shape the content of special rules to their advantage. Furthermore, the 21-day rule created opportunities not only for liberals, but also for members pushing special-interest bills opposed by Democratic and GOP leaders alike. By challenging the Rules Committee's gatekeeping power, the 21-day rule limited the committee's ability to perform its other traditional role, as a control committee protecting the House from ill-advised, special-interest legislation. Thus, adding the 21-day rule to this preexisting authority structure resulted in a process that no longer served any given collective interest particularly well.

In 1970–89, path-dependent layering again emerged as an important pattern compromising the effectiveness of reform. For example, the Budget Act of 1974 created budget committees without dismantling the long-standing structure of authorizing, appropriations, and revenue committees. Reformers' need to accommodate these preexisting power centers limited the budget committees' ability to coordinate fiscal policy. In like fashion, Democratic party-building efforts in the 1980s were limited by the persistence of reforms that had fragmented power in the preceding decade. Despite restrictive rules on the amending process and Jim Wright's revitalization of the speakership, such fragmenting reforms as the subcommittee bill of rights and the various sunshine reforms of the 1970s remained on the books, creating difficulties for Democratic leaders. The result, again, was a combination of institutions inspired by competing motivations.[8]

There have been a few occasions where reformers succeeded in the wholesale dismantlement of existing institutions. The best examples are the Reed rules of 1890 and Republicans' jettisoning of the subcommittee prerogatives in 1995 that had become entrenched under the Democrats. In both cases, a new majority party had just taken over the House after many years in the minority.[9] Since few party members had experience as committee leaders, resistance to transforming existing power bases apparently was lower than usual (see Evans and Oleszek 1997, and discussion in epilogue). Sweeping institutional reforms may therefore be more likely when a party gains majority status after an extended period in the minority. But that is a fairly unusual event; the more common outcome is for the interplay of coalitions promoting multiple interests to foster institutions that are historical composites, incorporating disparate elements that simultaneously promote a range of partially incompatible goals.

INNOVATION AND RESPONSE

Evidence from two of the four periods supports the fourth claim, that a series of changes that promote a single interest will typically provoke a response from members seeking to protect competing interests. In 1890–1910, the big push toward centralized party government sparked rank-and-file restiveness, leading House Republicans to install David Henderson as a figurehead Speaker and junior senators from both parties to decentralize control of appropriations in 1899. Henderson's failure to defend the House from Senate incursions enabled Cannon to initiate a further round of centralization in 1903, but this too provoked another, fiercer rank-and-file revolt in 1909–10.

A similar pattern characterized 1970–89: a series of fragmenting reforms in the early 1970s made the legislative process increasingly treacherous for majority party Democrats, leading to a concerted effort to strengthen the party. Jim Wright's decisive leadership in the 100th Congress (1987–88) represents the culmination of this Democratic party-building. But just as Cannon's bid to shut out Democrats and dissident Republicans led to his downfall in 1910, Wright's dominance provoked resentment among Republicans and rank-and-file Democrats. This in turn allowed Newt Gingrich to bring down Wright based on relatively minor ethical lapses.

The absence of a big push toward a single coherent model of organization in either the 1920s or 1937–52 makes this "innovation and response" dynamic less relevant to these periods. However, if one extends the time frame slightly, developments in these eras can be viewed as a response to the perceived excesses of earlier periods. Thus, the moves to decentralize power in the House and Senate in 1919–32 were, in part, a continuation of the 1909–10 revolt against party-based centralization. In particular,

House Republicans' fear of czar rule led them to create a Steering Committee and to separate their floor leader from the committee system. Similarly, the cross-party activism of 1937–52 was a reaction against the executive-led party government of Franklin Roosevelt's first term.

An important reason that successful reforms generate reactions rather than self-reinforcement has to do with the character of Congress as an institution: the "losers" in one round of institutional reform do not go away; instead, they (or successors with similar interests) typically remain to fight another day. The American electoral system, with its geographically based single-member districts and decentralized parties, generally prevents today's winners in Congress from completely vanquishing their opponents. This differs from many other contexts, in which the losers in one round—for example, a minor political party—often either vanish from the political scene or are forced to make more fundamental adjustments.[10] As long as members represent individual, independent constituencies, the ability of an ascendant coalition to create and consolidate a single, coherent model of organization will be severely limited.

CONDITIONS WHEN SPECIFIC INTERESTS MATTER

The evidence supporting the four claims of disjointed pluralism is not reason to reject other accounts of congressional organization. The alternative models outlined in chapter 1 are insufficient in that each focuses on a single collective interest, yet no single interest accounts for congressional development either within a period or across periods.[11] Table 6.1, which presents the distribution of cases across each period, makes this point quite clearly.

Nonetheless, single-interest models also generate hypotheses about the conditions under which a given interest will be more or less prominent. The empirical chapters provide support for some, but not all, of these hypotheses:

- Electoral interests will matter more as member careerism increases (Mayhew 1974).

Although careerism has clearly increased in the twentieth century (Polsby 1968; Price 1975), there is surprisingly little evidence that members' shared reelection interest has driven development in the four periods examined. It played a significant role in promoting only a handful of the changes: the increase in committee staff under the LRA of 1946, rules requiring open committee meetings in the 1970s, and the recent boom in Senate obstruction.[12]

This does not mean that members did not care about their individual electoral fortunes as they sought institutional changes. Recall from chap-

TABLE 6.1 Number of Changes in Each Period Motivated Primarily
by Each Collective Interest

Interest	1890–1910	1919–1932	1937–1952	1970–1989	Total
Majority party	5	3	1	4	13
Congress or chamber-centered interests	0	2	3.5[a]	4	9.5
Individual power bases	2	3	0	3.5[b]	8.5
Policy interests	2	2	3.5[a]	0	7.5
Reelection	0	0	0	.5[b]	.5
Minority party	1	0	1	1	3
Total	10	10	9	13	42

[a] The expansion in investigations in 1937–52 is credited equally to conservatives' policy interests and to members' stake in congressional capacity and power.

[b] The boom in Senate obstruction in the 1970s is credited equally to electoral and power base interests.

ter 1 that several collective interests can be derived from individual members' electoral goals, including a positive party reputation or the success of an ideological faction. But reelection, as a collective interest, encompasses only those cases in which incumbents' electoral interests do not conflict with one another.[13] There are numerous cases, however, when a change promoted the electoral prospects of some members at the expense of others. For example, the Dies Committee on Un-American Activities served the electoral interests of its members, while imperiling the reelection of liberal Democrats (see chapter 4). This is a much different dynamic from incumbents jointly creating institutions that provide electoral benefits for all members.

Notwithstanding the limited explanatory power of reelection as a collective interest, a series of changes, starting with the revolt against Cannon, continuing through the rules reforms of 1924 and 1931, and culminating with the innovations adopted in the early 1970s, have spread influence among more members. By dispersing power, these changes have created a system in which each individual member has plentiful resources to pursue reelection. However, these changes involved considerable conflict: the institutional "have-nots"—typically junior members, minority party members, or ideological dissidents in the majority party—forced changes that threatened those in power. Such zero-sum conflict means that all incumbents' common interest in reelection cannot explain these changes. Models that emphasize reelection as a collective interest downplay such pitched battles that involved junior-senior, partisan, and ideological cleavages.

- Congressional capacity and power will be more salient following episodes in which the president has gained influence at Congress's expense (Sundquist 1982; Dodd 1977).

Studies of presidential-congressional relations agree that major wars and economic crises tend to empower the president (Schlesinger 1973; Wander 1984; Fischer 1991). By that criterion, the years following World War I, the Great Depression, World War II, the Korean War, and the Vietnam War should be marked by congressional reassertion. These periods coincide quite closely with efforts to strengthen congressional capacity and power.[14] Indeed, *all* of the changes that primarily served this interest occurred either during or shortly after World War I, World War II, or Vietnam:

Recentralizing Appropriations, 1920–22
Senate committee consolidation, 1920
Investigations explosion, 1940s
Legislative Reorganization Act of 1946
Joint Committee on Atomic Energy, 1946
Budget Act of 1974
Multiple referrals, 1974
Stevenson committee reforms, 1977

This evidence shows that interest in congressional capacity and power depends on (perceived) presidential aggrandizement.[15] This interest also became more salient as the twentieth century unfolded. No changes in 1890–1910 primarily involved congressional capacity and power. Two changes in the 1920s did, yet neither was an assault on presidential power per se. Rather, members sought to boost congressional policymaking capacity, which members assumed sufficient to safeguard congressional influence. Amid FDR's dominance, however, members began to confront presidential excesses more directly. Thus, changes in 1937–52 included the 1946 LRA, creation of the JCAE, and the boom in investigations. The latter two changes involved much more than policymaking capacity: they challenged presidential control of the executive branch. Similarly, members hoped to use the Budget Act of 1974 to recapture the power of the purse, rather than simply to improve congressional capacity. Whereas budget reform in 1920 involved granting both the president and Congress new tools to manage fiscal policy, reform in 1974 meant providing new tools for Congress while cutting down on presidential prerogatives (i.e., eliminating impoundments). Therefore, a focus on Congress-centered interests is particularly useful for understanding institutional reform in the middle to late twentieth century.

- Members' interest in institutional power bases will generate pressure for decentralization following an influx of junior members that substantially alters the seniority distribution (Diermeier 1995).

Evidence for this hypothesis is limited. Several reforms did involve junior members' dispersing power: in the House, these include the 1909 and 1924 rules reforms, the amendments strengthening the Legislative Reorganization Act of 1970, and the assault on seniority in 1973–75. In the Senate, these include the 1899 Appropriations decentralization, the 1975 staffing and committee openness reforms, and the 1977 Stevenson committee reforms. In each of these cases, junior members were significantly more likely to favor reform.[16] Nonetheless, the timing of these reforms does not coincide closely with changes in the number of junior members.

Figure 6.1 shows the percentage of representatives and senators serving in their first Congress from 1881 to 1997. Since there is a strong, downward trend in turnover, what counts as an "influx" of new members has fallen over time. Therefore, it makes sense to compute change scores for each Congress: a positive score indicates increased turnover relative to the preceding Congress. In the House, change in the percentage of freshmen was positive in the Congresses when the 1924 rules reforms were adopted (68th Congress) and when the assault on seniority took place (93rd–94th Congresses) but was negative when the 1909–10 rules reforms and LRA of 1970 were adopted (61st and 91st Congresses). The same pattern holds if one looks at change in the percentage of members serving two terms or fewer or three terms or fewer. Therefore, the reform Congresses followed decreased turnover as well as increased turnover.

The Senate also provides little support for the hypothesis. Change in the percentage of senators in their first Congress was positive when the Stevenson reforms were adopted (95th Congress) but was negative when the staffing and openness reforms passed (94th Congress) and was unchanged when the appropriations decentralization passed (55th Congress). The results are identical if one examines change in the percentage of senators in their first six-year term.[17] In sum, the timing of changes that serve junior members' power interests does not correspond closely to changes in the proportion of new members.[18]

- Majority party interests will be particularly important when the majority party is internally unified and has policy preferences that are sharply different from those of the minority (Rohde 1991).

To assess this hypothesis, figure 6.2 displays majority party homogeneity in the House and Senate for 1881–1997. Homogeneity is measured by

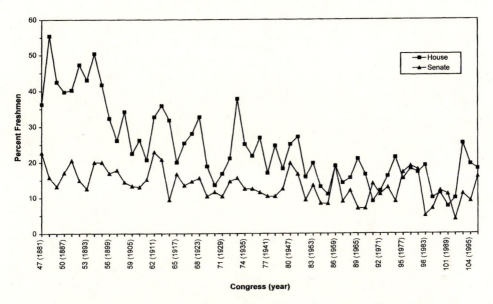

Figure 6.1 Percentage of freshmen in the House and Senate, 1881–1997

the standard deviation of majority party members' first-dimension NOM-INATE scores divided by the standard deviation of all House members' scores.[19] A high score on this variable indicates low majority party homogeneity (or, alternatively, high majority party heterogeneity).[20]

Turning first to the House data, at a broad level, trends in homogeneity are consistent with changes in institutions: the majority party was strongest in 1890–1910, which mostly consisted of homogeneous Republican majorities, and in the 1980s, when majority Democrats became increasingly homogeneous. Cross-party ideological coalitions were more successful in the 1920s, a decade of fairly heterogeneous GOP majorities, and in 1937–52 as Democrats became more heterogeneous.

There are several noteworthy exceptions: the decline in the speakership under Henderson occurred as GOP homogeneity peaked; Cannon's revitalization of the speakership coincided with the start of the decline in GOP homogeneity; Longworth's party-strengthening moves in 1925 did not correspond to a change in party homogeneity; and the 21-day rule passed in 1949 even as Democratic homogeneity continued its decline. Furthermore, Democrats' party building in the 1970s and 1980s was constrained by the need to accommodate earlier changes that had fragmented power. Nonetheless, the general pattern in the House supports the homogeneity hypothesis: majority party interests appear more salient when the party is homogeneous, while cross-party ideological coalitions are more successful when the majority party is internally divided.[21]

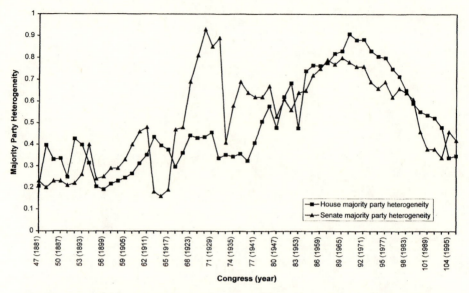

Figure 6.2 Majority party heterogeneity in the House and Senate, 1881–1997

Evidence for this hypothesis is less persuasive in the Senate. While Republicans were homogeneous in the mid-1890s when Aldrich and Allison centralized control, this homogeneity did not prevent reformers from undermining one of Allison's main power bases by decentralizing appropriations in 1899. The weak GOP majorities in the 1920s and weak Democratic majorities in 1937–52 are consistent with the sharp divisions revealed by the NOMINATE data. However, in contrast to the House, the major increase in homogeneity in the 1970s and 1980s did not lead to much party-based centralization in the Senate. The analysis in chapter 5 suggests that senators gain too much power as individuals from a fragmented authority structure to allow notable centralization.

Indeed, looking across the four periods, the House and Senate differ sharply in the relative importance of partisan interests, especially when compared to individual power base interests. At any given time, majority party leaders were stronger in the House than the Senate, while individual members had greater autonomy and influence in the Senate. Examining the changes individually, majority party interests motivated twelve changes in the House, but only two Senate changes. By contrast, power base goals drove five changes in the House, as compared to four Senate changes.[22] Senators can legitimately aspire to greater power as individuals than can House members, and as a result, power base interests have exerted an even stronger centrifugal force in the upper chamber. This, in turn, has greatly limited the Senate majority party's agenda control, whatever the level of majority party homogeneity.

- Policy-based interests will generate pressure for institutional change when electoral shocks and other exogenous factors substantially shift the location of the median voter on the floor (Krehbiel 1998; Schickler 2000).

Figure 6.3 displays the floor median and party medians for each Congress from 1881 to 1997. I focus on the House because the Senate's supermajority requirements complicate the relationship between the floor median and institutional change. In the House, progressive or liberal policy interests motivated rules changes adopted in 1909–10 (revolt against Cannon), 1924 and 1931 (liberalized discharge rule), and 1949 (adoption of 21-day rule). Liberal interests also motivated several cases in the 1970s and 1980s: the LRA of 1970 (recorded teller amendment), the reforms empowering subcommittees, the Democratic committee assignment changes in 1974, the unseating of three senior chairmen in 1975, the rise of restrictive rules after 1979, and the revitalization of the speakership in the 1980s. Conservatives' policy interests motivated the 1920 Appropriations Committee recentralization, the tightening of the discharge rule in 1925, the transformation in the role of the Rules Committee in 1937, the creation of the Dies committee in 1938, the boom in investigations in the 1940s, and the creation of COS in 1983.[23]

These changes correspond fairly well to shifts in the floor median. The progressive-liberal victories of 1909–10, 1924, 1931, and 1949 each coincided with a significant shift in the median to the left. Similarly, the conservative victories of 1920 and 1925, and the 1951 repeal of the 21-day rule, each coincided with a significant shift in the median to the right.[24] Similarly, the boom in (mostly conservative) investigations in the 1940s coincided with a fairly steady rightward movement in the floor median. The sole exceptions prior to 1970 are the transformation in the Rules Committee's mode of operations in 1937 and the creation of the Dies committee in 1938: both occurred in the 75th Congress, in which the median was unchanged from its previous (liberal) position. Even these cases are only partial exceptions, since notwithstanding the NOMINATE scores, most observers agree that House members moved noticeably to the right in 1937–38 (Patterson 1967; Barone 1990).

Starting in 1970, however, the results are more mixed. The LRA of 1970 constituted a limited victory for liberals in a Congress in which the median was essentially unchanged and fairly conservative. Furthermore, Democratic caucus changes empowering subcommittees occurred in the 92nd and 93rd Congresses (1971–74) amid little change in the floor me-

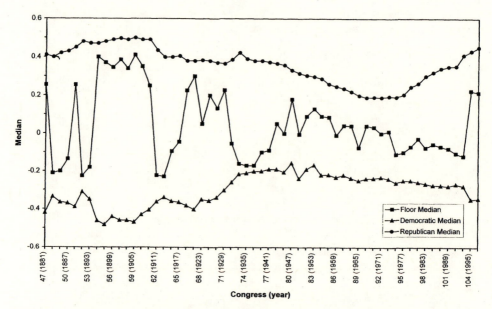

Figure 6.3 Floor and party medians in the House, 1881–1997

dian. Perhaps even more problematically, the rise in restrictive rules and revitalization of the speakership in the 1980s coincided with only a slight leftward drift in the floor median. Conservatives' one change—the formation of COS—occurred in the 98th Congress, when the median moved slightly left. The only case that supports the median voter approach is the 1975 deposal of three chairmen, which followed big Democratic gains in the 1974 election that shifted the median well to the left.

What explains these findings? It appears that the median voter model fares much better in explaining formal rules changes that need to be approved on the floor, than in explaining more informal changes (such as formation of COS and the revitalization of the speakership in the 1980s) or intraparty rules changes. It makes sense that the floor median would be more important when decisions are made directly on the floor. Thus, even when a faction lacks a floor majority, it can still influence House operations through internal caucus changes or other, informal changes. Indeed, the 1970s suggest that a faction of majority party members can pursue changes in caucus rules when it has the support of a majority of its party but lacks a clear floor majority. These caucus changes had a profound impact on the House (see chapter 5). Therefore, while the floor median substantially constrains the majority party's ability to manipulate House rules, it is less of a constraint on other types of changes. Different types of coalitions, responding to a range of different interests, are able to influence congressional organization.[25]

In sum, three of the hypotheses outlined in chapter 1 find at least some support.[26] Congressional capacity and power appears more salient following instances of presidential aggrandizement. In the House, majority party interests are most important when majority party homogeneity is high. Rules changes motivated by policy interests correspond fairly closely to shifts in the House floor median.

These findings are compatible with the argument that the interactions among coalitions promoting multiple interests drive congressional development. Single-interest models help specify when a given interest will be more or less prominent, and therefore the general *direction* in which institutions are likely to move in a particular Congress (i.e., toward or away from party government). But single-interest models are limited because no single interest has dominated congressional development and because few major institutional changes derive from just one member interest. As a result, fully understanding the *content* and *effects* of legislative reform requires a focus on the intersections among multiple interests.

For example, even when majority party interests are important (due to rising majority party homogeneity), these interests are rarely alone in shaping specific institutional changes. The effects of a given change depend on the particular combination of interests involved in its adoption. Furthermore, even when a homogeneous majority party centralizes power in party leaders' hands, a focus on multiple interests suggests that coalitions motivated by other interests will likely respond with countervailing changes. Thus, the decline in the speakership under Henderson, which is difficult to square with the homogeneity hypothesis, makes sense if one attends to the relationships among multiple interests: the party-based centralization of the mid-1890s threatened competing interests, provoking decentralization even amid rising GOP homogeneity. Finally, efforts to enhance party strength must typically accommodate preexisting institutions that were designed to promote other interests. For example, Jim Wright's efforts to centralize in the 1980s confronted an authority structure that empowered subcommittees and individual members. The result was an amalgam of institutions serving competing ends rather than a coherent party machine. In sum, disjointed pluralism focuses on how the intersections among multiple member interests drive congressional development and thus illuminates features of institutional development that are missing from single-interest models.

This raises the question of what combinations of interests are common. Table 6.2 shows the combinations of interests that were prominent in each period. One noteworthy pattern is that efforts to strengthen the majority party repeatedly intersected with members' stake in congressional capacity and power. This conjunction of interests arises fairly often because building up both a party and Congress as a whole typically involves centralizing the legislative process (see Cooper 1975).

But changes to promote congressional capacity and power have also taken other forms, pointing to the flexibility of institutional development. Most notably, majority party interests played little if any role in the 1937–52 moves to revive Congress's institutional standing. To the contrary, several of these changes gained support from conservatives eager to attack liberal Democratic administrations and from individual members eager to advance their personal careers. For example, Republicans and conservative Democrats united to support investigations that simultaneously undermined liberal Democratic administrations, promoted conservative causes, and gave publicity and power to individual members. While such changes did not make Congress a more centralized institution, they enabled the House and Senate to challenge executive branch primacy.

Another common combination is for junior members' power interests to intersect with either minority party interests or with the policy interests of a dissident faction in the majority party. Examples include the SAC decentralization in 1899, the revolt against Cannon in 1909–10, the House rules reforms in 1924 and 1931, and the Stevenson committee reforms and Senate staffing changes in the mid-1970s. This conjunction of interests occurs frequently because junior members, the minority, and dissident majority party members each (typically) stand to gain from fragmented agenda control. In a sense, the Democratic caucus reforms of the early 1970s also fit this pattern: with power in the hands of conservative committee chairmen, liberal Democrats believed they would benefit by fragmenting power; in doing so, they appealed to junior members and, on occasion, to Republicans, who also stood to gain from decentralization.

The case studies also show that tensions among competing interests often compromise the effectiveness of institutional changes. One notable pattern is that members' power base interests frequently undermine reforms motivated primarily by either the majority party's interests or by Congress-centered interests. For example, the Stevenson committee reforms of 1977 included numerous concessions that compromised the proposed reorganization. Reformers made these concessions to gain the support of senators determined to preserve their existing committee power bases.

Therefore, disjointed pluralism and single-interest models generate different types of insights concerning congressional development. Whereas single-interest models illuminate the conditions under which a given interest is likely to be more significant, disjointed pluralism shows how the interplay of competing coalitions promoting multiple, potentially con-

TABLE 6.2 Combinations of Interests That Occur in Each Period

Primary Interest	Other Interest Also Served?	1890–1910	1919–1932	1937–1952	1970–1989	Total
Majority party	Policy	0	1	0	4	5
	Congress or chamber-centered interests	3	0	0	1	4
	Individual power bases	0	1	0	1	2
	Minority party	0	0	0	0	0
	Reelection	0	0	0	0	0
	None	2	1	1	0	4
Congress or chamber-centered interests	Majority party	0	1	0	2	3
	Policy	0	1	1	0	2
	Individual power bases	0	0	3	3	6
	Minority party	0	0	0	1	1
	Reelection	0	0	1	1	2
	None	0	0	1	0	1
Individual power bases	Majority party	0	3	0	1	4
	Congress or chamber-centered interests	0	0	0	2	2
	Policy	1	1	0	2	4
	Minority party	0	0	0	3	3
	Reelection	0	0	0	1	1
	None	1	0	0	0	1

TABLE 6.2 Combinations of Interests That Occur in Each Period (cont.)

Primary Interest	Other Interest Also Served?	1890–1910	1919–1932	1937–1952	1970–1989	Total
Policy	Majority party	0	0	1	0	1
	Congress or chamber-centered interests	0	0	1	0	1
	Individual power bases	2	1	2	0	5
	Minority party	1	1	1	0	3
	Reelection	0	0	0	0	0
	None	0	1	1	0	2
Minority party	Majority party	1	0	0	0	1
	Individual power bases	0	0	0	1	1
	Congress or chamber-centered interests	1	0	1	0	2
	Policy	0	0	1	1	2
	Reelection	0	0	0	0	0
	None	0	0	0	0	0

Note: This table compiles cases where two or more interests support the same change (that is, cases of common carriers). Since a single change may serve more than two interests, column totals may exceed the total number of cases.

flicting interests shapes both the content of individual changes and the course of institutional development over time.

IMPLICATIONS FOR THE STUDY OF INSTITUTIONS

These findings suggest a view of legislative institutions that borrows from both rational choice and historical institutionalist approaches. Rational choice models plausibly claim that the goal-driven behavior of individual members shapes Congress's committee system, rules and procedures, and leadership structures. Furthermore, rational choice models have effectively isolated certain important interests and uncovered the implications of each of these interests for institutional design.

At the same time, in a departure from much (but by no means all) rational choice scholarship, disjointed pluralism suggests that congressional institutions are not necessarily sources of stability and coherence in legislative politics. The "new institutionalism" in rational choice theory involved an effort to find a source of stability amid the prevalence of Arrovian voting cycles in multidimensional policy spaces (Shepsle 1986). For example, Weingast and Marshall (1988) argue that the congressional committee system stabilizes distributive logrolls that benefit all members, while Cox and McCubbins (1994, 226, 215) theorize that the majority party binds its members to support "a specific structure of agenda power," which thereby "stabilizes the structure of the House, and hence the policy decisions made in the House." In each case, legislative institutions solve a specific collective action problem that plagues members and thereby impose stability on an otherwise chaotic legislative world.

By contrast, I show that legislative institutions are historical composites, full of tensions and contradictions.[27] Congressional development does not produce some stable, effective compromise that is reasonably satisfactory for all (or even most) members. Instead, it produces a set of institutions that often work at cross-purposes. For example, balancing individual rights and party interests has entailed inventing countervailing institutional devices with contradictory purposes. Elements of congressional organizations privilege party; other elements privilege individual members. In one sense, these provide balance and compromise. But in another sense, they grate against one another, producing tensions that provoke further demands for change. Rather than providing stability and coherence—as the metaphor of institutions as equilibria suggests—congressional institutions embody contradictory purposes, which provide for an ongoing, churning process of institutional development.

One might counter that rational members would quickly eliminate any dissonance in legislative institutions. But changes intended to improve the efficiency of legislative organization are subject to the same disjointed, plu-ralistic dynamics (see also Knight 1992). Members cannot simply block out the play of competing interests whenever "efficiency-inducing" changes are under consideration. Social choice theory demonstrates why. In consid-ering institutional design, Riker (1995) cites the well-known result that large social groups with many goals and diverse individual preferences will rarely produce a transitive preference ordering. Consequently, while "indi-viduals can, with effort, impose consistency on their goals and instruments, . . . groups seldom can" (121). Add to this the limited cognitive capacities of decision makers, who must evaluate the complex implications of pro-posed institutions (Braybrooke and Lindblom 1963), and it should be no surprise that legislative institutions are not coherent, optimal solutions.[28]

Historical dynamics reinforce conflicts within congressional institu-tions. As argued above, preexisting institutions create constituencies for their preservation that typically force reformers with new goals to build upon, rather than dismantle, these structures. The resulting path depen-dence limits the optimality of reforms. However, whereas path depen-dence suggests that legislative institutions likely will, in the long run, move toward a single organizational model, members' multiple goals have precluded such an outcome. Congressional development is prone to oscil-lation and changes in direction that belie the metaphor of steadily build-ing upon a single path. Successful innovations that serve a narrow set of interests generally provoke a reaction in which members seek to protect competing interests. The ultimate irreconcilability of members' multiple interests has thwarted the triumph of either an incumbent cartel, a major-ity party cartel, or any other coherent model of organization.

This recasting of congressional institutions may hold important lessons for the study of other social and political institutions that share certain basic features with Congress. In particular, when an organization's mem-bers have diverse goals and can each influence its structure and processes, a decisive, consistent ordering of institutional objectives is unlikely. Uni-versities, professional associations, national parties made up of semiautono-mous state or local units, and governmental agencies charged with multiple and technically complex missions are examples of institutions that may follow this logic. Disjointed pluralism should also apply to other legislative bodies, except where an electoral or constitutional system fosters strict party discipline. If a legislature has a single majority party and if that party controls its members' access to their seats, then the prospects for multiple, crosscutting coalitions fall dramatically. The institutional development of the British House of Commons would thus likely feature much less "dis-jointed pluralism" than the U.S. Congress. Again, disjointed pluralism is rooted in a constitutional framework and electoral system that help to pro-duce members for whom multiple collective interests are likely to be salient.

If one assumes that coherence is a critical objective, then one might conclude that disjointed pluralism is something that elites designing political or social institutions ought to avoid. However, the history of Congress suggests that coherence might not be a desirable outcome. Against Riker's (1995, 121) claim that institutions "reflecting diverse goals are likely to be ineffective and unstable," congressional history suggests that institutional incoherence has important benefits—especially in terms of accommodating intensely held but conflicting preferences (see Miller 1983 and March 1994 for related arguments). The congressional authority structure has arguably been most coherent during those rare eras of majority party dominance—notably, in the first decade of the twentieth century and during much of the 1983–94 period. Yet in both cases, this dominance provoked sustained, virulent attacks on the Congress itself by members of the minority. These attacks eventually undermined the electoral reputation of the majority party and contributed to serious party splits and disastrous electoral losses.[29]

Notwithstanding these (generally) ill-fated attempts to form party machines, Congress is ordinarily composed of complex institutions produced by interactions among members for whom multiple, competing collective goods are salient. In general, the result is not coherent: legislative institutions do not "fit" together as if designed with a clear and consistent set of objectives in mind. However, because the goals served by congressional institutions are diverse, conflicting, and at times not even clearly defined, the notions of optimality and coherence do not seem appropriate as either normative standards or empirical expectations.

Institutional Change in the 1990s

NO ACCOUNT of congressional institutions would be complete without addressing the major changes wrought by the Republican takeover of Congress in 1995. This epilogue briefly discusses the Democratic difficulties preceding the 1994 elections and the implications of the resulting Republican "revolution."[1]

DEMOCRATIC DISARRAY IN THE 103RD CONGRESS, 1993–1994

When Bill Clinton took office in 1993, Democrats had good reason for optimism: for the first time in twelve years, the party controlled both the White House and Congress. Furthermore, congressional Democrats had built a party leadership apparatus in the intervening years that appeared capable of shepherding through a major presidential program. However, the 103rd Congress produced a much different outcome.

From the outset, Democrats were plagued by dissension on both procedural and substantive matters. Newt Gingrich and his allies' persistent attacks on the House as an institution had continued after Wright's 1989 departure and took a heavy toll on Wright's successor, Thomas Foley (D-Wash.), and the Democrats. Foley's inability to quell the House bank and post office scandals led some Democrats to doubt both his effectiveness and existing institutional arrangements. As Dodd and Oppenheimer (1993, 48) point out, it appeared that "the scandals had the potential to undermine the power that had accrued to the party leadership since the late 1970s."

Party members' rebellious spirit first emerged in January 1993, when one-third of the Democrats surprised the leadership by joining with Republicans to deny funding for the Select Committee on Narcotics. By March, Democratic leaders conceded that they lacked the votes to preserve funding not only for the Narcotics Committee but also for the Select Committees on Hunger, Aging, and Children, Youth and Families (CQ Almanac 1993, 13). These committees had provided useful position-taking platforms for their Democratic chairs.

Conservative Democrats and Republicans also defeated six special rules in the 103rd Congress, a dramatic contrast to the Democrats' successes on these votes in previous sessions. In addition, the Conservative Democratic

Forum, which had declined in the 1980s, claimed fifty-four members in the 103rd Congress and showed signs of renewed activism (*National Journal,* October 29, 1994, 2507). The boll weevils had returned, though this time with support from beyond the South.

A further sign of declining Democratic effectiveness occurred in September 1993 when Republican James Inhofe (R-Okla.) succeeded in amending the discharge rule to make public the names of representatives who sign discharge petitions. This undermined party leaders' ability to discourage members from signing petitions for politically popular proposals. Democratic leaders opposed the change, but Inhofe, emulating Gingrich's use of television and radio, successfully focused media attention on this example of congressional secrecy. By raising the visibility of the issue, Inhofe forced reluctant Democrats to acquiesce (CQ Almanac 1993, 10).

In addition to procedural troubles, Democrats suffered numerous setbacks on substantive issues. While party unity on roll call votes continued to rise in the 103rd Congress, some of the most important Democratic defeats occurred without so much as a roll call. Mayhew (1995, 44) points out that health care reform, the issue that "dominated the news, politics, and policy processes" in 1994 and the matter on which Clinton and the Democrats had staked their credibility, "figured in no roll call votes at all in the House." Although Democrats managed to avoid floor defeats simply by scheduling no votes, this did nothing to negate the growing public perception that the party had failed to govern. The *Washington Post* proclaimed shortly before the November 1994 elections that "this will go into the record books as perhaps the worst Congress—least effective, most destructive, nastiest—in 50 years" (October 7, 1994, A24; see *NYT,* October 9, 1994, 14E for a similar assessment).

But there is a more recent precedent for Democrats' self-destruction in the 103rd Congress: the party's failures under Carter, the last time that it controlled both the presidency and Congress. The disarray, factionalism, and embarrassing defeats discussed in chapter 5 returned in 1993–94, notwithstanding the well-documented rise in party loyalty in the 1980s. While Democrats did enact several important measures proposed by Clinton, Mayhew (1995) finds that the volume of major legislation was about the same as during Jimmy Carter's first two years in office.[2]

One possible reason for the Democrats' difficulties in the late 1970s and in 1993–94 is that the dispersal of influence from committee chairs to subcommittee chairs and individual members in the 1970s impeded ambitious, controversial presidential programs. Strong party leadership in the 1980s did not remove this layer of fragmentation. Passing Carter's and Clinton's programs required coordinating more committee and subcommittee units than before, when full committee chairs had been the focal points for bargaining. This coordination proved elusive because Carter's and Clinton's proposals often exacerbated Democrats' internal divisions.

So why did Democratic leaders feel compelled to support divisive presidential initiatives? The reason derives from the contradictions structuring party leadership, as discussed in chapter 4. Starting in the late 1930s, under unified party government, majority party leaders have been responsible both to party members and to the president. Leaders know that they and their party will be judged by how successfully Congress enacts the president's program, regardless of whether the congressional party determined that program. As a result, Democratic leaders have repeatedly had to push members to adopt legislation that divides the party. It may well have been easier to work out accommodations between the president and the congressional party prior to the 1970s, when bargaining could be confined to the president, party leaders, and a handful of committee chairs.[3]

Clinton's first Congress thus demonstrates that the Democrats had built an authority structure featuring significant tensions, as party members sought simultaneously to enhance their power as individuals and to make their party more effective.[4] These tensions became particularly problematic under unified party government given earlier institutional developments that had closely tied the congressional party and its leadership to the success of presidential programs.

THE REPUBLICAN REVOLUTION OF 1995

Democrats' failure to govern as a team facilitated Republicans' stunning ascension to majority status in the House and Senate. After forty years in the minority, the Republican majority elected in November 1994 embraced numerous institutional changes intended to transform the House. Republicans enhanced the Speaker's power substantially, giving him more control over committee assignments and the selection of committee chairs (Aldrich and Rohde 1995). The GOP also made several moves to weaken committee chairs, most notably through a six-year term limit (which also applied to subcommittee chairs) and through Gingrich's efforts to ensure that individual chairs saw themselves as dependent on the leadership for their position.[5] Gingrich sent an important message when he bypassed the seniority system in appointing conservative loyalists to lead the Appropriations, Judiciary, and Commerce Committees (Evans and Oleszek 1997).

At the same time, the 1995 reforms strengthened full committee chairs vis-à-vis subcommittee chairs. In a major departure from the Democrats' subcommittee bill of rights, the GOP allowed committee chairs to appoint subcommittee chairs and to hire all majority staff, including those assigned to subcommittees (Evans and Oleszek 1997). Gingrich had learned from the Democrats' difficulties in combining subcommittee-based entrepreneurship with strong party leadership. Indeed, his determination to undercut subcommittees supports the view that the subcommittee reforms of the early 1970s had undermined the Democrats' ability to govern.

In contrast to most of the institutional changes analyzed in this book, Gingrich did not have to make significant compromises in realizing the GOP's partisan goals.[6] Furthermore, the new Speaker successfully swept away earlier innovations, rather than simply adding new mechanisms for leadership influence to the existing structure. It is noteworthy that rank-and-file Republicans did not defend the powers of subcommittees and their chairs, perhaps because, as members of the perennial minority party, they had little or no experience at using subcommittees as power bases. It would have been much more difficult to undo the Democratic subcommittee reforms had it required acting against entrenched subcommittee leaders. This is not to deny the insight from conditional party government models, that Republicans' homogeneous policy views also facilitated Gingrich's centralizing moves (Aldrich and Rohde 1995). But it nonetheless seems doubtful that the former Democratic majority would have ever repealed the subcommittee bill of rights, no matter how homogeneous the party became or how much the subcommittees' influence hurt the party. Overcoming entrenched subcommittee leaders' personal power interests would have posed too immense an obstacle.

As noted in chapter 6, this suggests that sweeping institutional reforms tend to occur when a party gains majority status after a long stint in the minority. The Republicans' 1994 changes have rightly been compared to Reed's "revolutionary" revision of House rules in 1890, which also followed a relatively long GOP stint in the minority (see, e.g., Forgette 1997).[7] Gingrich's centralized, highly visible, and fiercely partisan leadership in the 104th Congress does evoke Reed's towering presence a century earlier. But in both cases there are important ironies. The Republicans' vigorous partisanship in 1890 resulted in one of the most devastating election defeats in congressional history. A little over a hundred years later, the GOP came dangerously close to repeating that blunder. The party's aggressiveness, manifested most notably in the government shutdowns during the 1995–96 budget battles with President Clinton, nearly led to electoral disaster. Dodd and Oppenheimer (1997) argue persuasively that Republicans were saved from this only because party leaders reluctantly moved to the center in 1996, accepting compromises that fell well short of those desired by the median Republican (see also Brady and Volden 1998; Krehbiel 1998). That a House dominated by conservative Republicans had to accept an increase in the minimum wage shows that Republicans saved their "revolution" by jettisoning some of their key principles.

The lesson of the 51st and 104th Congresses is that creating vigorous party government and pursuing an ideologically charged agenda pose tremendous risks for individual members, who have electoral incentives to tailor their appeals to their particular constituents. By 1997, John Linder (R-Ga.), the head of the National Republican Congressional Campaign Committee, was urging party members to run on local issues rather than national Republican themes, noting that "it will be 435 separate races" in 1998 (*Post*, September 14, 1997).

After narrowly surviving the excesses of the 104th Congress, Republicans have displayed elements both of strong party leadership and of deleterious infighting. Party voting remained high in the 105th and 106th Congresses (1997–2000), and the GOP has continued the Democrats' practice of limiting the minority's role in House deliberations. Aldrich and Rohde (1999) thus document several examples of the Republicans' using the Rules Committee and other institutional power levers to advantage conservative policy proposals.[8]

Yet Republicans have also experienced internecine strife. In July 1997, a botched coup attempt against Gingrich, in which several top party leaders cooperated with a small faction of archconservatives seeking to topple the Speaker, embarrassed the party and signaled the precariousness of Gingrich's leadership (*NYT*, July 19, 1997).[9] For the remainder of the 105th Congress, Republican leaders were unable to shake an image of dissension and drift (*CQWR*, November 7, 1998, 2990–91; November 14, 1998, 3050–52). The result was a meager list of accomplishments to run on in 1998 and a disappointing loss of five House seats in the midterm elections. In the election's aftermath, Republican National Committee chairman Jim Nicholson warned House leaders "that they have to end the disarray that left them without a platform to run on in 1998" (*NYT*, March 8, 1999, 13).

Gingrich's problems stemmed in large part from his need to reconcile moderate Republicans' interest in compromising with the White House to pass centrist legislation, with many conservatives' insistence on a sharply ideological agenda. Indeed, ideological divisions between conservative and moderate Republicans have become surprisingly salient since the party's takeover of the Congress (see, e.g., *NYT*, July 10, 1997, B7; March 8, 1999, 13; *Post*, June 8, 1999, 1). Conservatives have repeatedly urged GOP leaders to push hard for policies that will likely provoke vetoes and that moderate Republicans worry will hurt their electoral prospects at home (*NYT*, June 18, 1997, 1; May 29, 1999, 1; *Post*, September 14, 1997, A8).

The Clinton impeachment fiasco nicely illustrates Republicans' dilemma. Republicans' focus on Clinton's affair with Monica Lewinsky is widely credited with causing the party's unusually poor performance in the 1998 midterm election (*CQWR*, November 7, 1998, 2990). Yet even after the election, conservative Republicans continued to pursue impeachment; the House ultimately passed the impeachment articles on a near party-line vote. This Republican "victory" is consistent with Aldrich and Rohde's (1999) emphasis on GOP strength: it is likely that the median voter on the floor—a moderate Republican by most accounts—favored censure instead of impeachment, but nonetheless stuck with the party on a procedural motion to block the censure option from a direct floor vote. However, the problem for moderate Republicans is that a few more victories of this sort may doom their electoral prospects. The impeachment case suggests both the strength of congressional parties and the dangers posed to individual members (and the future of the GOP majority) by party pressure to buck constituent opinion. The problem, put simply, is that the sort of party image that is attractive to safe-seat conservatives is not likely to help moderate Republicans from swing districts (see *National Journal*, October 23, 1999, 3060–61).

One legacy of the 1998 midterm was Gingrich's resignation as Speaker and departure from the House. The leader of the Republican revolution received the brunt of the blame for the party's limited accomplishments and poor electoral performance. Gingrich's replacement, Dennis Hastert (R-Ill.), bears some resemblance to Reed's successor, David Henderson. Just as Republicans in 1899 did not want a domineering Speaker to succeed Reed, Republicans in December 1998 chose a leader who is in many ways Gingrich's opposite (*NYT*, March 8, 1999, 13). Hastert was known for "his relaxed style and low profile," as compared to Gingrich's penchant for publicity and controversy (*CQWR*, December 22, 1998, 3333). At least initially, Hastert appeared to take on a secondary role as compared to other House leaders, especially GOP whip Tom DeLay of Texas (*NYT*, June 21, 1999, 1). The strong speakership of Gingrich proved no more durable than Jim Wright's experiment with assertive leadership.

Even as Republicans embraced a more collegial leadership structure under Hastert, they have continued to shut out the Democrats. But the party has also had great difficulty agreeing on and adopting an agenda and risks once again being tarred as responsible for a "Do-Nothing Congress" (*NYT*, May 29, 1999, 1; November 26, 1999, 1). The question for Republicans is whether they can devise leadership arrangements that simultaneously satisfy conservatives who emphasize ideological goals and moderates who believe those goals threaten both their own electoral survival and their party's prospects for solidifying its majority. After a brief respite in 1995 in which the House GOP provided an effective form of majority party government, the tensions among competing member interests that typically undermine any coherent legislative order have reemerged in full force. The Republicans of the 105th and 106th Congresses hardly resembled a cohesive team pursuing a set of shared goals.

Although a more detailed analysis is required before reaching any strong conclusions about the 1990s, the evidence appears to support the argument that disjointed pluralism continues to characterize congressional development. While Newt Gingrich's ascension to the speakership in 1995 seemed to herald the onset of a new era of vigorous party government, his downfall less than four years later suggests the continuing tensions confronting efforts to bring party government to the House.

Case Selection

As DESCRIBED in chapter 1, I define an "important" institutional change as one that historians or congressional specialists perceive to have had substantial effects on congressional operations. I operationalize this definition by counting a change as important if five sources each suggest that the institutional change in question had such effects. While reading each source, I recorded all cases of institutional change during the four periods that affected rules and procedures, the committee system, and leadership instruments. I generated a list of changes from each source and then compared the lists.

One issue is what constitutes a single change. This is not a problem for rules changes, which are discrete events. But alterations in leadership instruments and the committee system may result from an accumulation of numerous smaller steps. For example, the development of centralized Senate leadership under William Allison (R-Iowa) and Nelson Aldrich (R-R.I.) resulted from a series of decisions over the course of several years. One could consider each individual step in this process to be a single institutional change and apply the criteria listed above to each of these steps. However, this forces an emphasis on singular events that obscures the potential for institutional change to occur gradually. As a result, I treat a set of related changes as a single case if at least five scholars treat the individual changes as related parts of a single, common change that the scholars identify in specific terms and judge to be important.

THE SOURCES

I relied on approximately thirty sources for case selection in each period. I sought to use a wide variety of sources, which approach the topic of congressional politics from diverse vantage points.[1] The sources are listed in table A.1.

Since fewer histories are available for the 1970–89 period, I supplemented the sources listed by using the article entitled "Inside Congress" in each edition of *Congress and the Nation,* which is published every four years by Congressional Quarterly. Since the "Inside Congress" article typically aims to cover congressional changes comprehensively, I used only the

TABLE A.1 Sources Used in Case Selection

Type of Source	Chamber(s)	Periods Covered
Congressional histories		
Congressional Quarterly 1982	Both	All, except 1982–89
Josephy 1979	Both	All, except 1970–89
MacNeil 1963	House	All, except 1970–89
Galloway and Wise 1976	House	All, except 1970–89
Bolling 1968	House	All, except 1970–89
Byrd 1988	Senate	All
Haynes 1938	Senate	1890–1910, 1919–32
Young 1956	Both	1940–45
General histories of American politics		
Dunn 1922	Both	1890–1910
Morgan 1969	Both	1890–96
Faulkner 1959	Both	1890s
Williams 1993 [1978]	Both	1890s
Keller 1977	Both	1890–1900
Mowry 1958	Both	1900–10
Cooper 1990	Both	1900–10
Leuchtenberg 1993	Both	1919–32
Paxson 1948	Both	1919–23
Hicks 1960	Both	1921–32
Murray 1973	Both	1921–24
McCoy 1967	Both	1923–28
Warren 1959	Both	1929–32
Schwarz 1970	Both	1930–32
Barone 1990	Both	1937–52, 1970–88
Leuchtenberg 1963	Both	1937–39
Kirkendall 1974	Both	1937–45
Blum 1976	Both	1941–45
Grantham 1976	Both	1945–52
Grantham 1987	Both	1970–86
Rules and procedures		
Damon 1971	Both	All, except 1970–89
Riddick 1949	Both	All, except 1970–89
Galloway 1953	Both	All, except 1970–89
Ripley 1983	Both	All, except 1970–89
Smith 1989	Both	1970–89
Committee system		
Goodwin 1970	Both	All, except 1970–89
Smith and Deering 1990 (chaps. 1, 2)	Both	All, except 1970–89
Deering and Smith 1997 (chaps. 1, 2)	Both	1970–89
Cooper 1988	House	All, except 1970–89
Kravitz 1974	Senate	All, except 1970–89
Robinson 1954	Senate	All, except 1970–89

TABLE A.1 Sources Used in Case Selection (cont.)

Type of Source	Chamber(s)	Periods Covered
Leadership instruments		
Sinclair 1990	Both	All
Peabody 1976	Both	All, except 1970–89
Jones 1970 (minority party)	Both	All, except 1970–89
Peters 1990	House	All
Ripley 1967	House	All, 1970–89
Ripley 1969b	Senate	All, except 1970–89
Rothman 1966	Senate	1890–1910
Truman 1959a	House	1937–52
Huitt 1961	Senate	1937–52
Davidson 1989	Senate	1970–89
Smith 1993	Senate	1970–89
Sinclair 1989	Senate	1970–89
Dodd and Oppenheimer 1993	House	1970–89
Connelly and Pitney 1994	House	1970–89
Miscellaneous		
Wolf 1981	House	1890–1910
Taylor 1954	Both	1919–32, 1937–52
Griffith 1967	Both	1937–52
Patterson 1967	Both	1937–45
Rieselbach 1995	Both	1970–89
Davidson 1992	Both	1970–89
Jones 1995	Both	1970–89
Price 1992	House	1970–89
Ornstein, Peabody, and Rohde 1997	Senate	1970–89
Bader and Jones 1993	Both (GOP)	1970–89
Bailey 1988	Senate (GOP)	1970–84

introductory portion of each essay, which identifies the most important changes.[2] These articles are cited in the text as *CQ 19xx*, where *19xx* is the last of the four years covered in a given edition.

CLOSE CALLS

To convey a sense of the criteria I used, it is useful to note changes that do not qualify for one reason or another. For example, the Federal Elections Campaign Acts of 1971, 1974, and 1976 affected the financial resources available to members as they seek reelection. But it is hard to argue that these were institutional changes within the Congress (and they certainly were not a change in rules or procedures, the committee system, or congressional leadership instruments).

A few other cases are excluded because of concerns about timing. An example would be the development of the seniority system in the House, which is difficult to date precisely. Ripley (1983, 72) argues that the seniority system hardened in 1911–25, and Peters (1990, 96–97) emphasizes the growth in seniority under the Democrats in 1911–19.[3] Polsby et al. (1969, 794–95) agree that uncompensated seniority violations died out rapidly after the 1911 rules changes took committee assignments out of the hands of the Speaker. However, the Polsby data show that uncompensated violations continued to occur in the 1920s, albeit rarely. Because few authors specifically suggest that the seniority system tightened during the 1919–32 period, I exclude this case.

Still other cases fail to qualify because an insufficient number of authors identified them as significant. For example, numerous authors discuss the change in the Senate cloture rule in 1949 but typically conclude it did not significantly change Senate operations (see Barone 1990, 223; Grantham 1976, 46; Josephy 1979, 349; CQ 1982, 267–68; Galloway 1953, 561–67; Byrd 1988, 2:127–28; Truman 1959a, 18).

Votes Pertaining to Institutional Changes in Each Period

TABLE B.1 Votes Pertaining to Institutional Changes, 1890–1910

Description	All Members		Republicans		Democrats		Party Vote[a]
	Yes	No	Yes	No	Yes	No	
Reed rules, 1890							
Table appeal of Reed quorum ruling	162	0	161	0	0	0[b]	Yes
Table appeal of Reed ruling against dilatory motions	163	0	162	0	0	0[b]	Yes
Outhwaite (D-Ohio) amendment to drop rule setting 100 as quorum in Committee of the Whole	136	149	1	149	133	0	Yes
Crisp (D-Ga.) amendment to delete Reed's proposed quorum rule	136	156	0	156	134	0	Yes
Mills (D-Tex.) amendment to strike ban on dilatory motions	140	155	0	155	138	0	Yes
Final passage of Reed rules	161	144	161	0	0	142	Yes
Repeal of Reed rules, 1892							
Enloe (D-Tenn.) amendment to restore Reed's rule for the handling of private bills	172	74	60	0	105	74	No
Bynum (D-Ind.) amendment to limit dilatory motions	87	164	56	3	31	154	Yes
Burrows (R-Mich.) amendment to bar dilatory motions	34	96	(division vote)				
Reed amendment to keep order-of-business rule from 51st Congress	80	104	(teller vote)				
Final passage	(adopted on a voice vote)						
Readoption of quorum rule, 1894							
Previous question on adoption of new quorum rule	140	120	8	78	124	41	Yes
Adoption of new quorum rule	213	47	85	0	125	45	No
Increase in Rules Committee powers							
Oates (D-Ala.) amendment to enlarge Rules Committee and make it elective (Feb. 1892)	19	155	(teller vote)				

TABLE B.1   Votes Pertaining to Institutional Changes, 1890–1910 (cont.)

Description	All Members		Republicans		Democrats		Party Vote[a]
	Yes	No	Yes	No	Yes	No	
Hooker (D-Miss.) amendment to delete Rules Committee's new powers (Feb. 1892)	21	139	(division vote)				
O'Neill (D-Mo.) amendment to require Rules to report back on proposed rules changes within ten days (Feb. 1892)	39	73	(division vote)				
Hooker (D-Miss.) amendment to take away Rules Committee's exclusive jurisdiction over reporting special orders (Aug. 1893)	28	97	(division vote)				
Kilgore (D-Tex.) amendment to grant Coinage Committee the right to report at any time (Aug. 1893)	138	97	34	33	98	64	No
Springer (D-Ill.) amendment to grant Coinage and Banking and Currency Committees the right to report at any time (Aug. 1893)	102	58	(division vote)				
Senate appropriations decentralization, 1896–99							
Hale (R-Maine) motion to consider deficiency appropriations bill (Feb. 1896)	25	44	15	21	10	19	No
Dubois (R-Idaho) motion to consider decentralization of appropriations (Feb. 1896)	49	24	23	15	22	9	No
Harris (D-Tenn.) motion to adjourn (to put off consideration of rules change) (Feb. 1896)	34	29	15	15	19	12	No
Faulkner (R-W.Va.) motion to table amendment ordering Rules Committee to report favorably on decentralizing appropriations (Feb. 1896)	39	29	18	15	19	12	No
Allison (R-Iowa) motion to refer rules change proposal to Rules Committee (Feb. 1896)	40	29	20	13	20	11	No
Aldrich (R-R.I.) proposal to adopt amended version of appropriations decentralization (Jan. 1899)	(adopted on a voice vote)						

TABLE B.1   Votes Pertaining to Institutional Changes, 1890–1910 (cont.)

Description	All Members		Republicans		Democrats		Party Vote[a]
	Yes	No	Yes	No	Yes	No	
1909 House rules changes							
Proposal to readopt rules of 60th Congress	189	193	184	32	5	161	Yes
Previous question on Clark (D-Mo.) proposal for rules changes	180	203	29	187	151	16	Yes
Passage of Fitzgerald (D-N.Y.) substitute rules proposal	211	173	188	28	23	145	Yes
1910 House rules changes							
Dalzell (R-Pa.) motion to table appeal of Cannon ruling that Norris amendment is out of order	164	184	164	35	0	147	Yes
Vote to sustain Cannon ruling that Norris (R-Nebr.) amendment is out of order	160	182	160	35	0	147	Yes
Previous question on Norris's proposed rules changes	180	159	35	159	145	0	Yes
Adoption of Norris's proposed rules changes, as amended	191	156	43	156	148	0	Yes

[a] A party vote occurs when a majority of voting Democrats opposes a majority of voting Republicans.
[b] One hundred fifty-nine Democrats refused to vote on this roll call.

TABLE B.2   Votes Pertaining to Institutional Changes, 1919–1932

Description	All Members		Republicans		Democrats		Party Vote[a]
	Yes	No	Yes	No	Yes	No	
1920 House appropriations changes							
Special rule for House appropriations changes	158	154	106	59	52	93	Yes
Final passage of House appropriations changes	200	117	122	45	78	70	No
1922 Senate appropriations changes							
Lodge (R-Mass.) amendment guaranteeing legislative committees one member on appropriations conference committees	46	20	38	6	7	14	Yes
Norris (R-Nebr.) amendment for committees to elect ex officio members of SAC[b]	20	37	4	33	16	3	Yes
Norris amendment that ex officio provision expire at end of 67th Congress	14	39	9	26	4	13	No
Final passage of Senate appropriations changes	63	14	45	4	18	9	No
1924 rules reforms							
Garrett (D-Tenn.) germaneness amendment	208	177	26	177	178	0	Yes
Graham (R-Ill.) amendment to require 218 signatures on discharge petitions	184	206	157	44	27	158	Yes
Crisp (D-Ga.) amendment to require 100 signatures	164	224	19	180	141	44	Yes
Final passage of new discharge rule	253	114	87	101	162	13	Yes
1925 discharge rule changes							
Previous question on new rules	210	192	210	22	0	166	Yes
Adoption of new rules	207	196	207	22	0	168	Yes
1931 rules reforms							
Previous question on new rules	227	193	9	192	217	0	Yes
Adoption of new rules	403	7	191	7	211	0	No

[a] A party vote occurs when a majority of voting Democrats opposes a majority of voting Republicans.

[b] This later passed without a roll call when Norris deleted the requirement that one of the ex officio members be from the minority party.

Table B.3 Votes Pertaining to Institutional Changes, 1937–1952

Description	All Members		Nonsouthern Democrats		Southern Democrats		Republicans		Party Vote[a]	Conservative Coalition Vote[b]
	Yes	No	Yes	No	Yes	No	Yes	No		
Dies committee/HUAC										
Create special committee, 1938	191	41	(division vote)							
Renewal vote, 1939	344	35	90	34	96	9	154	0	No	No
Renewal vote, 1941	354	6	123	5	90	0	136	0	No	No
Renewal vote, 1943	302	94	35	65	85	13	180	13	No	Yes
Vote to make HUAC a standing committee, 1945	208	186	10	113	60	37	138	35	Yes	Yes
Legislative Reorganization Act of 1946										
Creat Joint Committee on Organization of Congress	(approved by voice vote in both chambers, 1945)									
Senate passage	49	16	17	4	9	9	23	3	No	No
House passage	229	61	(division vote)							
Senate acceptance of House amendments	(adopted on a voice vote)									
Investigations explosion[c]										
Smith NLRB, 1939 (H)	254	134	26	108	76	15	151	8	Yes	Yes
Woodrum WPA, 1939 (H): Previous question on resolution authorizing investigation[d]	351	27	101	24	94	2	152	16	No	No
Truman committee, 1941(S)	(adopted on a voice vote)									

TABLE B.3 Votes Pertaining to Institutional Changes, 1937–1952 (cont.)

Description	All Members		Nonsouthern Democrats		Southern Democrats		Republicans		Party Vote[a]	Conservative Coalition Vote[b]
	Yes	No	Yes	No	Yes	No	Yes	No		
Byrd Joint Committee on Nonessential Federal Expenditures, 1941 (J)[c]	(adopted on a voice vote)									
Smith Executive Agencies Committee, 1943 (H)	294	50	45	45	92	5	154	0	No	Yes
Cox FCC probe, 1943 (H)	(adopted on a voice vote)									
Montgomery Ward, 1944 (H)	300	60	37	55	80	4	181	0	No	Yes
Pearl Harbor Probe, 1945 (J): Senate authorization	(adopted on a voice vote)									
House authorization	308	0	89	0	80	0	138	0	No	No
Fulbright RFC, 1950 (S)	(adopted on a voice vote)									
Kefauver Crime Committee, 1950 (S): Kefauver substitute to create special committee[f]	35	35	22	0	13	4	0	31	Yes	No
Tydings investigation of McCarthy charges, 1950 (S)	(approved on a voice vote after Democrats accepted three GOP amendments)									
McCarran Internal Security, 1950 (S)	(adopted on a voice vote)									
Russell inquiry into firing of General MacArthur, 1951 (S)	(adopted by unanimous consent)									

TABLE B.3 Votes Pertaining to Institutional Changes, 1937–1952 (cont.)

Description	All Members		Nonsouthern Democrats		Southern Democrats		Republicans		Party Vote[a]	Conservative Coalition Vote[b]
	Yes	No	Yes	No	Yes	No	Yes	No		
Creation of Senate policy committees										
SAC amendment adding policy committees to Appropriations bill			(approved on a voice vote)							
21-day rule										
Previous question on adoption, 1949	275	143	145	2	80	29	49	112	Yes	No
Cox resolution to rescind, 1950	183	236	4	145	81	26	98	64	Yes	Yes
Block amendments to rules, 1951	179	247	117	6	24	83	37	158	Yes	Yes
Drop 21-day rule, 1951	244	179	9	112	83	24	152	42	Yes	Yes

[a] A party vote occurs when a majority of voting Democrats opposes a majority of voting Republicans.

[b] A conservative coalition vote occurs when a majority of nonsouthern Democrats opposes a majority of southern Democrats and a majority of Republicans.

[c] Unless otherwise noted, the vote is on the resolution authorizing each investigation. H: House; S: Senate; J: joint committee.

[d] The resolution then passed on a voice vote.

[e] The committee was created through a Senate Finance Committee amendment to a 1941 revenue bill.

[f] The Kefauver substitute passed on the vote of the vice president. The resolution was then approved 69–1. Subsequent extensions and funding increases were granted by voice votes, without controversy.

TABLE B.4 Selected Votes Pertaining to Institutional Changes, 1970–1989

Description	All Members		Nonsouthern Democrats		Southern Democrats		Republicans		Party Vote[a]	Conservative Coalition Vote[b]
	Yes	No	Yes	No	Yes	No	Yes	No		
Legislative Reorganization Act of 1970										
House votes										
Fascell (D-Fla.) amendment to make recorded votes in committee public	(adopted on a voice vote)									
Recorded teller vote amendment	(adopted on a voice vote)									
Schwengel (R-Iowa) amendment to bar proxy voting	156	187	23	106	26	46	107	35	Yes	No
House passage	326	19	127	1	59	12	140	6	No	No
Senate votes										
Mathias (R-Md.) amendment to make chairmen elective by majority party, and not by seniority	23	44	9	13	1	12	13	19	No	No
Senate passage	59	5	24	0	6	5	29	0	No	No
Open committee meetings										
House votes										
previous question on open meeting resolution[c]	197	196	130	6	67	11	0	179	Yes	No

TABLE **B.4** Selected Votes Pertaining to Institutional Changes, 1970–1989 (cont.)

Description	All Members		Nonsouthern Democrats		Southern Democrats		Republicans		Party Vote[a]	Conservative Coalition Vote[b]
	Yes	No	Yes	No	Yes	No	Yes	No		
Stratton (D-N.Y.) amendment to allow executive officials to attend closed meetings	201	198	21	121	45	33	135	44	Yes	Yes
Adoption of open meetings rules, 1973	371	27	138	3	61	15	172	9	No	No
Adoption of House rules, 1975 (open conference meetings)[d]	259	150	181	2	74	12	4	136	Yes	No
Senate votes										
Roth (R-Del.) amendment to require public vote to close meeting, 1973	38	47	18	15	4	10	17	22	No	Yes
Rules Committee substitute to allow individual committees to set own open meeting policies, 1975	16	77	4	36	4	13	8	28	No	No
Roth (D-Del.) amendment to require open conference committee meetings, 1975	81	6	37	2	12	2	32	2	No	No

TABLE **B.4** Selected Votes Pertaining to Institutional Changes, 1970–1989 (cont.)

Description	All Members		Nonsouthern Democrats		Southern Democrats		Republicans		Party Vote[a]	Conservative Coalition Vote[b]
	Yes	No	Yes	No	Yes	No	Yes	No		
Adopt open meeting rule, 1975	86	0	38	0	14	0	34	0	No	No
Budget Act of 1974										
House votes										
Bennett (D-Fla.) amendment to require pilot testing of programs	185	218	11	135	35	41	139	42	Yes	No
Bingham (D-N.Y.) amendment to delay sending appropriations to president until reconciliation bill passes	117	289	78	70	12	64	27	155	No	Yes
Martin (R-Nebr.) amendment to delete impoundment provisions	108	295	3	143	3	74	102	78	Yes	No
Passage of House version	386	23	134	14	72	6	180	3	No	No
Conference report approval	401	6	145	4	79	0	177	2	No	No

Description	All Members		Nonsouthern Democrats		Southern Democrats		Republicans		Party Vote[a]	Conservative Coalition Vote[b]
	Yes	No	Yes	No	Yes	No	Yes	No		
Senate votes										
Byrd (Ind-Va.) amendment to require balanced budget	35	52	6	32	9	4	20	16	Yes	Yes
Chiles (D-Fla.) amendment to require budget committee meetings to be open to public	55	26	30	5	7	6	18	15	No	No
Roth (R-Del.) amendment to require vote of either chamber to rescind an impoundment	28	60	0	39	4	9	24	12	Yes	No
Nelson (D-Wis.) amendment to put six-year term limit on Senate Budget Committee	24	56	17	18	1	12	6	26	No	No
Roth (R-Del.) amendment to tighten spending ceilings	23	57	2	33	3	11	18	13	Yes	No
Passage of Senate version	80	0	36	0	14	0	30	0	No	No
Conference report approval	75	0	39	0	11	0	25	0	No	No
Senate staffing, 1975										
Brock (R-Tenn.) motion to invoke cloture	77	19	40	3	8	9	29	7	No	No

TABLE B.4 Selected Votes Pertaining to Institutional Changes, 1970–1989 (cont.)

Description	All Members		Nonsouthern Democrats		Southern Democrats		Republicans		Party Vote[a]	Conservative Coalition Vote[b]
	Yes	No	Yes	No	Yes	No	Yes	No		
Cannon (D-Nev.) motion to table Gravel staffing amendment	40	55	20	22	11	5	9	28	Yes	No
Cranston-Brock amendment to provide more money for staff than Gravel version	47	49	16	26	4	12	27	11	Yes	No
Adoption of Gravel staffing resolution	63	35	30	13	7	11	26	11	No	No
Stevenson committee reforms, 1977										
Church (D-Idaho) amendment to restore Select Aging Committee	90	4	37	1	19	0	34	3	No	No
Table Burdick (D-N.Dak.) amendment to restore Post Office Committee	55	42	20	22	8	10	27	10	Yes	No
Table McGovern (D-S.Dak.) amendment to retain Nutrition Committee	49	44	15	25	15	3	19	16	No	Yes

TABLE **B.4** Selected Votes Pertaining to Institutional Changes, 1970–1989 (cont.)

Description	All Members		Nonsouthern Democrats		Southern Democrats		Republicans		Party Vote[a]	Conservative Coalition Vote[b]
	Yes	No	Yes	No	Yes	No	Yes	No		
Table Clark (D-Iowa) amendment to bar full committee chairmen from heading more than two subcommittees	42	47	16	23	13	3	13	21	Yes	No
Table Clark amendment requiring committees to have subcommittees	63	20	22	15	13	4	28	1	No	No
Table Nelson (D-Wis.) amendment to require rotation of committee chairmen	62	26	21	16	14	4	27	6	No	No
Pass Stevenson resolution	89	1	38	1	18	0	33	0	No	No

[a] A party vote occurs when a majority of voting Democrats opposes a majority of voting Republicans.
[b] A conservative coalition vote occurs when a majority of nonsouthern Democrats opposes a majority of southern Democrats and a majority of Republicans.
[c] Republicans opposed the previous question on motion due to its blocking a minority staffing amendment.
[d] Open meetings were part of a package of changes adopted. Republicans opposed the resolution due to other elements of the package.

Notes

Chapter One
Disjointed Pluralism and Institutional Change

1. Additional examples of works that emphasize members' multiple goals are Dodd 1977, Maltzman 1997, Rohde 1991, Sinclair 1989, and Smith 1993. See also Remington and Smith 1998, and Smith and Remington 2001, who show the importance of multiple goals for institutional development in the Russian Duma.

2. Shepsle and Weingast (1994) and Rohde (1994) suggest possible paths to such a synthesis.

3. Braybrooke and Lindblom (1963) use "disjointed incrementalism" to describe a decision-making strategy they attribute to policy analysts. I use the term *disjointed* to describe processes of institutional change, while Braybrooke and Lindblom primarily use the term to describe thought processes. Still, my usage of the term borrows from their understanding of decision making as a fragmented process.

4. The second column of table 1.1 refers to the group highlighted by theorists who focus on the collective interest in question while the third column refers to the authority structure expected based on such models. In practice, a few of the collective interests could apply to other groups. For example, party-centered interests can apply to the minority as well as the majority party. Similarly, power base interests apply to senior members as well as juniors. The analysis of individual cases addresses such interests when they are relevant, but table 1.1 simplifies matters by focusing only on the groups highlighted by the theoretical literature.

5. While Mayhew (1974) emphasizes members' electoral goals, his discussion of control committees highlights members' interest in congressional power.

6. Organizational theorists have long pointed out that individuals who acquire status from an organization will typically develop a vested interest in that organization's survival and growth. This leads members to pursue organizational maintenance goals in addition to the organization's stated goals (Scott 1998). As their status comes to depend on Congress's institutional standing, careerist members likely experience an analogous goal expansion.

7. A handful of scholars have also pointed to members' shared stake in congressional prestige (see table 1.1). But it is not clear what sorts of institutions boost Congress's reputation, and therefore it is difficult to derive predictions based on this interest.

8. Polsby (1968) also highlights how the committee system encourages specialization and therefore helps Congress meet modern policymaking challenges.

9. Krehbiel (1991) is agnostic as to whether members' primary motive for creating a specialized committee system is electoral or policy based. He argues that both individual goals can generate a collective interest in information.

10. The Cannon case would fit the Diermeier and Myerson model if Cannon had added to the number of veto points in the House. However, Cannon at times

used his power to bypass committees and push favored policies to enactment. As such, it is not clear whether Cannon's recentralization resulted in a net increase in House veto points.

11. By authority structure, I mean the allocation of resources, especially mechanisms for the exercise of influence, to leaders, committee units, and rank-and-file members.

12. Cox and McCubbins acknowledge variations in majority party effectiveness, but they emphasize the structural advantages of the majority party, which they contend are always substantial.

13. The supermajority requirement for cloture in the Senate means that shifts in the median may not be sufficient to generate changes in Senate institutions.

14. One might argue that since voting on policy tends to be dominated by a single ideological dimension (Poole and Rosenthal 1997), decisions about institutions should likewise be dominated by a single dimension. However, multiple dimensions are relevant to congressional organization precisely because such decisions not only affect policy, but also affect members' electoral, power, and partisan goals, which do not necessarily coincide perfectly with their policy interests.

15. Again, it is important to emphasize that I am not the first to argue that multiple interests matter. Indeed, several of the authors discussed above draw upon multiple interests. For example, Rohde argues that parties will be strong when members' partisan and policy interests overlap and will be weak when these goals conflict (due to intraparty ideological divisions). Similarly, Dodd's (1977) cyclical theory of congressional change is premised on a conflict between members' individual power goals and their shared interest in congressional power.

16. Although I use the term *pluralist* in this work, I depart from pluralist theory in focusing on interests that are, for the most part, institutional rather than societal in their origins. For example, public interest in congressional capacity and power is only sporadic and rarely leads to substantial pressure for change. But the constitutional separation of powers and checks and balances have continually motivated members to maintain Congress's standing within the larger political system. It simply would not occur to a member of the contemporary British Parliament that the power of the House of Commons needed protection from executive incursions. That such concerns have proven important in the United States stems from the constitutional provisions that structure Congress and its place in the American polity. Similarly, the characteristic features of the U.S. electoral system also help to shape members' party-based interests: the strength of congressional parties depends in part on the role played by state and national party organizations in recruiting candidates, financing campaigns, and otherwise structuring election outcomes (Cooper and Brady 1981). Power base goals are also fundamentally institutional: those with disproportionate power have an institutionally induced interest in defending the status quo, just as members with less power have an institutionally induced interest in reform.

17. A discharge petition can be used to force a floor vote on a bill or resolution that is being held up by a House committee.

18. An entrepreneur also may place an unusually high value on the collective interest that the change would benefit. The evidence in chapter 2 suggests that Reed believed strongly that ending minority obstruction was necessary for Congress to function effectively, and that he was therefore willing to take unusual risks to achieve that goal.

19. As Laver (1981) points out, entrepreneurs are not Hobbesian sovereigns. Baumgartner and Jones (1993) also discuss how policy entrepreneurs exercise influence by convincing others that their framing of an issue is more accurate than their opponents' framing.

20. This analysis owes much to Riker's (1986) work on heresthetics. See also Strahan (1999) and Aldrich and Shepsle (1997) for additional efforts to grapple with entrepreneurial leaders' role.

21. In a similar spirit, Humes (1989) likens congressional organization to the typical New England farmhouse: numerous additions are made to the farmhouse over the years, each with a conscious purpose in mind. However, there is no single architect with a master plan guiding this process, and the result, therefore, appears haphazard.

22. Braybrooke and Lindblom (1963, 127) make an analogous point in their treatment of policy analysis. They argue that "if the values of one analyst or one policy-making group neglect indefinitely some kinds of policy consequence, other analysts and groups whose values are adversely affected will make these neglected consequences focal points of their own problem-solving." For a related argument, see Dodd's (1986) cyclical analysis of congressional change.

23. In a sense, the decentralizing changes of the 1920s can be viewed as a response to the centralizing moves in earlier decades. But within the period itself, innovation-and-response is less evident.

24. This criterion is intended to provide a more difficult test for claims 3 and 4.

25. These cases do not include three periods of (mostly) Democratic majorities since 1890: 1911–18, 1933–36, and 1953–69. I do not believe that these omitted periods differ from those selected in the kinds of authority structures constructed or collective interests pursued, except that 1913–17, 1933–36, and 1964–66 are the premier cases of executive-led coalitions. However, periods of executive-led politics are rare, and their apparent lack of durability suggests the need for an investigation distinct from that undertaken here.

26. Primary sources have their own shortcomings when it comes to identifying cases. In particular, they tend to highlight those changes that are visible to many participants and that occur within a brief period of time, which presupposes a narrow vision of what constitutes institutional change. Primary sources also may confuse momentary controversy for lasting significance. It is important to emphasize that I do not argue that the changes I identify are the only important ones during the periods under consideration. My claim is that the cases I have selected are significant, and that a focus on the interactions among coalitions pursuing multiple interests is a useful way to understand the dynamics surrounding adoption and implementation of these changes.

27. An additional concern about case selection is whether focusing only on changes that are adopted, as opposed to changes that fail, amounts to selecting on the dependent variable. To gain additional leverage, I draw upon comparisons with failed changes when available. For example, comparing the 1890 adoption of the Reed rules in the House with a failed Senate effort to crack down on filibusters later in the same Congress helps illuminate the House changes. In addition, in analyzing each period I discuss paths that were considered but not taken. Finally, not all of the changes analyzed were "successful" (significance is not synonymous with success), and I can therefore capitalize on variation in success as well.

28. One might say that the hypothesis that majority party interests account for a change is the null for evaluating party theory versus disjointed pluralism, while the hypothesis that electoral interests account for a change is the null for evaluating reelection models versus disjointed pluralism, and so on. However, two caveats are important: first, not all cases are appropriate for testing certain theories (see discussion below). Second, my argument is not that single-interest theories are wrong, but that they are insufficient. I argue that a focus on multiple interests leads to important generalizations that are missed by single-interest models; I do not argue (or believe) that single-interest models are without merit.

29. Distinguishing partisan and policy interests can prove difficult, due to the often-high correlation between party and policy preferences. The key criterion for counting a case as partisan is whether party has an impact controlling for policy preferences. Likewise, policy goals will be cited when policy preferences have an impact controlling for party. Determining whether these conditions hold varies in difficulty, and as a result, in a few cases the conclusions about the relative weight of partisan and policy goals are tentative.

30. An example would be a reform that provides a resource that any incumbent could use.

. 31. Interests that fall outside my typology also play a significant role in a few cases. More specifically, on those rare occasions when the public is focused on congressional organization, members may vote for reforms simply to posture for constituents. This sort of position taking differs from the more institution-specific sense in which position taking enters my typology: namely, that members may share a collective interest in institutions that provide opportunities for *future* position taking (and thus promote reelection). In such a situation, there is a clear connection between position-taking interests and specific institutional devices: for example, investigative committees can serve as platforms for members to show off their skills. This differs from a situation in which voting for a change is *itself* an exercise in position taking, regardless of the change's actual institutional effects and regardless of whether the change is even implemented. Such posturing—which will be noted in the text when relevant—makes it even more unlikely that institutions will be well tailored to any single collective interest, since it allows the intrusion of factors other than the actual effects of a change.

32. One might argue that any change that promotes congressional capacity and power should have unanimous support. But this ignores the complex nature of changes, which may promote one interest while harming other interests. For example, a change that strengthens congressional capacity may undermine the personal power bases of some members.

Chapter Two
Institutional Development, 1890–1910:
An Experiment in Party Government

1. The bill to safeguard the voting rights of African-Americans was the only one of these measures to fail. A Senate filibuster killed that bill.

2. Reed's rulings have often been called "revolutionary" (see, e.g., Low 1906, 413; Cannon 1920).

3. Some of the leading participants in 1910 readily admitted that they were engaging in a revolution (see Oscar Underwood (D-Ala.), as quoted in Atkinson 1911, 120).

4. The 1890 rules also dropped the Holman rule, a Democratic invention that had allowed appropriations riders when their purpose was to cut spending. The rule was restored in 1892, only to be dropped again in 1896 (Stewart 1989). Seventeen sources treat the Reed rules as significant: Bolling 1968, 52–61; Byrd 1988, 1:342–43; CQ 1982, 120–22; Cooper 1988, 80–81; Damon 1971, 110–13; Dunn 1922, 1:23–34; Faulkner 1959, 99; Galloway and Wise 1976, 55–56; Josephy 1979, 260–62; Keller 1977, 301–3; MacNeil 1963, 49–52; Morgan 1969, 333–35; Peters 1990, 62–70; Ripley 1967, 18, 89; Sinclair 1990, 109, 120; Williams 1978, 20–25; and Wolf 1981, 304–24.

5. One might argue that conditional party government theory should not be applied to late-nineteenth-century Congresses. Party control over nominations was strong enough in this era so that member agreement on policy may not have been necessary for them to delegate substantial power to party leaders (Rohde 1991). However, Binder (1997) has successfully applied conditional party government theory to nineteenth-century Congresses, suggesting that the approach is potentially helpful even in this era (see also Dion 1997).

6. A difficult question is whether majority party interests were sufficient to account for this change, even if concerns about congressional capacity marginally reinforced partisan interests. If so, this should be classified as a change that can be explained by a single interest. Notwithstanding the party-line votes on the reform, I argue that there is considerable evidence that Republicans would not have passed this change if not for the additional push provided by the goal of bolstering congressional capacity. As discussed below, this evidence includes the GOP divisions that militated against centralizing power and the consistent advocacy of a crackdown on obstruction by GOP leaders even when the party was in the minority. However, further research into the private papers of key participants and rank-and-file members might help to resolve this issue with greater certainty.

7. The realignment led dissident silver Republicans to leave the GOP and cost Democrats much of their foothold in the North, thereby creating a much more sectionally polarized party system.

8. Similar results are obtained when simpler measures, such as the difference in party medians or the standard deviation of majority party members' scores, are used. Similar results also are obtained when census data on manufacturing employment are used. The census data were drawn from Parsons et al. (1990) and from data generously provided by Scott James at UCLA.

9. The other major issues were pension legislation, which did divide members along party lines, and antitrust policy, which was not a partisan issue.

10. The tariff arguably was the defining partisan issue in the late nineteenth century. Republicans generally favored high tariffs on imports in order to protect industry from foreign competition. Democrats typically opposed high tariffs because they represented agricultural areas that depended on exports and that faced less competition from cheap imports. See Stanwood 1903 for a classic discussion of tariff politics.

11. See *Chicago Tribune*, May 10, 1890; May 22, 1890, 5; and May 23, 1890, 4; *Public Opinion*, May 17, 1890, 120–22; and Faulkner 1959, 27, 38.

12. The political scientists are correct, however, that party voting rose dramatically in Reed's 51st Congress. But the evidence presented above suggests that this increase did not correspond to an increase in the homogeneity of party members' constituencies; conditional party government theory regards constituent homogeneity as the key variable affecting party strength.

13. See also CR, February 4, 1884, 998; and statements by Roswell Horr (R-Mich.) and Joseph Keifer (R-Ohio), CR, February 5, 1885, 1289–90.

14. Reed had defended minority obstruction in 1880, but he became a consistent supporter of majority rule by the mid-1880s—while the GOP was still in the minority (see Robinson 1930; Strahan 1999).

15. Since Reed's consistent commitment to limiting obstruction appears to have transcended the GOP's partisan interests, Cannon's claim that only Reed could have pushed such extensive reforms through the House bolsters the view that concern about congressional capacity played a significant role.

16. Riker (1986) defines a heresthetical maneuver as a move that helps to manipulate the political situation in a way that leads others to join your side.

17. Press accounts of the Republican caucus held on January 27, 1890, made it clear that Reed had not told his colleagues that he planned to count a quorum and had not received assurances of support in case he embarked on such a course. The *Post* noted that the caucus proceedings suggested that "the Speaker hardly contemplates adopting the radical course of counting as present members not voting in order to secure a quorum" (January 28, 1890, 3; see also *NYT*, January 29, 1890, 1).

18. On events in the Senate, see De Santis 1969 and Hoar 1903. Due to the overrepresentation of the West in the Senate, Republicans in the upper chamber were even more divided than were House Republicans. Furthermore, preexisting Senate institutions (especially the absence of a rule for calling the previous question) also impeded passage of the cloture rule (see Binder and Smith 1997).

19. The Bennett law barred the use of German in Wisconsin's public schools. Similar legislation was adopted in Illinois in 1889, also resulting in a voter backlash.

20. Republicans' aggressive behavior in the 104th Congress of 1995–96 provides another example of a majority party's self-destructive excesses (see the epilogue).

21. Five sources treat the repeal of the Reed rules as significant: Williams 1978, 90; Peters 1990, 72; Keller 1977, 303; Damon 1971, 114–15; Wolf 1981, 343–45.

22. Based on manufacturing levels, Democratic homogeneity in the 52nd Congress was only slightly lower than GOP homogeneity had been in the preceding Congress. Although party polarization was a bit lower in the 52nd Congress, the standard deviation of the value of manufacturing in Democratic districts was nearly identical to the standard deviation among Republicans in the preceding Congress (119.73 vs. 119.56).

23. Cox and McCubbins (1993) attend to both of these majority party interests. The interesting aspect of this case is that it suggests that legislative and reputational concerns may conflict in important ways.

24. None of these variables were significant predictors of voting behavior on the Bynum amendment. Ideology is measured using first- and second-dimension D-NOMINATE scores. NOMINATE scores measure members' policy preferences (Poole and Rosenthal 1997). Calculated based on all nonunanimous roll call votes, they place members in a two-dimensional space. The first dimension, which generally taps into an economic left-right cleavage, is usually a stronger predictor of members' votes than the second dimension, which tapped into sectional cleavages in the late nineteenth century and into civil rights issues in the 1930s through 1970s. NOMINATE scores range in value from −1 to +1 along each dimension.

25. An alternative explanation is that the more senior members had experienced the deficiencies of the pre-Reed bill introduction system and therefore better understood the advantages of Reed's system. The seniority variable is the number of two-year terms served by each member.

26. Six sources treat the 1894 restoration of Reed's quorum rule as important: Williams 1978, 90; Peters 1990, 72–73; Keller 1977, 303; Josephy 1979, 262; Damon 1971, 114; Wolf 1981, 347–48. In January 1896, the new GOP majority restored the remainder of Reed's rules.

27. A logit analysis of the roll call finds that the Democratic supporters of the change did not differ from Democratic opponents in ideology, seniority, region, or committee assignments.

28. Eight sources treat the increase in the Rules Committee's powers in 1892–95 as a significant change: Bolling 1968, 46; Ripley 1967, 19; Cooper 1988, 80–81; Damon 1971, 75–77, 205; Galloway 1953, 340; Riddick 1949, 113, 119–20; Wolf 1981, 344–46; Goodwin 1970, 184. The Rules Committee consisted of five members from 1890 to 1910. The Speaker, who chaired the committee, typically picked two close allies for the remaining majority party slots.

29. In a division vote, those in favor and then those opposed are asked to stand while a head count is taken. It is impossible to determine how any individual member voted when a division vote is conducted (Oleszek 1996).

30. Opponents of the 1895 change also decried giving the Rules Committee additional powers, but they mostly focused on the substance of the bill that Rules sought to extract from a legislative committee. No direct votes were taken on the 1895 ruling by Speaker Crisp.

31. For example, William Oates (D-Ala.) argued, "I am opposed to the adoption of rules which give the Speaker and his two [Rules] committee associates the power to determine whether my bills shall have a hearing in the House" (CR, February 1, 1892, appendix, 13; see also statement by Hooker, CR, August 31, 1893, 1106). As pointed out in chapter 1, although all members share a stake in congressional capacity and power, individuals may oppose changes that promote that goal when those changes threaten other interests.

32. Members' second-dimension NOMINATE scores were a strong, significant predictor of votes on this roll call. In the mid-1890s, the NOMINATE second dimension primarily tapped into the sectionally based currency issue. Coinage Committee members also were more likely to support passage than were nonmembers (b = 1.61; SE = 1.02; p = .06). The estimates for seniority, party, and first-dimension NOMINATE scores were small and insignificant.

33. Seven sources treat as significant the rise of the Senate Four to prominence in the late 1890s: Byrd 1988, 1:343, 362–63; CQ 1982, 225–27; Josephy 1979, 268; Mowry 1958, 115; Ripley 1969b, 27–28, 41; Rothman 1966; Smith and Deering 1990, 34.

34. Gamm and Smith (1999) have undertaken a major study of changes in Senate leadership that will add greatly to the evidence base for this case.

35. I relied on the Congressional Directory to classify members' party affiliations. Two of the six former Republicans are listed as belonging to the "Silver" party rather than the Silver Republican party.

36. As noted above, Allison's election appears to have been predicated simply on his seniority (Rothman 1966). Press coverage of the caucus decision to select Allison does not suggest that members had a major change in party operations in mind (see *Post*, March 7, 1897, 5).

37. However, the prospect of a bipartisan floor coalition did help shape the caucus agreement on the Hepburn Act (Blum 1954).

38. See, for example, Ben Tillman's (D-S.C.) filibuster in 1903 of an appropriations bill to force inclusion of pork for his state (Gwinn 1957, 73).

39. Seven sources treat this change as significant: CQ 1982, 227; Goodwin 1970, 12; Haynes 1938, 458; Ripley 1969b, 27; Rothman 1966, 65–67; Robinson 1954, 296–98; Smith and Deering 1990, 33–34. The 1896 proposal promised increased turf for roughly three-quarters of all senators; the version adopted in 1899 reduced this number somewhat but still provided a net gain in jurisdiction for a healthy majority.

40. The results are substantively the same if a logit analysis is performed on the individual roll calls, or if the six-point scale is analyzed using ordered logit.

41. Second-dimension NOMINATEs appear to offer a more precise measure for this sectional division than does the dummy variable for western residence, which misses the considerable variation in the conditions confronting western states. It is also worth noting that first-dimension NOMINATE scores do not have a significant impact on support for the reform. Schickler and Sides (2000) point out that the first-dimension scores do not map neatly onto opinions about spending levels at the turn of the century.

42. Membership on committees that stood to gain jurisdiction is not a significant predictor of votes on the change. However, this is largely due to the high negative correlation (−.72) between this variable and SAC membership: there were few members lacking seats on Appropriations who did not stand to gain jurisdiction from the change (Schickler and Sides 2000).

43. Presidential politics played a role because Allison was viewed as a contender for the White House (*Post*, February 8, 1896, 4).

44. Chandler had proposed that Appropriations keep its jurisdiction over the legislative, executive, and judicial, sundry civil expenses, and deficiencies bills.

45. Five sources discuss as significant the change in the mode of operations in House GOP leadership under Henderson: Mowry 1958, 115–18; CQ 1982, 125; Ripley 1967, 83, 90; MacNeil 1963, 62; Peters 1990, 75.

46. Evidence on the Senate leaders' motivations is indirect. More research, drawing upon the senators' personal papers, is necessary to be certain about their goals in helping Henderson.

47. These conclusions about the effects of Henderson's speakership are tentative as they are based on the assessments of the press and House members, rather than a direct examination of decision making. One step that might make the conclusion of increased Senate power less tentative would be to explore the extent to which major bills during these years were shaped primarily in the House or the Senate.

48. Moreover, since the House under Speaker Crisp (1891–95) does not resemble strong party government, the era of Speaker-led party government is further reduced to Reed's six years as Speaker and Cannon's first six years as presiding officer.

49. Six authors treat Cannon's revival of the speakership as an important institutional change: Mowry 1958, 117–18; Ripley 1967, 90; MacNeil 1963, 29–30, 53; Peters 1990, 75–78; CQ 1982, 125–26; Josephy 1979, 278.

50. Henderson declared that he would not be a candidate because there is "a growing sentiment among [Iowa] Republicans that I do not truly represent their views on the tariff question" (*Post*, September 17, 1902, 1). A farm district is defined here as one in which the value of farm production exceeds the value of manufacturing production.

51. See *Post*, September 19, 1902, 6, September 21, 1902, p.3; *NYT*, September 18, 1902, 1, September 19, 1902, 11. See also "Speaker Henderson's Retirement" 1902. Secondary sources provide a similar assessment of rising GOP divisions on the tariffs and trusts; see, e.g., Dunn 1922, 1:406–7; Mayhill 1942; Mowry 1958; Skowronek 1993, 233–49; Stephenson 1930, 206. Figure 2.1 also suggests that GOP homogeneity was slightly *lower* when Cannon was elected than when Henderson was elected.

52. Historian John Milton Cooper (1990) argues that the tariff was the only issue on which the two candidates adopted clearly different positions.

53. For example, Henderson's handling of the beet-sugar Republicans' revolt on the high-profile Cuba trade reciprocity bill in 1902 damaged party leaders' prestige (Thompson 1906, 152–54).

54. Cannon's motives for handing this power over to Williams are not entirely clear. His friendship with Williams likely played a role. He also may have hoped that Democrats would become more divided as they squabbled over assignments (Gwinn 1957).

55. Along these lines, it is intriguing that his NOMINATE scores suggest Cannon was not a conservative outlier relative to the floor median when he took office as Speaker in 1903 (Krehbiel and Wiseman 1999). Notwithstanding Cannon's archconservative reputation (which became increasingly well earned in 1907–10), the Speaker showed a surprising willingness to tolerate Roosevelt's progressive proposals early in his tenure, so long as Roosevelt kept his hands off the tariff.

56. In December 1907, Roosevelt called for regulation of railroad securities, income and inheritance taxes, workman's compensation, a ban on corporate political donations, and public financing of party campaigns (Hatch 1967).

57. Nine sources note the significance of the 1909 reforms: Riddick 1949, 228, 257; Ripley 1983, 62; Cooper 1988, 88–97; MacNeil 1963, 54, 171; Damon 1971, 12, 214–15; Peters 1990, 80, 95; Goodwin 1970, 209; CQ 1982, 126–27; Galloway 1953, 348.

58. The median is calculated using first-dimension D-NOMINATE scores. The floor median was .45 in the 59th Congress, leaving it just barely to the left of the GOP median, which was .55. The floor median shifted by .09 to the left following the 1906 election and by another .24 to the left following the 1908 election. After these shifts, the floor median stood at .24 in the 61st Congress, while the GOP median was .51. The Democratic median shifted slightly toward the center during these years, from −.52 to −.44.

59. Although the two NOMINATE dimensions may tap into different aspects of members' policy preferences, I treat policy goals as a single interest, rather than as two distinct interests. There is no evidence from the historical record that members drew a distinction between two separate dimensions of policy-based dissatisfaction with Cannon.

60. Though to the left of the median Republican, Gardner was far closer to the GOP median than to the Democratic median (based on first-dimension NOMINATE scores). Fowler was more of a progressive than Gardner but was still much closer to the GOP median than to the Democratic median. See Marguiles 1996 on both members.

61. Fowler chaired the Banking and Currency Committee (prior to his 1909 demotion by Cannon); Gardner was the second-ranking member of the Immigration and Naturalization Committee. In 1906, Cannon had used a restrictive rule and other stratagems to defeat Gardner when they disagreed over a key provision of an immigration bill reported by Gardner's committee (Marguiles 1996). Two years later, the Speaker appointed a special committee to report currency legislation when Fowler's committee insisted on promoting a bill sponsored by Fowler that Cannon found objectionable (Hechler 1940).

62. Krehbiel and Wiseman (1999) have recently presented data challenging the idea that Cannon punished dissident members. Nonetheless, of six committee chairmen in the 60th Congress who voted against Cannon on the rules in March 1909, four were no longer chairmen when Cannon made his appointments for the 61st Congress.

63. The technique relies upon examining transfer rates among committees.

64. I rely upon portfolio values in the 60th Congress because most committee assignments in the 61st Congress were made after the 1909 votes, creating the possibility that a low portfolio value in that Congress could have been an effect, rather than a cause, of voting against Cannon on the rules. Using values from the 60th Congress requires deleting freshmen in the 61st Congress. Substituting the number of terms served by each member for the committee assignments variable in model 1 avoids this missing-data problem and produces substantively similar results (with junior members more likely to support reform), though the seniority variable falls just short of significance ($p = .076$). Including both the number of terms and committee portfolio variables results in a significant coefficient only for the portfolio values.

65. The mean first-dimension NOMINATE score for the Republican defectors was .23, while the mean for Republicans who stuck with Cannon was .54 ($p < .01$). Among the Democrats, the mean score for those voting against Cannon was −.45, while the mean for those opposing Cannon was −.31 ($p < .01$). When an interaction term between party and first-dimension NOMINATE scores is added

to the models in table 2.3, the results show that NOMINATE scores have a substantial impact for both Democrats and Republicans.

66. Several Regulars had distanced themselves from Cannon during the 1908 campaign but believed replacing Cannon would create too much strife (Gwinn 1957; Bolles 1951).

67. The House did not adopt a discharge rule until June 1910, and it was another two decades before reformers came up with an effective discharge process.

68. Seventeen sources treat the changes as significant: Galloway and Wise 1976, 57–59, 169–70; Mowry 1958, 242; Cooper 1988, 101–4; Cooper 1990, 148; Peters 1990, 82–90; Smith and Deering 1990, 35; CQ 1982, 125–28; Josephy 1979, 288–89; Sinclair 1990, 112; Bolling 1968, 74–85; Jones 1970, 15, 113; Riddick 1949, 64; Ripley 1967, 19, 194; MacNeil 1963, 53–54; Damon 1971, 78–79; Goodwin 1970, 209; Peabody 1976, 41; and Wolf 1981, 386–87.

69. Restricting the analysis to Republicans cuts the number of cases substantially. Notice that second-dimension NOMINATEs are strong and significant in model 5, when the committee portfolio values variable is omitted (thereby allowing inclusion of additional cases).

70. One problem with the committee portfolio values variable is that it doubtless includes measurement error, which likely attenuates its coefficient estimate. Each committee's estimated value has a fairly large standard error attached to it, and some of the committee ratings appear implausible (for example, Disposition of Executive Papers ranks as the seventh most desirable committee, ahead of the Rules Committee and Military Affairs Committee). Alternative measures indicate that committee power bases were relevant: for example, of 21 Republicans who had been on what most would regard as the top three committees in the preceding, 60th Congress—Rules, Ways and Means, and Appropriations—none voted for the Norris motion, while 43 of the remaining 178 Republicans voted in its favor. Replacing committee portfolio values with this "top committee" variable does not affect the estimates for the remaining variables. Since "top committee" is a perfect predictor it has an essentially infinite coefficient and standard error ($b = 7.17$; $SE = 30.02$).

71. Cannon's opposition to a reduction in tariff duties on wood pulp and print paper added fuel to press anger (Rager 1991).

72. Members who voted for Clark's proposed rules changes in 1909 and for Norris's 1910 change are counted as resisting Cannon in both 1909 and 1910, while those voting against the Clark resolution in 1909 but in favor of final passage of the Norris resolution are counted as newcomers to insurgency.

73. This is based on a reanalysis of data presented in Baker 1973.

74. The position-taking interest in this case falls outside the typology of interests outlined in chapter 1. Republican defectors used their votes on reform to posture for constituents but were not seeking to create institutions that foster opportunities for future position-taking (see note 31 in chapter 1 for a discussion of this distinction).

75. Cannon had taken back control of committee assignments from Clark in 1909, making it difficult for the minority to punish the defectors in the short term.

76. See Gwinn 1957; Holt 1967; and Riker 1986 on Norris's maneuver.

77. Cannon based this claim on the constitutional provision stating that Congress is responsible for making laws pertaining to the census.

78. It is true, however, that several of the Republicans who changed their votes between 1909 and 1910 did stick with the Regulars on some of the procedural motions leading up to the vote on adoption of the Norris amendment.

79. Dedicated insurgents, such as Norris, Nelson, and Murdock, also made the rules issue more visible by writing articles and giving speeches that highlighted the abuses of "czar rule" (Hechler 1940, 196; Gwinn 1957).

80. Cooper (1988) finds that changes in Congress's workload do not account for this increase in the Rules Committee's activity.

81. Recall that the existence of these multiple interests is rooted in institutional features of American government, such as separation of powers and the relative weakness of national parties in controlling nominations (see note 16 in chapter 1).

Chapter Three
Institutional Development, 1919–1932: Cross-Party Coalitions, Bloc Government, and Republican Rule

1. In the House, the Agriculture, Post Office and Post Roads, Military Affairs, Naval Affairs, Foreign Affairs, Indian Affairs, and Rivers and Harbors committees could report appropriations. For a list of Senate committees with this authority, see chapter 2. Twelve sources treat the 1920 decision by the House, and the 1922 move by the Senate to follow suit, as an important institutional development: Cooper 1988, 137; CQ 1982, 132–34, 254; Bolling 1968, 108; MacNeil 1963, 395; Galloway and Wise 1976, 213; Smith and Deering 1990, 37; Haynes 1938, 458–60; Damon 1971, 62–63; Paxson 1948, 225–26; Goodwin 1970, 10–13; Robinson 1954, 319; Byrd 1988, 2:232. The change has also been discussed in recent treatments of the budget process (Brady and Morgan 1987; Stewart 1989; Kiewiet and McCubbins 1991).

2. Members on more than one committee losing jurisdiction are counted only once. The Senate number excludes six Appropriations Committee members who also served on committees which were losing jurisdiction.

3. For example, in 1920 a nearly unanimous Congress adopted a bill that would have repealed sixty wartime measures that had vested power in the executive. Only a Wilson pocket veto stopped its enactment (Binkley 1962).

4. Wilson's surprising decision to veto the budget bill delayed its ultimate enactment for another year.

5. The issue content of second-dimension NOMINATE scores is unclear in the 1920s (see Poole and Rosenthal 1997, 48). Therefore, the scores are excluded from the models in table 3.2. Adding the second dimension produces an insignificant coefficient estimate and does not affect the estimates for the remaining variables. Adding a control for the South also produces an insignificant coefficient and leaves the remaining estimates unaffected.

6. The high correlation between party and ideology (as measured by first-dimension NOMINATE scores) in the 66th Congress ($r = .90$) makes it difficult to distinguish statistically the effects of these two variables. When both variables are included in the model, the party variable is small and insignificant, while the effect

of ideology is significant and properly signed (see table 3.2). Furthermore, when the analysis is done separately for Democrats and Republicans, the coefficient for the ideology variable remains substantial and is borderline significant.

7. The Senate added it at the suggestion of Alabama Democrat Oscar Underwood (CR, March 6, 1922, 3419).

8. Norris sought to delete the ex officio membership provision but otherwise supported the reforms.

9. A rules change restricting House conferees' ability to agree to Senate amendments to spending bills also increased the leverage of House members in appropriations battles with the Senate (Haynes 1938, 469–70; Luce 1926, 85).

10. Six authors treat the elimination of the committees as significant: Smith and Deering 1990, 37; Kravitz 1974, 33–35; CQ 1982, 248; Haynes 1938, 285–87; Goodwin 1970, 12; Byrd 1988, 2:244. The House followed suit in 1927, eliminating thirteen committees. The House changes were more modest in scope and did not receive sufficient attention from scholars to qualify for consideration here (see Galloway and Wise 1976, 70–71; Damon 1971, 63, for discussions of the House changes).

11. Furthermore, when the GOP proposed increasing the size of committees by one in 1921, Democrat Harrison took the Republicans to task for their apparent change of heart: he accused them of hypocrisy because when committee sizes had been cut in 1920, "it was given out to the country that it was going to effect great economy and the saving of much expense to the Government" (CR, April 18, 1921, 399).

12. The 1920 consolidation has often been confused in the secondary literature with this 1921 increase in committee sizes (CQ 1982, 253; Haynes 1938, 285–87). This latter change was a partisan move, although Republicans' representation on the enlarged panels was quite close to their share of seats in the Senate as a whole.

13. Six authors specifically identify the farm bloc's creation as an important institutional development: Leuchtenberg 1993, 101–2; Murray 1973, 44–52; Paxson 1948, 252, 291; Josephy 1979, 309–13; Jones 1970, 70–71; Ripley 1967, 175. These sources tend to emphasize the Senate farm bloc far more than the House bloc. This is consistent with accounts from the early 1920s, which also generally identified the Senate bloc as more effective and organized than the House bloc (see, e.g., Welliver 1922; Bradley 1925).

14. Electoral interests clearly played a major role in this case, but they can be subsumed under the "sectoral/policy" collective interest because farm-state members' individual electoral goals generated a collective interest in new policies that was shared only by other farm-state members. A change is considered to promote "reelection" as a collective interest only if, at least in principle, it stands to benefit all members.

15. Republican leaders offered agriculture increased tariff rates—which many agrarians suspected were of little use to most farmers.

16. Welliver (1922, 160) notes that the farm bloc used threats of hostile amendments to sidetrack probusiness legislation favored by Republican leaders. The *Times* also cites the farm bloc's role in defeating the ship-subsidy bill, which was one of Harding's top priorities (November 19, 1922, 1, 17).

17. The "Coalition" was an informal Senate alliance of Democrats and dissident Republicans who were particularly active in the fight over the Smoot-Hawley tariff. The "Allied Progressives" comprised a group of about fifteen Republicans and a handful of Democrats in the House who fought for progressive legislation in the 72nd Congress.

18. Seven sources treat the rules changes as significant: Riddick 1949, 239; Josephy 1979, 310–11; Cooper 1988, 168–73; CQ 1982, 132–36; Galloway and Wise 1976, 176–77; Damon 1971, 216, 220; Bolling 1968, 111.

19. The bill for which the discharge petition was filed would then gain consideration if a majority of members present voted for the discharge motion. For the first time, the discharge rule was also made to apply to special orders from the Rules Committee (Beth 1994, 8).

20. The rule provided an exemption for the final three days of a session.

21. In a teller vote, members file up the center aisle of the House—the ayes first and then the nays—and are counted by two "tellers" (Oleszek 1996). Prior to 1970, it was impossible to know how any individual voted on a teller vote (see chapter 5 on the 1970 change).

22. The ideology effect is robust to changes in model specification, such as dropping the party variable or adding controls for the South and second-dimension NOMINATE scores. The significant estimate for western residence on several of the votes also likely reflects policy preferences: progressivism was particularly strong in the West.

23. The mean first-dimension NOMINATE score for the nineteen Republicans who voted for the most liberal version of the discharge rule was .01, as compared to a mean of .39 for the 189 Republicans who opposed the proposal ($p < .01$).

24. Since no Democrats voted against this change, the party variable is in essence a perfect predictor of members' votes. As a result, the logit analysis of the germaneness amendment is confined to Republicans.

25. A caveat should be added: first-dimension NOMINATE scores suggest that few, if any, Democrats were conservative when compared to the Republicans. However, scholarship on the 1920s counters this notion (see, for example, Murray 1973; Schwarz 1970; Hicks 1960, 102).

26. The effect of seniority remains robust when members' second-dimension NOMINATE scores are added to the model and when a control for the South is included.

27. The requirement for a one-day waiting period before voting on a special rule also suggests a membership concerned about defending itself from abuses by party leaders and committee elites (CR, January 18, 1924, 1139–41). The changes to the consent calendar also appealed to rank-and-file members' personal power interests: the new requirement of three objections to kill a measure facilitated noncontroversial legislation that nonetheless was important to individual members (Damon 1971, 216).

28. The progressives again caucused prior to floor consideration of the proposed rules reforms in January 1924 (*Post*, January 12, 1924, 4).

29. The average seniority of the defectors was 3.6 terms, as compared to 2.6 terms for the loyal Democrats ($p < .05$).

30. During floor debate on the rules change, John Nelson asserted it was necessary to allow specific amendments to the tax bill (CR, January 14, 1924, 958). In subsequent floor debates, however, Garrett denied that the now-repealed germaneness restriction (the "Underwood rule") had ever applied to tax bills and claimed it had only applied to tariff bills (CR, February 18, 1924, 2717). However, an examination of House precedents shows quite clearly that the Underwood rule had been interpreted to restrict amendments to tax bills and not just tariff bills (see, e.g., CR, May 27, 1920, 7745, 7764–65; CR, September 19, 1918, 10510–11). It also appears that the House presiding officer took into account the repeal of the Underwood rule when he ruled on the admissibility of amendments to the tax bill (see, e.g., CR, February 21, 1924, 2910).

31. The unruly tendencies of the Rules Committee were reinforced in December 1923 when progressives successfully pressured GOP leaders to place John Nelson on the committee. The progressives had threatened to ally with the Democrats to place both Nelson and an additional Democrat on the committee, unless the Republicans acceded to their demands that Nelson receive an assignment through the party caucus (*Post*, December 16, 1923, 3).

32. Five authors treat the 1931 changes as a significant reform (Riddick 1949, 240–41, 244, 257; Cooper 1988, 168–73; Galloway and Wise 1976, 80, 105; CQ 1982, 149; Damon 1971, 11, 223–29).

33. As shown in appendix B.2, the vote on the previous question motion was closely divided. However, the previous question vote was more symbolic than substantive: as noted below, many Republicans opposed the motion in the hopes of offering a competing package of rules changes. But the GOP package differed little from the Democratic proposal, and it therefore would be incorrect to code a vote against the previous question motion as a vote against reform.

34. Schwarz's book on the 72nd Congress demonstrates that Garner cooperated closely with Hoover and minority leader Bertrand Snell (R-N.Y.), particularly for the first four months of the Congress (Schwarz 1970, 100–103, 133–34, 233; see also Timmons 1948, 139). The March 1932 rank-and-file rebellion against the regressive sales tax that Garner and the Republican leaders sought to push through the House spelled the end of the "incongruous Republican administration–House Democratic leadership alliance" (Schwarz 1970, 133). La Guardia and Robert Doughton (D-N.C.) led the rebellion uniting progressive Republicans with restless Democrats (Schwarz 1970, 117–33).

35. Crisp took great care to make the discharge rule workable, apparently due to his principled belief in the right of the minority party to "smoke out the majority and make them face issues" (CR, January 14, 1924, 967). Beth (1994, 8) notes that "almost alone among those who discuss the rule over the years, his positions never seem tainted by ulterior attachment to interests of party or of political position in the House."

36. La Guardia worked with progressives in both parties throughout the 72nd Congress. For example, in the spring of 1932, he led an unofficial caucus of progressives that formed to develop relief legislation. The caucus included five Democrats and several progressive Republicans (Zinn 1959, 201; Kessner 1989, 184).

37. The Senate eventually rejected the veterans' bonus. The House voted down the motion to discharge on the other matters, but those presenting the discharge petition did succeed in forcing a recorded vote in each case.

38. This ruling was not reversed until the 1993 passage of a rules change initiated by that year's Republican minority (Schickler and Rich 1997a).

39. Ironically, the conservative coalition's control of the Rules Committee after 1937 gave majority Democrats reason to favor a less cumbersome discharge process (see chapter 4).

40. Six sources treat the creation and use of the Steering Committee as significant: Josephy 1979, 310; Peters 1990, 101–2; Ripley 1967, 48–49, 83, 100–101; Cooper 1988, 164–65; CQ 1982, 135; MacNeil 1963, 108. The Steering Committee grew out of a less formal and less important advisory body created in the preceding Congress, while the GOP was in the minority (Peters 1990, 101; Ripley 1967, 48–49).

41. Indeed, based on first-dimension NOMINATE scores Longworth was actually to the right of Mann.

42. Republican National Committee chairman Will C. Hays and Republican senators Lodge, Boies Penrose of Pennsylvania, and Reed Smoot of Utah convinced House Republicans to reject Mann for Speaker out of fear that his public relations troubles would damage the party (*NYT*, January 27, 1919, 8; Peters 1990, 99).

43. Interestingly, Gillett's voting record prior to the 66th Congress (he did not vote enough to have a NOMINATE score after becoming Speaker) placed him extremely close to the GOP median, while Mondell and Mann were both a bit to the right of the GOP median.

44. Six sources treat the 1919 innovation as an important institutional development: Cooper 1988, 165; CQ 1982, 134–35; Smith and Deering 1990, 37; Peabody 1976, 34; MacNeil 1963, 96–97; Galloway and Wise 1976, 175.

45. News reports in March–May 1919, the period surrounding the organization of the 66th Congress, do not discuss the change.

46. In 1926, newly installed floor leader John Tilson (R-Conn.) initiated the practice of providing a daily listing of upcoming committee hearings (Hasbrouck 1927, 111).

47. The clearest exception is Sam Rayburn's influence as floor leader in 1937–40. Speaker William Bankhead (D-Ala.) was in poor health, and Rayburn overshadowed him in House deliberations (Peters 1990, 120).

48. Seven authors identify Longworth's revival of the speakership as an important change: Peters 1990, 103–4; Ripley 1967, 101; MacNeil 1963, 81; Jones 1970, 113; CQ 1982, 137–38; McCoy 1967, 268; Bolling 1968, 111–15.

49. Begg (R-Ohio) owed his prominence entirely to his relationship with Longworth (MacMahon 1927, 299; Chiu 1928, 335).

50. A high standard deviation denotes a low level of party homogeneity.

51. Garner was ranking Democrat on Ways and Means and chair of the Democrats' Committee on Committees throughout Longworth's tenure as Speaker. Garner also had the title of minority leader from 1929–31.

52. Garner's rhetoric on tax matters did have a populist cast, but he was less committed to free trade than were most Democrats, and he was conservative on

many issues (Steinberg 1975, 85; Timmons 1948; Bolling 1968, 149; *New York Herald Tribune*, November 23, 1931, 8). By 1937, then–Vice President Garner had become a strident foe of President Roosevelt's liberal policies (Barone 1990).

53. Among other things, the rule required 218 members to second the discharge motion on a teller vote. Since a teller vote is not a record vote, attendance is generally poor—particularly on Mondays, when the discharge calendar was in order. The rule forbade a call of the House to encourage attendance. Six authors treat the 1925 change as significant: Peters 1990, 103; Cooper 1988, 170; CQ 1982, 137; Damon 1971, 222–23; Josephy 1979, 311; Riddick 1949, 240–44.

54. Since party is a perfect predictor of Democrats' votes on the 1925 change, they are excluded from the analysis.

55. These mean scores are based on first-dimension D-NOMINATE scores for the 68th Congress. Again, higher NOMINATE scores reflect more conservative policy positions.

56. The switchers might also have been chastened by the 1924 election. In the eyes of many, La Follette's failed third-party bid for the presidency had discredited the insurgent cause, perhaps making some former insurgents willing to cooperate with their GOP colleagues (see Murray 1973, 144).

57. Adding a dummy variable for freshmen to the logit analysis in table 3.3 produces a massive negative coefficient and an infinite standard error. The problem is that all fifty-seven Republican freshmen voted for the change. Ideology remains significant when the freshman variable is added to the model. Replicating this analysis using OLS produces significant estimates for both the freshman and ideology variables. It is also worth noting that the mean first-dimension NOMINATE score of freshmen was only slightly to the right of the mean for other Republicans (.40 vs. .35; $p = .04$).

58. The importance of the change was reinforced by restoring a clear majority for conservative Republicans on the Rules Committee. This meant that the committee would not be an appeals court for members dissatisfied with gatekeeping by other standing committees—except in those cases where the Regular Republicans opposed such gatekeeping.

59. A thirteenth House defector, Fiorello La Guardia of New York, was elected as a Socialist in 1924 and thus belongs in a separate category from the other defectors, who were each elected as Republicans.

60. La Follette and Ladd died before the new Congress convened, thus evading this punishment.

61. Interestingly, Keller voted against the new GOP discharge rule yet still was spared punishment.

62. Five sources describe the sanctions in the House as a significant institutional development: CQ 1982, 137; Peters 1990, 103–4; Ripley 1967, 22, 191–92; Bolling 1968, 112–14; Josephy 1979, 311. By contrast, few suggest that the punishment of the Senate defectors had a substantial influence on Senate operations or on member expectations about party loyalty (see, e.g., Byrd 1988, 1:440–41, 2:246; CQ 1982, 249–50).

63. Cooper was demoted to the bottom of the Foreign Affairs Committee but was allowed to stay on the committee.

64. Ernst initially proposed removing the defectors from their committees. This would have required approval by the full Senate in the now lame-duck 68th Congress. Such a proposal would have had "small chance of passage" (*NYT*, November 29, 1924, 2).

65. Indeed, in order to retain control of the Senate, the Republican leadership "yielded to further demands of five recalcitrant radicals for better committee assignments and for better opportunity to present their legislative program" (Berdahl 1949, 497).

66. Following his reelection as Speaker by a straight party vote, Longworth "gave a genial wave to Wisconsin as he took the chair" and addressed the insurgents by saying, "I welcome your return to the Republican party, where you rightfully belong" (MacMahon 1928, 652).

67. Defections among majority party members in the election of the Speaker were reduced to nil after the 1925 incidents (Schickler and Rich 1997a). A handful of progressive Republicans did vote against the party nominee for Speaker in December 1931, in the first speakership election following Longworth's death. However, Democrats were in the majority at the time.

68. The spate of progressive investigations of corruption in the 1920s narrowly failed to qualify for consideration as an institutional change (four sources treat the investigations as a significant institutional development: Haynes 1938, 519, 560; Robinson 1954, 328–41; Murray 1973, 117–19; Taylor 1954, 58–62). The two most important investigative bodies were the subcommittee of the Public Lands Committee led by Thomas Walsh (D-Mont.), which uncovered the Teapot Dome scandal in 1922–24, and the special committee led by Burton Wheeler (D-Mont.) targeting corruption in the Justice Department in 1924. These committees tarnished the reputation of the Harding administration and antagonized Harding's successor, Calvin Coolidge. Other noteworthy investigations include Couzens's vigorous attack on Treasury secretary Andrew Mellon in 1924, James Reed's (D-Mo.) investigation in 1926–28 of excessive campaign spending by Republicans William Vare of Pennsylvania and Frank Smith of Illinois, which resulted in both members losing their seats, Nye's investigation of campaign spending in 1930–31, Thaddeus Caraway's (D-Ark.) 1929–30 probe of the influence of lobbyists, and the Senate Banking Committee's 1932–34 investigation of Wall Street (known as the Pecora investigation), which was initially chaired by progressive Republican Norbeck, followed by Duncan Fletcher (D-Fla.) when the Democrats took over in March 1933.

Chapter Four
Institutional Development, 1937–1952:
The Conservative Coalition,
Congress against the Executive, and
Committee Government

1. I analyze the act's other significant legacy, the expansion in committee staffing, separately because it qualifies on its own for consideration and because the dynamics surrounding staffing differed somewhat from the committee consolidation.

2. Eleven sources treat the committee consolidation as significant: Smith and Deering 1990, 39; Goodwin 1970, 19; Byrd 1988, 1:548–49; Griffith 1967, 83; CQ 1982, 152, 265; Galloway and Wise 1976, 61; Kravitz 1974, 35–36; Cooper 1988, 181; Damon 1971, 12, 64–65; MacNeil 1963, 151; Riddick 1949, 159.

3. The estimated effect of being a committee chairman was -1.48 (SE = .80), while the estimate for the dummy variable for southern Democrats was -1.46 (SE = .66). Ideology (as measured by first-dimension NOMINATE scores) had an insignificant effect, net of the dummy variables for committee chairmen and southern Democrats.

4. Eugene Cox (D-Ga.) dissented from the committee jurisdiction changes and from the proposed creation of party policy committees, Thomas Lane (D-Mass.) disagreed with the pay raise, and Richard Russell (D-Ga.) refused to sign on to the proposal for home rule for the District of Columbia.

5. Other members making similar arguments included Homer Capehart (R-Ind.), Arthur Miller (R-Nebr.), Robert Ramspeck (D-Ga.), William Poage (D-Tex.), and Albert Gore (D-Tenn.) (Joint Committee 1945).

6. George Galloway and other scholars on the American Political Science Association Committee on Congress also functioned as catalysts for change. Created in 1941, the APSA committee issued its report in 1945.

7. Members' shared interest in improved pay falls outside the typology of interests outlined in chapter 1. This is the only case examined in which it played a significant role.

8. However, these limitations were not always enforced in practice.

9. Senate committees averaged five or six clerks and assistant clerks, but these staffers were assigned as part of the chairman's office staff and often divided their attention between committee and noncommittee duties.

10. Nine sources discuss the expansion of committee staff under the Reorganization Act as important: Smith and Deering 1990, 39, 43; Goodwin 1970, 22–24, 271; Byrd 1988, 1:548–49; Griffith 1967, 93, 96; CQ 1982, 154, 265; Galloway and Wise 1976, 60–62; Kravitz 1974, 37; Cooper 1988, 268, 295; Ripley 1983, 268.

11. Similar themes were touched upon at the hearings by Democrats Howard Smith of Virginia and E. C. Gathings of Arkansas and Republican Rees (Joint Committee 1945).

12. This claim is based on an examination of the La Follette–Monroney committee's hearings, and of floor debate on the Reorganization Act. Taft did propose professional staffing for the Senate policy committees, but it appears no one proposed that standing committee staff be selected by party leaders or by the party caucuses (see below).

13. Five sources suggest that creation of the JCAE was an important institutional change: Goodwin 1970, 43; Griffith 1967, 202–3; Ripley 1983, 164; Galloway and Wise 1976, 290; Cooper 1988, 416; see also Riddick 1949, 148.

14. See also McMahon's comments during the Special Committee on Atomic Energy's hearings (1946, 503) and statements by representatives Chester Holifield (D-Calif.) and John Sparkman (D-Ala.) (House Committee on Military Affairs 1946, 26, 37).

15. The House did adopt, on a voice vote and without debate, an amendment to set the size of the JCAE at twenty-two, with a 12–10 party ratio (CQ Almanac 1946, 513). The conference committee accepted the Senate version, which instead set the size of the JCAE at eighteen, with a 10–8 party ratio.

16. Until 1954, the JCAE did lack the power to authorize spending for the AEC, which was granted a blanket authorization in the 1946 Atomic Energy Act. The JCAE campaigned for authorization power starting in 1949 and gained it in a noncontroversial provision of the 1954 Atomic Energy Act (Green and Rosenthal 1963, 169–72). The omission of authorization power was not viewed as a significant weakness in 1946, but it reduced the JCAE's leverage over the AEC and made it more difficult for the committee to fight the House Appropriations Committee's efforts to slow spending on nuclear programs.

17. McMahon had chaired the JCAE when it was created in 1946 but had been replaced when the GOP gained a majority in the 1946 elections.

18. Green and Rosenthal (1963, 32–34) note that "from the beginning, there seemed to be a purposeful attempt to make the Committee regionally representative." Although states particularly affected (though often in different ways) by nuclear energy issues may have been overrepresented, this in no way mitigated the divisions among JCAE members on the key issue of public versus private development.

19. Again, it is worth emphasizing that the committee was generally ideologically representative of Congress as a whole.

20. Specifically, "national investment in atomic energy would have been substantially less and the present level of technology considerably lower" (Green and Rosenthal 1963, 266).

21. Young (1956, 227) contrasts the plethora of investigative committees created during World War II to the dearth of investigations during World War I and to the single, powerful Joint Committee to Investigate the Conduct of the War created to supervise the Civil War. The Republican-controlled 66th Congress (1919–21) did embark on significant investigations related to World War I, but hostilities had already concluded.

22. Important investigations in the postwar years included the Senate Committee on Expenditures in the Executive Department's probe of influence peddling by the White House staff (the "five percenters" investigation of 1949–50), the Senate Banking Committee investigation into corruption in the Reconstruction Finance Corporation (1950–51), the Senate Armed Services and Foreign Relations committees' joint investigation into the Truman administration's handling of the Korean War, and Senator Joseph McCarthy's (R-Wis.) probe of the State Department and army.

23. Five sources treat the marked expansion in special investigative committees during World War II as an important institutional development: Josephy 1979, 335–36; Robinson 1954, 379; Byrd 1988, 2:250–51; Riddick 1949, 152; Young 1956, 18–21, 226–29; see also Cooper 1988, 190; Griffith 1967, 47–48. In addition, six authors attribute significance to the expansion of investigative activity by standing committees following World War II: Galloway and Wise 1976, 62, 223; Damon 1971, 12, 256–57; Cooper 1988, 273–74; Griffith 1967, 13, 95; Josephy 1979, 343; Robinson 1954, 413. An examination of specialized sources on con-

gressional oversight supports dating the rise in investigative activism to the late 1930s and suggests the importance of the shift from special to standing committees after 1946 (see, e.g., Harris 1964, 263–66). Floyd Riddick's annual articles summarizing the most recent congressional session in the *American Political Science Review* (and later the *Western Political Quarterly*) also call attention to the expansion in investigations during World War II, and the efforts at systematization under the Reorganization Act.

24. Southern residence correlates highly with second-dimension NOMINATE scores in these years (Poole and Rosenthal 1997). When a dummy variable for the South is added to the model, it is significant only in the NLRB vote. The results for the remaining variables are unaffected. The high correlation between first-dimension NOMINATEs and party likely explains why the Democratic dummy variable is incorrectly signed (these correlations are consistently above .80). Dropping the party variable leaves the results for the remaining variables unchanged. When first-dimension NOMINATEs are excluded, party has a strong effect, with Republicans significantly more likely to vote for each investigation than Democrats. It is also worth noting that within each party, first-dimension NOMINATEs are strong predictors of members' votes on each investigation, again suggesting the importance of ideology.

25. Conservatives' ideological interests were also promoted by Eugene Cox's 1943 investigation of the Federal Communications Commission (Van Hollen 1951), Harry Byrd's Joint Committee for the Reduction of Nonessential Federal Expenditures (Blum 1976; Riddick 1944; *NYT,* February 7, 1943, 1), and the loyalty probes discussed below.

26. The Smith committee's accusations of agency misbehavior contributed to support for the Administrative Procedures Act of 1946, which facilitated public scrutiny of agency actions (Galloway 1953, 85).

27. Ironically, Republicans sought unsuccessfully to amend the resolution creating the Kefauver committee, believing that the Tennessee senator intended to "whitewash the iniquities perpetrated by Democratic political machines" (Wilson 1975a, 365). But the committee was renewed by a voice vote in March 1951, amid praise from Republicans who no doubt were pleased with the committee's rough treatment of Democratic machines (CR, March 29, 1951, 3005).

28. For example, Republican majority leader Taft took several steps in 1953 to prevent McCarthy from conducting disruptive investigations of the Eisenhower administration (Patterson 1972). But McCarthy surprised Taft by using his Government Operations Committee to embarrass the administration and its Senate Republican allies.

29. This led to efforts to regulate investigative committees. The House passed a set of "fair play" rules in 1955, but the Senate left committees free to set their own rules (CQ 1982, 165).

30. Ten authors treat the change in the Rules Committee's mode of operations as significant: Smith and Deering 1990, 38; Goodwin 1970, 182, 188; Bolling 1968, 40, 135; Josephy 1979, 328, 342; Ripley 1967, 166; Patterson 1967, 53, 186, 307–8; CQ 1982, 146–51; MacNeil 1963, 104–7, 413; Galloway and Wise 1976, 67, 180–81; Sinclair 1990, 113.

31. Lapham (1954), Van Hollen (1951), and House Committee on Rules (1983) provide several examples of this.

32. In the 71st Congress (1929–31), he ranked as the 58th most "left-leaning" out of 167 Democrats, and in the 72nd Congress (1931–33) he ranked 106th out of 224, based on first-dimension NOMINATE scores.

33. Smith ranked as the 167th most "left-leaning" out of 224 Democrats in the 72nd Congress (1931–33), and 229th out of 317 in the 73rd Congress (1933–34).

34. Dies ranked as the 29th most "left-leaning" out of 317 Democrats in the 73rd Congress (1933–34), and 97th out of 322 in the 74th Congress (1935–36). His scores on the second-dimension NOMINATE measure, which taps into civil rights issues, were more conservative. But Dies was within the mainstream of the party on that dimension prior to his appointment to Rules.

35. Colmer ranked as the 257th most "left-leaning" out of 334 Democrats in the 75th Congress (1937–38), and the 219th out of 266 in the 76th Congress (1939–40).

36. From 1939 to 1948, at least half of the Rules Democrats in each Congress were among the most conservative 20 percent of party members. In 1949–52, three of eight Rules Democrats were among the most conservative 10 percent, while a fourth was among the most conservative 30 percent of party members.

37. Cox, Smith, Dies, and Colmer clearly fit this category.

38. In August 1937, Rules member Byron Harlan (D-Ohio) recalled earlier cases where he and other Rules members had voted to report administration bills that they personally opposed and that they ended up voting against on the floor, and he decried how Rules had since then developed into "a committee of censorship, which has taken to itself the power of passing upon the wisdom or desirability of an administration measure" (CR, August 17, 1937, 9112–13). See Lapham 1954, Van Hollen 1951, and House Committee on Rules 1983 for additional quotes and examples.

39. An example would be the Rules Committee's role in creating the Smith committee in 1943, after Cox, Martin, and Woodrum settled on a course of action (see the discussion above).

40. For example, in 1938, the committee was discharged from consideration of what became the Fair Labor Standards Act.

41. Six sources treat the creation and operations of the Dies committee as a significant institutional change: Taylor 1954, 70–79; Kirkendall 1974, 129, 250–51; Leuchtenberg 1963, 280–81; Barone 1990, 171, 232–33; MacNeil 1963, 191–95; Byrd 1988, 2:249–50.

42. Southern Democrats' support for a ban on labor union political contributions (as part of the Smith-Connally Act, passed in 1944) illustrates their willingness to put regional and ideological concerns above party interests.

43. In 1943, the estimate for first-dimension NOMINATE scores is 11.53 (SE = 1.99) and the estimate for second-dimension scores is 3.30 (SE = 1.40).

44. One of the eight bills did not pass the House. Four others died in the Senate after passing the House. These were the anti–poll tax bill, bills to provide statehood for Alaska and Hawaii, and a veterans' hospitals bill. Three bills brought up under the rule were enacted into law: the bill creating the National Science Foundation, a Rivers and Harbors and Flood Control bill, and a bill dealing with American participation in international organizations.

45. Seven sources treat the 21-day rule as an important institutional change: Jones 1970, 15, 124–26; Goodwin 1970, 16, 212–14; Bolling 1968, 179–80; CQ 1982, 161; Grantham 1976, 46; Josephy 1979, 342; Galloway and Wise 1976, 67–68, 146, 185–86.

46. Second-dimension NOMINATE scores are highly correlated with southern residence (r = .79). A dummy variable for the South is insignificant when included alongside the second-dimension NOMINATEs in the logit analyses.

47. Furthermore, if party attachments generally affect members' votes and hence their ideological rankings (since NOMINATE scores are based on roll call votes), the total effects of party will be understated in this sort of analysis (see Jackson and Kingdon 1992 and Snyder and Groseclose 2000).

48. ADA scores from 1948 are used because the 1949 scores include members' votes on the 21-day rule. ADA scores are not available prior to 1945 and thus are not used in analyses of institutional changes before that date.

49. See *NYT*, January 2, 1949, 1; *Washington Post*, January 2, 1949, 1. This was the first binding caucus vote since 1935, and it turned out to be the last such vote until the 1970s.

50. Thirteen of fifteen chairmen (excluding nonexclusive committees) backed the change. Adding a dummy variable for committee chairmen to the analyses in table 4.3 yields a positive but insignificant coefficient estimate.

51. Some authors have suggested that Rayburn wanted the rule repealed in 1951 (MacNeil 1963; Lapham 1954). Robinson (1963, 67) provides solid reasons to reject that claim.

52. Liberal floor strength in 1961 was remarkably similar to liberal strength in 1949 (see Bolling 1968, 207). One difference, however, was that the Democratic Study Group made liberals better organized in 1961.

53. This is because each party ordinarily controls its own committee assignments. Thus, mainstream Democrats likely could have blocked any moves to remove liberals from the committee or to add more conservative Democrats. Conservatives could have stacked the committee only by increasing the number of Republicans on Rules, without adding any new Democrats.

54. A further caveat is that the significant coefficient estimate for second-dimension NOMINATE scores suggests that a unidimensional, median voter model is inadequate to capture the cleavages at work. At the same time, it is worth noting that the estimated effect of the first dimension is far greater in magnitude than the second dimension.

55. For example, the Rules Committee approved a rule for consideration of a bill to repeal the Taft-Hartley Act, but the rule granted favorable treatment to John Wood's (D-Ga.) substitute measure. Lapham (1954, 223) notes that the rule "best suited the plans—not of the House leadership—but of the coalition leadership."

56. Although formally charged with assisting the floor leader in scheduling matters, it did not meet often under Alben Barkley (D-Ky.), the Democratic leader from 1937 to 1948. His successors, Scott Lucas (D-Ill.) and Ernest McFarland (D-Ariz.), consulted the committee more often, but there is scant evidence to suggest that it played a major role during their tenure (Goodwin 1970, 227; Jewell 1959, 978–80). The committee gained some importance when Lyndon Johnson became floor leader in 1953 (Bone 1956).

57. Seven authors consider the creation of the Senate Republican policy committee important; Jones 1970, 53, 161; Goodwin 1970, 229; Griffith 1967, 158;

Cooper 1988, 282; Byrd 1988, 1:550, 587–88; Truman 1959b, 130–32; Ripley 1969b, 38, 102. With the exception of Cooper, each source comments on the importance of the GOP Policy Committee in more specific terms than the Democratic committee. Cooper does not compare the two committees.

58. However, committee staffing generally was not explicitly done along party lines.

59. The committee also performed service functions, often with a party-building element. For example, when the Republicans gained majority status in 1947, the Policy Committee staff supplied new committee chairmen with the names of qualified persons for committee staffs (Bone 1968, 180; Kampelman 1954, 544).

60. Five sources treat the onset of these weekly meetings as an important development in the position of congressional leaders: Riddick 1949, 92–93, 417–18; Ripley 1967, 77–78, 86, 92; Truman 1959b, 257, 295–98; MacNeil 1963, 34–35; Galloway and Wise 1976, 134, 146–47.

61. Alsop and Kintner (1941, 76) claim that Rayburn also wanted to protect the prestige of the speakership, and therefore of the House, which had suffered from Roosevelt's surprises. But there is no additional evidence to suggest that broad, institutional concerns played a significant role. The partisan stakes were most likely sufficient.

62. Truman (1959a) shows that party leaders' role as presidential agents dates back to Wilson's first administration, but notes that this role was dramatically expanded under FDR.

63. Barkley slowly gained a level of prestige that eluded his two successors, Scott Lucas and Ernest McFarland. But his stature never matched that of his predecessor, Joseph Robinson of Arkansas (Ritchie 1991; Bacon 1991).

64. Barkley's angry resignation in 1944 following Roosevelt's veto message attacking Congress for enacting an inadequate tax bill underscores the tensions characterizing Barkley's role. After Senate Democrats unanimously reelected Barkley, Senator Elbert Thomas (D-Okla.) claimed that ever since Barkley's election by a one-vote margin in 1937, the impression had been that Barkley "spoke to us for the President. Now that he has been unanimously elected, he speaks for us to the President" (as quoted in Byrd 1988, 1:535). Still, Barkley continued to regard himself as "the Administration's floor leader" and to claim that he was obliged to resign in the case of a "fundamental and irreconcilable disagreement with the President" (quoted in Truman 1959b, 306).

65. The interests of a divided Democratic party (at least as interpreted by Sam Rayburn) also influenced the decision to remove the policy committees and legislative-executive council from the Reorganization Act.

Chapter Five
Institutional Development, 1970–1989: A Return to Party Government or the Triumph of Individualism?

1. When a senator places a hold on legislation (or a nomination), his party leader agrees to object to the bill's consideration on his behalf.

2. The War Powers Act was an important element of this congressional resurgence but is not a change in rules and procedures, leadership instruments, or the committee system and thus is not analyzed here.

3. Eight sources treat the Budget Act as an important institutional development: CQ 1976, 744; Peters 1990, 176–83; Bailey 1988, 12–13; Dodd and Oppenheimer 1993, 46; Rieselbach 1995, 13, 17; Deering and Smith 1997, 39–40; Jones 1995, 51, 202; Price 1992, 76, 92.

4. "Backdoor" and "uncontrollable" spending refers to expenditures that are not subject to the annual appropriations process. Entitlement programs are a leading example.

5. Adding second-dimension NOMINATE scores to the equation yields an insignificant coefficient and does not affect the results for the remaining variables. The control for the South was also insignificant.

6. Kiewiet and McCubbins (1991, 63) argue that the Budget Act should be viewed as an innovation "adopted by the majority party to further its own policy objectives." My analysis of the act belies this interpretation.

7. At the instigation of the Democratic caucus, the term limitation was loosened a bit in 1979 to six years out of any ten.

8. Though four of the Rules Committee's five Republicans opposed the anti-impoundment procedures included in the revised bill, all five Republicans endorsed the budget reform procedures as a whole (CQ Almanac 1973, 249).

9. Six sources identify multiple referrals as an important change: Connelly and Pitney 1994, 72; Davidson 1992, 21; Dodd and Oppenheimer 1993, 46, 55; Smith 1989, 25; Sinclair 1990, 115, 117, 138; Rieselbach 1995, 18.

10. This interpretation of multiple referrals supports Krehbiel's (1991) informational model of committees.

11. The sole difference was that the Bolling committee and Martin plans allowed for appeals of the Speaker's referral decisions to the Rules Committee, while the Hansen version omitted provision for appeal. Bolling and Martin both served on Rules and thus stood to gain from such an appeals process (see CR, October 8, 1974, 34453–54).

12. Collie and Cooper (1989) point out that, paradoxically, this broadened participation undermined committee monopolies over specific issues. Members in effect "surrendered autonomy for access" (254). King (1997) counters that multiple referrals cost committees less in terms of control of legislation than Collie and Cooper (1989) suggest.

13. See Davidson (1980b) for a detailed description of the proposed jurisdiction changes.

14. The Senate's adoption of fairly extensive jurisdictional changes in 1977 led to a significant fall in its use of multiple referrals, just as the House began to make use of the procedure.

15. Under a joint referral, two or more committees simultaneously considered the same legislation.

16. Seven sources treat the Stevenson reforms as an important change: CQ 1980, 877; Bailey 1988, 9, 29–31; Byrd 1988, 2:260–65; Deering and Smith 1997, 41–42; Rieselbach 1995, 17; Ornstein, Peabody, and Rohde 1997, 23; Jones 1995, 92.

17. Stevenson's statement is consistent with Diermeier's (1995) hypothesis, from chapter 1, that an influx of new members can disrupt the distribution of power in the committee system. Chapter 6 assesses how well Diermeier's model fares in explaining this and other changes.

18. Length of service is measured by the number of contiguous Congresses of Senate service.

19. Since no committee chairmen voted for the Clark amendment, the logit model yields an essentially infinite coefficient and standard error for this variable. Dropping the chairmen from the analysis leaves the results for the remaining variables unaffected.

20. Adding second-dimension NOMINATE scores generates an insignificant coefficient estimate and does not appreciably change the estimates for the remaining variables.

21. Prior to this change, junior members on many committees received only those subcommittee assignments left over after senior members selected theirs.

22. Clark described his floor amendment in terms that echo the arguments for the decentralization of Senate appropriations in 1899 (see, e.g., *CQWR*, February 12, 1977, 281).

23. The Senate granted some exemptions to the assignment limits, so that by 1983 the average number of assignments had crept up to twelve (Ornstein, Peabody, and Rohde 1997). Concerns about sound organization could not dictate impermeable limits on assignments, given their value in promoting reelection and personal power.

24. The drop in multiple referrals in the Senate documented by Collie and Cooper (1989) indicates that the committee consolidation reduced jurisdictional overlaps.

25. Five sources identify opening committee meetings as a significant reform: CQ 1976, 744; Bailey 1988, 9, 108–9; Dodd and Oppenheimer 1993, 46; Sinclair 1989, 105–6; Davidson 1992, 7–8; see also Sinclair 1990, 46.

26. Junior members' frustrations surfaced in the House as well. For example, Representative Charles Vanik (D-Ohio), in urging open conference committee meetings, complained that conference "decisions are usually made by Members with more than ten years of service. The point of view of newer Members is seldom considered" (CR, March 7, 1973, 6718).

27. While in a sense the openness reforms were part of the more general liberal Democratic attack on conservative committee chairmen, large bipartisan majorities favored the reforms. Furthermore, there was apparently little ideological cleavage surrounding the issue (*CQWR*, January 20, 1973, 71–72). It is also worth noting that, in a move that displeased many liberals, the openness reforms spread to the House Democratic caucus in 1975. Conservative southern Democrat Joe Waggonner (D-La.) pushed for open caucus meetings as a ploy to make them far less useful to the Democrats (*CQWR*, May 3, 1975, 911).

28. Interestingly, first-dimension NOMINATEs and party each have a significant effect in 1973. These results indicate that liberals were more likely to vote for the Roth proposal than were conservatives, but that, all else equal, Republicans were more likely to favor the proposal than Democrats. The high correlation between NOMINATE scores and party ($r = -.71$) suggests one should interpret these somewhat opposing results cautiously. Furthermore, neither ideology nor party had a significant effect on the 1975 Senate vote on open meetings. It is also worth noting that the chairman variable is related to support for open meetings at the

bivariate level (r = −.29), but that this relationship is insignificant when the full model is estimated (see table 5.2).

29. I used the list of cosponsors published on January 15, 1975, in the Congressional Record.

30. The act transformed the old Legislative Research Service into the better-funded Congressional Research Service. Seven sources treat the Reorganization Act as a significant institutional change: Byrd 1988, 2:258–59; CQ 1972, 353; Connelly and Pitney 1994, 72; Peters 1990, 153–55; Dodd and Oppenheimer 1993, 46, 55; Smith 1989, 21–35; Sinclair 1989, 45–49, 211.

31. Seniority and ideology are also significantly related to cosponsorship at the bivariate level.

32. One cautionary note about the significant effect for party is that it is less robust than the other coefficients. It is insignificant when second-dimension NOMINATE scores are added to the model. However, it is significant when ADA scores are used in place of NOMINATE scores as a measure for policy preferences. The South is unrelated to support for the amendment in the multivariate logit analysis.

33. Ironically, the same liberal Democrats who had favored the recorded teller change found themselves the targets of GOP amendments when they took over an increasing share of floor management duties as subcommittee chairmen in the mid-1970s (Kravitz 1990).

34. The Democrats finally succeed in 1979 in slightly increasing the level of support required to obtain a recorded teller vote from twenty to twenty-five members.

35. Republicans were angered, however, by Democrats' January 1971 decision to renege on a guarantee of increased minority staffing.

36. Five sources identify the 1975 change as significant (CQ 1982, 289; Bailey 1988, 9, 28–29; Byrd 1988, 2:259; Ornstein, Peabody, and Rohde 1997, 9–10; Sinclair 1989, 78–79).

37. Junior senators' power interests were partly linked to their electoral interests. Prior to 1975, juniors often confronted the choice of whether to use their personal staff for committee business or to promote reelection (Malbin 1975). The additional staff provided in 1975 helped senators minimize this trade-off (Smith 1993).

38. Similar results characterize the closely contested vote on an unsuccessful amendment sponsored by Alan Cranston (D-Calif.) and Brock to provide even more money for staff than Gravel had proposed (see appendix B.4). The results are somewhat weaker when the lopsided final passage vote is analyzed, in part because several of the chairmen dropped their opposition to the Gravel resolution once its approval was a foregone conclusion (*CQWR*, June 21, 1975, 1294).

39. The version passed was actually sponsored by Humphrey, but it closely resembled the original Gravel proposal.

40. Earlier changes in party procedures for distributing committee assignments, such as the Democrats' Johnson rule of 1953 and GOP changes adopted in 1959 and 1965, also helped junior members obtain better committee assignments.

41. Eight sources treat the boom in obstruction as an important institutional change: Bailey 1988, 11–12, 76–77, 130; Byrd 1988, 2:154–57, 160–61; CQ 1980, 877; Davidson 1989, 290–93; Ornstein, Peabody, and Rohde 1997, 11, 26;

Sinclair 1989, 94–95, 128–31; Smith 1989, 94–98, 104, 110–13; Rieselbach 1995, 25–26. With the exception of Rieselbach, each source discusses the rise in filibusters along with either the postcloture filibuster or the spread of holds.

42. While first used in 1939 on the Executive Reorganization Bill, expedited procedures did not become common until the 1970s (Binder and Smith 1997).

43. Binder and Smith's (1997) list of statutes that include debate limitations contains many cases involving congressional efforts to respond to executive branch challenges. Adoption of such restrictions may also be facilitated because their ultimate policy impact is often uncertain; for example, the budget process set up in 1974 did not systematically favor either party or ideological camp.

44. Seven sources consider the subcommittee reforms important: CQ 1976, 743; Deering and Smith 1997, 38, 42; Dodd and Oppenheimer 1993, 46, 49–51; Peters 1990, 177; Rieselbach 1995, 18; Sinclair 1990, 114; Price 1992, 58, 75, 78.

45. Another Rosenthal staffer, David Rohde, also played an important role in devising the reforms (Ornstein 1975).

46. The caucus approved the subcommittee changes on voice votes in 1971 and 1973.

47. Empowering subcommittees may also have made sense from an informational standpoint: as the agenda facing Congress became more complex, the need for highly specialized work units became more pressing. But there is little evidence that this interest played a significant role.

48. Seven sources identify the Democrats' changes in the committee assignment process as significant: Peters 1990, 177, 192; Dodd and Oppenheimer 1993, 54–55; Sinclair 1990, 114–15, 138; Deering and Smith 1997, 38–39; Rieselbach 1995, 16–19; Connelly and Pitney 1994, 72; Price 1992, 75–76.

49. The mean ADA rating in 1974 for Ways and Means Democrats was 47.0 (SE = 8.0), as compared to a mean rating of 51.7 (SE = 1.9) for the caucus as a whole. The mean ADA for Steering and Policy members in 1974 was 56.9 (SE = 5.8). Though the gap between Ways and Means and the full caucus is not statistically significant, see Rohde 1991 and Rieselbach 1994 for additional evidence that liberals perceived Ways and Means Democrats as too conservative.

50. Six authors treat this as an important institutional development (CQ 1976, 743; Barone 1990, 539; Peters 1990, 193, 209; Dodd and Oppenheimer 1993, 46, 50; Davidson 1992, 11; Deering and Smith 1997, 38).

51. However, it is also worth noting that the attack on seniority began in 1970–71, before turnover began to rise. Chapter 6 includes a more sustained assessment of evidence concerning Diermeier's model.

52. The estimated effect of first-dimension NOMINATE scores on support for the reform is −5.11 (SE = 1.52). The estimated effect of terms of service is −.20 (SE = .06). Controlling for ideology and seniority, dummy variables for committee chairmen and the South are insignificant. The survey results mirrored the caucus vote: 70 percent of the 150 members who stated a position on the reform in the survey claimed to support it, as compared to 67 percent of members voting at the caucus.

53. Some have alleged that the leadership worked to have Hays purged (Hinckley 1976; Sheppard 1985). But several members of Steering and Policy denied this was the case (*National Journal*, January 25, 1975, 131).

54. Along these lines, it is noteworthy that the first major inroads against seniority occurred in 1965, when Democrats demoted two members who had endorsed Goldwater for president in the 1964 election. As in 1975, the Democrats enjoyed an overwhelming majority in 1965.

55. Seven sources treat the rise of restrictive rules as important: CQ 1984, 799; Connelly and Pitney 1994, 72–73; Davidson 1992, 21; Dodd and Oppenheimer 1993, 55–56; Peters 1990, 269–70, 283–85; Price 1992, 76, 87; Smith 1989, 40–85.

56. Examining a set of Congresses different from Krehbiel's, Sinclair (1994) finds weaker effects for informational variables. However, Sinclair does obtain a statistically significant estimate for committee specialization.

57. Members' interest in preserving their committee power bases may have also contributed to this change, but the evidence for this interest is sketchy. Committee chairmen have increasingly requested restrictive rules from the Rules Committee (*CQWR*, October 10, 1987, 2452). But there is little evidence that the chairmen were a driving force behind the change.

58. The case of welfare reform in 1987 is illustrative (Barry 1989).

59. As noted above, a leadership effort to raise from twenty to forty the number of members who could together force a record teller vote was rejected in 1974. The House approved a slight increase, to twenty-five members, in 1979.

60. Six sources identify the reemergence of the strong speakership under Wright as a significant institutional change: CQ 1988, 871–72; Davidson 1992, 21–22; Dodd and Oppenheimer 1993, 55–57, 63; Peters 1990, 210, 262–80; Price 1992, 77–78; Sinclair 1990, 138–39.

61. Though the House as a whole adopted the multiple referral rule, the committee assignment changes were made by the Democratic caucus.

62. While President Harrison backed Reed's program in 1889–91, most of the initiative rested with the House.

63. Wright deleted the bill's controversial welfare reform provisions before bringing it up the second time.

64. The so-called Gephardt amendment split the Democrats on trade. Democratic liberals and conservatives could not agree on how much to spend on welfare reform or on defense. John Murtha (D-Pa.) led a group of more than twenty Democrats who demanded higher defense spending than most liberals were willing to countenance. On taxes, many Democrats voted for Wright's tax increase despite their skepticism about the move's political wisdom. The *contra* aid issue featured a camp of about seventy-five liberals who would refuse to vote for any assistance and a somewhat smaller, but often pivotal, group of conservative Democrats who insisted on providing at least some funding. The importance of a group of fiscal conservatives led by Tim Penny (D-Minn.) and Buddy MacKay (D-Fla.) is an indication of the Democrats' divisions. This group, which had about forty members or sympathizers, often was displeased by the leadership's decisions on budget matters and constantly threatened Wright's ability to pass a Democratic budget. See Barry 1989 and the accounts of specific legislation provided by *Congressional Quarterly*.

65. Six sources discuss the formation and activities of COS as an important institutional development: Bader and Jones 1993, 294–95; CQ 1984, 799, 1988, 872; Connelly and Pitney 1994, 27–29, 77–78; Dodd and Oppenheimer 1993, 60–61; Peters 1990, 252–53, 275; Smith 1989, 65–68.

66. The model estimated controls for the South, length of service, and being a ranking member on a committee. Adding second-dimension NOMINATE scores to the model results in an insignificant coefficient estimate and does not impact the remaining coefficients. The list of COS members was obtained from *Conservative Digest* ("Conservative Opportunity Society" 1984).

67. Edwards' first-dimension D-NOMINATE score placed him slightly to the right of the GOP median in the 98th Congress (1983–84).

Chapter Six
Understanding Congressional Change

1. These cases include all of the rules changes and decisions to create new committees or to reorganize (formally) existing committees.

2. These sixteen changes include six cases that involved formal decisions by one party (e.g., changes in party rules), seven informal changes in party leadership instruments, and three informal changes that were not confined to one party.

3. Changes in party rules also may have binding force, at least on party members. But the binding nature of caucus rules cannot be taken for granted. For example, the Democratic caucus adopted a rule in 1911 allowing it to set binding party positions when two-thirds of its members agree. However, there are numerous instances in which Democrats defected on the floor in defiance of a "binding" caucus vote, without apparent punishment (Schickler and Rich 1997a).

4. Their success was limited by Cannon's entrepreneurial efforts: the Speaker worked with James Mann (R-Ill.) and John Fitzgerald (D-N.Y.) to frame an alternative that capitalized on the policy and power goals of dissident Democrats.

5. The restrictive rules case is difficult to classify, since it was a gradual development. I classify it as a formal, floor-approved change because each special rule requires a floor majority for approval.

6. There are several additional cases in which entrepreneurs may have played a significant role, but the evidence is less clear: these include the Senate Appropriations decentralization of 1899 (Dubois and Chandler) and House rules reforms adopted in 1924 (John Nelson and his allies).

7. The DSG's activism in the early 1970s is the best example of backbencher entrepreneurs promoting majority party interests. In a sense, the DSG's leaders constituted an alternative leadership cadre, seeking to strengthen and then take over their party.

8. Excepting Wright's centralization, most of the cases of path-dependent layering involved formal changes approved on the floor. Therefore, restricting attention to this subset of changes does not reduce the support for this claim. Path-dependent layering occurred in other cases as well, but these are the instances in which the layering process clearly compromised the effectiveness of individual changes.

9. Prior to the 51st Congress, the Republicans had been in the majority for only two years (1881–83) since the party's setback in the 1874 elections. The GOP majority elected in 1994 was the first in forty years.

10. I owe this point to discussions with Paul Pierson.

11. Conditional party government theory is an exception in that it highlights both partisan and policy interests, but it too is insufficient (see discussion below).

12. In a few other cases, the reelection interest forced compromises upon reformers. For example, Democrats seeking to repeal the Reed rules in 1892 were forced to retain Reed's bill introduction process.

13. This is consistent with Mayhew (1974) and Fiorina (1977), who argue that congressional organization is tailored to the electoral goals of *all* incumbents. Each member is able to cultivate her own "market" without hurting her colleagues.

14. The period following Korea is not included in this study, but in any case it is the one major war that did not feature substantial presidential power gains (Barone 1990; Fischer 1991).

15. Divided party control of Congress and the presidency fails to explain the timing of these changes: four of the eight occurred when the same party controlled both branches.

16. In 1909, the value of members' committee assignments is significant. Seniority falls just short of significance (see note 64 in chapter 2). For the assault on seniority, the quantitative analysis focused on Democrats' support for an automatic vote on committee chairmen, but a similar cleavage apparently characterized Republicans (see chapter 5). Excepting the assault on seniority, each case involved formal, floor-approved changes.

17. One might also add a handful of cases that served junior members' power interests, but where there were no data to demonstrate a seniority effect statistically: Henderson's ascension to the speakership in 1899, the House GOP decisions to create a Steering Committee and to take away the floor leader's committee duties in 1919, House rules reforms of 1931, and changes empowering House subcommittees in 1971–73. These cases provide no additional support for the seniority distribution hypothesis: turnover was not higher in these Congresses than in the preceding Congresses.

18. An alternative test is to regress the proportion of newcomers on time and then to examine the residuals. A positive residual indicates a Congress with more new members than expected. In the House, two of the reform Congresses had positive residuals and two had negative residuals. In the Senate, the results are also mixed: focusing on members in their first Congress, two positive residuals are obtained (55th and 95th Congresses) along with one negative residual (94th Congress). However, when one examines the percentage in their first six-year term, the 55th and 94th Congresses have negative residuals, while the 95th remains positive. It is also worth noting that Senate turnover peaked in 1979–80, after the burst of junior-initiated reform.

19. Aldrich and Rohde (1998) find this measure is a valid indicator for majority party homogeneity. It is highly correlated with alternative measures, such as the difference in party medians divided by the majority party standard deviation ($r = -.93$). DW-NOMINATE scores are used in the figure. These scores are virtually identical to the more commonly used D-NOMINATE scores but have been computed for more recent Congresses.

20. One weakness of NOMINATE scores as a homogeneity measure is that they may reflect majority party strength (instead of being a cause of such strength). Constituency-based measures avoid this problem and are used in chapter two (see figure 2.1). However, it is difficult to find valid constituency measures applicable for a long time-span (see Jenkins and Schickler 2000).

21. The repeated successes of cross-party coalitions opposed by a majority of the majority party is inconsistent with the view that the majority party dominates House institutions (Cox and McCubbins 1993) but is consistent with conditional party government theory (Cooper and Brady 1981; Rohde 1991).

22. When a change involved both the House and Senate (i.e., weekly leadership meetings and the LRA of 1970), it is counted separately for both chambers. There were several other cases in which partisan or power base goals were a secondary motivation for a change; adding these cases results in a similar House-Senate difference.

23. In some of these cases, policy interests were not the primary motivation but nonetheless were significant.

24. The average absolute change in the floor median in these seven Congresses was .19, as compared to an average absolute change of .09 in the other thirty Congresses in the four periods (difference-in-means significant at $p < .05$).

25. It is also noteworthy that majority party interests have generally been associated with changes in party rules, party leadership instruments, and, at times, House rules concerning floor procedure. Few committee system changes have been motivated *primarily* by partisan interests. By contrast, coalitions promoting congressional capacity and power have focused on the committee system. Thus, the committee system has been shaped largely by bipartisan coalitions, while other features of congressional organization have more often been molded for partisan purposes. This suggests that Krehbiel's (1991) informational theory may illuminate the development of the committee system, while partisan theories are more applicable to other aspects of congressional organization.

26. It is also worth noting that distributive models find little support. Only one change primarily served sectoral interests: the Senate farm bloc of 1921–22. While a few other changes may have also promoted cross-party distributive log-rolls, other forces, such as battles between partisan and cross-party ideological coalitions, have been far more important.

27. See Orren and Skowronek (1994) and March and Olsen (1984) for related arguments concerning other political and social institutions.

28. Internally consistent legislative institutions are plausible only if one assumes that very few types of member coalitions influence institutional design. This might be accurate if the costs of organizing to pursue a shared interest could be absorbed only by certain types of groups, such as parties. But the case studies show that many different kinds of coalitions mold legislative institutions to advance their goals, and the analysis of these cases suggests some of the techniques members use to pursue nonpartisan coalitional interests. Collective action problems, therefore, do not minimize the tensions within congressional institutions.

29. See the epilogue for a discussion of events in 1993–94 and of Republicans' post-1994 experiment with party government.

Epilogue
Institutional Change in the 1990s

1. I focus on the House because Senate changes have been less dramatic in the 1990s.

2. The number of major laws was also no higher than during George Bush's first two years in office (Mayhew 1995). Furthermore, the total number of laws passed in 1993–94 was 465, as compared to 650 in Bush's first two years and 633 in Carter's first Congress (CQ Almanac 1995).

3. This basic argument applies to the Senate as well, except that power in the upper chamber is less tied to formal position. Senate changes over the past two decades did less to empower subcommittee leaders than to give each individual member more opportunities to participate.

4. Clinton's difficulties were likely exacerbated by the moderate status quo on most issues and the tenuous Democratic margins in the House and Senate, which meant that there were few new policies that could garner both the supermajority required for Senate approval and the floor majority required for House passage (see Brady and Volden 1998; Krehbiel 1998). One might conjecture that it would have been easier for the Democrats to find bipartisan compromises that appealed to swing voters had committee chairs still served as focal points for coalition formation (especially if these chairs had close working relations with ranking Republicans, as had been the case prior to the 1970s).

5. An eight-year limit was also set on the Speaker's tenure.

6. Gingrich and his allies sought only relatively minor changes to committee jurisdictions, out of fear of provoking intraparty squabbles as members sought to defend their existing turf. While the GOP eliminated three minor committees with primarily Democratic constituencies, the party made few other jurisdictional changes.

7. The Republicans had been in the majority for only two years (1881–83) since the party's defeat in the 1874 elections.

8. Brady and Volden (1998) and Krehbiel (1998) counter that actual policy outputs are generally consistent with a nonpartisan model. Although Republican leaders may have used their agenda control and other devices to win specific House votes, presidential vetoes and Senate filibusters have sharply limited their ability to adopt noncentrist policies. Resolving this debate requires a more detailed analysis than can be offered here. However, as argued below, even if Republicans have succeeded in adopting noncentrist policies, doing so threatens the electoral survival of party moderates and thus the viability of the party's majority.

9. A series of articles in *Roll Call* in summer 1997 documents the coup and provides evidence for the depth of the GOP's internal troubles.

Appendix A
Case Selection

1. A handful of individuals are authors or coauthors of multiple sources, but no author is counted more than once when considering whether a particular change qualifies. For example, if Galloway (1953) and Galloway and Wise (1976) both

attribute importance to a specific change, this counts for only one of the five sources required for inclusion of a case.

2. I also excluded any boxed sections in the "Inside Congress" essays. For the 1968–72 period, I used the introduction to the "Congressional Affairs" article in *Congress and the Nation;* in subsequent editions, the "Congressional Affairs" article was replaced by the "Inside Congress" section.

3. Abram and Cooper (1968, 70–74) also argue that seniority was firmly established by 1919.

References

Abram, Michael, and Joseph Cooper. 1968. "The Rise of Seniority in the House of Representatives." *Polity* 1:52–85.

Aldrich, John H. 1994. "Rational Choice and the Study of American Politics." In C. Lawrence Dodd and Calvin Jillson, eds., *Dynamics of American Politics*. Boulder, Colo.: Westview Press.

———. 1995. *Why Parties? The Origin and Transformation of Party Politics in America*. Chicago: University of Chicago Press.

Aldrich, John H., and David W. Rohde. 1995. "Theories of the Party in the Legislature and the Transition to Republican Rule in the House." Paper presented at the Annual Meeting of the American Political Science Association, Chicago.

———. 1996. "A Tale of Two Speakers: A Comparison of Policy-Making in the 100th and 104th Congresses." Paper presented at the Annual Meeting of the American Political Science Association, San Francisco.

———. 1998. "Measuring Conditional Party Government." Paper presented at the Annual Meeting of the American Political Science Association, Chicago.

———. 1999. "The Consequences of Party Organization in the House: Theory and Evidence on Conditional Party Government." Paper presented at the Annual Meeting of the American Political Science Association, Atlanta.

Aldrich, John H., and Kenneth Shepsle. 1997. "Explaining Institutional Change: Soaking, Poking, and Modeling in the U.S. Congress." Paper presented at a conference in honor of Richard Fenno, University of Rochester, October 24–25, 1997.

Alexander, Albert. 1955. "The President and the Investigator: Roosevelt and Dies." *Antioch Review* 55:106–17.

Alexander, De Alva. 1916. *History and Procedure of the House of Representatives*. Boston: Houghton Mifflin.

Allen, Robert S., and Drew Pearson. 1931. *Washington Merry-Go-Round*. New York: Horace Liveright.

Alsop, Joseph, and Robert Kintner. 1941. "Never Leave Them Angry." *Saturday Evening Post*, January 18, 1941, 21.

Anderson, Sydney. 1921. "The Latest Thing in Blocs." *Country Gentlemen*, December 31, 1921, 3, 21.

Arnold, Douglas R. 1990. *The Logic of Congressional Action*. New Haven: Yale University Press.

Arrow, Kenneth J. 1951. *Social Choice and Individual Values*. New Haven: Yale University Press.

Atkinson, Charles R. 1911. *The Committee on Rules and the Overthrow of Speaker Cannon*. New York: Columbia University Press.

Bach, Stanley. 1990. "Suspension of the Rules, the Order of Business, and the Development of Congressional Procedure." *Legislative Studies Quarterly* 15:49–63.

Bach, Stanley, and Steven S. Smith. 1988. *Managing Uncertainty in the House.* Washington, D.C.: Brookings Institution.

Bacon, Donald. 1991. "Joseph Taylor Robinson: The Good Soldier." In Richard A. Baker and Roger H. Davidson, eds., *First among Equals: Outstanding Senate Leaders of the Twentieth Century.* Washington, D.C.: CQ Press.

Bader, John B., and Charles O. Jones. 1993. "The Republican Parties in Congress: Bicameral Differences." In Lawrence C. Dodd and Bruce Oppenheimer, eds., *Congress Reconsidered.* 5th ed. Washington, D.C.: CQ Press.

Bailey, Christopher J. 1988. *The Republican Party in the U.S. Senate, 1974–1984.* Manchester: Manchester University Press.

———. 1989. *The US Congress.* Oxford: Basil Blackwell.

Baker, John D. 1973. "The Character of the Congressional Revolution of 1910." *Journal of American History* 60:679–91.

Baker, Ross K. 1991. "Mike Mansfield and the Birth of the Modern Senate." In Richard A. Baker and Roger H. Davidson, eds., *First among Equals: Outstanding Senate Leaders of the Twentieth Century.* Washington, D.C.: CQ Press.

Balogh, Brian. 1991. *Chain Reaction: Expert Debate and Public Participation in American Commercial Nuclear Power, 1945–1975.* Cambridge: Cambridge University Press.

Balz, Dan, and Ronald Brownstein. 1996. *Storming the Gates: Protest Politics and the Republican Revival.* Boston: Little, Brown.

Barfield, Claude E. 1970. " 'Our Share of the Booty': The Democratic Party, Cannonism, and the Payne-Aldrich Tariff." *Journal of American History* 57:308–23.

Barkley, Frederick R. 1939. "Martin Dies of Texas." *Current History* 51:29–30.

Barnes, John K. 1922. "The Man Who Runs the Farm Bloc." *World's Work* 45 (November): 51–59.

Barone, Michael. 1990. *Our Country: The Shaping of America from Roosevelt to Reagan.* New York: Free Press.

Barry, John M. 1989. *The Ambition and the Power.* New York: Penguin.

Baumgartner, Frank, and Bryan Jones. 1993. *Agendas and Instability in American Politics.* Chicago: University of Chicago Press.

Bensel, Richard. 1984. *Sectionalism and American Political Development.* Madison: University of Wisconsin Press.

Berdahl, Clarence A. 1949. "Some Notes on Party Membership in Congress." *American Political Science Review* 43:309–321, 492–508, 721–34.

Berg, John. 1978. "The Effects of Seniority Reform on Three House Committees in the 94th Congress." In Leroy N. Rieselbach, ed., *Legislative Reform: The Policy Impact.* Lexington, Mass: Lexington Books.

Beth, Richard S. 1994. "Control of the House Floor Agenda: Implications from the Use of the Discharge Rule, 1931–1994." Paper presented at the Annual Meeting of the American Political Science Association, New York.

———. 1995. "What We Don't Know about Filibusters." Paper presented at the Annual Meeting of the Western Political Science Association, Portland, Oregon.

Bibby, John F., and Roger H. Davidson. 1972. *On Capitol Hill.* 2d ed. Hindale, Ill.: Dryden Press.

Binder, Sarah. 1997. *Minority Rights, Majority Rule.* Cambridge: Cambridge University Press.

Binder, Sarah, and Steven S. Smith. 1996. "Revisiting the Senate Filibuster: Political Goals and Procedural Choice in the Senate." Paper presented at the Annual Meeting of the Midwest Political Science Association, Chicago.

———. 1997. *Politics or Principle?* Washington, D.C.: Brookings Institution.

Binkley, Wilfred E. 1962. *President and Congress.* 3d ed. New York: Vintage.

Black, John D. 1928. "The McNary-Haugen Movement." *American Economic Review* 18: 405–27.

Blakey, Roy, and Gladys Blakey. 1940. *The Federal Income Tax.* London: Longmans, Green.

Blum, John Morton. 1954. *The Republican Roosevelt.* Cambridge: Harvard University Press.

———. 1976. *V Was for Victory.* New York: Harcourt Brace Jovanovich.

Bolles, Blair. 1951. *Tyrant from Illinois: Uncle Joe Cannon's Experiment with Personal Power.* New York: W. W. Norton.

Bolling, Richard. 1968. *Power in the House.* New York: Dutton.

Bone, Hugh. 1956. "An Introduction to the Senate Policy Committees." *American Political Science Review* 50:339–59.

———. 1968. *Party Committees and National Politics.* 3d ed. Seattle: University of Washington Press.

Born, Richard. 1990. "The Shared Fortunes of Congress and Congressmen." *Journal of Politics* 52:1223–42.

Bovitz, Greg. 1999. "Electoral Incentives and Institutional Change: Re-centralizing the U.S. House Appropriations Process, 1919–20." Typescript, Michigan State University.

Brady, David W., and Phillip Althoff. 1974. "Party Voting in the U.S. House of Representatives, 1890–1910: Elements of a Responsible Party System." *Journal of Politics* 36:753–75.

Brady, David W., Richard Brody, and David Epstein. 1989. "Heterogeneous Parties and Political Organization: The U.S. Senate, 1880–1920." *Legislative Studies Quarterly* 14:205–23.

Brady, David W., and Charles S. Bullock III. 1980. "Is There a Conservative Coalition in the House?" *Journal of Politics* 42:549–59.

Brady, David W., Joseph Cooper, and Patricia A. Hurley. 1979. "The Decline of Party in the U.S. House of Representatives, 1887–1968." *Legislative Studies Quarterly* 4:381–407.

Brady, David W., and David Epstein. 1995. "Intraparty Preferences, Heterogeneity, and the Origins of the Modern Congress," *Journal of Law, Economics, and Organization* 13:26–49.

Brady, David W., and Mark A. Morgan. 1987. "Reforming the Structure of the House Appropriations Process." In Mathew McCubbins and Terry Sullivan, eds., *Congress: Structure and Policy.* New York: Cambridge University Press.

Brady, David W., and Craig Volden. 1998. *Revolving Gridlock: Politics and Policy from Carter to Clinton.* Boulder, Colo.: Westview Press.

Braybrooke, David, and Charles E. Lindblom. 1963. *A Strategy of Decision.* New York: Free Press.

Britt, Stewart Henderson, and Seldon C. Menefee. 1939. "Did the Publicity of the Dies Committee in 1938 Influence Public Opinion?" *Public Opinion Quarterly* 3:449–57.

Brock, Bill. 1974. "Committees in the Senate." *Annals of the American Academy of Political and Social Sciences* 41:15–26.

Brown, George Rothwell. 1922. *The Leadership of Congress.* Indianapolis: Bobbs-Merrill.

Bullock, Charles S. III. 1978. "Congress in the Sunshine." In Leroy N. Rieselbach, ed., *Legislative Reform: The Policy Impact.* Lexington, Mass: Lexington Books.

Burdette, Franklin L. 1940. *Filibustering in the Senate.* Princeton: Princeton University Press.

Burns, James McGregor. 1963. *The Deadlock of Democracy.* Englewood Cliffs, N.J.: Prentice-Hall.

Busbey, L. White. 1927. *Uncle Joe Cannon.* New York: Henry Holt.

Byrd, Robert C. 1988. *The Senate: 1789–1989, Addresses on the History of the United States Senate.* Washington, D.C.: Government Printing Office.

Cannon, Joseph G. 1920. "Dramatic Scenes in My Career in Congress: II. When Reed Counted a Quorum." *Harper's* 65:433–41.

Capper, Arthur. 1922. *The Agricultural Bloc.* Westport, Conn.: Greenwood Press.

Carmichael, Otto. 1903. " 'Uncle Joe' Cannon as Speaker." *World's Work* 7 (December): 4195–99.

Cater, Douglass. 1964. *Power in Washington.* New York: Random House.

Chambrun, Clara Longworth. 1933. *The Making of Nicholas Longworth.* New York: Ray Long and Richard R. Smith.

Chiu, Chang-Wei. 1928. *The Speaker of the House of Representatives since 1896.* New York: Columbia University Press.

Clark, Champ. 1920. *My Twenty Years of American Politics.* New York: Harper and Brothers.

Clements, Kendrick. 1992. *The Presidency of Woodrow Wilson.* Lawrence: University of Kansas Press.

Cochrane, James D. 1964. "Partisan Aspects of Congressional Committee Staffing." *Western Political Quarterly* 17:338–48.

Cohen, Richard E. 1979. "A Report Card for Congress—an 'F' for Frustration." *National Journal* 11, no. 32 (August 11): 1326–30.

Collie, Melissa, and Joseph Cooper. 1989. "Multiple Referral and the 'New' Committee System in the House of Representatives." In Lawrence C. Dodd and Bruce Oppenheimer, eds., *Congress Reconsidered.* 4th ed. Washington, D.C.: CQ Press.

Common Cause. 1973. "Responses to Common Cause 'Open up the System' Questionnaire.' " Seeley Mudd Manuscript Library, Princeton University.

Congressional Quarterly (CQ). 1972. *Congress and the Nation.* Washington, D.C.: CQ Press.

———. 1976. *Congress and the Nation.* Washington, D.C.: CQ Press.

———. 1980. *Congress and the Nation.* Washington, D.C.: CQ Press.

———. 1982. *Origins and Development of Congress.* 2d ed. Washington, D.C.: CQ Press.

———. 1984. *Congress and the Nation.* Washington, D.C.: CQ Press.

———. 1988. *Congress and the Nation.* Washington, D.C.: CQ Press.

———. 1992. *Congress and the Nation.* Washington, D.C.: CQ Press.

Connelly, William F., Jr., and John J. Pitney Jr. 1994. *Congress' Permanent Minority? Republicans in the U.S. House.* Lanham, Md.: Rowman and Littlefield.

"The Conservative Opportunity Society: New Directions, New Leaders for the GOP?" 1984. *Conservative Digest* 10 (August): 4–20.

"Contemporary Celebrities." 1900. *Current Literature* 27 (February): 114–15.

Cooper, John Milton, Jr. 1990. *Pivotal Decades: The United States, 1900–1920.* New York: W. W. Norton.

Cooper, Joseph. 1975. "Strengthening the Congress." *Harvard Journal on Legislation* 2:301–68.

———. 1981. "Organization and Innovation in the House of Representatives." In Joseph Cooper and G. Calvin Mackenzie, eds., *The House at Work.* Austin: University of Texas Press.

———. 1988 [1960]. *Congress and Its Committees.* New York: Garland.

Cooper, Joseph, and David Brady. 1981. "Institutional Context and Leadership Style: The House from Cannon to Rayburn." *American Political Science Review* 75:411–25.

Cooper, Joseph, and Cheryl D. Young. 1989. "Bill Introduction in the Nineteenth Century: A Study of Institutional Change." *Legislative Studies Quarterly* 14:67–105.

Cooper, Joseph, and Garry Young. 1997. "Partisanship, Bipartisanship, and Crosspartisanship in Congress since the New Deal." In Lawrence C. Dodd and Bruce Oppenheimer, eds., *Congress Reconsidered.* 6th ed. Washington, D.C.: CQ Press.

Cox, Gary, and Mathew D. McCubbins. 1993. *Legislative Leviathan: Party Government in the House.* Berkeley and Los Angeles: University of California Press.

———. 1994. "Bonding, Structure, and the Stability of Political Parties: Party Government in the House." *Legislative Studies Quarterly* 19 (May): 215–31.

Crawford, Kenneth. 1939. *The Pressure Boys.* New York: Julian Messner.

Crook, Sara Brandes, and John R. Hibbing. 1985. "Congressional Reform and Party Discipline." *British Journal of Political Science* 15:207–26.

" 'Czar' Reed's Successor Presumptive." 1899. *American Monthly Review of Reviews* 20 (July): 19.

Dahl, Robert, and Ralph Brown. 1951. *Domestic Control of Atomic Energy.* New York: Social Science Research Council.

Damon, Richard E. 1971. "The Standing Rules of the U.S. House of Representatives." Ph.D. diss., Columbia University.

David, Paul T. 1963. "The Changing Political Parties." In Marian D. Irish, ed., *The Continuing Crisis in American Politics.* Englewood Cliffs, N.J.: Prentice-Hall.

Davidson, Roger H. 1980a. "Subcommittee Government: New Channels for Policy Making." In Thomas Mann and Norman Ornstein, eds., *The New Congress.* Washington, D.C.: American Enterprise Institute.

———. 1980b. "Two Roads of Change: House and Senate Committee Reorganization." *Congressional Studies* 7:11–32.

———. 1988. "The New Centralization on Capitol Hill." *Review of Politics* 50:345–64.

Davidson, Roger H. 1989. "The Senate: If Everybody Leads, Who Follows?" In Lawrence C. Dodd and Bruce Oppenheimer, eds., *Congress Reconsidered*. 4th ed. Washington, D.C.: CQ Press.

———. 1990. "The Legislative Reorganization Act of 1946 and the Advent of the Modern Congress." *Legislative Studies Quarterly* 15:357–73.

———. 1992. "The Emergence of the Postreform Congress." In Roger Davidson, ed., *The Postreform Congress*. New York: St. Martin's Press.

Davidson, Roger H., and Walter J. Oleszek. 1976. "Adaptation and Consolidation: Structural Innovation in the U.S. House of Representatives." *Legislative Studies Quarterly* 1:37–65.

———. 1977. *Congress against Itself*. Bloomington: Indiana University Press.

Davidson, Roger H., Walter J. Oleszek, and Thomas Kephart. 1988. "One Bill, Many Committees." *Legislative Studies Quarterly* 13:3–28.

Deering, Christopher J., and Steven S. Smith. 1985. "Subcommittees in Congress." In Lawrence C. Dodd and Bruce I. Oppenheimer, eds., *Congress Reconsidered*. 3d ed. Washington, D.C.: CQ Press.

———. 1997. *Committees in Congress*. 3d ed. Washington, D.C.: CQ Press.

De Santis, Vincent. 1969. *Republicans Face the Southern Question*. New York: Greenwood Press.

Dierenfield, Bruce J. 1987. *Keeper of the Rules: Congressman Howard W. Smith of Virginia*. Charlottesville: University Press of Virginia.

Diermeier, Daniel. 1995. "Commitment, Deference, and Legislative Institutions." *American Political Science Review* 89:8344–55.

Diermeier, Daniel, and Roger B. Myerson. 2000. "Bicameralism and Its Consequences for the Internal Organization of Legislatures." *American Economic Review* 89:1182–96.

Dion, Douglas. 1997. *Turning the Legislative Thumbscrew*. Ann Arbor: University of Michigan Press.

Dodd, Lawrence C. 1977. "Congress and the Quest for Power." In Lawrence C. Dodd and Bruce I. Oppenheimer, eds., *Congress Reconsidered*. New York: Praeger.

———. 1986. "The Cycles of Legislative Change: Building a Dynamic Theory." In Herbert F. Weisberg, ed., *Political Science: The Science of Politics*. New York: Agathon Press.

Dodd, Lawrence C., and Bruce I. Oppenheimer. 1977. "The House in Transition." In Lawrence C. Dodd and Bruce I. Oppenheimer, eds., *Congress Reconsidered*. New York: Praeger.

———. 1989. "Consolidating Power in the House: The Rise of a New Oligarchy." In Lawrence C. Dodd and Bruce I. Oppenheimer, eds., *Congress Reconsidered*. 4th ed. Washington, D.C.: CQ Press.

———. 1993. "Maintaining Order in the House: The Struggle for Institutional Equilibrium." In Lawrence C. Dodd and Bruce I. Oppenheimer, eds., *Congress Reconsidered*. 5th ed. Washington, D.C.: CQ Press.

———. 1997. "Congress and the Emerging Order: Conditional Party Government or Constructive Partisanship?" In Lawrence C. Dodd and Bruce I. Oppenheimer, eds., *Congress Reconsidered*. 6th ed. Washington, D.C.: CQ Press.

Drury, Allen. 1963. *A Senate Journal, 1943–1945*. New York: McGraw-Hill.

Dunn, Arthur Wallace. 1922. *From Harrison to Harding*. New York: G. P. Putnam's Sons.

Ellwood, John W. 1985. "The Great Exception: The Congressional Budget Process in an Age of Decentralization." In Lawrence C. Dodd and Bruce I. Oppenheimer, eds., *Congress Reconsidered*. 3d ed. Washington, D.C.: CQ Press.

Ellwood, John W., and James A. Thurber. 1981. "The Politics of the Congressional Budget Process Reexamined." In Lawrence C. Dodd and Bruce I. Oppenheimer, eds., *Congress Reconsidered*. 2d ed. Washington, D.C.: CQ Press.

Evans, C. Lawrence. 1991. *Leadership in Committee*. Ann Arbor: University of Michigan Press.

Evans, C. Lawrence, and Walter J. Oleszek. 1997. *Congress under Fire: Reform Politics and the Republican Majority*. Boston: Houghton-Mifflin.

Evans, Rowland, and Robert Novak. 1966. *Lyndon B. Johnson: The Exercise of Power*. New York: New American Library.

"The 'Farmers' Party' in Congress." 1921. *Literary Digest*. July 2, 14.

Faulkner, Harold U. 1959. *Politics, Reform, and Expansion, 1890–1900*. New York: Harper and Brothers.

Fenno, Richard F. 1966. *Power of the Purse*. Boston: Little, Brown.

———. 1973. *Congressmen in Committees*. Boston: Little, Brown.

Fiorina, Morris. 1977. *Congress: Keystone of the Washington Establishment*. New Haven: Yale University Press.

Fisher, Louis. 1977. "Congressional Budget Reform: The First Two Years." *Harvard Journal on Legislation* 14:413–57.

———. 1991. *Constitutional Conflicts between Congress and the President*. 3d ed. Lawrence: University Press of Kansas.

Follett, Mary Parker. 1896. *The Speaker of the House of Representatives*. New York: Longmans, Green, and Co.

Forgette, Richard. 1997. "Reed's Rules and the Partisan Theory of Legislative Organization." *Polity* 29:375–96.

Forum. 1899. "A Word to the Next Speaker." 28 (December): 57–65.

Fox, Harrison W., and Susan W. Hammond. 1977. *Congressional Staffs*. New York: Free Press.

Frohlich, Norman, Joe Oppenheimer, and Oran Young. 1971. *Political Leadership and Collective Goods*. Princeton: Princeton University Press.

Froman, Lewis A., Jr., and Randall B. Ripley. 1965. "Conditions for Party Leadership: The Case of the House Democrats." *American Political Science Review* 59:52–63.

Galloway, George B. 1953. *The Legislative Process in Congress*. New York: Thomas Y. Crowell.

Galloway, George B., and Sidney Wise. 1976. *History of the House of Representatives*. 2d ed. New York: Crowell.

Gamm, Gerald, and Steven S. Smith. 1999. "Policy Leadership and the Development of the Modern Senate." Paper presented at the Annual Meeting of the Midwest Political Science Association, Chicago.

Gellerman, William. 1944. *Martin Dies*. New York: John Day.

Gilfond, Duff. 1927. "Mr. Speaker." *American Mercury*, August, 451–58.

Gilligan, Thomas W., and Keith Krehbiel. 1987. "Collective Decision-Making and Standing Committees." *Journal of Law, Economics, and Organization* 3:287–335.

Goodman, Walter. 1968. *The Committee: The Extraordinary Career of the House Committee on Un-American Activities.* New York: Farrar, Straus, and Giroux.

Goodwin, George, Jr. 1959. "The Seniority System in Congress." *American Political Science Review* 53:412–36.

———. 1970. *The Little Legislatures.* Amherst: University of Massachusetts Press.

Graff, Leo W., Jr. 1988. *The Senatorial Career of Fred T. Dubois of Idaho, 1890–1907.* New York: Garland.

Grantham, Dewey W. 1976. *The United States since 1945: The Ordeal of Power.* New York: McGraw-Hill.

———. 1987. *Recent America: The United States since 1945.* Arlington Heights, Ill.: Harlan Davidson.

Green, Harold. 1971. "The Joint Committee on Atomic Energy: A Model for Legislative Reform?" In Ronald C. Moe ed., *Congress and the President.* Pacific Palisades, Calif.: Goodyear.

Green, Harold, and Alan Rosenthal. 1963. *Government of the Atom: The Integration of Powers.* New York: Atherton Press.

Griffith, Ernest S. 1967. *Congress: Its Contemporary Role.* 4th ed. New York: New York University Press.

Groseclose, Tim, and Charles Stewart III. 1998. "The Value of Committee Seats in the House, 1947–91." *American Journal of Political Science* 42:418–52.

Gwinn, William Rea. 1957. *Uncle Joe Cannon: Archfoe of Insurgency.* Bookman Associates.

Haines, Lynn. 1923. "The Battle with the Bosses in Congress." *Searchlight on Congress* 8 (December): 9–15.

———. 1924. "Reforming the Rules." *Searchlight on Congress,* January 31, 14–17.

Hall, Richard L., and C. Lawrence Evans. 1990. "The Power of Subcommittees." *Journal of Politics* 52:335–55.

Hammond, Susan Webb. 1978. "Congressional Change and Reform: Staffing the Congress." In Leroy N. Rieselbach, ed., *Legislative Reform: The Policy Impact.* Lexington, Mass: Lexington Books.

Hansen, John Mark. 1987. "Choosing Sides: The Creation of an Agricultural Policy Network in Congress, 1919–1932." *Studies in American Political Development* 2:183–229.

———. 1991. *Gaining Access: Congress and the Farm Lobby, 1919–1981.* Chicago: University of Chicago Press.

Hard, William. 1924. "Nicholas Longworth." *Nation* 118, no. 3055 (January 23): 88–89.

———. 1925. "Nicholas Longworth." *American Review of Reviews* 71:370–73.

Hardeman, D. B., and Donald C. Bacon. 1987. *Rayburn: A Biography.* Austin: Texas Monthly Press.

Harris, Joseph P. 1964. *Congressional Control of Administration.* Washington, D.C.: Brookings Institution.

Hasbrouck, Paul. 1927. *Party Government in the House of Representatives.* New York: Macmillan.

Hatch, Carl E. 1967. *The Big Stick and the Congressional Gavel.* New York: Pageant Press.

Haynes, George H. 1938. *The Senate of the United States.* Boston: Houghton-Mifflin.

Hechler, Kenneth W. 1940. *Insurgency: Personalities and Politics of the Taft Era.* New York: Columbia University Press.

Herring, E. Pendleton. 1932. "First Session of the Seventy-second Congress." *American Political Science Review* 26:846–74.

Hewlett, Richard G., and Oscar E. Anderson Jr. 1962. *A History of the United States Atomic Energy Commission.* University Park: Pennsylvania State University Press.

Hicks, John D. 1960. *Republican Ascendancy: 1921–1933.* New York: Harper and Brothers.

Hinckley, Barbara. 1976. "Seniority, 1975: Old Theories Confront New Facts." *British Journal of Political Science* 6:383–99.

Hirshson, Stanley P. 1962. *Farewell to the Bloody Shirt.* Bloomington: Indiana University Press.

Hoar, George F. 1903. *Autobiography of Seventy Years.* Vol. 2. New York: Scribners' Sons.

Hoing, Willard L. 1957. "David B. Henderson: Speaker of the House." *Iowa Journal of History* 55:1–34.

Holcombe, Arthur Norman. 1925. *The Political Parties of Today.* New York: Harper and Brothers.

Holt, James. 1967. *Congressional Insurgents and the Party System, 1909–1916.* Cambridge: Harvard University Press.

House Committee on Rules. 1924. *Revision of the Rules: Hearings before the Committee on Rules.* Washington, D.C.: Government Printing Office.

———. 1983. *A History of the Committee on Rules.* Washington, D.C.: Government Printing Office.

House Committee on Military Affairs. 1946. *Atomic Energy: Hearings.* Washington, D.C.: Government Printing Office.

House Select Committee on Committees. 1973. *Committee Organization in the House: Hearings.* Washington, D.C.: Government Printing Office.

House Select Committee on the Budget. 1919. *National Budget System—Changes in the Rules of the House.* 66th Congress, 1st session, H. Rept. 373. Washington, D.C.: Government Printing Office.

Hughes, Jonathan R. T. 1991. *The Governmental Habit Redux.* Princeton: Princeton University Press.

Huitt, Ralph K. 1961. "Democratic Party Leadership in the Senate." *American Political Science Review* 55:331–44.

Humes, Brian. 1989. "Congress at the Bicentennial: A Comment." *Legislative Studies Quarterly* 14:135–45.

Huntington, Samuel. 1965. "Congressional Responses to the Twentieth Century." In David B. Truman, ed., *Congress and America's Future.* Englewood Cliffs, N.J.: Prentice-Hall.

Hurley, Patricia, and Rick K. Wilson. 1989. "Partisan Voting Patterns in the U.S. Senate, 1877–1986." *Legislative Studies Quarterly* 14:225–50.

Jackson, John E., and John W. Kingdon. 1992. "Ideology, Interest Group Scores, and Legislative Votes." *American Journal of Political Science* 36:805–23.

Jacobson, Gary. 1993. "Deficit-Cutting Politics and Congressional Elections." *Political Science Quarterly* 108:375–402.

Jensen, Richard. 1971. *The Winning of the Midwest: Social and Political Conflict, 1888–1896.* Chicago: University of Chicago Press.

Jewell, Malcolm E. 1959. "The Senate Republican Policy Committee and Foreign Policy." *Western Political Quarterly* 12:966–80.

Jewell, Malcolm E., and Samuel C. Patterson. 1966. *Legislative Politics in the United States.* New York: Random House.

Joint Committee on the Organization of Congress. 1945. *Organization of Congress: Hearings.* 79th Congress, 1st sess. Washington, D.C.: Government Printing Office.

———. 1946. *Organization of the Congress: Report of the Joint Committee on the Organization of Congress.* Washington, D.C.: Government Printing Office.

———. 1965. *Organization of Congress: Hearings.* 89th Congress, 1st sess., part 1. Washington, D.C.: Government Printing Office.

Jones, Charles O. 1968. "Joseph G. Cannon and Howard W. Smith: An Essay on the Limits of Leadership in the House of Representatives." *Journal of Politics* 30:617–46.

———. 1970. *The Minority Party in Congress.* Boston: Little, Brown.

———. 1995. *Separate but Equal Branches.* Chatham, N.J.: Chatham House.

Josephy, Alvin M. 1979. *On the Hill: A History of the American Congress.* New York: Simon and Schuster.

Kammerer, Gladys M. 1951a. *Congressional Committee Staffing since 1946.* Lexington: University of Kentucky.

———. 1951b. "The Record of Congress in Committee Staffing." *American Political Science Review* 45:1126–36.

Kampelman, Max M. 1954. "The Legislative Bureaucracy: Its Response to Political Change, 1953." *Journal of Politics* 16:539–50.

Keller, Morton. 1977. *Affairs of State.* Cambridge: Belknap Press of Harvard University Press.

Kessner, Thomas. 1989. *Fiorello H. La Guardia and the Making of Modern New York.* New York: McGraw-Hill.

Key, V. O. 1962 [1949]. *Southern Politics in State and Nation.* New York: Vintage.

Kiewiet, Roderick D., and Mathew D. McCubbins. 1991. *The Logic of Delegation.* Chicago: University of Chicago Press.

King, David C. 1997. *Turf Wars: How Congressional Committees Claim Jurisdiction.* Chicago: University of Chicago Press.

Kirkendall, Richard S. 1974. *The United States, 1929–1945: Years of Crisis and Change.* New York: McGraw-Hill.

Knight, Jack. 1992. *Institutions and Social Conflict.* Cambridge: Cambridge University Press.

Kofmehl, Kenneth. 1977. *Professional Staffs of Congress.* 3d ed. West Lafayette, Ind.: Purdue University Press.

Kravitz, Walter. 1974. "Evolution of the Senate's Committee System." *Annals of the American Academy of Political and Social Science* 411:27–38.

————. 1990. "The Legislative Reorganization Act of 1970 and the Advent of the Modern Congress." *Legislative Studies Quarterly* 15:375–99.

Krehbiel, Keith. 1991. *Information and Legislative Organization*. Ann Arbor: University of Michigan Press.

————. 1993. "Where's the Party?" *British Journal of Political Science* 23:235–66.

————. 1998. *Pivotal Politics: A Theory of U.S. Lawmaking*. Chicago: University of Chicago Press.

Krehbiel, Keith, and Alan Wiseman. 1999. "Joseph G. Cannon: Majoritarian From Illinois." Paper presented at the Conference on the History of Congress, Stanford University, January 15–16.

Lapham, Lewis J. 1954. "Party Leadership and the House Committee on Rules." Ph.D. diss., Harvard University.

Latham, Earl. 1966. *The Communist Controversy in Washington*. Cambridge: Harvard University Press.

Laver, Michael. 1981. *The Politics of Private Desires*. New York: Penguin.

LeLoup, Lance T. 1989. "Fiscal Policy and Congressional Politics." In Christopher Deering, ed., *Congressional Politics*. Washington, D.C.: CQ Press.

Lemann, Nicholas. 1985. "Conservative Opportunity Society." *Atlantic* 255:22–36.

Lester, Robert Leon. 1969. "Developments in Presidential-Congressional Relations: F.D.R. to J.F.K." Ph.D. diss., University of Virginia.

Leuchtenburg, William. 1963. *Franklin D. Roosevelt and the New Deal, 1932–1940*. New York: Harper and Row.

————. 1993 [1958]. *The Perils of Prosperity, 1914–1932*. 2d ed. Chicago: University of Chicago Press.

Leupp, Francis. 1910. "Personal Recollections of Thomas B. Reed." *Outlook*, September 3, 36–40.

Lindblom, Charles E. 1965. *Intelligence of Democracy*. New York: Free Press.

Lodge, Henry Cabot. 1889. "The Coming Congress." *North American Review* 149 (September): 293–301.

Loomis, Burdette. 1988. *The New American Politician*. New York: Basic Books.

Low, A. Maurice. 1906. "Thomas Reed." In Orlando O. Stealey, ed., *Twenty Years in the Press Gallery*. New York: Orlando Stealey.

Lowe, Margaret. 1975. "Additional Committee Staff." *Congressional Quarterly Weekly Report*, June 14, 1235–36.

Luce, Robert. 1922. *Legislative Procedure*. Boston: Houghton Mifflin.

————. 1926. *Congress: An Explanation*. Cambridge: Harvard University Press.

Maass, Arthur. 1983. *Congress and the Common Good*. New York: Basic Books.

MacMahon, Arthur W. 1927. "Second Session of the Sixty-Ninth Congress." *American Political Science Review* 21:297–317.

————. 1928. "First Session of the Seventieth Congress." *American Political Science Review* 22:650–83.

————. "Third Session of the Seventy-First Congress." *American Political Science Review* 25:932–55.

MacNeil, Neil. 1963. *Forge of Democracy*. New York: David McKay.

Malbin, Michael J. 1974. "New Democratic Procedures Affect Distribution of Power." *National Journal* 6, no. 50 (December 14): 1881–90.

Malbin, Michael J. 1975. "Senate Preparing for Study of Committee, Staffing Problems." *National Journal* 7, no. 18 (May 3):647–51.

———. 1977. "You Can Please Some of the Senators Some of the Time." *National Journal* 9, no. 3 (January 15): 106–11.

Maltzman, Forrest. 1997. *Competing Principals: Committees, Parties, and the Organization of Congress.* Ann Arbor: University of Michigan Press.

Manley, John F. 1973. "The Conservative Coalition in Congress." *American Behavioral Scientist* 17:223–47.

Mann, Arthur. 1959. *La Guardia.* Philadelphia: Lippincott.

March, James G. 1994. *A Primer on Decision Making.* New York: Free Press.

March, James G., and Johan Olsen. 1984. "The New Institutionalism: Organizational Factors in Political Life." *American Political Science Review.* 78: 734–749.

Marguiles, Herbert F. 1996. *Reconciliation and Revival: James R. Mann and the House Republicans in the Wilson Era.* Westport, Conn.: Greenwood Press.

Marx, Fritz Morstein. 1951. "Congress Investigates: Significance for the Legislative Process." *University of Chicago Law Review* 18:503–20.

Matthews, Donald R. 1960. *U.S. Senators and Their World.* New York: Vintage Books.

Mayer, George H. 1964. *The Republican Party, 1854–1964.* New York: Oxford University Press.

Mayhew, David R. 1974. *Congress: The Electoral Connection.* New Haven: Yale University Press.

———. 1995. "Clinton, the 103rd Congress, and Unified Party Control: What Are the Lessons." Paper presented at conference honoring Stanley Kelley Jr., Princeton University, October 27–28.

Mayhill, George Roger. 1942. "Speaker Cannon under the Roosevelt Administration: 1903–1907." Ph.D. dissertation, University of Illinois.

McCall, Samuel W. 1914. *The Life of Thomas Brackett Reed.* Boston: Houghton Mifflin.

McClellan, George B. 1911. "Leadership in the House of Representatives." *Scribner's Magazine* 49:594–99.

McCoy, Donald R. 1967. *The Quiet President.* New York: Macmillan.

McGreary, M. Nelson. 1951. "Congressional Investigations: Historical Development." *University of Chicago Law Review* 18:425–48.

McKelvey, Richard D. 1976. "Intransitivities in Multidimensional Voting Models and Some Implications for Agenda Control." *Journal of Economic Theory* 12:472–82.

Merrill, Horace Samuel, and Marion Galbraith Merrill. 1971. *The Republican Command, 1897–1913.* Lexington: University Press of Kentucky.

Miller, Nicholas. 1983. "Pluralism and Social Choice." *American Political Science Review* 77:734–47.

Morgan, H. Wayne. 1969. *From Hayes to McKinley: National Party Politics, 1877–1896.* Syracuse, N.Y.: Syracuse University Press.

Morrison, Geoffrey. 1974. "Champ Clark and the Rules Revolution of 1910." *Capitol Studies* 2:43–56.

Mowry, George E. 1958. *The Era of Theodore Roosevelt.* New York: Harper and Brothers.

Murray, Robert K. 1973. *The Politics of Normalcy: Governmental Theory and Practice in the Harding-Coolidge Era.* New York: W. W. Norton.

North, Douglass. 1990. *Institutions, Institutional Change, and Economic Performance.* Cambridge: Cambridge University Press.

O'Neill, Thomas P. 1987. *Man of the House.* New York: Random House.

Ogden, August R. 1945. *The Dies Committee.* Washington, D.C.: Catholic University of America Press.

Ogden, R. 1903. "Larger Aspects of the Late Congress." *Nation* 76, no. 1967 (March 12): 204.

Oleszek, Walter J. 1996. *Congressional Procedures and the Policy Process.* 4th ed. Washington, D.C.: CQ Press.

Olssen, Erik. 1980. "The Progressive Group in Congress." *Historian* 42:244–63.

Oppenheimer, Bruce I. 1977. "The Rules Committee: New Arm of the Leadership in a Decentralized House." In Lawrence C. Dodd and Bruce I. Oppenheimer, eds., *Congress Reconsidered.* New York: Praeger.

———. 1985. "Changing Time Constraints on Congress: Historical Perspectives on the Use of Cloture." In Lawrence C. Dodd and Bruce I. Oppenheimer, eds., *Congress Reconsidered.* 3d ed. Washington, D.C.: CQ Press.

Ornstein, Norman J. 1975. "Causes and Consequences of Congressional Change." In Norman J. Ornstein, ed., *Congress in Change.* New York: Praeger.

———. 1985. "Minority Report." *Atlantic* 256:30–38.

Ornstein, Norman J., Robert L. Peabody, and David W. Rohde. 1997. "The U.S. Senate: Toward the Twenty-First Century." In Lawrence C. Dodd and Bruce I. Oppenheimer, eds., *Congress Reconsidered.* 6th ed. Washington, D.C.: CQ Press.

Ornstein, Norman J., and David W. Rohde. 1974. "The Strategy of Reform: Recorded Teller Voting in the U.S. House of Representatives." Paper presented at the Annual Meeting of the Midwest Political Science Association, Chicago.

———. 1977. "Shifting Forces, Changing Rules, and Political Outcomes." In Robert Peabody and Nelson Polsby, *New Perspectives on the House of Representatives.* 3d ed. Chicago: Rand McNally.

———. 1978. "Political Parties and Congressional Reform." In Jeff Fishel, ed., *Parties and Elections in an Antiparty Age.* Bloomington: Indiana University Press.

Ornstein, Norman J., et al. 1982. *Vital Statistics on Congress.* Washington, D.C.: American Enterprise Institute.

Orren, Karen, and Stephen Skowronek. 1994. "Order and Time in Institutional Study." In James Farr et al., eds., *Political Science in History.* Cambridge: Cambridge University Press.

Palazzolo, Daniel J. 1992. *The Speaker and the Budget.* Pittsburgh: University of Pittsburgh Press.

Parris, Judith H. 1979. "The Senate Reorganizes Its Committees, 1977." *Political Science Quarterly* 94:319–37.

Parsons, Stanley, Michael Dubin, and Karen Toombs Parsons. 1990. *United States Congressional Districts, 1883–1913.* New York: Greenwood Press.

Patterson, James T. 1966. "A Conservative Coalition Forms in Congress, 1933–39." *Journal of American History* 52:757–72.

———. 1967. *Congressional Conservatism and the New Deal.* Lexington: University of Kentucky Press.

Patterson, James T. 1972. *Mr. Republican: A Biography of Robert A. Taft*. Boston: Houghton-Mifflin.

Paxson, Frederick L. 1948. *American Democracy and the War. III, Postwar Years, Normalcy, 1918–1923*. Berkeley and Los Angeles: University of California Press.

Peabody, Robert L. 1976. *Leadership in Congress*. Boston: Little, Brown.

Peters, Ronald. 1990. *The American Speakership: The Office in Historical Perspective*. Baltimore: Johns Hopkins University Press.

———. 1998. "Institutional Context and Leadership Style: The Case of Newt Gingrich." Paper presented at the Florida International Conference on the Republican Control of the U.S. House of Representatives, Miami.

Pierson, Paul. 1998. "Increasing Returns, Path Dependence, and the Study of Politics." Typescript, Harvard University.

Pitney, John J., Jr. 1988. "The Conservative Opportunity Society." Paper presented at the Annual Meeting of the Western Political Science Association, San Francisco.

———. 1996. "Understanding Newt Gingrich." Paper presented at the Annual Meeting of the American Political Science Association, San Francisco.

Pitney, John J., Jr., and William F. Connelly Jr. 1996. " 'Permanent Minority' No More: House Republicans in 1994." In Philip A. Klinkner, ed., *Midterm*. Boulder, Colo.: Westview Press.

Polsby, Nelson W. 1968. "The Institutionalization of the U.S. House of Representatives." *American Political Science Review* 62:144–68.

Polsby, Nelson W., Miriam Gallagher, and Barry S. Rundquist. 1969. "The Growth of the Seniority System in the U.S. House of Representatives." *American Political Science Review* 63:787–807.

Poole, Keith T., and Howard Rosenthal. 1997. *Congress: A Political-Economic History of Roll Call Voting*. New York: Oxford University Press.

Porter, David L. 1980. *Congress and the Waning of the New Deal*. Port Washington, N.Y.: Kennikat Press.

Price, David E. 1992. *The Congressional Experience*. Boulder, Colo.: Westview Press.

Price, H. Douglas. 1975. "Congress and the Evolution of Legislative Professionalism." In Norman J. Ornstein ed., *Congress in Change*. New York: Praeger.

Rager, Scott William. 1991. "The Fall of the House of Cannon: Uncle Joe and His Enemies, 1903–1910." Ph.D. diss., University of Illinois.

"Record of Political Events." 1925. *Political Science Quarterly* 40:59–70.

———. 1926. *Political Science Quarterly* 41:49–53.

Reed, Thomas B. 1889. "Obstruction in the National House." *North American Review* 149 (October): 421–28.

Reeves, Andree E. 1993. *Congressional Committee Chairmen*. Lexington: University Press of Kentucky.

Remington, Thomas F., and Steven S. Smith. 1998. "Theories of Legislative Institutions and the Organization of the Russian Duma." *American Journal of Political Science* 42:545–72.

Rice, Stuart. 1925. "The Behavior of Legislative Groups: A Method of Measurement." *Political Science Quarterly* 40:60–72.

Riddick, Floyd M. 1944. "The First Session of the Seventy-Eighth Congress." *American Political Science Review* 38:301–17.

———. 1949. *The United States Congress: Its Organization and Procedure*. Manassas, Va.: National Capitol Publishers.

Riddle, Donald. 1964. *The Truman Committee*. New Brunswick, N.J.: Rutgers University Press.

Rieselbach, Leroy N. 1994. *Congressional Reform: The Changing Modern Congress*. Washington, D.C.: CQ Press.

———. 1995. "Congressional Change: Historical Perspectives." In James Thurber and Roger Davidson, eds., *Remaking Congress*. Washington, D.C.: CQ Press.

Rieselbach, Leroy N., and Joseph K. Unekis. 1981–82. "Ousting the Oligarchs." *Congress and the Presidency* 9:83–117.

Riker, William H. 1986. *The Art of Political Manipulation*. New Haven: Yale University Press.

———. 1995. "The Experience of Creating Institutions: The Framing of the United States Constitution." In Jack Knight and Itai Sened, eds., *Explaining Social Institutions*. Ann Arbor: University of Michigan Press.

Ripley, Randall B. 1967. *Party Leaders in the House of Representatives*. Washington, D.C.: Brookings Institution.

———. 1969a. *Majority Party Leadership in Congress*. Boston: Little, Brown.

———. 1969b. *Power in the Senate*. New York: St. Martin's Press.

———. 1983. *Congress: Process and Policy*. 3d ed. New York: W. W. Norton.

Ritchie, Donald A. 1991. "Alben W. Barkley: The President's Man." In Richard A. Baker and Roger H. Davidson, eds., *First among Equals: Outstanding Senate Leaders of the Twentieth Century*. Washington, D.C.: CQ Press.

Robertson, James Oliver. 1983 [1964]. *No Third Choice: Progressives in Republican Politics, 1916–1921*. New York: Garland.

Robinson, George Lee. 1954. "The Development of the Senate Committee System." Ph.D. diss., New York University.

Robinson, James A. 1963. *The House Rules Committee*. Indianapolis: Bobbs-Merrill.

Robinson, William A. 1930. *Thomas B. Reed: Parliamentarian*. New York: Dodd, Mead.

Rogers, Lindsay. 1922. "The First (Special) Session of the Sixty-Seventh Congress." *American Political Science Review* 16:41–52.

———. 1925. "First and Second Sessions of the Sixty-Eighth Congress." *American Political Science Review* 19:761–72.

———. 1926. *The American Senate*. New York: Alfred A. Knopf.

Rohde, David W. 1991. *Parties and Leaders in the Postreform House*. Chicago: University of Chicago Press.

Rohde, David W. 1994. "Parties and Committees in the House: Member Motivations, Issues, and Institutional Arrangements." *Legislative Studies Quarterly* 19:341–59.

Rohde, David W., and Kenneth A. Shepsle. 1987. "Leaders and Followers in the House of Representatives." *Congress and the Presidency* 14:111–33.

Rosenthal, Alan. 1981. *Legislative Life*. New York: Harper and Row.

Rothman, David J. 1966. *Politics and Power: The United States Senate, 1869–1901*. Cambridge: Harvard University Press.

Rudder, Catherine E. 1977. "Committee Reform and the Revenue Process." In Lawrence C. Dodd and Bruce I. Oppenheimer, eds., *Congress Reconsidered*. New York: Praeger.

Sarasohn, David. 1979. "The Insurgent Republicans: Insurgent Image and Republican Reality." *Social Science History* 3:245–61.

Saunders, D. A. 1939. "The Dies Committee: First Phase." *Public Opinion Quarterly* 3:223–38.

Schick, Allen. 1980a. *Congress and Money.* Washington, D.C.: Urban Institute.

———. 1980b. "The Three-Ring Budget Process." In Thomas E. Mann and Norman J. Ornstein, eds., *The New Congress*. Washington, D.C.: American Enterprise Institute.

Schickler, Eric. 1994. "Position-Taking, Policy Goals, and the House Committee on Rules." Paper presented at the Annual Meeting of the American Political Science Association, New York.

———. 2000. "Institutional Change in the House of Representatives, 1867–1998: A Test of Partisan and Ideological Power Balance Models." *American Political Science Review* 94:267–88.

Schickler, Eric, and Andrew Rich. 1997a. "Controlling the Floor: Parties as Procedural Coalitions in the House." *American Journal of Political Science* 41:1340–75.

———. 1997b. "Party Government in the House Reconsidered: A Response to Cox and McCubbins." *American Journal of Political Science* 41:1387–94.

Schickler, Eric, and John Sides. 2000. "Intergenerational Warfare: The Senate Decentralizes Appropriations." *Legislative Studies Quarterly* 35 (November): 551–75.

Schlesinger, Arthur M. 1973. *The Imperial Presidency.* Boston: Houghton-Mifflin.

Schneier, Edward V. 1963. "The Politics of Anti-Communism: A Study of the House Committee on Un-American Activities and Its Role in the Political Process." Ph.D. diss., Claremont Graduate School.

Schneier, Edward V., and Bertram Gross. 1993. *Congress Today.* New York: St. Martin's Press.

Schwarz, Jordan A. 1970. *The Interregnum of Despair: Hoover, Congress, and the Depression*. Urbana: University of Illinois Press.

Scott, W. Richard. 1998. *Organizations: Rational, Natural, and Open Systems.* 4th ed. Upper Saddle River, N.J.: Prentice-Hall.

Senate Committee on Rules and Administration. 1988. *Report on Senate Operations*. Washington, D.C.: Government Printing Office.

Sheppard, Burton D. 1985. *Rethinking Congressional Reform.* Cambridge, Mass.: Schenkman Books.

Shepsle, Kenneth A. 1986. "Institutional Equilibrium and Equilibrium Institutions." In Herbert Weisberg, ed., *Political Science: The Science of Politics*. New York: Agathon Press.

Shepsle, Kenneth A., and Barry R. Weingast. 1984. "Legislative Politics and Budget Outcomes." In Gregory B. Mills and John L. Palmer, eds., *Federal Budget Policy in the 1980s*. Washington, D.C.: Urban Institute.

———. 1994. "Positive Theories of Congressional Institutions." *Legislative Studies Quarterly* 19:149–79.

Shideler, James H. 1957. *Farm Crisis: 1919–1923.* Berkeley and Los Angeles: University of California Press.

Sinclair, Barbara. 1983. *Majority Leadership in the U.S. House.* Baltimore: Johns Hopkins University Press.

———. 1989. *The Transformation of the U.S. Senate.* Baltimore: Johns Hopkins University Press.

———. 1990. "Congressional Leadership: A Review Essay and a Research Agenda." In John J. Kornacki, ed., *Leading Congress: New Styles, New Strategies.* Washington, D.C.: CQ Press.

———. 1993. "House Majority Party Leadership in an Era of Divided Control." In Lawrence Dodd and Bruce Oppenheimer, eds., *Congress Reconsidered.* 5th ed. Washington, D.C.: CQ Press.

———. 1994. "House Special Rules and the Institutional Design Controversy." *Legislative Studies Quarterly* 19:477–94.

———. 1995a. "Changes and Continuity in the Legislative Process: The U.S. House and Senate from the 1970s to the 1990s." Paper presented at the Annual Meeting of the American Political Science Association, Chicago.

———. 1995b. *Legislators, Leaders, and Lawmaking.* Baltimore: Johns Hopkins University.

Skowronek, Stephen. 1993. *The Politics Presidents Make.* Cambridge: Belknap Press of Harvard University Press.

Smith, Steven S. 1989. *Call to Order.* Washington, D.C.: Brookings Institution.

———. 1993. "Forces of Change in Senate Party Leadership and Organization." In Lawrence C. Dodd and Bruce Oppenheimer, eds., *Congress Reconsidered.* 5th ed. Washington, D.C.: CQ Press.

Smith, Steven S., and Christopher J. Deering. 1990. *Committees in Congress.* 2d ed. Washington, D.C.: CQ Press.

Smith, Steven S., and Bruce A. Ray. 1983. "The Impact of Congressional Reform: House Democratic Committee Assignments." *Congress and the Presidency* 10:219–40.

Smith, Steven S., and Thomas F. Remington. 2001. *The Politics of Institutional Choice: The Formation of the Russian State Duma.* Princeton: Princeton University Press.

Smith, William Wolff. 1906. "David Henderson." In Orlando O. Stealey, ed., *Twenty Years in the Press Gallery.* New York: Orlando Stealey.

Snyder, Jim, and Tim Groseclose. 2000. "Estimating Party Influence in Congressional Roll Call Voting." *American Journal of Political Science* 44:193–211.

Socolofsky, Homer E., and Allan B. Spetter. 1987. *The Presidency of Benjamin Harrison.* Lawrence: University of Kansas Press.

"The Speaker and His Critics." 1890. *North American Review,* August, 237–50.

"Speaker Henderson's Retirement." 1902. *American Monthly Review of Reviews* 26 (October): 387–92.

Special Committee on Atomic Energy. 1946. *Atomic Energy Act of 1946: Hearings.* Washington, D.C.: Government Printing Office.

Stanwood, Edward. 1903. *American Tariff Controversies in the Nineteenth Century.* Vol. 2. Boston: Houghton-Mifflin.

Stephenson, Nathaniel Wright. 1930. *Nelson W. Aldrich: A Leader in American Politics.* New York: Charles Scribner's Sons.

Stewart, Charles H. 1989. *Budget Reform Politics.* Cambridge: Cambridge University Press.

Strahan, Randall. 1990. *New Ways and Means.* Chapel Hill: University of North Carolina Press.

———. 1999. "Leadership in Institutional Time: The Nineteenth Century House." Paper presented at the History of Congress Conference, Stanford University, January 15–16.

Sundquist, James L. 1981. *The Decline and Resurgence of Congress.* Washington, D.C.: Brookings Institution.

———. 1983. *Dynamics of the Party System.* Washington, D.C.: Brookings Institution.

Swenson, Peter. 1982. "The Influence of Recruitment on the Structure of Power in the U.S. House, 1870–1940." *Legislative Studies Quarterly* 7:7–36.

Taylor, Telford. 1954. *Grand Inquest: The Story of Congressional Investigations.* New York: Simon and Schuster.

Thomas, Morgan. 1956. *Atomic Energy and Congress.* Ann Arbor: University of Michigan.

Thompson, Charles W. 1906. *Party Leaders of the Time.* New York: G. W. Dillingham.

Tiefer, Charles. 1989. *Congressional Practice and Procedure.* New York: Greenwood Press.

Timmons, Bascom N. 1948. *Garner of Texas.* New York: Harper and Brothers.

Truman, David B. 1959a. *The Congressional Party.* New York: John Wiley and Sons.

———. 1959b. "The Presidency and Congressional Leadership." *Proceedings of the American Philosophical Society* 103:687–92.

Uslaner, Eric. 1978. "Policy Entrepreneurs and Amateur Democrats in the House of Representatives." In Leroy Rieselbach, ed., *Legislative Reform: The Policy Impact.* Lexington, Mass: Lexington Books.

Vandenberg, Arthur. 1952. *The Private Papers of Senator Vandenberg.* Boston: Houghton-Mifflin.

Van Hollen, Christopher. 1951. "The House Rules Committee 1933–1951: Agent of Party and Agent of Opposition." Ph.D. diss., Johns Hopkins University.

Voorhis, Jerry. 1944. "Stop Kicking Congress Around!" *American Mercury* 58:647–55.

Waldman, Sidney. 1981. "Majority Leadership in the House of Representatives." *Political Science Quarterly* 95:373–93.

Wander, W. Thomas. 1982. "Patterns of Change in the Congressional Budget Process, 1865–1974." *Congress and the Presidency* 9:23–49.

———. 1984. "The Politics of Congressional Budget Reform." In W. Thomas Wander, F. Ted Hebert, and Gary W. Copeland, eds., *Congressional Budgeting: Politics, Process, and Power.* Baltimore: Johns Hopkins University Press.

Warren, Harris Gaylord. 1959. *Herbert Hoover and the Great Depression.* New York: Oxford University Press.

Weingast, Barry R., and William Marshall. 1988. "The Industrial Organization of Congress." *Journal of Political Economy* 96:132–63.

Wellborn, Fred. 1928. "The Influence of the Silver Republican Senators, 1889–1891." *Mississippi Valley Historical Review* 14:462–80.

Welliver, Judson C. 1922. "The Agricultural Crisis and the 'Bloc.'" *American Review of Reviews* 65:158–65.

Whalen, Charles W. 1982. *The House and Foreign Policy: The Irony of Congressional Reform*. Chapel Hill: University of North Carolina Press.

White, William S. 1954. *The Taft Story*. New York: Harper and Brothers.

———. 1957. *Citadel: The Story of the U.S. Senate*. New York: Harper and Brothers.

Widenor, William C. 1991. "Henry Cabot Lodge: The Astute Parliamentarian." In Richard A. Baker and Roger H. Davidson, eds., *First among Equals: Outstanding Senate Leaders of the Twentieth Century*. Washington, D.C.: CQ Press.

Williams, John Alexander. 1973. "The Bituminous Coal Lobby and the Wilson-Gorman Tariff of 1894." *Maryland Historical Magazine* 68:273–87.

Williams, R. Hal. 1993 [1978]. *Years of Decision: American Politics in the 1890s*. Prospect Heights, Ill.: Waveland Press.

Wilson, Theodore. 1975a. "The Truman Committee, 1941." In Arthur Schlesinger and Roger Bruns, eds., *Congress Investigates*. New York: Chelsea House.

———. 1975b. "The Kefauver Committee, 1950." In Arthur Schlesinger and Roger Bruns, eds., *Congress Investigates*. New York: Chelsea House.

Winters, Donald L. 1970. *Henry Cantwell Wallace as Secretary of Agriculture, 1921–1924*. Urbana: University of Illinois Press.

Wolf, Thomas W. 1981. "Congressional Sea Change: Conflict and Organizational Accommodation in the House of Representatives, 1878–1921." Ph.D. diss., Massachusetts Institute of Technology.

Wreszin, Michael. 1975. "The Dies Committee." In Arthur Schlesinger and Roger Bruns, eds., *Congress Investigates*. New York: Chelsea House.

Wrighton, J. Mark, and Kristin Kanthak. 1997. "Parliamentary Siege: Obstructionism in the United States Senate over Time." Paper presented at the Annual Meeting of the Midwest Political Science Association, Chicago.

Young, Garry, and Joseph Cooper. 1993. "Multiple Referral and the Transformation of House Decision-Making." In Lawrence C. Dodd and Bruce I. Oppenheimer, eds., *Congress Reconsidered*. 5th ed. Washington, D.C.: CQ Press.

Young, Roland A. 1956. *Congressional Politics in the Second World War*. New York: Columbia University Press.

Zinn, Howard. 1959. *La Guardia in Congress*. Ithaca, N.Y: Cornell University Press.

Index

PRINCETON STUDIES IN AMERICAN POLITICS:
HISTORICAL, INTERNATIONAL, AND COMPARATIVE PERSPECTIVES